College Vergil

Latin Text with Facing Vocabulary and Commentary

Geoffrey Steadman

College Vergil
Latin Text with Facing Vocabulary and Commentary

First Edition

The Latin text is the Oxford Classical Text edited by J. B. Greenough in 1900.

ISBN-13: 978-0-9991884-4-6

Published by Geoffrey Steadman
Cover Design: David Steadman

geoffreysteadman@gmail.com

Table of Contents

Preface to the Series

This commentary includes all selected passages from Vergil's *Aeneid* for the Advanced Placement Latin course divided into 63 Lessons:

Book 1: lines 1-209, 418-440, 494-578
Book 2: lines 40-56, 201-249, 268-297, 559-620
Book 4: lines 160-218, 259-361, 659-705
Book 6: lines 295-332, 384-425, 450-476, 847-899

Each lesson is two facing pages in length. Each even page includes 12-18 lines of Latin text from J.B. Greenough's 1900 Latin edition with all corresponding vocabulary and grammar notes below the Latin on the same page. The vocabulary contains all words occurring 4 or fewer times, arranged alphabetically in two columns. The grammatical notes are organized according to line numbers and likewise arranged in two columns. On the facing odd page there are high frequency word lists (occurring 5 or more times), short-answer questions, and finally information boxes, which include literary, historical, and grammatical explanations.

To complement the vocabulary within the commentary, I have added a core running list of words occurring 5 or more times in the introduction of this book and recommend that readers review this list before they read each lesson. An alphabetized list of the same core words is found in the glossary. Together, this book has been designed in such a way that, once readers have mastered the core vocabulary list, they will be able to rely solely on the Latin text and commentary and not need to turn a page or consult dictionaries as they read.

The grammatical notes are designed to help intermediate readers read the text, and so I have passed over literary and historical explanations in favor of short, concise, and frequent entries that focus on grammar and morphology. Detailed literary and historical explanations are included in information boxes on the facing page. Assuming that readers complete their initial study of Latin with varying levels of ability, I draw attention to all subjunctive and accusative-infinitive constructions, identify unusual verbs forms and noun constructions, and in general explain aspects of the Latin that they should have encountered in their initial review of Latin grammar but perhaps forgotten. As a rule, I prefer to offer too much assistance rather than too little.

One of the virtues of this commentary is that it eliminates time-consuming dictionary work. While there are occasions where a dictionary is necessary for developing a nuanced reading of the Latin, in most instances any advantage that may come from looking up a word is outweighed by the time and effort spent in the process. Many continue to defend this practice, but I am convinced that such work has little pedagogical value for intermediate and advanced students and that the time saved can be better spent reading Latin, memorizing vocabulary, mastering principal parts, and rereading the text.

As an alternative to dictionary work, I recommend that readers review the running core vocabulary list (5 or more times) before they begin each lesson and continue to review the relevant words daily until they are thoroughly learned. Many of the remaining, less frequent words can be learned in the context of reading and rereading the lessons. Altogether, I am confident that readers who follow this regimen will learn the vocabulary more efficiently and develop fluency more quickly than with traditional dictionary work.

If you would like to suggest changes or download a free pdf copy of this commentary and ancillaries, please see the website below. All criticisms are welcome, and I would be very grateful for your help.

Geoffrey Steadman, Ph.D.
geoffreysteadman@gmail.com
http://www.geoffreysteadman.com

How to Use this Commentary

1. Skim and familiarize yourself with the introduction, glossary, and all information boxes.

Familiarity with the book will help relieve anxiety and enhance your enjoyment as you read.

2. Download free pdf copies of the commentary, translation sheets, and useful ancillaries.

The translation sheets correspond to the 63 lessons in this book and include text and lined spaces for you to write out translations, scan lines, or simply take notes as you read and review. You are encouraged to download and print out these pages as needed. The pdf of the book offers an accessible alternative to the paperback edition. The website is www.geoffreysteadman.com.

3. Review and master the core vocabulary in the shaded box before you read each lesson.

High frequency core words that occur 5 or more times are found in only three places in the commentary: (1) in a running list in the introduction, (2) in an alphabetized list in the glossary, and (3) in a shaded box in the lesson where the core word first occurs. For each lesson, review the core words in the shaded box before you read the Latin text. Since you have likely seen many of these words in earlier Latin levels, single out and review the words that you do not know. Ideally, you should use digital flashcards and review the core words daily until they are learned.

Shaded core word lists are manageable in most cases but overwhelmingly large in the initial few lessons. Still, review before you read and then review daily until the words are mastered.

All non-core words (4 or fewer times) are included in two columns below the Latin text in each lesson. If you have to look up a Latin word and it is not found in the non-core list, then the word is either a new core word in the shaded box or a previously reviewed core word that you must now look up in the alphabetized vocabulary list in the glossary.

4. Review the titles of the information boxes before you read each lesson.

Information boxes include either literary context or extended explanations of new grammar that readers will encounter in the lesson. Skimming the titles will let you know when you will want to interrupt your reading and read through a relevant grammar explanation in a box.

5. Develop the habit of making educated guesses as you read the Latin.

As you read, make an educated guess before you consult the vocabulary entries or grammar notes below the text. If you guess correctly, the commentary will confirm your knowledge of the Latin. If you guess incorrectly, you will become more aware of your weaknesses and more likely to remember the correct answer when you review the passage later.

6. After you complete a lesson, read through any unread information boxes and questions.

7. Reread a passage or lesson immediately after you have completed it.

Resist the temptation to shut down immediately and rush off to another task. The extra 5 minutes of repetition will strengthen your ability to recognize vocabulary and forms quickly, bolster your confidence, and most importantly offer you the pleasure of reading that is often missed during the initial reading. Since the Latin in the lesson is still fresh in your mind, the repetition will take just a few extra minutes but will make future review much, much easier. Repetition works.

8. Have fun.

Through the miracle of writing, you are reading the same words arranged in the same order and in the same rhythm as they were composed by another human being 2000 years ago in a different language and in a different part of the world. It is only through your effort that Vergil can speak to you today. Approach each reading with joy and wonder, and you will be rewarded.

Why Read Vergil?

What book would you copy by hand for the next generation?

For over 2000 years the *Aeneid* has been copied by hand, often by free people, more frequently by slaves for the booksellers' shops, still later by monks in monastaries, in papyrus, then in parchment made from animal skins, and finally in paper. Even after the invention of the printing press, craftsmen had to mold each letter in lead or tin, arrange the movable type into rows of words and lines, and then print individual pages that would be gathered in nested folds, sewn together, and finally glued to a binding to form a single book. All of this effort made it possible for us to read the *Aeneid* today.

We call the *Aeneid* "classical" because it has *enduring value*. Generation after generation, people chose to copy this work rather than some other piece of literature; and, more importantly, they chose to copy this work rather than do something else entirely. These two factors, the desire to preserve literature of enduring value and the passing of time, created a 2000-year old filter that allowed the *Aeneid* and other selected works to survive and those writings believed to be inferior to be lost.

One of the reasons that we read the *Aeneid* is to consider what those enduring qualities are that make the *Aeneid* a "classic" and what insights into the human condition the epic might offer today.

Great thinkers were in conversation with Vergil

Vergil's *Aeneid* was immediately influential. After Vergil's death, the emperor Augustus insisted that the poem be copied and published. Vergil's works became standard texts in Roman education. Ovid and other Roman poets alluded to the *Aeneid* and offered their own creative responses. In the late 3rd century Saint Augustine lamented that he cried more for Vergil's Dido than for his own soul, and in the *City of God* he sought to challenge the *Aeneid's* role in education. The 13th century Italian poet Dante wrote the *Inferno*, a poem that imitates Vergil's depiction of the Underworld and imagines Vergil as Dante's guide on a journey through Hell. Foundational works in English literature such as Spencer's *Fairie Queene* and Milton's *Paradise Lost* were inspired and even modeled on the *Aeneid.* As late as the early 1900s, Ivy league schools required students to have read multiple books of the epic in Latin for admission, and today the *Aeneid* is a standard text in secondary and university-level Latin courses.

The *Aeneid* is important to us, in part, because it was important to many great thinkers, who for two millennia were inspired by Vergil's reflections on myth and history to imitate and offer their own unique responses. We cannot fully understand these thinkers unless we have an understanding of Vergil. This 2000-year-old conversation between the poet and subsequent authors made the epic a foundational text in the Western tradition, and the *Aeneid's* place in education ensured that future generations could read and take part in that larger discourse on ideas which the *Aeneid* helped to inspire.

Reading the *Aeneid* allows us to join that same conversation.

Vergil was in conversation with great thinkers in his own past

Many readers will never encounter an author who imitates and repurposes previous literary works as much as Vergil. The poet models the first half of the *Aeneid* on Homer's *Odyssey* and the second half on Homer's *Iliad*, epics composed in Greek 700 years before Vergil's *Aeneid*. He models the love affair between Aeneas and Dido in part on the one between Jason and Medea in Apollonius of Rhodes' 3rd c. BC epic *Argonautika* and draws inspiration from Ennius' *Annales*, an epic on Roman history, and from Lucretius' *De Rerum Natura*, an epic on Epicurean philosophy. The works that he imitates are numerous, but for practical reasons only allusions to the *Odyssey* are noted in this commentary.

Vergil challenges the modern view that something must be brand new to be original. The poet is not plagiarizing other writers. He expects his readers to recognize the imitations and, more importantly, to notice when he offers a variation or twist from the traditional account. This combination of imitation of tradition with variation makes what is original in Vergil's poem intelligible to readers. Readers derive immediate pleasure and meaning when they recognize a familiar character, scene, or verse taken from the *Odyssey*, for example, and then Vergil's novel use of those allusions challenge readers to consider what those differences mean for the *Aeneid*. In short, Vergil engages in the same dialogue and exchange of ideas with previous writers as future writers will engage with him.

The *Aeneid* convincingly shows how knowledge of an historical and literary tradition can greatly enhance the quality of a literary work as well as the meaning and pleasure that readers derive from it.

The *Aeneid* is a Mediterranean epic that asks big philosophical questions

Vergil's ambitions take readers from the heights of Olympus to the depths of the Underworld, from Troy in modern Turkey and Tyre in modern Lebanon, through Greece, Crete, and Sicily, to Carthage in North Africa and Rome in Italy. The poet weaves together the ancient Greek traditions of myth, epic, tragedy, and philosophy with Roman culture and history, which pays respect to the contribution of the Etruscans, Latins, and other Italians and makes Augustus heir to Aeneas himself. The result is a work of propaganda that asserts that there is purpose in history, and that the purpose is to give rise to Augustus and Roman rule which will pacify and unite the Mediterranean world with the approval of the gods.

Against this backdrop the *Aeneid* invites readers to ask big questions: What does it mean to be a good person? Why must the pious suffer? What obligations do we have to one another? What role do emotions play? What role do the gods play in our lives? Does religion make us successful? If there is an afterlife, what do we imagine it to be? Why not live a life of pleasure and ignore these concerns?

Today, in school and in public spaces we are largely silent about these questions precisely because they are so personal and important. But, because Vergil wrote the *Aeneid* far removed from Christian, Judaic, and Islamic traditions, we can engage in deep and meaningful discussions without challenging our fellow readers' traditions directly. Vergil's legacy, once more, is to keep the conversation going.

A Few Preliminary Questions

Who is Vergil?

Publius Vergilius Maro (70 – 19 BC)

70 BC	born near Mantua in northern Italy
42	farm confiscated by Octavian (the emperor Augustus)
37	completes *Eclogues*, "Selections," a poem about shepherding
37	Maecenas, friend of Octavian, becomes Vergil's patron
31	completes *Georgics*, "On Farming," a poem about farming
29-19	composes the *Aeneid* (3 lines per day on average)
19	falls ill and dies in Brundisium at age 52

Vergil, also spelled "Virgil," was born in northern Italy to a family of equestrian rank in 70 BC. In 42 BC Octavian, Julius Caesar's grand-nephew and future emperor, confiscated Vergil's farm in order to resettle soldiers. Vergil was later able to recover that estate with the influence of friends. Shortly before or after the publication of the *Eclogues* in 37 BC, Vergil gained the financial support of Maecenas, a patron of the arts and both friend and advisor to Octavian. Vergil dedicated the *Georgics* to his patron Maecenas in 31 BC, and both the *Eclogues* and *Georgics* continue to be read to this day.

Since Maecenas was part of Octavian's inner circle of advisors, it is reasonable to assume that Octavian, i.e. Augustus, was indirectly or directly Vergil's patron. From 29-19 BC, Vergil composed the *Aeneid*, "Song of Aeneas," a work of propaganda that connected Aeneas and the mythology of the Trojan war directly to the rule of Augustus. In 19 BC Vergil accompanied Augustus in Athens, where the poet fell ill. Vergil died on his return home in Brundisium, Italy and requested that his unfinished *Aeneid* not be published. Augustus instead had the poem edited and published on Vergil's behalf.

Who is Augustus?

Caesar Augustus (63 BC – AD 14)

63-44	Gaius Octavius
43-27	Octavian (Gaius Julius Caesar Octavianus)
27- AD 14	Caesar Augustus (Gaius Julius Caesar Octavianus Augustus)

Gaius Octavius, Octavian, and Caesar Augustus refer to the same person at different periods of time. When Gaius Julius Caesar (100-44 BC) was assassinated in 44 BC, his only child Julia had already died while giving birth in 54. And so, Julius Caesar adopted his 17-year old grand-nephew Gaius Octavius posthumously in his will and made him his heir. Since it was common for an adoptee to assume the name of his adopted father and make his own nomen a cognomen, Gaius Octavius was renamed in 44 BC as Gaius Julius Caesar Octavianus, whom we today call Octavian. In 27 BC, the Senate bestowed on the emperor the honorific name Augustus, "the Enricher" or "Venerable one." Today, we typically call him Octavian between 44 and 31 BC (Battle of Actium) and either Augustus or Caesar Augustus when he became sole ruler and emperor from 31 BC until his death in AD 14. Other relevant details about Augustus are revealed in individual lessons throughout this commentary.

When was the *Aeneid* written?

509-31 BC	Roman Republic: government with a senate, public assemblies, consuls, praetors, etc.
133-122	**Gracchi** brothers: rival factions of senators appeal to senators or to the people for power
91-88	**Social Wars**: Italian allies (*socii*) fight with Rome over citizenship and rights
88-7, 82-1	Civil wars lead to the **dictatorship of Sulla**: rivals are executed, property is confiscated
73-71	**Spartacus** and a slave revolt throughout Italy is eventually suppressed by **Crassus**
63	**Catiline's conspiracy**: attempted coup to kill senators and redistribute land, suppressed
58-49	**Julius Caesar** conquers Gaul and refuses to relinquish power to the senate
49-45	Civil war: Caesar defeats **Pompey** and senatorial leaders around the Mediterranean
44-42	Civil war: Octavian and Marc Antony defeat Caesar's assassins, **Cassius** and **Brutus**
32-30	Civil war: **Octavian** defeats the naval forces of **Marc Antony** and Egyptian **Cleopatra**
31	**Battle of Actium** (Sept. 2, 31 BC): Octavian defeats Antony and Cleopatra decisively
29-19	**Vergil composes the *Aeneid***
27 - AD 14	First emperor **Augustus** consolidates power under *Pax Romana* until his death in AD 14

After 375 years of what Vergil's contemporaries viewed as unified government, imperial expansion, and prosperity (509-133 BC), the Roman republic suffered a century of civil wars, social upheaval, and political unrest that led to what we now call the "Fall of the Republic" (133-31 BC) and consolidation of power under Augustus. The details are too numerous to review, but readers should note that Vergil wrote the *Aeneid* (29-19 BC) when the republican government existed in form (consuls, senate, assemblies), but Augustus alone possesssed the loyalty of all legions and real decision-making power.

What are the 12 books of the *Aeneid* about?

Books 1-6 imitate the *Odyssey*

1 Juno sends a storm, Aeneas lands in Carthage
2 Aeneas recalls the fall of Troy for Dido
3 Aeneas recalls his travels at sea for Dido
4 Love affair with Dido
5 Funeral games for father Anchises
6 Aeneas visits the Underworld

Books 7-12 imitate the *Iliad*

7 Aeneas arrives in Latium, Juno incites war
8 Visits Evander at Rome, Shield of Aeneas
9 War: Nisus and Euryalus episode
10 War: Turnus kills Evander's son Pallas
11 War: mourning for Pallas, minor episodes
12 Truce among gods, Aeneas kills Turnus

The first 6 books are an imitation of Homer's *Odyssey* and the second 6 are an imitation of Homer's *Iliad*, ancient Greek epics composed 700 years before the *Aeneid* but well known to Rome's Greek-educated aristocracy. In Book 1 Juno sends a storm that shipwrecks Aeneas and the Trojans at Carthage. At a banquet hosted by Queen Dido, Aeneas recalls in Book 2 the Fall of Troy and in Book 3 his travels at sea for 7 years. In Book 4 Dido and Aeneas fall in love, and, when Aeneas is urged by the gods to leave, Dido commits suicide. In Book 5 he travels to Sicily and celebrates funeral games for his father Anchises, and in Book 6 Aeneas enters the Underworld in Italy to seek advice from his father.

In Book 7 Aeneas lands in Latium, and King Latinus offers to the Trojan his daughter Lavinia—and the future rule of the Latins. Juno incites the Latin Turnus, who was engaged to marry Lavinia before Aeneas' arrival, to wage war. In Book 8 Aeneas seeks help from Evander and the Greeks who settled near the site of Rome and from the Etruscans. In this war (Books 9-12), Aeneas is likened to the Greek Achilles, and just as Achilles kills the Trojan Hector to avenge the death of Achilles' friend Patroclus, so in Book 12 Aeneas kills Turnus to avenge the death of Aeneas' friend Pallas.

Scanning Epic Song

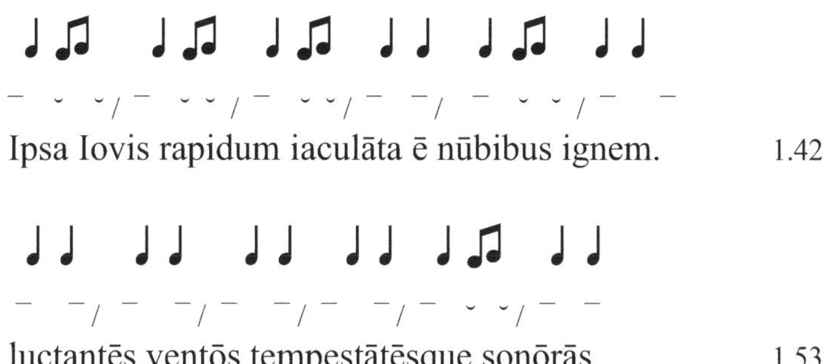

While the rhythms of English poetry are based on word-stress (stressed and unstressed syllables), Latin poetry relies on the length of syllables (long and short syllables). Long syllables are pronounced twice as long as short ones, as shown in the musical notation above. To mark the length of a syllable, we place the notation ¯ (here equal to ♩) above a long syllable and the notation ˘ ˘ (here equal to ♫) above the two short syllables.

I. Epic meter: Dactylic Hexameter

A. dactyl = "finger"

♩ ♫
¯ ˘ ˘

B. spondee = "(solemn) libation"

♩ ♩
¯ ¯

♩ = ♫
¯ ˘ ˘

Every line of the *Aeneid* includes six (*hex*) metrical feet (*metra*) of **dactyls** and **spondees**. A **dactylic** foot is a combination of 3 syllables, long-short-short (¯ ˘ ˘), just like the long and short segments of a finger. A **spondaic** foot has 2 syllables, long-long (¯ ¯), which takes just as long to pronounce as a dactylic foot. Slight metrical stress (Lat. **ictus**) is placed on the first syllable of each foot.

An epic poet uses a combination of six dactyls and spondees in every line of verse. The combination can vary from line to line depending on the poet's needs. Note in line 1.42 above (Book 1, line 42), the line has 4 dactyls and 2 spondees (d-d-d-s-d-s). In line 1.53, the poet uses 1 dactyl and 5 spondees (s-s-s-s-d-s). Although the first verse contains more syllables and appears visibly longer than the second verse, the second takes just as long as the first a to pronounce. Every line takes an equal amount of time to pronounce.

While the first four feet vary between dactyls and spondees, the last two feet are dactyl-spondee (¯ ˘ ˘ / ¯ ¯) in most—but not all—verses. The final syllable, called an **anceps**, "two-headed," may be short or long but is considered long for scanning purposes. Some mark the anceps with the letter "x" but most will scan the syllable long (¯) to complete the final spondee.

¯ / ¯ ˘ ˘ / ¯ X
…rēgīna Iovisque

but, more common…

¯ / ¯ ˘ ˘ / ¯ ¯
…rēgīna Iovisque 1.46

II. Dividing up Syllables in a Latin Word

A. A Latin word has as many syllables as vowels. There is one vowel in each syllable, and diphthongs (ae, au, oe, etc.) count as one vowel.

Ar-ma vi-rum-que ca-nō, Tro-jae quī prī-mus ab ō-rīs I.1

B. When there is one consonant between vowels, that consonant is pronounced with the 2nd syllable.

Ar-ma vi-rum-que ca-nō, Tro-jae quī prī-mus ab ō-rīs I.1

C. When there are two or more consonants between vowels, the first is pronounced with the preceding syllable and the rest are pronounced with the following syllable. There are a few exceptions.

Ar-ma vi-rum-que ca-nō, Tro-jae quī prī-mus ab ō-rīs I.1

D. qu- is considered a single consonant, and a mute consonant (t, d, b, p, c, g) followed by a liquid (l, r)—most often tr—in the same word often count as one consonant and fall in the second syllable.

Al-bā-nī-que pa-trēs at-que al-tae moe-ni-a Rō-mae. I.7

III. Three Easy Rules to Determine the Length of a Syllable

A. A syllable is long (¯) by nature if it contains…

1. a long vowel (ā, ē, ī, ō, ū)

2. a diphthong – two vowels that together produce one sound (ae, au, ei, eu, oe, ui)

B. A syllable is long (¯) by position if…

3. a short vowel is followed by 2 consonants (in the same or different words).

(x (=cs), z (=sd), and often j are considered double consonants)

C. Any syllable that does not follow the rules 1, 2, or 3 above is by default a short syllable (˘).

Lines Scanned According to the Three Easy Rules

When you scan a line of epic verse—as you will on the facing page—it is common to include long and short marks but NOT include the rule number. I have included the rule numbers below and in the answer keys just for clarification and instruction. Note that the final syllable is an **anceps**, "two-headed," (marked 'x'). It may be long or short, but is always considered long for scanning purposes.

3 3 3 1 1 1 3 x
– ˘ ˘ / – ˘ ˘ / – ˘ ˘ / – – / – ˘ ˘ / – –
Ipsa Iovis rapidum jaculāta ē nūbibus ignem. 1.42

3 3 1 3 1 3 3 1 1 1 1
– – / – – / – – / – – / – ˘ ˘ / – –
luctantēs ventōs tempestātēsque sonōrās 1.53

Scansion Rules Simplified

A syllable is long (¯) if…

1. long vowel (ā, ē, ō, ū, ī)
2. diphthong (ae, au, ei, eu, oe, ui)
3. short vowel followed by two consonants (or double consonants x, z, and sometimes j)

…all other syllables are short (˘)

Check:
(1) that you end up with a combination of six dactyls (¯ ˘ ˘) and spondees (¯ ¯)
(2) and that the last two feet most often—but not always—scan as a dactyl-spondee (¯ ˘ ˘ / ¯ ¯)

IV. Scansion Practice (Set 1)

For many, it is easier to recite hexameter aloud than to write out the long and short marks. There are variations to the rules, but before you learn them, use the rules above and mark out the long (¯) and short (˘) notations above the lines below. Before you consult the answers on the next page, perform the following check: (1) Are there six dactyls and spondees? (2) Are the final two a dactyl-spondee?

1. Ar-ma vi-rum-que ca-nō, Tro-jae quī prī-mus ab ō-rīs 1.1 remember qu = k; j is a double cons.
2. Ī-ta-li-am fā-tō pro-fu-gus Lā-vī-na-que vē-nit 1.2 qu = k
3. vī su-pe-rum, sae-vae me-mo-rem Jū-nō-nis ob ī-ram, 1.4
4. īn-fer-ret-que de-ōs La-ti-ō—ge-nus un-de La-tī-num I.6 qu = k
5. Mū-sa, mi-hī cau-sās me-mo-rā, quō nū-mi-ne lae-sō I.8 au is a diphthong

V. Scansion Practice with Ellisions (Set 2)

Elision ("cutting out"):

When a short vowel (or short vowel + m) at the end of a word is followed by a word beginning with a vowel, the short vowel (or vowel + m) is elided, "cut out," and omitted during scansion. This is similar to contraction in English. As you scan the lines below, use the rules at the top of the page. When a vowel or vowel + m at the end of a word is followed by a vowel (as underlined below), omit the final vowel from scansion (i.e. -um, -e, -e, -e) but scan the vowel that begins the following word.

6. lī-to-ra—mul-~~tum~~ il-le et ter-rīs jac-tā-tus et al-tō 1.3 -um, -e are elided
7. mul-ta quo-que et bel-lō pas-sus, dum con-de-ret ur-be 1.5 -e is elided; remember qu = k
8. Al-bā-nī-que pa-trēs at-que al-tae moe-ni-a Rō-mae. 1.7 -e is elided, tr = 1 consonant

Why is the final vowel + m elided? Linguists think that the Romans pronounced the final -m nasally, and that this nasal -m sounded enough like a vowel to be treated as such when scanning.

Scansion Rules Simplified

A syllable is long (¯) if…

1. long vowel (ā, ē, ō, ū, ī)
2. diphthong (ae, au, ei, eu, oe, ui)
3. short vowel followed by two consonants (or x, z, or j)

…all other syllables are short (˘)

Answer Key for Set 1 and 2

3 3 1 3 2 1 1 1 1
¯ ˘ ˘ / ¯ ˘ ˘ / ¯ ¯ / ¯ ¯ / ¯ ˘ ˘ / ¯ ¯
1. Ar-ma vi-rum-que ca-nō, Tro-jae quī prī-mus ab ō-rīs 1.1
remember qu = k
j is a double cons.

1 3 1 1 3 1 1 1 x
¯ ˘ ˘ / ¯ ¯ / ¯ ˘ ˘ / ¯ ¯ / ¯ ˘ ˘ / ¯ ¯
2. Ī-ta-li-am fā-tō pro-fu-gus Lā-vī-na-que vē-nit 1.2

1 3 2 2 3 1 1 1 x
¯ ˘ ˘ / ¯ ¯ / ¯ ˘ ˘ / ¯ ¯ / ¯ ˘ ˘ / ¯ ¯
3. vī su-pe-rum, sae-vae me-mo-rem Jū-nō-nis ob ī-ram, 1.4

1 3 3 1 1 3 1 x
¯ ¯ / ¯ ˘ ˘ / ¯ ˘ ˘ / ¯ ˘ ˘ / ¯ ˘ ˘ / ¯ ¯
4. īn-fer-ret-que de-ōs La-ti-ō—ge-nus un-de La-tī-num 1.6
qu = k

1 1 2 1 1 1 1 2 1
¯ ˘ ˘ / ¯ ¯ / ¯ ˘ ˘ / ¯ ¯ / ¯ ˘ ˘ / ¯ ¯
5. Mū-sa, mi-hī cau-sās me-mo-rā, quō nū-mi-ne lae-sō 1.8
au is a diphthong

1 3 3 3 3 1 3 1 3 1
¯ ˘ ˘ / ¯ ¯ / ¯ ¯ / ¯ ¯ / ¯ ˘ ˘ / ¯ ¯
6. lī-to-ra—mul-~~tum~~ il-le et ter-rīs jac-tā-tus et al-tō 1.3
-um/-e are elided

3 3 3 1 3 3 3 3 3 x
¯ ˘ ˘ / ¯ ¯ / ¯ ¯ / ¯ ¯ / ¯ ˘ ˘ / ¯ ¯
7. mul-ta quo-que et bel-lō pas-sus, dum con-de-ret ur-be 1.5
-e is elided

3 1 1 1 3 2 2 1 2
¯ ¯ / ¯ ˘ ˘ / ¯ ¯ / ¯ ¯ / ¯ ˘ ˘ / ¯ ¯
8. Al-bā-nī-que pa-trēs at-que al-tae moe-ni-a Rō-mae. 1.7
-e is elided,
tr = 1 consonant

VI. Oral Recitation

Finally, it is common when first reading hexameter to give stilted, mechanical recitations that place excessive word stress (**ictus**) on the first long syllable of each of the six feet in each verse at the expense of the natural accentuation. This tendency is both useful and perhaps necessary when you first learn to recite in meter. In classroom settings, teachers sometimes encourage exaggeration because they recognize that new readers are accustomed to hearing word stress and that stilted recitations will help students recognize the individual feet within the verse.

Many readers choose never to pass beyond this stage. Over time, however, you should focus on natural accentuation and try to develop an ear for the rhythmic long and short syllables of each line.

Scansion Rules Simplified

A syllable is long (ˉ) if…

1. long vowel (ā, ē, ō, ū, ī)
2. diphthong (ae, au, ei, eu, oe, ui)
3. short vowel followed by two consonants (or double consonants j, x, or z)

…all other syllables are short (˘)

VII. Extra Scansion Practice (Set 3): Juno' Initial Speech

Mark out the long (ˉ) and short (˘) notations above the lines below. You must find the ellisions and mark them yourself, but the end of each line provides a hint. Before you consult the answers on the next page, perform the following check: (1) Are there six dactyls and spondees? (2) Are the final two a dactyl-spondee?

9. Vix ē cōn-spec-tū Si-cu-lae tel-lū-ris in al-tum 1.34 x is a double cons.

10. vē-la da-bant lae-tī et spū-mās sa-lis ae-re ru-ē-bant, 1.35 1 ellision

11. cum Jū-nō ae-ter-num ser-vāns sub pec-tore vul-nus 1.36 1 ellision

12. haec sē-cum: "Mē-ne in-cep-tō dē-sis-te-re vic-tam I.37 1 ellision

13. nec pos-se Ī-ta-li-ā Teu-crō-rum ā-ver-te-re rē-gem? I.38 2 ellisions
eu is a diphthong

14. Quip-pe ve-tor fā-tīs. Pal-las-ne ex-ū-re-re clas-sem 1.39 1 ellision
remember qu = k

15. Ar-gī-vum at-que ip-sōs po-tu-it sum-mer-ge-re pon-tō 1.40 2 ellision

16. ū-ni-us ob no-xam et fu-ri-ās A-jā-cis O-ī-leī*? 1.41 1 ellision
x, j are double cons.

17. Ip-sa Jo-vis ra-pi-dum ja-cu-lā-ta ē nū-bi-bus ig-nem I.42 1 ellision
j is a single cons.

18. dis-iē-cit-que ra-tēs ē-ver-tit-que ae-quo-ra ven-tīs, I.43 1 ellision

19. il-lum ex-spī-ran-tem trāns-fī-xō pec-to-re flam-mās I.44 1 ellision

20. tur-bi-ne cor-ri-pu-it sco-pu-lō-que īn-fī-xit a-cū-tō; I.45 1 ellision

* Synizesis is one of the rare exceptions to the rules. It occurs when two vowels that should be pronounced in separate syllables are pronounced as a single syllable. The final -eī in O-ī-leī should be pronounced as two syllables (e-ī) but is here pronounced as a single long syllable.

Answer Key for Set 3

3 1 1 3 1 2 3 1 3 x

9. Vix ē cōn-spec-tū Si-cu-lae tel-lū-ris in al-tum 1.34 x is a double cons

1 3 2 3 1 1 2 1 3

10. vē-la da-bant lae-~~tī~~ et spū-mās sa-lis ae-re ru-ē-bant, 1.35 1 ellision

3 1 2 3 3 3 1 3 3 3 x

11. cum Jū-~~nō~~ ae-ter-num ser-vāns sub pec-tore vul-nus 1.36

2 1 3 1 3 3 1 1 3 3 x

12. haec sē-cum: “Mē-ne in-cep-tō dē-sis-te-re vic-tam I.37 1 ellision

3 3 1 1 2 1 1 3 1 x

13. nec pos-~~se~~ Ī-ta-li-ā Teu-crō-~~rum~~ ā-ver-te-re rē-gem? I.38 2 ellision
eu is a diphthong

3 3 1 1 3 3 3 1 3 x

14. Quip-pe ve-tor fā-tīs. Pal-las-~~ne~~ ex-ū-re-re clas-sem 1.39 1 ellision
remember qu = k

3 1 3 3 1 3 3 3 3 1

15. Ar-gī-~~vum~~ at-~~que~~ ip-sōs po-tu-it sum-mer-ge-re pon-tō 1.40 2 ellision

1 3 3 3 1 3 1 1 1

16. ū-ni-us ob no-~~xam~~ et fu-ri-ās A-jā-cis O-ī-leī*? 1.41 1 ellision with -m
x, j are double cons.

3 3 3 1 1 1 3 x

17. Ip-sa Jo-vis ra-pi-dum ja-cu-lā-~~ta~~ ē nū-bi-bus ig-nem I.42 1 ellision
j is a single cons.

3 1 3 1 1 3 3 2 3 1

18. dis-iē-cit-que ra-tēs ē-ver-tit-~~que~~ ae-quo-ra ven-tīs, I.43 1 ellision

3 3 1 3 3 1 1 1 3 3 1

19. il-~~lum~~ ex-spī-ran-tem trāns-fī-xō pec-to-re flam-mās I.44 1 ellision with -m

3 3 3 1 1 1 1 1

20. tur-bi-ne cor-ri-pu-it sco-pu-lō-~~que~~ īn-fī-xit a-cū-tō; I.45 1 ellision

Running Core Vocabulary (5 or more times)

The following list includes all 275 words in the Vergil selections that occur five or more times arranged in a running vocabulary list. The number on the left of the dictionary entry indicates the lesson in which the word first appears. The number on the end of the entry indicates how many times the word occurs in the commentary. These same dictionary entries are found in an alphabetized list in the glossary.

1 **ā, ab, abs**: (away) from, by, 25
1 **altus, -a, -um**: high; deep; **altum, ī n.**: (deep) sea, 28
1 **animus, -ī m**: mind; spirit; courage; anger, 19
1 **arma, -ōrum n**: arms; weapons and armor, 18
1 **atque, ac**: and; as, 38
1 **bellum, -ī n**: war, 11
1 **causa, -ae f**: reason, cause; for the sake of (gen), 7
1 **deus, -ī m**: god, 19
1 **dum**: while, as long as, until; provided that, 6
1 **ego, meī** (pl **nōs, nostrum**): I (pl. we), 43
1 **et**: and; also, even, too, 173
1 **fātum, -ī n**: fate, 18
1 **genus, -eris n**: birth, lineage, family, race; kind, 7
1 **iactō** (1): to throw (back and forth), toss, 7
1 **ille, illa, illud**: that, those, 41
1 **īra, -ae f**: anger, rage; passion, 11
1 **Ītalia, -ae f**: Italy, 11
1 **Iūnō, Iūnōnis f**: Juno, 9
1 **labor, -ōris m.**: labor, hardship, task, 8
1 **lītus, -oris n**: shore, coast, beach, 15
1 **moenia, -ium n**: walls; defense, city-walls; 7
1 **multus, -a, -um**: much, many, 9
1 **-ne**: *indicates a yes/no question*; whether, or, 9
1 **nūmen, -inis n**: divine power, approval, 7
1 **ōra, -ae f.**: shore, coast, border, 5
1 **pater, -tris m**: father; ancestor, 13
1 **pietās, -tātis f**: piety, devotion, 6
1 **prīmus, -a, -um**: first; leading, 23
1 **que**: and, 273
1 **quī, quae, quod (quis? quid?)**: who, which, what, that; *after sī*: any, some, 136
1 **rēgīna, -ae f**: queen, 10
1 **saevus, -a, -um**: savage, fierce, 7
1 **tantus, -a, -um:** so great, so much, so many, 18
1 **terra, -ae f:** land, ground, earth, 20
1 **tot**: so many, 8
1 **Troia, ae f:** Troy, 13
1 **urbs, urbis f:** city, 27
1 **ve, vel:** or (either or both options hold true), 8
1 **veniō, -īre, vēnī, ventus:** come, go, 14
1 **vir, -ī m:** man, husband, 22
1 **vīs, vīs f :** force, power; *pl.* **vīrēs**, strength, 7
1 **volvō, -ere, -ī, volūtus:** turn, roll (over), revolve, 6
2 **arx, arcis f**: citadel, (fortifed) hilltop, 12
2 **dea, -ae f**: goddess, 7
2 **dūcō, -ere, dūxī, ductus**: lead, draw; consider, 9
2 **sum, esse, fuī, futūrus:** be, 55
2 **ferō, ferre, tulī, lātus**: bear, endure, carry, report, 25
2 **gēns, gentis f**: race, people, clan, 11
2 **hīc**: here, 13
2 **hinc**: from here, hence, from this place, 7
2 **hic, haec, hoc**: this, these, 73
2 **iam**: now, already, 19
2 **lātus, -a, -um**: wide, 6
2 **Libya, -ae f**: Libya, 5
2 **longus, -a, -um**: long; *adv*. far, 10
2 **omnis, -e**: all, every, whole, entire, 27
2 **populus, -ī m**: people, 6
2 **rēgnum, -ī n**: kingdom, kingship, rule, 14
2 **sanguis, -inis m**: blood, 6
2 **sed:** but, 15
2 **sī:** if, whether, 26
2 **sīc:** thus, so, in this way, 17
2 **tendō, -ere, -dī, tentus:** stretch; strive, hasten, 8
2 **teneō, -ēre, -uī, -tus:** hold; grab, 11
2 **tum, tunc:** then, at that time; 18
2 **Tyrius, -a, -um:** Tyrian, of Tyre; Carthaginian, 8
2 **ūnus, -a, -um:** one, alone; **ūnā**, together, 10
3 **ad:** to, toward, at, near (acc.), 29
3 **aequor, -oris n**: sea, the level (sea), 11
3 **agō, -ere, ēgī, āctus**: drive, lead, do, 9
3 **annus, -ī m**: year, 5
3 **circum**: around (acc.), 12
3 **Danaus, -a, -um**: Danaan (Greek), 7
3 **dolor, -ōris m**: pain, grief, 6
3 **errō** (1): wander, 10
3 **etiam**: also, even, 7
3 **gerō, -ere, gessī, gestus**: carry (on), wage, 5
3 **invideō, -ēre**: hate, envy, 6
3 **is, ea, id**: he, she, it, they; this, that, these, those; 5
3 **mare, -is n**: sea, 5
3 **mōlēs, -is f**: mass, structure; burden, 5
3 **per**: through, over, by, 45
3 **rapiō, -ere, rapuī, raptum**: snatch, seize; kidnap, 7

3 **Rōmānus, -a, -um**: Roman, 5

3 **tōtus, -a, -um:** total, entire, whole, 8

3 **Trōs, Trōis**: Trojan, 5

4 **classis, -is f**: fleet, 8

4 **corripiō, -ere, -uī, -reptus**: snatch (up), 6

4 **cum**: with; when, since, although, 23

4 **dō, dare, dedī, datum**: give; grant, allow, 27

4 **ē, ex**: out of, from (abl.), 8

4 **flamma, -ae f**: flame, 8

4 **ignis, -is m**: fire; lightning, 15

4 **incipiō, -ere, incēpī, inceptum**: begin, undertake, 6

4 **ipse, -a, -um**: himself, herself, myself, -self; very, 22

4 **Iuppiter, Iovis, Iovī, Iovem Iove m**: Jupiter, 9

4 **laetus, -a, -um**: happy; fertile, 5

4 **nec**: nor, and not; **nec…nec**: neither…nor, 30

4 **nūbēs, -is f**: cloud, 6

4 **pectus, -oris n**: chest, breast; heart, 12

4 **pontus, -ī m**: sea, 9

4 **possum, posse, potuī**: be able, can, 5

4 **ruō, ruere, -ī**: rush (over), fall; plow, 8

4 **scopulus, -ī m.**: rock, cliff, crag, 6

4 **sē:** him-, her-, it-, themselves, 20

4 **servō** (1)**:** save, perserve, keep, 6

4 **sub:** under, beneath; near, 13

4 **tellūs, -ūris f.**: land, earth, 6

4 **Teucrus, a, um:** Teucrian, Trojan, 10

4 **ventus, -ī m.:** wind, 11

4 **vincō, -ere, vīcī, victus:** conquer, 5

4 **vulnus, -eris n.**: wound, injury, 7

5 **Aeolus, -ī m.**: Aeolus (king of the winds), 5

5 **antrum, -ī n.**: cave, 5

5 **āra, -ae f.**: altar, 8

5 **at, ast**: but, yet, however, at least, 10

5 **aura, -ae f.**: breeze, air, 6

5 **aut:** or; **aut…aut**: either…or, 31

5 **caelum, -ī n.**: sky, 13

5 **coniūnx, -iugis m/f**: spouse, husband, wife, 6

5 **cor, cordis n.**: heart, 5

5 **dīvus, -a, -um**: divine; *noun*, god, goddess, 12

5 **faciō, -ere, fēcī, factum**: do, make, 7

5 **furō, -ere, -uī**: rage, rave, seethe, 7

5 **imperium, -ī n.**: power, command; empire, 6

5 **imponō, -ere, -posuī, -positus**: impose, place on, 5

5 **in**: in, on, among (abl.); into, against (acc.), 55

5 **locus, -ī m.** (pl. locī, loca): place, 8

5 **magnus, -a, -um**: great, large, 19

5 **mōns, montis m.**: mountain, 5

5 **patria, -ae f.**: fatherland, country, 8

5 **premō, -ere, pressī, pressum**: (sup)press, control, 5

5 **soror, sorōris f.**: sister, 5

5 **tālis, -e:** such, 15

5 **vastus, -a, -um:** vast, enormous, 7

6 **āter, ātra, ātrum**: dark, black, 7

6 **corpus, -oris n.**: body, 11

6 **flūctus, -ūs** m: wave, 11

6 **iubeō, -ēre, iussī, iussus**: order, command, 9

6 **nam, namque**: for; indeed, truly, 6

6 **pulcher, -chra, -chrum**: beautiful, pretty; noble, 5

6 **puppis, -is f.**: deck, ship, 5

6 **tollō, -ere, sustulī, sublātus:** raise, lift up; destroy, 5

6 **vōx, vocis f.:** voice, utterance; word, 8

7 **agmen, -inis n.**: column, formation (of troops), 5

7 **clāmor, -ōris m.**: shout, noise, 5

7 **dīcō, -ere, dīxī, dictus**: say, speak, tell, 18

7 **īmus, -a, -um**: bottom of, lowest (part) of, 5

7 **latus, -eris n.**: side, 5

7 **Ō**: O! oh!, 14

7 **parēns, -entis m./f.**: parent, 6

7 **porta, -ae f.**: gate, 6

7 **sēdēs, -is f.**: seat; home, dwelling, foundation, 7

7 **tū, tuī** (*pl.* **vōs, vestrum**) **:** you, 44

7 **tuus, -a, -um:** your, yours, 11

7 **ubi:** where; when, 10

7 **ut:** so that, that; as, when; how, 11

8 **Aenēās, -ae, acc. -ān m.**: Aeneas, 23

8 **anima, -ae f.**: breath, life; soul, spirit, 5

8 **ante**: before, in front of (acc.); before, previously, 10

8 **dexter, -tra, -trum**: right (hand), favorable, 9

8 **fortis, -e**: strong, brave, 5

8 **ingēns, -entis**: huge, immense, 13

8 **nōn**: not, 22

8 **nox, noctis, f.**: night, 7

8 **oculus, -ī m.**: eye, 12

8 **ōs, ōris n.**: mouth, face, 10

8 **referō, -ferre, -tulī, -lātus**: carry back; report, say, 5

8 **sīdus, -eris n.:** star, constellation, 7

8 **tēlum, -ī n.:** spear, arrow, projectile, 6

8 **unda, -ae f.:** wave, 14

9 **adversus, -a, -um**: facing, opposite, straight on, 5

9 **aperiō, -īre, -uī, apertus**: open; reveal, 5

9 **harēna, -ae f.**: sand, 6

9 **immānis, -e**: immense, huge, 6

9 **inter**: between, among, during (acc.), 8

9 **lateō, -ēre, -uī**: lie hidden, hide; escape notice, 5

9 **medius, -a, -um**: middle (part) of, middle, 12

9 **saxum, -ī n.**: rock, 11

9 **summus, -a, -um:** top of, highest, 9

9 **torqueō, -ēre, torsī, tortum**: twist, turn, 5

9 **videō, -ēre, vīdī, vīsus:** see; *videor*, seem, 24
9 **vocō (1):** call, name; summon, 8
10 **accipiō, -ere, -cēpī, -ceptus**: receive, take, 7
10 **caput, -itis n.**: head; life, 10
10 **gravis, -e**: heavy, serious, severe 5
10 **intereā**: meanwhile, in the meantime, 5
10 **misceō, -ēre, -uī, mīxtum**: mix (up), 7
10 **nāvis, -is f.**: ship, 11
10 **vertex, -icis m.**: peak; whirlpool, 5
11 **domus, -ūs f.**: home, house(hold); 8
11 **for, fārī, fātus sum**: speak, say, tell, 7
11 **fuga, -ae f.**: flight; haste, 5
11 **meus, -a, -um**: my, mine, 10
11 **moveō, -ēre, mōvī, mōtus**: move, upset, 7
11 **poena, -ae f.**: punishment, penalty, 5
11 **post**: after, behind (acc.), later, 5
11 **sors, sortis f.**: lot, lottery; luck, 5
11 **vester, -ra, -rum**: your, yours, 5
12 **aiō, ais, ait; aiunt:** say, speak; assert, 7
12 **cūnctus, -a, -um**: all, whole, entire, 5
12 **regō, -ere, rēxī, rectus**: rule, lead, direct, 13
12 **simul:** at the same time, together, 7
13 **cursus, -ūs m.**: course, running; haste, 6
13 **dulcis, -e**: sweet, pleasant, fresh, 7
13 **petō, -ere, -īvi**: seek, head for; ask, 14
13 **ūllus, -a, -um:** any(one, thing), 5
13 **umbra, -ae f.:** shade, shadow, ghost, 12
14 **amor, -ōris m.**: love, 9
14 **hūc**: to this place, hither, 5
14 **pōnō, -ere, posuī, positum**: put, place (aside), 5
14 **rēs, reī, f.**: thing, matter, affair; circumstance, 11
14 **subeō, -īre, -iī, itus:** go up to, approach, 6
15 **celer, -eris, -ere**: swift, quick, 6
15 **manus, -ūs f.**: hand, 9
15 **nūllus, -a, -um**: not any, no(one, thing), 6
15 **prior, prius**: earlier, before, 6
15 **socius, -ī m.:** comrade, ally, 6
15 **tergum, -ī n.**: back (part of the body), rear, 5
16 **cūra, -ae f.**: care, concern; worry, anxiety, 7
16 **fīnis, -is m./f.**: end, border; territory 5
16 **spēs, -eī f.**: hope, expectation, 6
16 **varius, -a, -um**: various, 5
16 **vultus, -ūs m.**: expression, face, 6
17 **alius, -a, -ud** : other, another, else, 9
17 **ardeō, -ēre, arsī, arsus**: burn, be eager to (inf.), 8
17 **mīror, -ārī, -ātus sum**: wonder, be amazed at, 5
17 **mūrus, ī m.**: wall, 8
17 **pars, -tis f.**: part, side, direction; some...others, 5
17 **tectum, -ī n.:** roof; shelter, house, building, 6
18 **Dīdō, -ōnis f.**: Dido, 11
18 **quālis, -e**: which/what sort; such as, just as, like, 7
18 **surgō, -ere, -rēxī, -rēctus:** raise, rise up, surge, 5
18 **templum, -ī n.**: temple, 5
19 **rīpa, -ae f.**: bank, 8
19 **tacitus, -a, -um**: silent, speechless, still, 5
20 **eō, īre, iī, itus**: go, 10
20 **metus, -ūs f.**: dread, fear, 5
21 **aspiciō, -ere, spexī, spectus**: to look at, see, 9
21 **dē**: (down) from; about, concerning, 10
21 **fāma, -ae f.**: fame, rumor, reputation, 9
21 **ferrum, -ī n.**: iron; sword, weapon, tool, 7
21 **miser, -era, -rum**: miserable, wretched, 6
21 **nōmen, -inis n.**: name, fame, renown 5
21 **noster, -ra, -rum**: our, ours, 10
21 **nunc**: now, 15
23 **crūdēlis, -e**: cruel, bloody, 6
24 **dēmittō, -ere, -mīsī, -missum**: drop, sink, 5
25 **crēdō, -ere, -didī**: believe, trust, 5
25 **dōnum, -ī n.**: gift, offering, prize, 6
25 **extrēmus, -a, -um:** farthest, outermost, 5
25 **īdem, eadem, idem**: same, the same, 6
26 **gemitus, -ūs m.**: groan, lament, sob, 5
26 **nē**: lest, that not, so that not; no, not, 5
26 **stō, -āre, stetī, status:** stand, stop, 6
28 **fugiō, -ere, fūgī**: flee, escape; avoid, 5
28 **nātus, -ī m.**: son (male having been born) 8
29 **ōrō (1)**: plead, beg; pray for, entreat, 8
29 **pēs, pedis m.**: foot, 5
29 **puer, -ī m.**: boy, child, 6
29 **sacer, -cra, -crum**: sacred, holy; rite, ritual, 5
30 **līmen, -inis n.**: threshold, doorway, 5
31 **lux, lūcis f.**: light, daylight; life, 5
31 **somnus, -ī m.:** sleep; dream 5
32 **capiō, -ere, -cēpī, captus**: take, seize, catch, 5
32 **comes, -itis m./f.**: companion; comrade, 5
32 **heu**: hail! hey! (to grab attention); alas! ah! 7
32 **quaerō, -ere, quaesīvī, -sītus**: search for, ask, 5
33 **dēsero, -ere, -ruī**: desert, forsake, abandon, 6
35 **Anchīsēs, -ae, acc. -ēn m.**: Anchises 8
39 **lūmen, -inis n.**: light, lamp; eye; life, 5
44 **morior, morī, mortuus sum**: die, 5
44 **tandem:** finally; at length, pray, 5
45 **lacrima, -ae f.**: tear, 5
45 **sōlus, -a, -um:** alone, only, sole, 5

Abbreviations

abs.	absolute	gen.	genitive	p. pl.	plural
acc.	accusative	imper.	imperative	PPP	perfect passive pple.
act.	active	impers.	impersonal	pple.	participle
adj.	adjective	impf.	imperfect	pass	passive
adv.	adverb	ind.	indirect	pf.	perfect
app.	appositive	indic.	indicative	plpf.	pluperfect
comp.	comparative	inf.	infinitive	pred.	predicate
dat.	dative	inter.	interrogative	pres.	present
dep.	deponent	l. (ll.)	line (lines)	s. sg.	singular
dir.	direct	m.	masculine	seq.	sequence
disc.	discourse	n.	neuter	subj.	subject, subjunctive
f.	feminine	nom.	nominative	superl.	superlative
fut.	future	obj.	object	voc.	vocative
1s, 2s, 3s	1st, 2nd, 3rd person singular			1p, 2p, 3p	1st, 2nd, 3rd person plural

---

Citations: The *Aeneid* consists of 9,896 lines of epic verse (dactylic hexameter) divided among 12 books that vary between 705 and 952 lines each. A Roman *liber*, "book," is the length of a single scroll—the equivalent of a long chapter today. And so, the 12 books of the *Aeneid* are equivalent to 12 lengthy chapters in a single modern book. All of the selections in this commentary come from Books 1, 2, 4, and 6 in the first half of the epic.

These 12 books do not have titles. Instead, when we refer to a specific book in the *Aeneid*, we capitalize the word "book" and add the number as a Roman or Arabic numeral: Book III or Book 3.

When citing a passage in the *Aeneid*, it is common to include the book as a Roman or Arabic numeral and the line number as an Arabic numeral: I.34 or 1.34 therefore refer to line 34 in the first book. If you cite an extended passage, add a hyphen: 2.42-49 refers to lines 42 through 49 in the second book. Finally, if it is unclear that you are referring to the *Aeneid* or if you refer to several different works in the same passage, you should add the title in italics before the book number: e.g. *Aeneid* 2.42-49.

When you include an accurate English translation of the Latin, it is common to include the translation in quotation marks and immediately follow the translation with the original Latin and line number in parentheses. A comma separates the Latin text from the book and line number. If the Latin is more than three words, often you may include the first and last Latin word and use ellipses (...) inbetween:

> The first words of the epic are "I sing of arms and a man" (*Arma virumque cano*, I.1).
>
> Aeolus "sits on the high citadel, holding his scepter" (*celsā... tenēns*, I.55-6).

In a classroom setting teachers may allow a range of citation formats, but in all cases (a) an accurate translation is placed in quotation marks, (b) the specific lines are cited in the sentence, and (c) the original Latin is cited immediately after the translation so readers can decide whether the translation is in fact an accurate interpretation of the Latin. Note that the example below includes all three elements:

> When in lines 139-41 Neptune refers to Aeolus' domain with the derogatory words "rock" (*saxa*) and "prison" (*carcere*), the god draws attention to how little power Aeolus has relative to Neptune's power over the entire sea.

The Virgilian connection between love and the constitution of civic life is significant. Certainly the wars between Rome and Carthage had economic and political causes, not the abandonment of Dido by Aeneas, not the removal of love, which is only a poetic cause. But why "only"? I—like anyone who loves literature—believe that the poetic causes say more than the political and economic causes, in fact they go to the heart of the political and economic causes.

- Elena Ferrante
La Frantumaglia

To make the ancients speak, we must feed them with our own blood.

- von Wilamowitz-Moellendorff

Arma virumque canō, Troiae quī prīmus ab ōrīs
Ītaliam, fātō profugus, Lāvīnaque vēnit
lītora—multum ille et terrīs iactātus et altō
vī superum, saevae memorem Iūnōnis ob īram,
multa quoque et bellō passus, dum conderet urbem
inferretque deōs Latiō—genus unde Latīnum
Albānīque patrēs atque altae moenia Rōmae.
  Mūsa, mihī causās memorā, quō nūmine laesō
quidve dolēns rēgīna deum tot volvere cāsūs
insignem pietāte virum, tot adīre labōrēs
impulerit. Tantaene animīs caelestibus īrae?

---

adeō, -īre, i(v)ī, itus: go to, approach, 2
Albānus, -a, -um; Alban, of Alba Longa
caelestis, -e: celestial, heavenly
canō, -ere, cecinī, cantus: sing (about), 3
cāsus, -ūs m: misfortune; chance, 4
condō, -ere, condidī, -ditum: found; hide, 4
doleō, -ēre, doluī: grieve, feel pain, suffer
impellō, -ere, -pulī, -pulsus: drive, set into motion, 3
inferō, -ferre, -tulī: carry or bring on, 2
insignis, -e: distinguished, marked, 3
labōrō (1): work, toil
laedō, -ere, -sī, -sus: hurt, harm; offend, 2
Latīnus, -a, -um: Latin, of Latin, 2
Latium, -ī n: Latium, 4
Lāvīnus, -a, -um: Lavinian (of the town Lavinium)
memor, -oris: mindful, remembering (gen) 4
memorō (1): recall, recount, 2
Mūsa, -ae f: Muse
ob: on account of, because of (acc), 3
patior, -ī, passus sum: suffer, endure; allow, 4
profugus, -a, -um: exiled, fugitive
quoque: also, 2
Rōma, -ae f: Rome
superus, -a, -um: above, higher; *noun* god above, 3
unde: whence, from which, 2

1 **virumque**: et virum; i.e. Aeneas
Troiae...ab ōrīs: abl. from ōra, -ae f. 'shore'
quī prīmus...vēnit: *who was the first to come...*; several groups of Trojans left Troy, and Aeneas' was the first to arrive at Italy

2 **Ītaliam...Lāvīniaque lītora**: *to...*; acc. place to which; Lavinium is a town founded by Aeneas
fātō: *by...*; 'because of...' abl of cause
profugus: in apposition to nom. sg. quī

3 **multum**: *much*; adverbial acc.
ille: *that one*; i.e. Aeneas
et terrīs...et altō...: *both on...and on...*; abl. place where; for altō, see note below
iactātus (est): 3s pf. pass.
altō: *the sea*; 'the deep,' metonymy: this neut. substantive is often used to mean 'the sea'
vī: *by force*; abl. of means, irreg. abl. sg. vīs

4 **super(ōr)um**: *of (those)...*; gen. pl.; i.e. gods
memorem: transferred epithet: the adj. agrees logically with īram but describes Juno

5 **multa**: *many things*; neut. acc. pl. substantive
passus (est): 3s pf. dep. patior: translate active

6 **dum conderet...inferretque**: *until he could... and could...*; 3s impf. anticipatory subj.; dum + subj. can express intention equiv. to a purpose clause and reveals the fatō expressed in line 2

7 **Latiō**: *into...*; dat. of compound verb in-ferret
unde (veniunt): *from where...come...*; ellipsis: add a verb to agree with all three nom. subjects

8 **Mūsa**: vocative, direct address; Vergil invokes the goddess to narrate the epic through him
memorā: sg. imperative
quō nūmine laesō: *by what the numen having been insulted*; 'because of what...' ind. question in apposition to causās: abl. abs + abl. of cause

9 **quidve dolēns...impulerit**: *or grieving what...*; ind. question with pf. subj. impellō; -ve = 'or'
de(ōr)um: gen. pl. deus
virum insignem pietāte volvere tot cāsūs (et) adīre tot labōrēs: *that a man...*; ind. disc. with anaphora, asyndeton (lack of conjunction 'et')

10 **pietāte**: *in...*; abl. of respect with insignem
volvere: *undergo*; 'turn over'

11 **Tantae-ne animīs caelestibus īrae (erant)?**: animīs caelestibus is dat. of possession: either make the dative possessive (1) 'Was the anger of the celestial spirits so great?' or make dative the subject: (2) 'Did the celestial spirits have such great anger?' ellipsis: add a linking verb; īrae is often pl. but may be translated as sg.

ā, ab, abs: (away) from, by, 25
altus, -a, -um: high; deep; **altum, ī n.**: (deep) sea, 28
animus, -ī m: mind; spirit; courage; anger, 19
arma, -ōrum n: arms; weapons and armor, 18
atque, ac: and; as, 4
bellum, -ī n: war, 11
causa, -ae f: reason, cause; for the sake of (gen), 7
deus, -ī m: god, 19
dum: while, as long as, until; provided that, 6
ego, meī (pl **nōs, nostrum**): I (pl. we), 43
et: and; also, even, too, 173
fātum, -ī n: fate, 18
genus, -eris n: birth, lineage, family, race; kind, 7
iactō (1): to throw (back and forth), toss, 7
ille, illa, illud: that, those, 41
īra, -ae f: anger, rage; passion, 11
Ītalia, -ae f: Italy, 11
Iūnō, Iūnōnis f: Juno, 9
labor, -ōris m.: labor, hardship, task, 8
lītus, -oris n: shore, coast, beach, 15
moenia, -ium n: walls; city-walls; 7
multus, -a, -um: much, many, 9
-ne: *indicates a yes/no question*; whether, or, 9
nūmen, -inis n: divine power, approval, 7
ōra, -ae f.: shore, coast, border, 5
pater, -tris m: father; ancestor, 13
pietās, -tātis f: piety, devotion, 6
prīmus, -a, -um: first; leading, 23
que: and, 273
quī, quae, quod (quis?quid?): who, which, what, 136
rēgīna, -ae f: queen, 10
saevus, -a, -um: savage, fierce, 7
tantus, -a, -um: so great, so much, so many, 18
terra, -ae f: land, ground, earth, 20
tot: so many, 8
Troia, ae f: Troy, 13
urbs, urbis f: city, 27
-ve, vel: or (either or both options hold true), 8
veniō, -īre, vēnī, ventus: come, go, 14
vir, -ī m: man, husband, 22
vīs, vīs f : force, power; *pl.* **vīrēs**, strength, 7
volvō, -ere, -ī, volūtus: turn, roll (over), revolve, 6

Introduction (ll. 1-7) and Invocation (ll. 8-11)

1. **arma virumque (I.1)**: The first word summarizes an epic in the same way as the title of a music album encapsulates the songs in the album. The first word in Homer's *Odyssey* is *andra*, 'man,' and the first word in Homer's *Iliad*, about Achilles and the last year of the Trojan war, is *mēnin*, 'wrath.' Both were written in Greek in 750-720 BC. Here, Vergil alludes to both epics and effectively asserts: 'This is my *Odyssey* and this is my *Iliad*, a Latin work that will rival the greatest Greek epics.'

2. **fatō profugus (I.2)**: Vergil suggests that his work will not merely rival but surpass the epics of Homer. The suggestion that the man, i.e. Aeneas, was a fugitive *by fate* is provocative. The Greeks, on this view, did not win the Trojan war because of their military prowess or the favor of the gods but because fate had a greater purpose: to drive the defeated Trojans to Italy and give rise to Rome. And so, just as Christians call the *Hebrew Bible* the 'Old Testament' and thereby assert that their *New Testament* is more important, so Vergil suggests that his epic and the story of Rome is more important than the Greek epics and all the Greek art and literature influenced by those epics.

3. **multum ille et terrīs iactātus et altō (1.3)...multa quoque et bellō passus (l. 5)**: This is the narrative of Books 1-6 and 7-12 respectively. As readers will discover, the first six books imitate the *Odyssey* while the second six imitate the *Iliad*. By alluding to the travels of Odysseus and war with Achilles, Vergil elevates the minor hero Aeneas to the heroic status of both Odysseus and Achilles.

4. **dum conderet urbem inferretque deōs...Rōmae (ll. 5-7)**: The use of the subjunctive indicates purpose and offers a partial explanation for the word 'fatō' in line 2. Vergil connects the world of Greek myth and literature with the founding of Rome. As Vergil later reveals, Aeneas will found the city Lavinium and rule the Latins for 3 years; his son Ascanius will found Alba Longa and rule the Albans for 30 years; and, after 300 years of kings at Alba Longa, Romulus will found the city of Rome (I.265-74). Note how Vergil begins the introduction with the word 'Troiae' and ends the final line with 'Rōmae.' In doing so, Vergil explicitly connects the gods of Troy with those of Rome itself.

5. **Mūsa, mihī causās memorā (l. 8)**: The invocation of the muse is a common epic convention, found in the *Odyssey* and *Iliad*. In effect, the rest of the epic is told by the goddess of creativity through Vergil. This allows the poet to be an omniscient narrator and relate details about the divine world and private conversations that humans would not know otherwise.

6. **insignem pietāte virum (l. 10)**: The entire poem is composed to answer one question: Why must the pious suffer? The word *pietās* signifies devotion to family, community, and the gods, and the Romans closely identified such devotion with success. How can Aeneas be pious and yet still suffer?

Urbs antīqua fuit (Tyriī tenuēre colōnī)
Karthāgō, Ītaliam contrā Tiberīnaque longē
ōstia, dīves opum studiīsque asperrima bellī;
quam Iūnō fertur terrīs magis omnibus ūnam
posthabitā coluisse Samō: hīc illius arma,
hīc currus fuit; hoc rēgnum dea gentibus esse,
sī quā fāta sinant, iam tum tenditque fovetque.
Prōgeniem sed enim Troiānō ā sanguine dūcī
audierat Tyriās ōlim quae verteret arcēs;
hinc populum lātē rēgem bellōque superbum
ventūrum excidiō Libyae: sīc volvere Parcās.

---

antīquus, -a, -um: ancient, old, 4
asper, aspera, asperum: harsh, rough, 2
audiō, -īre, -ivī, -ītus: hear, listen to, 3
colōnus, -î m: settler, colonist
colō, -ere, coluī, cultum: till, farm, cultivate, 3
contrā: opposite, facing (acc.), 3
currus, -ūs m: chariot, carriage, 2
dīves, dīvitis: rich, wealthy in (gen), 2
enim: for, indeed, 4
excidium, -ī n: destruction
foveō, -ēre, fōvī, fōtus: nuture, foster; caress, 4
Karthāgō, -inis f: Carthage, 4
magis: more, rather, 2
ōlim: once, once upon a time, 2
ops, opis f: resources, power, wealth, 3
ōstium, -ī n: mouth, entrance
Parcae, -ārum f: the Fates
posthabeō, -ēre, -uī, -itus: hold after (i.e. 2nd place)
prōgeniēs, ēī f: offspring, race
rēx, rēgis m: king, 4
Samos, -ī f: Samos (an island)
sinō, -ere, sīvī, situs: allow, permit, 2
studium, -ī n: zeal, pursuit
superbus, -a, -um: proud, arrogant, 3
Tiberīnus, -a, -um: of the Tiber river, Tiber river's, 2
Trōiānus, -a, -um: Trojan, 3
vertō, -ere, vertī, versum: to turn; overturn, 3

12 **fuit**: *there was...*; pf. sum
tenuē(runt): syncopated 3p pf.; supply 'urbem'
13 **Karthāgō**: nom. sg. in apposition to urbs
contrā: + both accusatives; Carthage faces Rome across the Mediterranean
longē: *far*
14 **dīves...asperrima**: both sg. modify fem. sg. Karthāgō; asperrima is a superlative adj.
studiīs: *in...*; abl. of respect with asperrima
15 **quam**: *which...*; relative, acc. obj. of coluisse; the antecedent is fem. sg. Karthāgō
fertur: *is said*; 'is reported,' + pf. inf. cōlō.
omnibus: *than...*; abl. of comparison
16 **posthabitā Samō**: abl. abs.; i.e. the island Samos holds second place in Juno's affection
Hīc illius (fuērunt) arma, hīc currus fuit: *Here...here...*; anaphora and ellipsis: add pf. of sum as a verb; note the macron: hīc is an adv., hic, 'this,' is a pronoun; These possessions of Juno are honored as sacred relics in Carthage.
illius: gen. sg. illa; i.e. Juno
17 **hoc rēgnum...esse**: *that this be....*; ind. disc. governed by tenditque fovetque.; hoc is acc. subj. and refers to fem. sg. Karthāgō, but is attracted into the neut. by the predicate rēgnum
regnum: *ruling power*
gentibus: *for (all)...*; dat. of interest
18 **sī quā...sinant**: *if in any way...*; quī, quid is indefinite (some, any) after sī, nisī, num and nē; pres. subj. of subordinate verb in ind. disc.
-que...-que: *both...and...*
19 **sed enim**: *but indeed*; place at first in sentence
Prōgeniem...dūcī: *that...*; first of 3 ind. disc. governed by audi(v)erat; pres. pass. inf. dūcō
Tyriās...quae verteret arcēs: *which would...*; a relative clause of purpose with impf. subj.; the antecedent is fem. Prōgeniem; Tyriās arcēs refers to Carthage, a colony of Phoenician Tyre
21 **(et) hinc populum...ventūrum (esse)**: *(and) that ..would.*; asyndeton and ellipsis; ind. disc. with fut. act. inf. veniō governed by audi(v)erat
lātē: adv. lātus with rēgem
rēgem: *ruling*; equiv. to pres. pple reg(ent)em
bellō: *in...*; abl. of respect with superbum
22 **excidiō**: *for...*; dat. of purpose
sīc...Parcās: *that thus the Fates were spinning*; ind. disc.; the Fates are personified as women who spin and cut threads that decide one's fate

arx, arcis f: citadel, (fortifed) hilltop, 12
dea, -ae f: goddess, 7
dūcō, -ere, dūxī, ductus: lead, draw; consider, 9
sum, esse, fuī, futūrus: be, 55
ferō, ferre, tulī, lātus: bear, endure, carry, say 25
gēns, gentis f.: race, people, clan, 11
hīc: here, 13
hinc: from here, hence, from this place, 7
hic, haec, hoc: this, these, 73
iam: now, already, 19
lātus, -a, -um: wide, 6
Libya, -ae f: Libya, 5
longus, -a, -um: long; *adv*. far, 10
omnis, -e: all, every, whole, entire, 27
populus, -ī m: people, 6
rēgnum, -ī n: kingdom, kingship, rule, 14
sanguis, -inis m: blood, 6
sed: but, 15
sī: if, whether, 26
sīc: thus, so, in this way, 17
tendō, -ere, -dī, tentus: stretch; strive, hasten, 8
teneō, -ēre, -uī, -tus: hold; grab, 11
tum, tunc: then, at that time; 18
Tyrius, -a, -um: Tyrian, of Tyre, Carthaginian, 8
ūnus, -a, -um: one, alone; **ūnā**, together, 10

Rome and Carthage

First Punic War	261-241 BC
Second Punic War	218-201 BC
Third Punic War	149-143 BC

The three Punic Wars fought between Rome and Carthage, a city-state in North Africa, transformed Rome into a naval power with a vast western Mediterranean empire. By the end of the wars, Rome had acquired the provinces of Sicily, Sardinia, Corsica, Hispania, and much of Libya (North Africa).

The Carthaginians were originally colonists from the Phoenician cities of Tyre and Sidon, located in modern day Lebanon. The Romans acknowledged this origin by calling the Carthaginians *Poenī* or *Pūnī*, 'Phoenicians.' Since the name *Carthāginiēnsēs* does not fit in epic meter, Vergil refers to the people eight times as *Tȳriī*, 'Tyrians,' twice as *Poenī*, 'Phoenicians,' and once as *Sidōniī*, 'Sidonians.'

In lines 19-22, Vergil ingeniously suggests that not only the rise of Rome but the Punic wars and rise of the Romans as a Mediterranean power were preordained by fate and the gods.

Syncopated Verbs

Vergil will sometimes abbreviate a verb form by omitting letters or shortening the ending in order to fit the meter. Verbs that are abbreviated in this way are called syncopated verbs (Grk. *syncoptein*, 'to cut off'). Note three recent examples from our reading:

tenuēre (tenuērunt)	*they held* (I.12)	3p perfect ending -ērunt shortened to –ēre
audierat (audīverat)	*she had heard* (I.20)	-v or -vi omitted from the perfect stem
repostum (repositum)	*having been stored* (I.26)	-i omitted from the perfect passive stem

There are 13 syncopated 3p perfects similar to tenuēre above. They look like present infinitives but are easy to identify because (1) they have perfect stems (e.g. tenu-, conspēx-) and (2) are found with nominative rather than accusative subjects (e.g. Tyriī tenuēre colōnī).

Ablative of Respect [27]

There are 27 labeled instances of the ablative of respect (also called the ablative of specification). This noun accompanies an adjective and both explains and limits the meaning of the adjective. It is often translated 'in X' or 'in respect to X.'

insignem pietāte virum	*A man distinguished* (in horse-racing? in speaking? No…) *in respect to piety* (I.10)
asperrima studiīs bellī	*most harsh* (in punishing criminals? in criticism? No…) *in the pursuits of war* (14)

Id metuēns veterisque memor Sāturnia bellī,
prīma quod ad Troiam prō cārīs gesserat Argīs
(necdum etiam causae īrārum saevīque dolōrēs
exciderant animō; manet altā mente repostum
iūdicium Paridis sprētaeque iniūria formae
et genus invīsum et raptī Ganymēdis honōrēs)
hīs accēnsa super iactātōs aequore tōtō
Trōās, relliquiās Danaum atque immītis Achillī,
arcēbat longē Latiō, multōsque per annōs
errābant actī fātīs maria omnia circum.
Tantae mōlis erat Rōmānam condere gentem.

---

accendō, -ere, -ī, ênsus: kindle, enflame, enrage, 3
Achillēs, -is (ī) m: Achilles, 2
arceō, -ēre, -uī: fend or keep off, defend, 2
Argus, -ī m: Argive (Greek)
cārus, -a, -um: dear, 3
condō, -ere, condidī, -ditum: found; hide, 4
excidō, -ere, -ī: fall from, slip from, perish
forma, -ae, f: shape; beauty (shapeliness), 4
Ganymēdēs, -is m: Ganymede
honor, -ōris m: honor; offering, sacrifice, 3
immītis, -e: pitiless, unmerciful
iniūria, -ae f: injury, insult, injustice, 2
iūdicium, -ī n: decision, judgment
Latium, -ī n: Latium, 4
maneō, -ēre, mānsī: stay, remain, wait, 4
memor, -oris: mindful of, remembering (gen) 4
mēns, mentis f.: mind, intent, purpose, 4
metuō, -ere, -uī: fear, dread, 2
necdum: not yet, nor yet
Paris, -idis m: Paris, 3
prō: before; for, in behalf of (*abl*), 3
relliquiae, -ārum f: survivors, remains, 2
repono, -ere, -suī, -situm: put up, store up
Sāturnia, -ae f: Saturnian one, Juno, (patronymic), 2
spernō, -ere, sprēvī, sprētum: spurn, scorn, reject, 2
super: above, beyond (*acc.*); *adv.* in addition, 3
vetus, -eris: old, former

23 **id**: *this*;; i.e. all that Juno had heard in ll. 19-23
metuēns: pres. pple
24 **prīma quod...gesserat**: *which she had been the first to wage...*; relative clause; nom. prīma points to Juno's leadership against the Trojans
prō cārīs...Argīs: *on behalf of..., for...*
gesserat: plpf. gerō
25 **etiam**: *also*
īrārum: *of (her) anger*; as often, translate as sg.
26 **animō**: *from...*; abl. of separation (place from which) or dat. of compound verb
manet: *there remain...*; 3s with a 3p subject
altā mente: *deep in her mind*; 'in her deep mind,' neut. altum attracted into fem. of mente
repos(i)tum: syncopated PPP, repōnō
27 **iūdicium Paridis**: *the judgment of Paris*
sprētae...formae: gen. sg.; PPP, spernō; i.e. Juno was insulted because she and Athena lost the judgment of Paris to Venus
28 **genus invīsum**: *hated race, hated stock*; i.e. the Trojan people
raptī: gen. sg. PPP, rapiō, 'kidnap,' the Trojan prince Ganymede was kidnapped and made Jupiter's cupbearer; Juno is envious of the attention that Ganymede receives from Jupiter
29 **(Iūno) hīs accēnsa...arcēbat**: *(Juno) having been...*; add a subject for arcēbat; PPP accensō
hīs: *by...*; abl. means, i.e. all the reasons above
super: *in addition*; 'on top of this,' adv.
(in) aequore tōtō
30 **Trōās**: *Trojans*; masc. acc. pl.
relliquiās: in apposition to Trōās
Danaum: *of the Greeks*; 3rd decl. gen. pl.
immītis Achillī: Achilles was the foremost fighter of the Greeks at Troy and was killed by the arrow of Paris shortly before the Greeks sacked the city of Troy
31 **longē**: *far*
Latiō: *from...*; abl. of separation (place from which)
(Troiānī) actī: *(the Trojans) having been driven...*; PPP agō + abl. means fātīs
32 **maria omnia circum**: circum omnia maria; anastrophe (reversal of normal word order)
33 **Tantae mōlis**: *(of) so great a burden*; gen. of description (quality) as predicate following erat
erat: *it was...*; condere is the infinitive subject

ad: to, toward, at, near (acc.), 29
aequor, -oris n: sea, the level (sea), 11
agō, -ere, ēgī, āctus: drive, lead, do, 9
annus, -ī m: year, 5
circum: around (acc.), 12
Danaus, -a, -um: Danaan (Greek), 7
dolor, -ōris m: pain, grief, 6
errō (1): wander, 10
etiam: also, even, 7
gerō, -ere, gessī, gestus: carry (on), wage, 5
invideō, -ēre: hate, envy, 6
is, ea, id: he, she, it, they; this/these, that/those; 5
mare, -is n: sea, 5
mōlēs, -is f: mass, structure; burden, 5
per: through, over, by, 45
rapiō, -ere, -uī, raptum: snatch, seize; kidnap, 7
Rōmānus, -a, -um: Roman, 5
tōtus, -a, -um: total, entire, whole, 8
Trōs, Trōis: Trojan, 5

Reasons for Juno's Anger

In addition to **1. the future destruction of Carthage by the descendants of Troy** in I.19-22, Vergil mentions several additional reasons why Juno feels anger toward Aeneas and the Trojans.

2. **iūdicium Paridis (sprētaeque iniūria formae)**: After the goddess Discord throws an apple inscribed with the words "to the most beautiful" into the wedding party of Thetis and Pelias, Achilles' parents, Mercury whisks the apple away and gives it to Paris, one of the fifty sons of King Priam of Troy. Soonafter, the goddesses Juno (Hera), Minerva (Athena), and Venus (Aphrodite) approach Paris and offer rewards in return for the apple. Juno offers political power; Minerva, victory in battle; and finally Venus, the most beautiful woman. Paris awards the apple to Venus and thus incurs the anger of both Juno and Minerva in the Trojan war and beyond.

3. **genus invīsum**: Although the phrase can be translated as the "hated race" and refer to the Trojans in general, it more likely means "hated stock" and refers to one of the founders of the Trojans, Dardanus, a local king and grandfather of Trōs, who gave his name to the Trojans. Dardanus was the offspring of an illicit affair between Jupiter and the mortal Electra. Juno undoubtedly knew about the affair and blamed Dardanus, who served as a reminder of her husband's infidelity.

4. **raptī Ganymēdis honōrēs**: Dardanus' grandson Trōs gave birth to three sons, Ilus, Assaracus, and Ganymede, whom Homer describes as the most handsome of mortal men. In the form of an eagle, Jupiter kidnapped Ganymede and made the boy his personal cupbearer. Juno appears to have envied the affection that Jupiter gave to the young man.

Trojans and Greeks

Review the list of proper names that Vergil uses to refer to the Trojans and Greeks:

Trōiānus, -a, -um: Trojan, 3
Trōs, Trōis: Trojan, 5
Trōius, -a, -um: Trojan, 1

Teucrus, -a, -um: Teucrian, Trojan, 10
Dardanius, -a, -um: Dardanian, Trojan, 4
Dardanidēs, -ae m.: Dardanian, Trojan, 2

Phrygius, -a, -um: Phrygian, Trojan, 3
Īliacus, -a, -um: of Ilium, Trojan, 2
Īlias, -adis: Trojan, 1

Argus, -ī m: Argive (Greek), 1
Argīvus, -a, -um: Argive (Greek), 1
Danaus, -a, -um: Danaan (Greek), 7

Graius, -a, -um: Greek, 2

The names Teucrians, Dardanians, and Trojans are patronymics that refer to the Trojans as the descendants of King Teucer, King Dardanus, and King Tros. Teucer was a distant relative who gave his name to the land around Troy, Teucria, until Dardanus arrived and the land was renamed Dardania. Dardanus's grandson Tros gave his name to the Trojans, while Tros' son Ilus, founded the city of the Trojans, which is called 'Ilium' as well as 'Troia.' Phrygia is the name of the entire region in western Asia Minor (modern day Turkey).

The names Argives and Danaans refer to the Greeks and are frequently used in the *Iliad* and *Odyssey*.

Vix ē cōnspectū Siculae tellūris in altum
vēla dabant laetī et spūmās salis aere ruēbant,
cum Iūnō aeternum servāns sub pectore vulnus
haec sēcum: “Mēne inceptō dēsistere victam
nec posse Ītaliā Teucrōrum āvertere rēgem?
Quippe vetor fātīs. Pallasne exūrere classem
Argīvum atque ipsōs potuit summergere pontō
ūnius ob noxam et furiās Aiācis Oīleī?
Ipsa Iovis rapidum iaculāta ē nūbibus ignem
disiēcitque ratēs ēvertitque aequora ventīs,
illum exspīrantem trānsfīxō pectore flammās
turbine corripuit scopulōque īnfīxit acūtō;

---

acūtus, -a, -um: sharp, pointed, 2
aes, aeris n.: bronze, 2
aeternus, -a, -um: eternal, everlasting 4
Aiās, Aiācis m: Ajax
Argīvus, -a, -um: Argive (Greek)
āvertō, -ēre, āvertī, āversum: turn away, 4
conspectus, -ūs, f: sight, view, 2
dēsistō, -ere, -stitī, -stitus: cease (from), desist
disiciō, -ere, -iēcī, -iectum: scatter, throw apart, 4
ēvertō, -ere, -vertī: overturn, turn over, 3
exspīrō (1): breathe out, exhale
exūrō, -ere, -ussī, -ustum: burn up
furia, -ae f: madness, fury
iaculor, -ārī, iaculātus sum: throw, hurl, 2
infīgō, -ere, -fīxī, -fīxus: fix, fasten on, 2
noxa, -ae f: crime
ob: on account of, because of (*acc*), 3
Oīleus, -ī m: Oileus (father of Ajax)
Pallas, -adis f: Pallas, Athena (Minerva), 2
quippe: of course, truly; surely, 3
rapidus, -a, -um: swift, grasping, 3
ratis, -is f.: raft, boat, ship, 2
rēx, rēgis m.: king, 4
sal, salis n.: salt (water); sea, 2
Siculus, -a, -um: Sicilian, of Sicily, 2
spūma, -ae f.: foam, spray
summergō, -ere, -rsī, -rsus: sink, drown, 2
turbō, -binis m.: whirlwind, 3
vēlum, -ī n.: sail, 2
vetō, -āre, -uī, -itus: forbid, prevent, 2
vix: scarcely, hardly, with difficulty

34 **in altum**: *into the deep (sea)*; metonomy
35 **laetī**: *happily*; nom. predicative adj. as adv.
salis: *of the salt (sea)*; metonomy
aere: abl. of means; metonymy, the fronts of the ships have a bronze rostrum, ‘beak,’ made to withstand daily wear from the water.
36 **cum...haec sēcum (dīxit)**: *when...(said)*; ellipsis: add verb; temporal cum
servāns: pres. pple servō, ‘preserve’
37 **haec**: *these things*; neut. acc. pl. substantive
sēcum: cum sē; reflexive pronoun; soliloquy: Juno is speaking alone to herself
Mē-ne...dēsistere...nec posse...: *Am I to...and am I not able...?*; acc. + inf. in an exclamatory question, often used without a main verb to express anger or surprise; mē is acc. subject
inceptō: *from my undertaking*; ‘from the thing having been begun,’ PPP and abl. of separation
38 **Ītāliā**: *from...*; abl. of separation
Teucrōrum: *of the Trojans*; patronymic; Teucer was one of the founders of Troy
39 **vetor**: 1s pres. pass.
Pallasne...potuit: *Was Pallas (Athena) able...*; pf. possum; Pallas Athena, also called Minerva
40 **(virōs) ipsōs**: *(the men) themselves*
(in) pontō
41 **ūnius...Aiācis Oīleī**: *of one man, Ajax, (son) of Oileus*; ūnus is a pronominal adj. (gen. -ius) Ajax had assaulted Cassandra in Pallas’ temple
42 **ipsa**: *(she) herself*; i.e. Pallas
Iovis: gen. sg. Iuppiter, who is Pallas’ father
iaculāta: pf. dep. pple: translate ‘having Xed’
rapidum ignem: i.e. Jupiter’s thunderbolt
-que...-que: *both...and...*
44-45 **illum...acutō**: hysteron proteron (‘later earlier’): events in line 44 occur after line 45
illum: *that one*; i.e. Ajax; obj. of corripuit
exspirantem...flāmmās: pres. pple; Ajax’s lung is pierced, and flames or his life spirit exits from his chest rather than from his mouth
trānsfīxō pectore: *from...*; PPP, trānsfīgō
45 **scopulō...acūtō**: *on...*; dat. of compound

classis, -is f: fleet, 8
corripiō, -ere, -uī, -reptus: snatch (up), 6
cum: with; when, since, although, 23
dō, dare, dedī, datum: give (the power); grant, 27
ē, ex: out of, from (abl), 8
flamma, -ae f: flame, 8
ignis, -is m: fire; lightning, 15
incipiō, -ere, -cēpī, -ceptum: begin, undertake, 6
ipse, -a, -um: himself, herself, -self; very, 22
Iuppiter, Iovis, Iovī, Iovem, Iove m.: Jupiter 9
laetus, -a, -um: happy; fertile, 5
nec: nor, and not; **nec…nec**: neither…nor, 30
nūbēs, -is f: cloud, 6
pectus, -oris n: chest, breast; heart, 12
pontus, -ī m: sea, 9
possum, posse, potuī: be able, can, 5
ruō, ruere, -ī: rush (over), fall; plow, 8
scopulus, -ī m.: rock, cliff, crag, 6
sē: him-, her-, it-, themselves, 20
servō (1): save, perserve, keep, 6
sub: under, beneath; near, 13
tellūs, -ūris f.: land, earth, 6
Teucrus, a, um: Trojan, Teucrian, 10
ventus, -ī m.: wind, 11
vincō, -ere, vīcī, victus: conquer, 5
vulnus, -eris n.: wound, 7

Eight Words Referring to the Sea

Vergil uses a variety of words to refer to the sea. Sometimes a specific word is necessary, but he often will include a particular word for variation or metrical purposes. Review the list below and notice that commonly used forms are metrically different and fit in different places in the dactylic line.

aequor, -oris n: sea, level sea, 11	aequora, aequore (¯ ˘ ˘)
altum, -ī n.: sea, deep sea	altum, altō (¯ ¯)
mare, -is n: sea, 5	maria, (˘ ˘ ˘) marī (˘ ¯)
pelagus, -ī n.: sea, 4	pelagī, pelagō (˘ ˘ ¯)
pontus, -ī m: sea, 9	pontum, pontō (¯ ¯)
sal, salis n.: sea, salt water, 2	salis, sale (˘ ˘)
salum, -ī n.: sea, swelling sea, 2	salō (˘ ¯)

Pallas Athena (Minerva) and Ajax

According to tradition, the Trojan princess Cassandra sought sanctuary in the temple of Minerva while the Greeks sacked the city. In one account, the Greek Ajax, son of Oileus, dragged Cassandra away as a prisoner and denied her Minerva's protection. In another account, Ajax assaulted Cassandra in the temple of Minerva where Cassandra sought sanctuary.

Juno suggests that Minerva was able to destroy Ajax's entire Greek fleet on the return from Troy in response to Ajax's behavior in the temple. Since Minerva is Jupiter's daughter (she leapt out of his head!), Vergil feels no need to explain why she so easily borrows her father's thunderbolt.

Short Answer

1. Vergil begins his Trojan narrative in ll. 34-35 *in medias res*. What does *in medias res* mean?

2. What rhetorical/stylistic device does Vergil use at the beginning of Juno's speech in ll. 37-41 to reveal Juno's bewilderment and anger? (Hint: Juno does not us a nominative and finite verb.)

3. How do the initial lines of Juno's speech in ll. 37-41 reinforce the idea expressed by Vergil that the Trojans were destined to come to Italy?

4. How is the example of Ajax supposed to support Juno's case for turning away Aeneas from Italy?

ast ego, quae dīvum incēdō rēgīna Iovisque
et soror et coniūnx, ūnā cum gente tot annōs
bella gerō. Et quisquam nūmen Iūnōnis adōret
praetereā aut supplex ārīs impōnet honōrem?"
  Tālia flammātō sēcum dea corde volūtāns
nimbōrum in patriam, loca fēta furentibus Austrīs,
Aeoliam venit. Hīc vastō rēx Aeolus antrō
luctantēs ventōs tempestātēsque sonōrās
imperiō premit ac vinclīs et carcere frēnat.
Illī indignantēs magnō cum murmure montis
circum claustra fremunt; celsā sedet Aeolus arce
scēptra tenēns mollitque animōs et temperat īrās;
nī faciat, maria ac terrās caelumque profundum
quippe ferant rapidī sēcum verrantque per aurās.

---

adōrō (1): pray to, plead to, honor
Aeolia, -ae f.: Aeolia
Auster, -trī m.: wind; Auster wind, (south) wind, 2
carcer, -eris m.: prison, 2
celsus, -a, -um: high, towering, 2
claustrum, -ī n.: enclosure; bar, bolt
fetus, -a, -um: teeming, pregnant (dat.), 2
flammō (1): enflame, kindle
fremō, -ere, -uī, -itus: roar, 3
frēnō (1): to bridle, restrain (a bit used with horses), 2
honor, -ōris m.: honor; offering, sacrifice, 3
incēdō, -ere, -cessī: strut; march, proceed, 2
indignor, -ārī, -ātus sum: be angry or indignant
luctor, -ārī, -ātus sum: wrestle, struggle, 2
molliō, -īre, -iī, -ītus: soften, soothe, 2
murmur, -uris n.: murmur, rumble, 4
nī, nisī: if not, unless 2
nimbus, -ī m.: (storm) cloud, rain/dark cloud 3
praetereā: besides, moreover
profundus, -a, -um: deep, vast, 2
quippe: of course, truly; surely, 3
quisquam, quaequam, quicquam: any(one), any(thing), 4
rapidus, -a, -um: swift, grasping, 3
rēx, rēgis m.: king, 4
scēptrum, -ī n.: scepter, staff, 2
sedeō, -ēre, sēdī, sessum: sit, 4
sonōrus, -a, -um: resounding, sonorous
supplex, -icis: suppliant, 3
temperō (1): refrain, calm, control, 2
tempestās, tempestātis f.: storm 2
verrō, -ere, -ī, -rsus: sweep, 2
vinculum, -ī n.: chain, 4
volūtō (1): roll or turn over; ponder, think about,

46 **ast**: *but*; alternative form for 'at'
quae...incēdō: *who...*; the antecedent is 1s, and so the verb in the relative clause is 1s
dīv(ōr)um: gen. pl. substantive: i.e. the gods
rēgīna Iovisque et soror...et coniūnx: *as...and as both...and...*; nom. in apposition; gen. sg. Iuppiter modifies soror and coniūnx
47 **tot annōs**: *for...*; acc. of duration
48 **et quisquam...adōret**: *would anyone...?*; 'Is anyone to,' 3s deliberative pres. subj.; the lack of an interrogative suggests shock or surprise
49 **aut (quisquam) supplex impōnet**: *or will (anyone) as a suppliant...?*; 3s fut.
ārīs: *on...*; dat. of compound verb
50 **Tālia**: *such things*; neut. acc. obj. of volūtāns; **sēcum**: cum sē; reflexive pronoun; i.e. she is speaking alone to herself in a soliloquy
flammātō corde: *in...*; abl. place where, PPP
51 **in patriam, loca...Aeoliam**: neut. acc. loca and Aeoliam are both in apposition to patriam
fēta: *pregnant with* + abl.; 'teeming with' the mountain filled with winds is likened here to a belly pregnant with a child
52 **(in) vastō...antrō**
luctantēs: pres. pple
53 **imperiō**: *with...*; abl. of means
vinc(u)līs et carcere: *with...*; abl. of means likely hendiadys: 'with the chains of a prison'
Illī (ventī): *those (winds)*
indignantēs: pres. pple
55 **magnō cum murmure montis**: alliteration and onomatopoeia; the next line continues with the hard-c sounds as if clanging against a cage
56 **(in) celsā...arce**

57 **sceptra**: poetic plural: translate as sg. obj. of pple tenēns;
animōs: *their spirits*; the plural of animus often means 'courage,' 'anger,' or 'passion'
īrās: *anger, passions*; the pl. of īra often refers to passions in general or can be translated as sg.
58 **nī faciat,...ferant...verrant**: *if he should not do (this),...would...and would...*; a fut. less vivid condition (sī pres. subj., pres. subj.), otherwise known as a should-would condition; nī = nisi (if not)
59 **rapidī (ventī)**: nom. subject
verrant: supply subject and obj. from ferant

Aeolus, -ī m.: Aeolus (king of the winds), 5
antrum, -ī n.: cave, 5
āra, -ae f.: altar, 8
at, ast: but, yet, however, at least, 10
aura, -ae f.: breeze, air, 6
aut: or; **aut...aut**: either...or, 31
caelum, -ī n.: sky, 13
coniūnx, -iugis m./f.: spouse, husband, wife, 6
cor, cordis n.: heart, 5
dīvus, -a, -um: divine; *noun*, god, goddess, 12
faciō, -ere, fēcī, factum: do, make, 7
furō, -ere, -uī: rage, rave, seethe, 7
imperium, (i)ī n.: power, command; empire, 6
impono, -ere, -posuī, -positus: impose, place on, 5
in: in, on, among (abl.); into, against (acc.), 55
locus, -ī m. (pl. locī, loca): place, 8
magnus, -a, -um: great, large, 19
mōns, montis m.: mountain, 5
patria, -ae f.: fatherland, country, 8
premō, -ere, pressī, pressum: (sup)press, control, 5
soror, sorōris f.: sister, 5
tālis, -e: such, 15
vastus, -a, -um: vast, enormous, 7

Ancient Science: Four Primary Elements and Natural Place

A prevailing view in the ancient world is that there are four primary elements and that each has its own **natural place**. Objects made of earth and water naturally move down to the land and water, while objects made of air and fire naturally move up to the sky and aether (upper sky) that contains the sun, moon, and stars. This view explains the effects of gravity as well as the tendency of air bubbles and flames to travel upward. These elements correspond to the following places in Vergil:

aether, -eris m.: aether, (upper) sky, 3
caelum, -ī n.: sky, 13
aqua, -ae f.: water, 3
terra, -ae f: land, ground, earth, 20

As you read the storm episode, note how often the **disorder** stirred up by the winds is depicted as the unnatural mixing of elements and **order** as the separation of these elements into their natural places.

Emotional winds create disorder in nature, just as emotions create disorder in individuals

Violent emotions are associated with disorder in Vergil—whether in an individual, in a society, or in the natural world—while emotional restraint in these same areas is associated with order. Almost every line from 51 to 59 identifies the winds as violent emotions or beasts with unrestrained emotions.

The gods restrain the emotional winds to impose order on nature.

The winds, unrestrained, create chaos by moving the four elements from their natural place. Jupiter, Aeolus, and later Neptune impose order on nature by restraining the winds and allowing the elements to take their natural place. The same emotional restraint that works in an individual works in nature.

1. In Roman religion, prayer and sacrifice are transactional: Romans honor a god in order to gain a reward or to avoid suffering. What does Juno say will happen if she cannot punish the Trojans?

2. Identify at least one word in each line (51, 53-57) that depicts the winds as unrestrained emotions. or animals with unrestrained emotions.

3. What Latin verbs in 54 and 57 portray Aeolus as one who imposes restraint on emotional beasts?

4. How can the idea in the four elements and their natural order explain why Vergil chose to use the words *maria*, *terrās*, and *caelum* in l. 58 to describe what happens if the winds are unrestrained?

Sed pater omnipotēns spēluncīs abdidit ātrīs
Hoc metuēns mōlemque et montēs īnsuper altōs
imposuit rēgemque dedit quī foedere certō
et premere et laxās scīret dare iussus habēnās.
Ad quem tum Jūnō supplex hīs vōcibus ūsa est:
"Aeole, namque tibī dīvum pater atque hominum rēx
et mulcēre dedit flūctūs et tollere ventō,
gēns inimīca mihī Tyrrhēnum nāvigat aequor
Īlium in Ītaliam portāns victōsque Penātēs:
incute vim ventīs summersāsque obrue puppēs,
aut age dīversōs et disiice corpora pontō.
Sunt mihi bis septem praestantī corpore nymphae,
quārum quae formā pulcherrima, Dēiopēa,
cōnūbiō iungam stabilī propriamque dicābō,

---

abdō, -ere, -didī, -ditus: hide, put away, 2
bis: twice, 3
certus, -a, -um: sure, reliable, definite, 4
conūbium, -iī n.: marriage, wedlock, 4
Dēiopēa, -ae f.: Deiopea (nymph)
dīcō (1): to declare, dedicate, consecrate
disiciō, -ere, -iēcī, -iectum: scatter, throw apart, 4
dīversus, -a, -um: in different directions, apart, 2
foedus, -eris n.: treaty, agreement, 2
habēna, -ae f.: rein
homō, -inis m./f.: person, people; human, 4
Īlium, -ī n.: Ilium, Troy, 2
incutiō, -ere, -cussī, -cussum: strike upon, 2
inimīcus, -a, -um: unfriendly, rival (dat), 4
insuper: on top; in addition, 2
iungō, -ere, iunxī, -iunctum: to join, 3
laxus, -a, -um: free, loosened, lax, 2
metuō, -ere, -uī: fear, dread, 2
mulceō, -ēre, -lsī, -lsus: calm, soothe, 3
nāvigō (1): to sail
nympha, -ae f.: nymph (minor woodland goddess), 4
ob-ruō, -ere, -uī, -utus: rush over, overwhelm
omnipotēns, -entis: all-powerful, 3
Penātēs, -ium m.: Penates (household gods), 3
portō (1): carry, bear, bring
praestō, -āre: set before, prefer; present; *praestāns*, outstanding; *praestat*: it is preferable/better, 2
proprius: one's own (here, 'your own'), 2
rēx, rēgis m.: king, 4
sciō, -īre, -īvī, -ītus: know (how)
spēlunca, -ae f.: cave, 2
stabilis, -e: stable, lasting
summergō, -ere, -rsī, -rsus: sink, drown, 2
supplex, -icis: suppliant, 3
Tyrrhēnus, -a, -um: Tyrrhenian Sea (west of Italy)
ūtor, -ī, ūsus sum: use, employ (*abl.*)

60 **abdidit (ventōs)**
(in) spēluncīs ātrīs
61 **hoc**: *this*; i.e. that the winds will carry off the elements; acc. obj. of pres. pple metuēns
mōlem et montēs...altōs: *a mass of high mountains*; 'mass and high mountains,' hendiadys (two items describing a single obj.) and alliteration
62 **dedit (ventīs)**: add 'to the winds'; pf. dō, dare
quī...scīret: *who would know how to...* + inf.; relative clause of purpose with impf. subj.
foedere certō: *in...*; i.e. in a patron-client
laxās...dare...habēnās: i.e. let go of the reins so that the winds, just as horses, can go fast
63 **iussus**: *(when)...*; PPP iubeo; i.e. Aeolus will act when called upon by Jupiter
64 **Ad quem**: *to this one*; 'to whom' a connective relative is often translated as a demonstrative
supplex: *as a suppliant*
hīs vocibus: *these words*
65 **namque**: *indeed*
pater atque rēx dīv(ōr)um (et) hominum: i.e. Jupiter; dīvōrum is a substantive: 'of the gods'
66 **Et mulcēre...et tollere**: *both to...and to...*
dedit: *granted* + inf.; 'gave (the power),' pf. dō
68 **Īlium**: *Troy*; i.e. the Trojan people and culture
portāns: pres. pple with gēns
victōsque Penātēs: PPP vincō; Juno notes that these gods failed to project the Trojans and are therefore worthless
69 **incute vim...**: *strike force into...*!; + dat. of compound verb; acc. vīs; 1 of 4 imperatives

69 **puppēs**: *ships*; 'decks,' synecdoche (the part suggests the whole)
age (virōs): *drive (the men)…*;
70 **diversōs:** predicative adj. with missing virōs
(in) pontō
sunt mihi: *I have…*; 'there are to me,' dat. of possession: as often, translate the dat. as subject and the nom. as object of the verb 'have;' Juno offers a bride in return for the favor
praestantī corpore: *of…*; i.e. beautiful; abl. of quality (description) modifying nymphae
quārum (nympham) quae (est)…Dēiopēa: *of whom (the nymph) who (is)…*; the missing antecedent of quae (add 'nympham') is the object of the two verbs iungam and dicābō
formā: *in…*; abl. of respect
73 **cōnūbiō…stabilī**: *in…*; abl. of means or place where, 3rd decl. i-stem abl.
iungam: 1s fut.
propriam dīcābō: *I will call…your own*; dīcō governs a double acc. (obj. and pred.): 'call (x) (y)' supply nympham as object

āter, ātra, ātrum: dark, black, 7
corpus, -oris n.: body, 11
flūctus, -ūs m: wave, 11
iubeō, -ēre, īussī, iussus: order, command, 9
nam, namque: for; indeed, truly, 6
pulcher, -chra, -chrum: beautiful, pretty; noble, 5
puppis, -is f.: deck, ship, 5
tollō, -ere, sustulī, sublātus: raise, lift up; destroy, 5
vōx, vocis f.: voice, utterance; word, 8

Jupiter and Aeolus as Patron and Client

The Romans likely viewed the relationship between Jupiter and Aeolus as one between a patron and client. As patron, Jupiter gives Aeolus the power to control the winds and all the honors that go with the position "when ordered," (iussus, I.63). In return, Jupiter expects his client Aeolus to be loyal (a client can have only one patron) and to treat the patron's allies and enemies as his own.

Vergil's description of the patron-client relationship in ll. 60-64 is critical for our understanding of Juno's speech, where the goddess behaves as if she were Aeolus' patron. Readers are left with several questions. Are Juno and Aeolus acting according to proper Roman social custom? If a client can have only one patron, why does Aeolus do what Juno rather than Jupiter says? Does Aeolus obey Juno because she is the spouse of his patron (just as an employee today may obey the spouse of a boss)? Is Aeolus confused? If Jupiter would never have allowed Aeolus to send the winds, is Juno deliberately breaking social customs and the patron-client relationship in order to have Aeolus fulfill her request?

The contrast between the narrative before the speech and Juno's own words suggest that Juno is indeed breaking the patron-client relationship and social customs in order to punish the Trojans.

1. Give the single Latin word and translation in lines 62-4 that suggests that Aeolus must wait for Jupiter's permission to use the powers that Jupiter has given to him.

2. To what particular animal does Vergil liken the winds with the words 'laxās habēnās' (l. 63) and 'frēnat' (l. 54)?

3. Analysis of Juno's Speech to Aeolus

   a. How do the two lines ll. 65-66 remind Aeolus of his obligation to Jupiter and indirectly to Juno?

   b. If the enemy of a patron becomes the enemy of the client, what is the significance of ll. 67-68?

   c. How do the form of the verbs in ll. 69-70 reflect Juno's superior status over Aeolus? What does she demand that Aeolus do to her enemy?

   d. Patrons often give rewards to clients in return for their continuing loyalty. What does Juno offer to Aeolus in order to reaffirm this relationship? (N.B. Political alliances between aristocrat families in Rome were often strengthened in the same way.)

omnēs ut tēcum meritīs prō tālibus annōs
exigat et pulchrā faciat tē prōle parentem."
  Aeolus haec contrā: "Tuus Ō rēgīna, quid optēs
explōrāre labor; mihi iussa capessere fās est.
Tū mihi quodcumque hoc rēgnī, tū scēptra Iovemque
conciliās, tū dās epulīs accumbere dīvum
nimbōrumque facis tempestātumque potentem."
  Haec ubi dicta, cavum conversā cuspide montem
impulit in latus: ac ventī velut agmine factō,
quā data porta, ruunt et terrās turbine perflant.
Incubuēre marī tōtumque ā sēdibus īmīs
ūnā Eurusque Notusque ruunt crēberque procellīs
Āfricus et vastōs volvunt ad lītora flūctūs:
insequitur clāmorque virum strīdorque rudentum.

---

accumbō, -ere, -uī: recline at
Āfricus, -ī m.: (southwest) wind
capessō, -ere, -īvī, -ītus: to carry out, execute, take, 2
cavus, -a, -um: hollow, 3
conciliō (1): win over
contrā: opposite, facing (*acc.*); in reply, 3
convertō, -ere, -ī, -rsus: turn (around)
crēber, -bra, -brum: frequent, crowded, 2
cuspis, -idos f.: point, spearpoint, 2
epulae, -ārum f.: banquet, feast
Eurus, -ī m.: Eurus wind, 4
exigō (ex+agō), -ere, -ēgī: spend, live; drive out
explorō (1): explore, search
fās n.: right, righteous; **fās (est)**, it is right, 3
impellō, -ere, -pulī, -pulsus: drive, set into motion, 3
incumbō, -ere, -cubuī,: lie on, 2
insequor, -sequī, -secūtus sum: follow, ensue, 3
meritum, -ī n.: favor, benefit, merit, 2
nimbus, -ī m.: (storm) cloud, rain/dark cloud 3
Nōtus, -ī m.: Notus wind, South wind (= Auster), 3
optō (1): desire, choose, hope (for), 4
perflō (1): blow through, blow over
potēns, -entis: powerful (over) (gen) 4
prō: before; for, in behalf of (*abl.*), 3
procella, -ae f.: blast, gust, 2
prōlēs, -is f.: offspring, 2
quī-, quae-, quodcumque: whoever, whatever
rudēns, -ntis m.: rope
scēptrum, -ī n.: scepter, royal staff, 2
strīdōr, -ōris m: screeching, creaking
tempestās, tempestātis f.: storm 2
turbō, -binis m.: whirlwind, 3
velut, velutī: just as, 2

74 **ut...exigat...faciat**: *so that she may...*; purpose clause with pres. subj.
omnēs...annōs: acc. obj.
tēcum: cum tē
prō: *in return for..., for...*

75 **pulchrā...prōle**: *of...*; abl. of quality (description) with parentem
faciat: *make* (x) (y); a double acc. (obj., pred.)

76 **haec (dīxit)**: ellipsis; neut. pl.: i.e. words
Tuus...labor (est): *your task (is)...*
quid optēs: *what...*; ind. question with pres. subj.; object of explōrāre

77 **mihi**: *for...*; dat. of interest
iussa: *orders*; 'things ordered,' neut. pl. PPP
fās est: *it is right...*; impersonal verb

78 **Tū...(et) tū...(et) tū...**: anaphora

78 **quodcumque hoc (est) rēgnī**: *whatsoever this (is) of a kingdom*; regnī is partitive gen.; Aeolus is modest about the extent of his kingdom; this relative clause is obj. of conciliās
scēptra Iōvemque: *scepter of Jupiter*; hendiadys (two items describing a single obj.) and metonomy: scēptra suggests 'power'

79 **dās (mihi)**: *you grant (for me), you allow (for me)*; 'give (the power) to' + inf.
epulīs...dīv(ōr)um: *at...*; dat. compound verb

80 **facis (mē)...**: *make* (x) (y); governs a double acc. (obj. and pred.); supply mē as acc. obj.

81 **dicta (sunt)**: 3p pf. pass.
conversā cuspide: *with...*; alliteration, abl. of means.; the spearpoint is turned to the ground

82 **velut agmine factō**: *just as...*; simile likening the winds to soldiers storming a city; here an abl. abs.; an agmen is a column of soldiers

83 **quā**: *where...*; a relative adverb
data (est): 3s pf. pass.
turbine: *with...*; abl. of means
84 **incubuē(runt)**: syncopated 3p pf.
marī: *on...*; dat. of compound verb or abl. place where (3rd decl. i-stem with -ī in abl.)
tōtum (mare): *(over)...*; obj. of ruunt
ūnā: *together*; ablative as adv.

Eurusque Notusque...Africus: polysyndeton, three subjects of ruunt and volvunt
86 **crēber procellīs**: modifying Āfricus; abl. means or respect ('in...') with crēber
87 **insequitur**: 3s pres. dep., governing a 3p subject: translate as active
-que...-que...: *both...and...*
vir(ōr)um, rudentum: both gen. pl.

agmen, -inis n.: column, formation (of troops), 5
clāmor, -ōris m.: shout, noise, 5
dīcō, -ere, dīxī, dictus: say, speak, tell, 19
īmus, -a, -um: bottom of, lowest (part) of, 5
latus, -eris n.: side, 5
Ō: O! oh!, 14
parēns, -entis m./f.: parent, ancestor, 6
porta, -ae f.: gate, 6
sēdēs, -is f.: seat; home, 7
tū, tuī (*pl.* **vōs, vestrum**) **:** you, 44
tuus, -a, -um: your, yours, 11
ubi: where; when, 10
ut: so that, that; as, when; how, 11

Political Alliances through Marriage

Members of the Roman aristocracy often intermarried for political purposes. Pompey the Great, for example, married Julius Caesar's daughter Julia in 59 BC in order to strengthen the political alliance between the members of the first Triumvirate: Caesar, Pompey, and Crassus. Julia died in 54 while giving birth, and many attribute this death as the cause of the break between Caesar and Pompey. Juno's offer to arrange Aeolus' marriage to a woodland nymph is consistent with this custom. Since Aeolus is a minor figure, however, Juno offers marriage not to her immediate family but to a nymph, a minor woodland goddess of little importance.

Summary of Subjunctives Through Lesson 7

1. Purpose, adverbial	ut/nē + pres./impf.	may/might	ut...exigat...faciat (I.74-75) *so that she might spend...*
2. Purpose, relative	quī, quae, quod + pres./impf.	may/might would	quī...scīret (I.62) *who would know how...*
3. Indirect Question	interrogatives: e.g. quis, cūr	none	quidve dolēns...impulerit (I.9-11) *or grieving what he set in motion*
4. Anticipatory Subj.	dum + pres./impf.	none	dum conderet...inferretque (I. 6) *until he could found... and bring*
5. Deliberative Subj.	main verb (interrogative)	am I to X should we?	et quisquam...adōret (I.48) *Is anyone to pray to...?*
6. Future Less Vivid Condition	sī pres. subj., pres. subj.	should/would	nī faciat, ferant...verrant (I.59) *if he should not do it...they would carry off...and sweep...*

1. What reason does Aeolus give for helping Juno in 76-80? How does this reason explain why Aeolus is perhaps confused and breaks his patron-client relationship with Jupiter. (N.B. Aeolus does not ask whether the command comes from Jupiter himself.)

2. Explain in one sentence how Juno's own inner disorder (i.e. her emotional response ot the Trojans) lead to (a) social disorder in the patron-client relationship and finally (b) disorder in nature.

3. Explain how the winds are likened to soldiers in the simile 'velut agmine factō, quā data porta, ruunt' (I.82-3).

Ēripiunt subitō nūbēs caelumque diemque
Teucōrum ex oculīs; pontō nox incubat ātra.
intonuēre polī et crēbrīs micat ignibus aethēr
praesentemque virīs intentant omnia mortem.
Extemplō Aenēae solvuntur frīgore membra;
ingemit et duplicēs tendēns ad sīdera palmās
tālia vōce refert: "Ō terque quaterque beātī,
quīs ante ōra patrum Troiae sub moenibus altīs
contigit oppetere! Ō Danaum fortissime gentis
Tȳdīdē! Mēne Īliacīs occumbere campīs
nōn potuisse tuāque animam hanc effundere dextrā
saevus ubi Aeacidae tēlō iacet Hector, ubi ingēns
Sarpēdon, ubi tot Simoīs correpta sub undīs
scūta virum galeāsque et fortia corpora volvit!"

Aeacides, -ae m.: Achilles, descendant of Aeacus
aether, -eris m.: aether, (upper) sky, 3
beatus, -a, -um: blessed, happy
campus, -ī m.: field, 3
contingō, -ere, contigī: touch, border; happen, 2
crēber, -bra, -brum: frequent, crowded, 2
diēs, diēī m./f.: day, day(light), 4
duplex, -icis: double
effundō, -ere, -fūdī, -fūsum: pour out, 3
ēripiō, -ere, -uī, -reptus: rescue, snatch from, 4
extemplō: immediately, forthwith, 2
frīgus, -ōris n.: cold, chill, 2
galea, -ae f.: helmet
Hector, -oris m.: Hector, 4
iaceō, iacēre, iacuī: lie, 2
Īliacus, -a, -um: of Ilium, Trojan, 2
incubō (1): lie on
ingemō, -ere, -uī: groan, sigh
intentō (1): threaten, stretch or extend over
intonō, -ere, -uī: thunder
membrum, -ī n.: limb
micō (1): flicker, flash
mors, -rtis f.: death, 3
occumbō, -ere, -cubuī: lie (dead)
oppetō, -ere, īvī, ītus: meet (death), encounter
palma, -ae f.: palm, hand
polus, -î m.: pole, sky
praesēns, -ntis: present, instant
quater: four times, 3
Sarpēdon, -ōnis m.: Sarpedon
scūtum, -ī n.: shield
Simoīs, -entis m.: Simois river
solvō, -ere, solvī, solūtum: loosen; set sail; pay
subitō: suddenly, 4
ter: thrice, three times, 4
Tȳdīdēs, ae m.: son of Tydeus, Diomedes

88 **caelumque diemque**: *both...and...*; acc. objs. diem here refers to 'daylight'
89 **Teucōrum**: *of the Trojans*; patronymic
pontō: *on...*; dat. of compound verb
90 **intonuēr(unt)**: syncopated 3p pf.
crēbrīs...ignibus: *with...*; i.e. lightning; abl. of cause or means
91 **intentant**: *threaten* (dat) *with* (acc); 'hold (acc) over (dat)' a dat. of compound verb; omnia is nom. subject
92 **solvuntur**: *are loosened*; i.e. his knees buckle
frīgore: *by chilly fear*; i.e. cold shudder of fear; metonomy (shudder suggests fear); abl. cause
93 **ingemit**: Aeneas is subject
94 **tālia**: *such things*; i.e. the following things; neut. acc. pl. substantive
vōce: *with (his)...*; i.e. aloud; Aeneas yells into the wind
refert: *says*; 'reports'
Ō...beātī: voc. direct address and apostrophe (turning off to address one not present); Aeneas addresses the Trojans who died at Troy below the city walls as their parents watched safely from the top of the walls
95 **quī(bu)s**: *to whom...*; dat. of interest
ōra: *faces*; 'mouths,' synecdoche
contigit oppetere: *it happened to meet (death)* impersonal pf. verb + inf.
96 **Ō...Tȳdīdē**: *O Diomedes*; 'O Son of Tydeus,' voc. direct address; patronymic and apostrophe; Aeneas now addresses the Greek Diomedes, who almost killed Aeneas at Troy in the *Iliad*

Mē-ne...potuisse: *Was I not able to...*; or 'could I not...' acc. + inf. of exclamation (see also I.37) expressing surprise or bewilderment
tuā...dextrā (manū): abl. means
animam hanc: i.e. Aeneas' last breath and life
99 **ubi...ubi...(iacet et) ubi**: *where...*; anaphora, asyndeton, and ellipsis; add 'et' and a verb
Aeacidae: *of Achilles*; 'of the descendant of Aeacus,' patronymic; Achilles is the grandson
telō: *by the spear*; abl. of cause
iacet: *lies (dead)*; in Bk 22 of the *Iliad*, Achilles kills Hector with a spear and then drags his body around the walls of Troy
ubi ingēns Sarpēdon (iacet): ellipsis; Patroclus, a friend of Achilles, kills the Greek Sarpedon, son of Jupiter, in Bk 16 of the *Iliad*
100 **tot**: adj. modifying all three acc. objects
correpta sub undīs: PPP modifies all three objs. but agrees with neuter pl. scūta
vir(ōr)um: of men; syncopated gen. pl.

Aenēās, -ae, acc. ān m.: Aeneas 23
anima, -ae f.: breath, life; soul, 5
ante: before, in front of (acc.); previously, 10
dexter, -tra, -trum: right (hand), favorable, 9
fortis, -e: strong, brave, 5
ingēns, -entis: huge, immense, 13
nōn: not, 22
nox, noctis, f.: night, 7
oculus, -ī m.: eye, 12
ōs, ōris n.: mouth, face, 10
referō, -ferre, -tulī, -lātus: carry back; report/say, 5
sīdus, -eris n.: star, constellation, 7
tēlum, -ī n.: spear, arrow, projectile, 6
unda, -ae f.: wave, 14

Aeneas's 1st Speech and *Odyssey* Book 5 (1 of 3)

In the following speech from *Odyssey* Book 5, Odysseus is lost at sea during a storm and laments his fate. Note how Aeneas' speech in ll. 92-101—particularly the underlined sections—is an imitation of this speech below.

Then were the knees of Odysseus loosened and his heart
melted, and deeply moved he spoke to his own mighty spirit:
"Ah me, wretched that I am! What is to befall me at the last?
I fear me that verily all that the goddess said was true, when
she declared that on the sea, before ever I came to my native land,
I should fill up my measure of woes; and lo, all this now is being brought to pass.
In such wise does Zeus overcast the broad heaven with clouds,
and has stirred up the sea, and the blasts
of all manner of winds sweep upon me; now is my utter destruction sure.
Thrice blessed those Danaans, aye, four times blessed, who of old perished
in the wide land of Troy, doing the pleasure of the sons of Atreus.
Even so would that I had died and met my fate on that day
when the throngs of the Trojans hurled upon me bronze-tipped spears,
fighting around the body of the dead son of Peleus.
Then should I have got funeral rites, and the Achaeans would have spread my fame,
but now by a miserable death was it appointed me to be cut off."

Odyssey V.297-312 (tr. A. T. Murray, 1919)

This imitation tells us several things: (1) Vergil expected his readers to know the *Odyssey* in Greek and recognize the imitation. (2) By having Aeneas mimic Odysseus' words, Vergil elevates Aeneas, who is a very minor figure in myth and legend, and encourages readers to view him as a hero of equal status to the famed Odysseus. (3) Vergil wishes for us to view Aeneas' fear and wish for death as an expression of the heroic ideal (below).

The Traditional Epic Hero

At first glance Aeneas and Odysseus may appear to be cowards wishing for death, but in fact both are expressing the ideal of the epic hero. A traditional epic hero strives though deeds to achieve immortal glory. Both Aeneas and Odysseus express this same ideal when they wish that they had died in battle and were remembered rather than die without glory at sea. When Aeneas recalls the fallen Trojans Hector and Sarpedon, he is lamenting that, while they will be remembered for their heroism after death, Aeneas will most certainly be forgotten at sea.

1. Identify in Latin and English the 3 behaviors that reveal Aeneas' emotional state before he speaks.
2. Aeneas turns off and addresses two different audiences in his speech. Who are they?
3. How does the heroic ideal explain that Aeneas is not behaving cowardly when he wishes for death?
4. How does the mention of Hector and Sarpedon reveal that Aeneas still has the heroic ideal in mind?

Tālia iactantī strīdēns Aquilōne procella
vēlum adversa ferit, flūctūsque ad sīdera tollit.
Franguntur rēmī, tum prōra āvertit et undīs
dat latus, insequitur cumulō praeruptus aquae mōns.
Hī summō in flūctū pendent; hīs unda dehīscēns
terram inter flūctūs aperit, furit aestus harēnis.
Trēs Notus abreptās in saxa latentia torquet
(saxa vocant Italī mediīs quae in flūctibus Ārās,
dorsum immāne marī summō), trēs Eurus ab altō
in brevia et syrtēs urget, miserābile vīsū,
inlīditque vadīs atque aggere cingit harēnae.

---

abripiō, -ere, -ripuī, -reptum: snatch away
aestus, -ūs f.: tide
agger, -eris m.: mound, heap
aqua, -ae f.: water, 3
Aquilō, -ōnis m.: Aquilo wind, north wind, 2
āvertō, -ēre, āvertī, āversum: turn away, 4
brevis, -e: short, shallow, 4
cingō, -ere, cīnxī, cīnctus: surround
cumulus, -ī m.: heap, mass
dehīscō, -ere, -hīvī: gape, split, yawn
dorsum, -î n.: back, reef, ridge
Eurus, -ī m.: Eurus wind, 4
feriō, ferīre: strike, 2
frangō, -ere, frēgī, frāctus: break 3
inlīdō, -ere, -līsī: dash, beat, strike
insequor, -sequī, -secūtus sum: follow, ensue, 3
Italus, -a, -um: Italian
miserābilis, -e: miserable
Nōtus, -ī m.: Notus wind, South wind (= Auster), 3
pendō, -ere, pependī, pensum: pay, weigh 2
praeruptus, -a, -um: steep, towering
procella, -ae f.: blast, gust; storm 2
prōra, -ae f.: prow (front of the ship)
rēmus, -ī m.: oar, 3
strīd(e)ō, -ēre, -dī: rustle, whir, hiss, screech, creak, 3
syrtēs, -um f.: sand bar
trēs, tria: three, 4
urgeō, -ēre, ursī: drive, push
vadum, -ī n.: shallows, shoals, flats, 4
vēlum, -ī n.: sail, 2

102 **Tālia**: *such things*; marking the end of the speech; obj. of iactantī
iactantī: *for the (one)...*; i.e. Aeneas; this pres. pple iactō and dat. of reference (i.e. point of view) can mean 'yell' in this context (i.e. throw with his voice) or simply 'ponder'
103 **adversa**: *straight on*; nom. pred. adj. as adv.
Franguntur...(et) tum...(et) insequitur: asyndeton, marking abrupt action in the storm
104 **dat latus**: in this position an oncoming wind can easily overturn and sink a ship
105 **cumulō**: *in...*; abl. of manner
106 **Hī (virī)**: masculine pronouns in this passage refer to the men while the feminine pronouns refer to ships (nāvēs f.)
summō: *top of...*; not 'highest'
hīs (virīs): *to these*; dat. of reference/interest
107 **(et) furit**
harēnīs: *with...*; abl. of association; the water and land are mixing
108 **Trēs (nāvēs)...abreptās**: acc. obj. with PPP abripiō; Latin prefers a finite verb and PPP (i.e. twists the snatched ships) where English prefers 2 finite verbs (i.e. snatches and twists)
latentia: neut. pl. pres. pple lateō
109 **saxa quae**: *rocks which...*; or 'which rocks' saxa is in apposition to saxa above
vocant: *call* (x) (y); verb governs a double acc. (obj. and pred.)
Ārās: *the Altars*; a proper name for the reef
110 **dorsum immāne**: in apposition to saxa; i.e. a reef; immane is a neut. sg. 3rd decl. adj.
(in) marī summō: i.e. on the surface of the water; marī is an 3rd decl. i-stem abl. noun
(et) trēs (nāvēs): acc. obj.; ellipsis
ab altō: *from the sea*; metonomy
111 **brevia**: *shallows*; i.e. shallow water; syrtēs, brevia, and vadīs are often synonyms
miserābile: neut. sg. adj. describing the entire scene just described
vīsū: *to behold*; 'in respect to seeing,' a supine (PPP + ū) and abl. of respect; translate as inf.
112 **inlīdit...cingit**: the obj. is still trēs (nāvēs)
vadīs: *into...*; dat. of compound verb

adversus, -a, -um: facing, opposite, straight on, 5
aperiō, -īre, -uī, apertus: open; reveal, 5
harēna, -ae f.: sand, 6
immānis, -e: immense, huge, 6
inter: between, among, during (acc.) 8
lateō, -ēre, -uī: lie hidden, hide, escape notice, 5
medius, -a, -um: middle (part) of, middle, 12
saxum, -ī n.: rock, 11
summus, -a, -um: top of, highest, 9
torqueō, -ēre, torsī, tortum: twist, turn, 5
videō, -ēre, vīdī, vīsus: see; *videor*, seem, 24
vocō (1): call, name; summon, 8

Winds mentioned by Vergil

Aquilō (North-Northeast)

Notus/Auster (South)

Eurus (Southeast)

Zephyr (West)

Africus (Southwest)

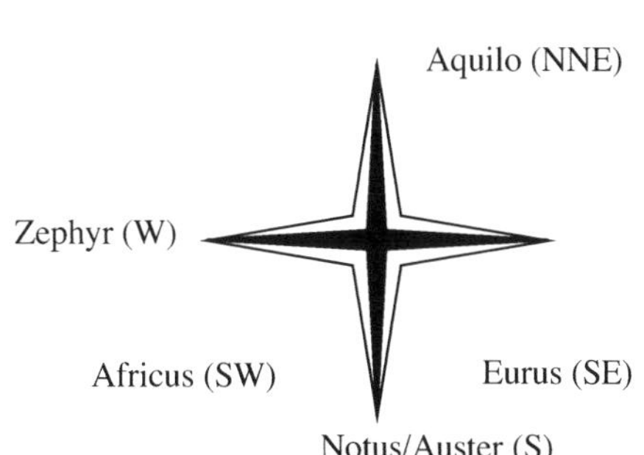

Both Romans and Greeks gave proper names to the winds of the Mediterranean. Farmers recognized that different winds had different characteristics—some brought cool air, others dry air, and others brought humid air and rain—and used the direction of the wind to predict the weather that would affect their crops. Sailors, who often lacked landmarks at sea, might also use the direction of a wind to orient the ship toward their destination.

Ancient Science: Four Primary Elements and Natural Place (part 2)

As we saw on page 11, the prevailing view in the ancient world is that there are four primary elements (earth, water, air, and fire), and each has its own natural place from top to bottom:

aether, -eris m.: aether, (upper) sky, 3
caelum, -ī n.: sky, 13
aqua, -ae f.: water, 3
terra, -ae f: land, ground, earth, 20

Reminder: As you read the storm episode, note how often the **disorder** stirred up by the winds is depicted as the unnatural mixing of elements from their natural places: e.g. water high in the air, land where there should be water, water described as land masses, etc. You will enjoy the passage much more if you notice these details.

A **Supine** [3] is a verbal noun formed by adding **-ū** in ablative and **-um** in accusative to the 4th principal part stem. The ablative is an ablative of respect and is often translated as an infinitive in English. These forms are rare but easy to spot:

miserābile vīsū [1] *miserable to behold (in beholding)*

mīrabile dictū [2] *amazing to speak of (in speaking)*

Ūnam, quae Lyciōs fīdumque vehēbat Orontēn,
ipsius ante oculōs ingēns ā vertice pontus
in puppim ferit: excutitur prōnusque magister
volvitur in caput; ast illam ter flūctus ibīdem
torquet agēns circum et rapidus vorat aequore vertex.
Appārent rārī nantēs in gurgite vastō,
arma virum tabulaeque et Trōia gaza per undās.
Iam validam Īlioneī nāvem, iam fortis Achātae,
et quā vectus Abās, et quā grandaevus Alētēs,
vīcit hiems; laxīs laterum compāgibus omnēs
accipiunt inimīcum imbrem rīmīsque fatīscunt.
  Intereā magnō miscērī murmure pontum
ēmissamque hiemem sēnsit Neptūnus et īmīs
stāgna refūsa vadīs, graviter commōtus; et altō
prōspiciēns summā placidum caput extulit undā.

Abās, Abantis m.: Abas
Achātēs, -ae m.: Achates (companion of Aeneas), 4
Alētēs, -ae m.: Trojan leader
appareō, -ēre, -uī, -itus: appear
commoveō, -ēre, -mōvī: upset, trouble, set in motion, 2
compāgēs, -is f.: seam, joint, 2
efferō, -ferre, extulī, ēlātus: raise, lift up 2
ēmittō, -ere, -mīsī, -missum: send away 2
excutiō, -ere, -cussī, -cussum: strike or shake off, 2
fatīscō, -ere: to gape, open. split
feriō, ferīre: strike, 2
fīdus, -a, -um: faithful, trustworthy, 3
gaza, -ae f.: treasure, wealth
grandaevus, -a, -um: very-aged, aged, old
gurges, -itis m.: whirl (of water), whirlpool, 3
hiems, hiemis f.: winter, storm, 3
ibīdem: in the same place
Ilioneus, -î m.: Ilioneus, 3
imber, imbris m.: rain
inimīcus, -a, -um: unfriendly, rival (dat), 4
laxus, -a, -um: free, loosened, lax, 2
Lycius, -a, -um: Lycian, of Lycia, 2
magister, magistrī m.: helmsman
murmur, -uris n.: murmur, rumble, 4
Neptūnus, -ī m.: Neptune, 3
nō, nāre, nāvī: swim, float
Orontēs, -is m.: Orontes (a Lycian leader)
placidus, -a, -um: peaceful, calm, 2
prōnus, -a, -um: leaning/bending forward, prone
prōspiciō, -ere, -spexī, -spectus: look out on, survey, 4
rapidus, -a, -um: swift, grasping, 3
rārus, -a, -um: scattered, far apart
refundō, -ere, -fūdī, -fūsus: pour back
rīma, -ae f.: crack, fissure
sentiō, -īre, -sī: feel, realize, 2
stagnum, -ī n.: pool, standing water, 3
tabula, -ae f.: plank, board
ter: thrice, three times, 4
vadum, -ī n.: shallows, shoals, 4
validus, -a, -um: strong, sturdy, 2
vehō, -ere, vēxī, vectum: convey, carry, 4
vorō (1): to devour

113 **Ūnam (nāvem)**: obj. of ferit
Lyciōs: *the Lycians*; a people in Asia Minor who fought alongside the Trojans in the war
Orontēn: Grk. acc. sg.; leader of the Lycians
ipsius: *of (Aeneas) himself*; 'of the (one) himself,' -ius is gen. sg.; modifies oculōs
114 **ā vertice...**: i.e. the wave strikes down after reaching its highest peak in the air
115 **puppim**: irreg. acc. sg.
excutitur: i.e. off of the ship and into the water; now, no one is steering the ship
-que: joins the two verbs
116 **ast**: *but*; alternative form for 'at'
illam (nāvem)
117 **agēns circum**: *driving (it) around*; pres. pple, tmesis (see p. 29) for circum-agō
(in) aequore
vertex: i.e. a whirlpool (but 'peak' in l. 114)
118 **Appārent**: *(there) appear*; with four subjects
nantēs: *swimmers*; '(men) swimming,' pres. pple
119 **vir(ōr)um**: syncopated gen pl.
Trōia: *Trojan*; neut. pl. adj. Trōius, -a, -um

120 **iam (hiems vīcit) validam Īlioneī nāvem (et) iam (nāvem) fortis Achātae**: anaphora and asyndeton with heavy ellipsis throughout; add the subject and verb from l. 122; the use of personal names humanizes the victims and therefore makes the terror more meaningful

121 **et (nāvem) quā...et (nāvem) quā**: *(the ship) by which...and (the ship) by which...*; anaphora; both relatives are abl. of means
vectus (est) Abās: 3s pf. pass. vehō
grandaevus Alētēs (vectus est)

122 **laxīs...compāgibus**: *with the joints of the sides loosened*; abl. abs., water is entering the ships through the seams between the boards on the sides of the ships
omnēs (nāvēs): nom. subj.

123 **inimīcum**: i.e. unwelcome
rīmīs: *with...*; abl. means or cause

124 **magnō miscērī...pontum**: *that...*; ind. disc. with pres. pass. inf.; see box below
magnō...murmure: *with...*; alliteration and onomatopoeia; abl. of manner, which omits the preposition 'cum' when it includes an adj.

125 **ēmissam (esse) hiemem**: *that...*; ind. disc. with pf. pass. inf. ēmittō; see box below.
īmīs...vādīs: *from...*; abl. of place from which

126 **stāgna refūsa (esse)**: *and that the still waters were poured up*; i.e. the water at the bottom of the sea, normally still, is being disturbed by the storm and the waters above; ind. disc.
altō: *over ...*; dat. of compound verb prōspiciēns or simple abl. of place where

127 **prospiciēns**: pres. pple, supply Neptunus as subject
summā...ūndā: *from...*; or 'on...' summus refers to 'the top of' not the 'highest'

accipiō, -ere, -cēpī, -ceptus: receive, take, 7
caput, -itis n.: head; life, 10
gravis, -e: heavy, serious, severe, 5
intereā: meanwhile, in the meantime, 5
misceō, -ēre, -uī, mīxtum: mix (up), 7
nāvis, -is f.: ship, 11
vertex, -icis m.: peak; whirlpool, 5

3rd I-Stem Nouns and Adjectives

All 3rd decl. adjectives and a small subset of 3rd decl. nouns are i-stem and have an extra 'i' not found in some forms of regular 3rd declension. Note the endings in boldface below.

	omnis, omne: every, all				ignis, is f.: fire		mare, -is n.: sea	
	m/f.		neut.		masc./fem.		neuter	
Nom.	omnis [5]	omnēs [5]	omne	**omnia** [1]	ignis	ignēs [4]	mare	**maria**
Gen.	omnis	**omnium**	omnis	**omnium**	ignis	**ignium**	maris	**marium**
Acc.	omnī	omnibus	omnī	omnibus	ignī	ignibus [1]	marī [1]	maribus
Acc.	omnem[4]	omnēs [5]	omne	**omnia** [5]	ignem [4]	ignēs [2]	mare	**maria** [3]
Abl.	**omnī** [1]	omnibus[1]	**omnī**	omnibus	**ignī** [2]	ignibus [1]	**marī** [1]	maribus

Present participles are also i-stem (e.g. in maria latentia, 'into hiding rocks'), but use the abl. sg. ending -ī when they behave as an adjective and abl. sg. ending -e when they behave as a verb form (e.g. abl. abs. or participial phrase).

pple as adj.	praestantī corpore	*of outstanding body*	(I.71)
abl. abs.	magnā comitante catervā	*a great retinue accompanying*	(II.40)

Indirect Discourse in Secondary Sequence: When the main verb is past tense, the infinitives in indirect discourse are translated slightly more in the past:

	sentit (he senses that)		sēnsit (he sensed that)
miscērī...pontum	*sea **is** mixed*	(pres. → impf.)	*sea **was being** mixed*
ēmissam (esse) hiemem	*storm **was** sent*	(pf. → plpf.)	*storm **had been** sent up*
stāgna refūsa (esse)	*stillwaters **were**...*	(pf. → plpf.)	*stillwaters **had been** poured up*

1. How does Vergil's use of personal names when referring to individual ships in 113-121 make the terror and loss more meaningful? Would we read the passage differently if the victims were nameless?

Disiectam Aenēae tōtō videt aequore classem,
flūctibus oppressōs Trōas caelīque ruīnā.
Nec latuēre dolī frātrem Iūnōnis et īrae.
Eurum ad sē Zephyrumque vocat, dehinc tālia fātur:
"Tantane vōs generis tenuit fīdūcia vestrī?
Iam caelum terramque meō sine nūmine, ventī,
miscēre et tantās audētis tollere mōlēs?
Quōs ego—! sed mōtōs praestat compōnere flūctūs.
Post mihi nōn similī poenā commissa luētis.
Mātūrāte fugam rēgīque haec dīcite vestrō:
nōn illī imperium pelagī saevumque tridentem,
sed mihi sorte datum. Tenet ille immānia saxa,
vestrās, Eure, domōs; illā sē iactet in aulā
Aeolus et clausō ventōrum carcere rēgnet."

---

audeō, -ēre, ausus sum: dare (+ inf.), 2
aula, -ae f.: hall, palace, 2
carcer, -eris m.: prison, 2
claudō, -ere, -sī, -sus: close (in)
committō, -ere, -mīsī: commit, commence
compōnō, -ere, -suī, -situs: compose, arrange, calm, 2
dehinc: then, thereupon, 2
disiciō, -ere, -iēcī, -iectum: scatter, throw apart, 4
dolus, -ī m.: trick, deceit, 3
Eurus, -ī m.: Eurus wind, 4
fīdūcia, -ae f.: confidence, trust
frāter, -tris m.: brother, 2
luō, -ere, -ī: atone for, pay for
mātūrō (1): hasten
opprimō, -ere, -pressī, -pressum: crush, overwhelm
pelagus, -ī n.: sea, 4
praestō, -āre: set before, prefer; present; *praestāns*, outstanding; *praestat*: it is preferable/better, 2
regnō (1): reign, rule as a king
rēx, rēgis m.: king, 4
ruīna, -ae f.: downfall, fall
similis, -e: like, similar, (*dat.*, *gen.*)
sine: without (*abl.*)
tridēns, -ntis m.: trident, 3
Zephyrus, -ī m.: (west) wind

128 **disiectam...classem**: PPP with fem. classem
(in) tōtō...aequore
129 **fluctibus...caelīque ruīnā**: abl. means
(et) oppressōs Trōās: PPP with masc. Trōās
130 **latuēr(unt)**: syncopated 3p pf.; dolī et īrae are the subject; i.e. Neptune knows that Juno played a role in stirring up the storm
131 **Eurum Zephyrumque**: acc. objs. of vocat
tālia: *such things*; i.e. the following
fātur: 3s pres. dep. for, fārī; translate as active
Tanta-ne...fīdūcia...vestrī?: a golden line (interlocking word order with verb in middle)
generis...vestrī: *of your lineage*; or 'of your birth,' Neptune refers to the winds' lower status in society compared to his own status
133 **meō sine nūmine**: nūmen here refers to 'divine permission' or 'approval'
ventī: voc. direct address
134 **audētis**: 2p pres. audeō—not audiō; + 2 infs.
tantās...mōlēs: i.e. the swells of seawater
135 **Quōs ego—!**: *whom I...!*; aposiopoesis (a breaking off): Neptune stops mid-sentence as he restrains his anger and composes himself
praestat: *it is better...*; impersonal verb
mōtōs: *set in motion*; PPP
136 **Post...luētis**: *Afterwards, you will pay for (the crimes) committed by no similar punishment*; i.e. by more than a strong verbal rebuke; litotes (understatement); 2p fut. with a neut. acc. pl. PPP used as a substantive
137 **rēgī...vestrō**: dat. ind. obj.; i.e. Aeolus
haec: neut. acc. pl., substantive: add 'things'
138 **nōn illī...sed mihi**: *not to...but to..*; i.e. Aeolus; dat. ind. obj. and both made emphatic by position at the beginning of each line; note the anaphora (illī...ille...illā...)
imperium...datum (esse): *(namely) that...*; ind. disc. with pf. pass. inf. in apposition to haec; verb is sg. but there are two acc. subjects
sorte: *by lot*; the brothers Jupiter, Neptune, and Pluto had drawn lots to decide which one ruled the sky, sea, and the underworld

140 **vestrās...domōs**: in apposition to immania saxa; domōs is 2nd decl. fem.; note how the god belittles Aeolus' home and domain of power by calling it 'saxa' and later 'carcere'

Eure: voc. dir. address

sē iactet: *let him boast himself*; i.e. let him throw his power/commands around; 3s jussive pres. subj. and reflexive pronoun

140 **(in) clausō...carcere**: PPP claudō

regnet: *let him*...; 3s jussive pres. subj.

domus, -ūs f.: home; house(hold), 8
for, fārī, fātus: speak, say, tell, 7
fuga, -ae f.: flight; haste, 5
meus, -a, -um: my, mine 10
moveō, movēre, mōvī, mōtus: move, upset, 7
poena, -ae f.: punishment, penalty, 5
post: after, behind (acc.), later, 5
sors, sortis f.: lot, lottery; luck, 5
vester, -ra, -rum: your, yours (pl. of tuus), 5

nūmen, nūminis n.

Roman divinities initially had no personalities or no myths attributed to them. Instead, they possessed solely the power to nod in approval (*adnuere*) or disapproval (*abnuere*) to prayers and offerings by humans. The word *nūmen*, literally 'a nod,' reflects this belief. And so, while we can at times translate *nūmen* as synonymous with 'god' or 'divinity,' it more often means 'divine approval' or 'divine will.'

Notice that Neptune's use of the word *nūmen* in line 133 means 'approval' or 'permission.'

Domains of Power

Neptune's speech (132-141) reveals that the gods have well-defined domains of power, and conflict can arise when one god interferes with the domain of another. When Neptune says that his power 'was given by lot,' (*sorte...dātum*) Vergil is alluding to the account that in the beginning Neptune, Jupiter, and Pluto drew lots and decided randomly who would rule over the sea, sky, and underworld.

Stoicism and Emotional Restraint

One of the modern misconceptions about Stoicism, a Greek philosophy popular among the Romans, is the belief that a Stoic should not show any emotion at all. This is simply not true. Stoics can in fact cry and show fear, just as Aeneas does, or feel anger, just as Neptune. The difference is that Stoics do not allow emotions to prevent them from *acting according to reason* and what is right.

Compare Juno's and Neptune's speeches and responses to anger. Both become angry when they see the Trojan ships on the sea—for different reasons, obviously—but, while Juno acts out of emotion when she directs Aeolus to send the winds, Neptune quickly redirects his initial anger away from the winds in line 135 with the famous *aposiopoesis* (a rhetorical device where one breaks off mid-sentence), and reestablishes order within the domains of power. From a Stoic's point of view, Neptune's initial anger and subsequent emotional restraint is the appropriate course of action.

Neptune's Speech

1. How does I.132 suggest that gods are like aristocrats fighting over relative status of their families?

2. Where in I.133-4 does the god say that the winds do not have permission to interfere in his domain?

3. Lines 133-135 show once again the gods' role in imposing order on the four elements. Which three of the four elements does Neptune mention in those lines?

3. When Neptune breaks off mid-sentence, what course of action does he decide to pursue in 135?

4. Note that while Juno uses imperatives when speaking to Aeolus, Neptune uses imperatives with the winds and jussive subjunctives with Aeolus. If we assume that a jussive is more polite than an imperative, what do these verbs suggest about Neptune's status relative to the winds and Aeolus?

5. What words does Neptune use in lines 139-40 to belittle Aeolus' domain of power and emphasize that Aeolus' domain is far less important than Neptune's power over the sea and the trident?

Sīc ait et dictō citius tumida aequora plācat
collēctāsque fugat nūbēs sōlemque redūcit.
Cȳmothoē simul et Trītōn adnixus acūtō
dētrūdunt nāvēs scopulō; levat ipse tridentī
et vastās aperit syrtēs et temperat aequor
atque rotīs summās levibus perlābitur undās.
Ac velutī magnō in populō cum saepe coörta est
sēditiō saevitque animīs ignōbile vulgus;
iamque facēs et saxa volant, furor arma ministrat;
tum, pietāte gravem ac meritīs sī forte virum quem
conspexēre, silent arrēctīsque auribus astant;
ille regit dictīs animōs et pectora mulcet:
sīc cūnctus pelagī cecidit fragor, aequora postquam
prōspiciēns genitor caelōque invectus apertō
flectit equōs currūque volāns dat lōra secundō.

---

acūtus, -a, -um: sharp, pointed, 2
adnītor, -ī, -xus sum: lean on, strive, exert onself (dat)
arrigō, -ere, -rēxī, -rectus: raise, prick up, 3
astō, -āre, abstiti: stand by or near, 2
auris, -is: **f.**: ear, 3
cadō, cadere, cecidī: to fall, 3
citius: more quickly (comparative adv. of cito)
colligō, -ere, -lēgī, -lēctum: gather, collect, 2
conspiciō, -ere, spexī, spectus: see, behold 2
coörior, -īrī, coörtus sum: arise
currus, -ūs m.: chariot, carriage, 2
Cȳmothoē, -ēs f.: Cymothoe (a sea nymph)
dētrūdō, -ere, -sī, -sus: push off, dislodge, thrust off
dictum, -ī n.: word, speech, 4
equus, -ī m.: horse, 4
fax, facis f.: torch, firebrand
flectō, -ere, -ēxī, -ectus: bend, turn
fors, fortis f.: fortune; **forte**: by chance
fragor, -ôris m.: crash, fall
fugō (1): put to flight, 2
furor, -ōris m.: rage, fury, madness, 3
genitor, -ōris m.: begetter, father, 4
ignōbilis, -e: ignoble, common
invehō, -ere, -ēxī, ectus: carry, convey into
levis, -e: light
levō (1): lift up, raise; relieve, 2
lōrum, -ī n.: rein, leather strap, 2
meritum, -ī n.: favor, benefit, merit, 2
ministrō (1): supply; manage, assist, 2
mulceō, -ēre, -lsī, -lsus: calm, soothe, 3
pelagus, -ī n.: sea, 4
perlabor, -ī, -lapsus sum: glide or slide over
placeō, -ēre, -uī, -itus: please, placate
postquam: after, 3
prōspiciō, -ere, -spexī, -spectus: look out on, survey, 4
redūcō, -ere, -dūxī, -ductus: to reduce, bring back, 2
rota, -ae f.: wheel, 2
saepe: often
saeviō, -īre, -īvī (iī), -ītus: rage, be fierce or savage, 2
secundus, -a, -um: following; favorable, obedient, 3
sēditiō, -ōnis f.: riot
sileō, -ēre, -uī: be silent, be still, 2
sōl, sōlis m.: sun, 4
syrtēs, -um f.: sand bar
temperō (1): refrain, calm, control, 2
tridēns, -ntis m.: trident, 3
Trītōn, -ōnis m.: Triton
tumidus, -a, -um: swelling, swollen, 2
velut, velutī: just as, 2
volō (1): to fly, 3
vulgus, -ī n.: masses, multitude, 2

142 **dictō citius**: *faster than said*; 'more quickly than (the thing) having been said,'' comparative adv. and abl. of comparison
144 **adnixus**: pf. dep. pple: translate 'having Xed'
acūtō...scopulō: *from*...; abl. of separation
145 **levat (nāvēs)**: ellipsis; i.e. off from the rocks
(Neptūnus) ipse
tridentī: i-stem 3rd decl. abl. means
147 **rōtīs...levibus**: *with*...; abl. means, Neptune, god of horses and the sea, is in a flying chariot
summās...undās: 'top of...' not 'highest'
perlābitur: pres. dep., translate as active
148 **Ac velutī...cum**: *and just as when*...; simile that lasts until the word sīc in l. 154
magnō in populō: *in a great crowd*
coörta est: *has arisen*; 3s pf. dep.

149 **animīs**: *with passion, with spirit*; abl. of cause; the pl. often means 'anger,' or 'passion'
ignobile vulgus: neut. nom.
furor arma ministrat: i.e. people in a frenzy will pick up anything and throw it
151 **sī forte...conspēxēr(unt)**: *if by chance they...*; a syncopated 3p pf.; the crowd is the subject; forte is an common abl. as adv.
pietāte...meritīs: *in...and in...*; abl. respect modifying grāvem, which modifies virum
virum quem: *some man*; quem is an indefinite adj. after sī (see below)
152 **arrectīs auribus**: abl. abs.
153 **ille**: i.e. the pious orator mentioned in l. 151
dictīs: *with words*; substantive from the PPP
pectora: i.e. hearts, the seat of emotion in the body is in the chest
154 **sīc**: marks the end of the simile
postquam: *afterwards*
155 **genitor**: *the father*; 'begetter,' i.e. Neptune
caelō...apertō: *into...*; dat. of compound verb; Neptune's chariot can fly through the air
currū...sēcundō: *to his obedient chariot*; dat. ind. obj.; currū is a variant of 4th decl. curruī
dat lōra: i.e. let go of the reins and allow the horses to go unrestrained as fast as they wish

aiō, ais, ait; aiunt: say, speak; assert, 7
cūnctus, -a, -um: all, whole, entire, 5
regō, -ere, rēxī, rectus: rule, lead, direct, 13
simul: at the same time, together, 7

After sī, nisi, num and nē, all the ali's go away: *aliquis, aliquid* is an indefinite pronoun, 'anyone/ anything, someone/something).' After the four words in the mnemonic above, the prefix *alī-* (=alius) is omitted. If you encounter *quis*, *quid* after these words, translate *quis*, *quid* as 'any' or 'some.'

Sī quā fāta sinant	*if in any (way) the fates allow*
Sī virum quem conspēxērunt	*if they have caught sight of some man*

animus, animī m. in the plural can be translated as 'spirits,' 'courage,' 'passions,' or even 'anger' and reflects a heightened emotional state. Compare the word 'spirited' in English.

mollitque animōs	*he softens their spirits (i.e. calms their anger)*	I.57
ille regit...animōs	*that one rules their spirits (i.e. restrains their passions)*	I.153

The Simile of the Pious Orator (I.148-153) is unique because it uses human behavior to explain nature, while most similes in epic use nature to explain human behavior.

Just as	the pious orator	restrains an emotional crowd	to reestablish order in society,
so	the god Neptune	restrains the emotional winds	to reestablish order in nature.

Emotional Restraint and the Broader View in Book I

Vergil has shown readers how unrestrained emotion creates disorder in individuals, in society (e.g. the riot), and in nature (i.e. storm) and has hinted that *pietās*, devotion to family, community, and the gods is one path to restraining these same emotions and creating order. The evidence for this framework remains incomplete but note the pattern below as it applies to Juno, Neptune, and the Pious Orator:

Individual	**Juno** defies fate and shows a lack of emotional restraint,	**Neptune** is initially angry but shows restraint for the better,	**The Pious Orator** acts out of duty to family, community, and gods,
Society	which leads to disorder in the patron-client relationship (who is the proper patron? enemy?),	which leads to reestablishing order in the domains of power (I control the sea; you, a rock),	and as leader restrains the emotions of the people to bring social order
Nature	which leads to releasing the emotional winds and creating disorder in nature (storm).	which leads to restraining the emotional winds and creating order in nature (calm).	and as suppliant strives to gain the favor of the gods and act in accordance with fate.

Aeneas and the Pious Orator: Not surprisingly, Vergil will have Aeneas plays the role of orator and calm his own people in a speech in Il.198-207. Just as the orator 'soothes hearts with words' (*dictīs... pectora mulcet*, 153), so Aeneas will do the same with the same words (*dictīs...pectora mulcet*, 197).

Dēfessī Aeneadae quae proxima lītora cursū
contendunt petere, et Libyae vertuntur ad ōrās.
Est in sēcessū longō locus: īnsula portum
efficit obiectū laterum, quibus omnis ab altō
frangitur inque sinūs scindit sēsē unda reductōs.
Hinc atque hinc vastae rūpēs geminīque minantur
in caelum scopulī, quōrum sub vertice lātē
aequora tūta silent; tum silvīs scaena coruscīs
dēsuper, horrentīque ātrum nemus imminet umbrā;
fronte sub adversā scopulīs pendentibus antrum,
intus aquae dulcēs vīvōque sedīlia saxō
nymphārum domus. Hīc fessās nōn vincula nāvēs
ūlla tenent, uncō nōn alligat ancora morsū.

---

adversus, -a, -um: facing, opposite, straight on, 5
Aeneadae, -(ār)um m.: followers/sons of Aeneas
alligō (1): bind to, tie to
ancora, -ae f.: anchor
aqua, -ae f.: water, 3
contendō, -ere, -ī, -ntus: strive; hasten
coruscus, -a, -um: waving, quivering, flashing
dēfessus, -a, -um: wearied, exhausted, worn out, 3
dēsuper: from above, 3
efficiō, -ere, -fēcī, -fectus: make, produce
fessus, -a, -um: tired, weary, worn, 3
frangō, -ere, frēgī, frāctus: break 3
frōns, frontis f.: forehead, 2
geminus, -a, -um: twin, double, two 4
horreō, -ēre, -uī; bristle at, shudder at; fear, dread, 3
immineô, -êre: overhang, tower over, 2
insula, -ae, f.: island
intus: within, inside
minor, -ārī, -ātus sum: threaten, tower, 2
morsus, -ūs m.: bite, 2
nemus, -oris n.: wood, forest, grove, 4
nympha, -ae f.: nymph, 4
obiectus, -ūs m.: projection, extension; barrier
pendō, -ere, pependī, pensum: pay, weigh 2
portus, -ūs m.: port, harbor, 3
proximus, -a, -um: nearest, very close
redūcō, -ere, -dūxī, -ductus: to reduce, bring back, 2
rūpēs, rūpis f.: rock, cliff, 2
scaena, -ae f.: background, backdrop, stage, 2
scindō, -ere, scidī, scissum: cut back
sēcessus, -ūs m.: recess, inlet
sedīle, -is n. (pl. sedīlia): seat, bench
sileō, -ēre, -uī: be silent, be still, 2
silva, -ae f.: woods, 4
sinus, -ūs m.: curve; bosom, lap, 2
tūtus, -a, -um: safe, secure, 4
uncus, -a, -um: curved
vertō, -ere, vertī, versum: to turn, 3
vinculum, -ī n.: chain, 4
vīvus, -a, -um: living, alive, 3

157 **Aeneadae**: i.e. the Trojans, a patronymic
quae (sunt) proxima lītora: *the shores which...*
cursū: *on (their) course*; abl. manner
158 **Est**: *there is...*; ecphrasis (a vivid description of a scene, often superfluous to the narrative)
obiectū laterum: *with...*; abl. means and gen. pl. latus; an island with extended sides lies off the shore and breaks up incoming waves that approach the shore to create a natural harbor
160 **quibus**: *by which...*; abl. means or cause
omnis...unda: subject of two verbs
ab altō: *from the sea*; metonomy
161 **in sinūs...reductōs**: i.e. smaller ripples; PPP redūcō
162 **hinc atque hinc**: *here and there*; 'from here and from here'
163 **quōrum sub...**: *under whose...*
164 **tūta**: i.e. safe for ships to lie at harbor
scaena (est): *(there is)...*
silvīs coruscīs: *of...*; abl. quality with scaena
165 **horrentī...umbrā**: *of...*; abl. of quality with nemus; pres. pple with 3rd decl. i-stem abl.
166 **scopulīs pendentibus**: *of...*; abl. of quality with pres. pple
antrum (est): *(there is)...*; nom. subj.
167 **aquae dulcēs (sunt)**: *(there are)...*; i.e. fresh water not saltwater
vīvō...saxō: *of...*; abl. of quality (material) modifying sedīlia
168 **domus**: nom. in apposition to aquae, sedīlia
nōn ūlla: *not any...*; = nūlla, with vincula
uncō...morsū: abl. of means

cursus, -ūs m.: course, running; haste, 6
dulcis, -e: sweet, pleasant, fresh, 7
petō, -ere, -īvi: seek, head for; ask, 14
ūllus, -a, -um: any(one, thing), 5
umbra, -ae f.: shade, shadow, ghost, 12

An **Ecphrasis** is a rhetorical device where the author offers an unusually vivid description of a scene or work of art: in the case of I.159-69, a detailed description of the calm bay where the Trojans find refuge for their ships. Thre are a number of examples of this device, but perhaps the most famous ecphrasis in the *Aeneid* is the depiction of scenes from Roman history depicted on the shield that Venus will give to Aeneas in VIII.629-719.

60 Deponent Verbs

Deponents put aside (*dēpōnere*) their active forms, and their passive forms translate as active. Often the presence of an acc. object and other context clues will suggest that the verb is active in meaning. Do not feel overwhelmed by this list. Verbs that look intimidating in isolation are often easier to grasp when read in context. For now, note the high frequency deponents and compound forms below:

adnītor, -ī, -xus sum: lean on, strive, exert oneself (dat)
  obnitor, -nitī -nixus sum: struggle, strive, resist
adorior, -īrī, -ortus sum: attack, rise to, undertake +inf.
  coörior, -īrī, coörtus sum: arise
  oborior, -orīrī, -ortus sum: rise up, appear
amplector, -ī, -plexus sum: wind around, embrace, 3
baccor, -ārī, -ātus sum: to rave, rage (like a Bacchante)
comitor, -ārī, comitātus sum: accompany, attend
confiteor, -ērī, -fessus sum: acknowledge, confess
cōnor, -ārī, cōnātus sum: to try
epulor, -ārī, epulātus sum: to feast together, feast on
experior, -īrī, expertus sum: experience, try, test
fabricor, -ārī, -ātus sum: make, fashion
for, fārī, fātus sum: speak, say, tell, utter, 7
  adfor, -fārī, -fātus sum: address, speak to
  profor, -fārī, -fātus sum: speak, say
fungor, -ī, functus sum: perform, execute (*abl.*)
  dēfungor, -ī, dēfunctus sum: finish, die; perform
gradior, -ī, gressus sum: march, go, proceed
  adgredior, -ī, aggressus sum: attack
  ēgredior, -ī, -gressus sum: go out, disembark
  ingredior, -ī, -gressus sum: step in, enter; begin, 3
  intrōgredior, -ī, -gressus sum: enter
iaculor, -ārī, iaculātus sum: throw, hurl, 2
indignor, -ārī, -ātus sum: be angry or indignant
lābor, -ī, lapsus sum: glide, slide, 2
  conlābor, -lābī, -lapsus sum: collapse, slide down
  dīlābor, -ī, -lapsus sum: glide apart, slip apart
  inlābor, -ī, lapsus sum: glide on, slide on
  perlabor, -ī, -lapsus sum: glide or slide over
  praeterlābor, -ī, lapsus sum: glide past, slide past
laetor, -ārī, -ātus sum: rejoice, exult
loquor, -ī, locūtu sum: speak, say, 2
  adloquor, -ī, -locūtus sum: address, speak to
luctor, -ārī, -ātus sum: wrestle, struggle, 2
meditor, -ārī, meditātus sum: ponder, consider, reflect
minor, -ārī, -ātus sum: threaten, tower, 2
mīror, -ārī, -ātus sum: to wonder, be amazed at, 5
  admīror, -ārī, admīrātus sum: admire, wonder at
misereor, -ērī: pity, have compassion for
miseror, -ārī, -ātus sum: pity, 4
mōlior, -īrī, -ītus sum: set in motion, bring about, 4
moror, -ārī, -ātus sum: delay, linger, 2
partior, -īrī: to partition, distribute, divide
pascor, -ī, pāstus sum: feed, graze
  dēpascor, -ī, pāstus sum: feed or graze from
patior, -ī, passus sum: suffer, endure; allow, 4
potior, -īrī, -ītus: possess, take possession of (*abl.*), 2
prōmereor, -ērī, prōmeritus sum: deserve, merit
queror, querī, questus sum: complain, lament
sequor, -ī, secūtus sum: follow, pursue, 4
  insequor, -sequī, -secūtus sum: follow, ensue, 3
  prōsequor, -sequī, -secūtus: follow, pursue, escort, 2
speculor, -ārī, -ātus sum: spy out, watch
testor, -ārī, testātus sum: bear witness, attest
tueor, tuērī, tutus(tuitus) sum: look on, watch, 3
ulciscor, -ī, ultus sum: avenge, take vengeance
ūtor, -ī, ūsus sum: use, employ (*abl.*)
vagor, -ārī, vagātus sum: wander, roam
vescor, vescī, --: feed on, eat (*abl.*)

Deponent Participles translate in the active but can be active or passive in form. Note that the perfect deponent participle (also called 'PPP dep.') translates as 'having Xed' rather than 'having been Xed.'

Present	sequēns, sequentis *following*	
Perfect		secūtus, -a, -um *having followed*
Future	secūtūrus, -a, -um *going/about to follow*	

PUFF-V is the mnemonic for deponent verbs that govern an ablative (originally, ablative of means) rather than accusative object: **P**otior [2], **Ū**tor [1], **F**ungor [2], **F**ruor [0], and **V**escor [1].

hūc septem Aenēās collēctīs nāvibus omnī
ex numerō subit; ac magnō tellūris amōre
ēgressī optātā potiuntur Trōes harēnā
et sale tābentēs artūs in lītore pōnunt.
Ac prīmum silicī scintillam excūdit Achātēs
suscēpitque ignem foliīs atque ārida circum
nūtrīmenta dedit rapuitque in fōmite flammam.
Tum Cererem corruptam undīs Cereāliaque arma
expediunt fessī rērum, frūgēsque receptās
et torrēre parant flammīs et frangere saxō.
  Aenēās scopulum intereā cōnscendit, et omnem
prōspectum lātē pelagō petit, Anthea sī quem
iactātum ventō videat Phrygiāsque birēmēs
aut Capyn aut celsīs in puppibus arma Caīcī.

Achātēs, -ae m.: Achates (companion of Aeneas), 4
Antheus, -eī, *acc.* **ea m.**: Antheus (a Trojan leader), 2
aridus, -a, -um: dry
artus, -ūs m.: joint, limb, 4
birēmis, -is f.: bireme (two-oared ship), ship
Caīcus, -ī m.: Caecus (a Trojan)
Capys, -yos, *acc.* **yn m.**: Capys (comrade of Aeneas)
celsus, -a, -um: high, towering, 2
Cereālis, -e: of Ceres, of grain
Cerēs, -eris f.: Ceres, grain
circumdō, -dāre, -dedī, -datum: put around, 2
colligō, -ere, -lēgī, -lēctum: gather, collect, 2
conscendō, -ere, -ī, -ēnsus: climb, mount, 2
corrumpō, -ere, -rūpī, -ruptum: to spoil, destroy
ēgredior, -ī, -gressus sum: go out, disembark
excūdō, -ere: strike out, hammer out, 2
expediō, -īre: make ready, prepare; set free
fessus, -a, -um: tired, weary, worn, 3
folium, -ī n.: leaf, foliage, 2
fōmes, -it is m.: tinder
frangō, -ere, frēgī, frāctus: break 3
frūx, frūgis f.: grain, 2
numerus, -ī m.: number, 2
nutrimentum, -î n.: food, fuel, nourishment
optō (1): desire, choose, hope (for), 4
parō (1): prepare, make ready, get, 4
pelagus, -ī n.: sea, 4
Phrygius, -a, -um: Phrygian, Trojan, 3
potior, -īrī, -ītus: take possession of, possess (*abl.*), 2
prospectus, -ūs m.: view, survey
recipiō, -ere, -cēpī, -ceptum: take back, recover, 3
sal, salis n.: salt (water); sea, 2
scintilla, -ae f.: spark
septem: seven, 3
silex, -icis m./f.: flint
suscipiō, -ere, -cēpī, -ceptum: undertake, take up, 2
tābeō, -ēre: drip, melt
torreō, -ēre: roast

170 **hūc**: i.e. into the calm harbor
  septem collectīs nāvibus: abl. abs., Aeneas has 7 of the original 20 ships. 13 ships were lost in the storm but will later be found safe.
  omnī : 3rd decl. i-stem abl. with numerō
171 **subit**: *comes up, approaches*; 3s subeō, the prefix 'sub' often means 'up (from under)'
  magnō...amōre: *with...*; abl. of manner
  tellūris: *for...*; objective gen. with amōre
172 **ēgressī...Troēs**: *the Trojans...*; pf. dep. pple ēgredior: translate as 'having Xed'
  potiuntur: 3p pres. dep. + abl. obj.
173 **sale**: *with salt water*; 'with salt,' <u>metonymy</u>
174 **tābentēs**: pres. pple, modifies Troēs
  prīmum: adv.
  silicī: *from...*; dat. of compound verb
175 **foliīs**: *under...*; dat. of compound verb
  circum...dedit: *puts...around*; <u>tmesis</u>: from the compound verb circumdō, 'surround'
  Cererem: *grain*; <u>metonomy</u>
  Cereālia arma: *utensils/tools of Ceres*; i.e. tools used to prepare grain to eat
178 **(virī) fessī rērum**: *(the men) weary of their circumstances;* objective gen.; rēs can often mean 'situation' or 'circumstance'
178 **receptās**: PPP, i.e. not spoiled by the waves
179 **et torrēre...et frangere**: *both...and...*
  flammīs, saxō: abl. of means
180 **omnem prōspectum**: *an entire view*
181 **(in) pelagō**

Anthea…quem: *something of Antheus*; i.e. some sign of Antheus; quem is an indef. adj. before sī; Anthea is a Grk acc. sg.; Antheus, and the rest are Trojan leaders on the lost ships
sī…videat: *if he should see…*; i.e. in the hope that he may…; 3s pres. subj. expressing the equiv. of purpose with four acc. objects
183 **arma Caīcī**: *the arms of Caecus*; shields were tied to the fencing of the decks facing outward; Aeneas hopes to recognize a particular ship led by Caecus by the display of shields tied to the decking

amor, -ōris m.: love, 9
hūc: to here, hither, to this place, 5
pōnō, -ere, posuī, positum: put, place (aside), 5
rēs, reī, f.: thing, matter, affair; circumstance, 11
subeō, -īre, -iī, itus: go up to, approach, 6

Ablative Absolutes [28] are circumstantial, causal, or concessive in sense, even if the translation does not reveal it. In polished translations, readers often add conjunctions (in boldface) and make the participle into a finite verb. Note that the PPP often becomes pluperfect in translation.

septem collēctīs nāvibus	1. raw translation	*(with) seven ships having been gathered*
(pf. pass. participle)	2. Circumstantial	***When/After*** *seven ships had been gathered*
	3. Causal	***Since/Because*** *seven ships had been gathered*
	4. Concessive	***Although*** *seven ships had been gathered*
magnā stīpante catervā:	1. raw translation	*(with) a great retinue crowding around*
(pres. act. participle)	2. Circumstantial	***When/While*** *a great retinue is/was crowding*
	3. Causal	***Since/Because*** *a great retinue is/was crowding*
	4. Concessive	***Although*** *a great retinue is/was crowding*

Cum Clauses [11] can also be translated at least three ways, but most uses in this book are temporal with the indicative. Note that in 12 of the 23 total instances, *cum* is just the preposition 'with.'

Cum haec verba audīvit	1. temporal [10]	***When*** *he heard these words*
Cum haec verba audīvisset	2. circumstantial [1]	***When/After*** *he had heard these words*
	3. causal	***Since/Because*** *he had heard these words*
	4. concessive	***Although*** *he had heard these words*

Tmesis ('cutting') is a rhetorical device involving the separation of a prefix from the compound verb by one or more words (e.g. *circumdāre* below). In English, tmesis is more generally the separation of prefixes or even syllables: e.g. abso-freaking-lutely, un-frickin'-believable, a-whole-nother.

ārida circum nūtrīmenta dedit — *he put the dry fuel around* — I.175-6

A poet may do this for no other reason than to fit the words to the meter.

Feasting Scenes are common in the *Odyssey*, and many are formulaic, where groups of lines are repeated verbatim from elsewhere in the *Odyssey*. It should not be surprising that Vergil chooses to imitate this convention found in epic and have Aeneas' companion Achates prepare a similar feast.

Aeneas' Leadership (1 of 3)

The use of personal names in I.180-83 reflects Aeneas' character as a leader. In the *Odyssey* Odysseus sets out from Troy with 12 ships of men, and all die before Odysseus returns alone to Ithaca. Since Odysseus seldom addresses the men by name, most remain nameless to readers today.

When Aeneas mounts a hill to look for the thirteen missing ships, the use of personal names suggests that Aeneas cares deeply about those under his leadership. They are not mere numbers but individuals, and the use of names shows that Aeneas has genuine concern for those whom he leads.

Nāvem in cōnspectū nūllam, trēs lītore cervōs
prōspicit errantēs; hōs tōta armenta sequuntur
ā tergō et longum per vallēs pascitur agmen.
Cōnstitit hīc arcumque manū celerēsque sagittās
corripuit, fīdus quae tēla gerēbat Achātēs,
ductōrēsque ipsōs prīmum capita alta ferentēs
cornibus arboreīs sternit, tum vulgus et omnem
miscet agēns tēlīs nemora inter frondea turbam;
nec prius absistit quam septem ingentia victor
corpora fundat humī et numerum cum nāvibus aequet.
Hinc portum petit et sociōs partītur in omnēs.
Vīna bonus quae deinde cadīs onerārat Acestēs
lītore Trīnacriō dederatque abeuntibus hērōs
dīvidit, et dictīs maerentia pectora mulcet:

---

abeō, -īre, -ivī, itus: go away, 2
absistō, -ere, -stitī: cease, stop, 2
Acestēs, -ae m.: Acestus, from Crete, 4
Achātēs, -ae m.: Achates (companion of Aeneas), 4
aequō (1): make equal, 3
arboreus, -a, -um: branching, tree-like
arcus, -ūs m.; bow
armenta, -ī n.: herd, cattle
bonus, -a, -um: good, noble
cadus, -ī m.: jar
cervus, -ī m.: deer
consistō, -ere, -stitī: stop, stand still, 3
conspectus, -ūs, f.: sight, view, 2
cornū, -ūs n.: horn, 2
deinde: then, next, 2
dictum, -ī n.: word, speech, 4
dīvidō, -ere, -vīsī, -vīsus: divide 3
ductor, -ōris m.: leader
fīdus, -a, -um: faithful, trustworthy, 3
frondeus, -a, -um: leafy
fundō, -ere, -fūdī, fūsus: pour (out), lay low, 3
hērōs, -hērōis m. gen. pl. -um: hero, 3
humus, -ī m.: ground; **humī**, on the ground, 2
maereō, -ēre: grieve, mourn
mulceō, -ēre, -lsī, -lsus: calm, soothe, 3
nemus, -oris n.: wood, forest, grove, 4
numerus, -ī m.: number, 2
onerō (1): load, store, burden
partior, -īrī: to partition, distribute, divide
pascor, -ī, pāstus sum: feed, graze
portus, -ūs m.: port, harbor, 3
prōspiciō, -ere, -spexī, -spectus: look out on, survey, 4
sagitta, -ae f.: arrow
septem: seven, 3
sequor, -ī, secūtus sum: follow, pursue, 4
sternō, -ere, strāvī, strātum: to lay (low), layer, 4
trēs, tria: three, 4
Trīnacrius, -a, -um: Sicilian, 2
turba, -ae f.: crowd, mob, 4
vallis, -is m.: vale, lowland
victor, -ōris m.: victor, 2
vīnum, -ī n.: wine
vulgus, -ī n.: masses, multitude, 2

184 **Nāvem...nūllum, (sed) trēs...cervōs prōspicit**: asyndeton: supply 'sed,' the lack of disjunction reflects the abruptness of looking for one thing but finding something different
(in) lītore: with errantēs
185 **hōs (cervōs)**: acc. obj.
sequuntur: pres. dep.: translate as active
186 **ā tergō**: *from the rear*; 'from the back,' this and 'agmen' are military terminology; Vergil suggests that Aeneas ambushes the deer just as one ambushes enemy soldiers
pascitur: pres. dep.: translate as active
187 **cōnstitit**: Aeneas is the subject
arcumque...celerēsque sagittās: *both...and*
188 **quae tēla fīdus Achātēs gerēbat**: *which weapons...*; quae is a relative adj.
189 **Ductōrēsque...prīmum...sternit, tum vulgus**: *and he lays low first...then...*; ductōrēs and neut. vulgus are acc. objs. of sternit; prīmum is an adv.
capita alta ferentēs: pres. participial phrase modifying ductōrēs
190 **cornibus arboreīs**: *with...*; abl. of quality modifying capita
omnem...turbam: acc. obj.; hyperbaton (distortion of normal word order)

191 **agēns tēlīs**: *driving (them)...*; pres. pple,
192 **prius...quam...fundat...aequet**: *before...* 'earlier than;' usually as one word priusquam, prius is a comparative adv. prīmus; both verbs are pres. anticipatory subj. expressing purpose
victor: *as victor*; nom. predicate
194 **partitur**: pres. dep.: translate as active
in omnēs sociōs: *among...*
195 **bonus...Achātēs**: *noble Achates*
cadīs: *in...*; or 'with...' abl. means
onerā(ve)rat: syncopated 3s plpf.
(in) lītore Trīnacriō: *on...*; in I.34 the Trojans are just leaving King Acestes, who had led a group of Trojan colonists to Sicily before the war. The wine comes from that recent visit.
abeuntibus: *to (those)...*; i.e. the Trojans, dat. ind. object, pres. pple abeō
hērōs: nom. subj., i.e. Acestes
197 **dīvidit, mulcet**: Aeneas is the subject
dictīs: *with words*; substantive; N.B. the pious orator also 'dictīs...pectora mulcet' in 1.153

celer, -eris, -ere: swift, quick, 6
manus, -ūs f.: hand, 9
nūllus, -a, -um: not any, no(one, thing), 6
prior, prius: earlier, before, 6
socius, -ī m.: comrade, ally, 6
tergum, -ī n.: back (part of the body), rear, 5

Aeneas' Hunt and *Odyssey* Book 10 (2 of 3)

In Book 10 of the *Odyssey*, Odysseus recalls that during his adventures he landed on the island of Circe and had to search for food. Notice how Aeneas' hunt is a clear imitation of Odysseus' hunt below.

There **we brought our ship in to the shore**, in silence,
at a harbor fit for ships to lie, and some god guided us in...

I climbed to a point of observation and stood there,
and got a sight of smoke which came from the halls of Circe...

But on my way, as I was close to the oar-swept vessel,
some god, because I was all alone, took pity upon me,
and sent a **great stag with towering antlers** right in my very
path; and he had come from his range in the forest down to the river
to drink, for the fierce strength of the sun was upon him. As he
stepped out, I hit him in the middle of the back, next to
the spine, so that the brazen spearhead smashed its way clean through.
He screamed and dropped in the dust and the life spirit fluttered from him...

...**I threw him down by the ship and roused my companions**,
standing beside each man and speaking to him in kind words:

Odyssey X.140-141, 148-149, 156-170, 172-173 (tr. A. T. Murray, 1919)

This imitation reinforces details highlighted in the imitation from lines I.92-101: (1) Vergil expected his readers to know the *Odyssey* in Greek and recognize the imitation. (2) By having Aeneas imitate Odysseus' words, Vergil encourages readers to view Aeneas as a hero of equal status to Odysseus.

Aeneas' Leadership (2 of 3)

1. Vergil' use of military terms such as *ā tergō*, *agmen* (186) and *victor* (192) suggests that the hunt is a demonstration of Aeneas' military skill. How does the hunt and its outcome show that Aeneas is a worthy military leader?

2. A common military tactic is to kill an enemy's leaders first so that the soldiers lose organizational discipline to fight back effectively. Even today on the battlefield, officers do not wear shiny insignia indicating their rank, and soldiers are instructed not to salute officers for fear that an enemy sniper will target and kill the officers first. How do I.189-191 show that Aeneas has similar military skill?

3. What do lines 192-193 reveal about Aeneas' leadership and ability to meet the needs of his people?

4. The introduction to Aeneas' speech to his men in I.197, 'dictīs maerentia pectora mulcet,' echo the ending line of the simile of the pious orator: 'ille regit dictīs animōs et pectora mulcet' (153). What, if anything, does this similarity suggest about Aeneas' character as leader of the Trojans?

"Ō sociī (neque enim ignārī sumus ante malōrum) 198
Ō passī graviōra, dabit deus hīs quoque fīnem. 199
Vōs et Scyllaeam rabiem penitusque sonantēs 200
accestis scopulōs, vōs et Cyclōpia saxa 201
expertī: revocāte animōs maestumque timōrem 202
mittite; forsan et haec ōlim meminisse iuvābit. 203
Per variōs cāsūs, per tot discrīmina rērum 204
tendimus in Latium, sēdēs ubi fāta quiētās 205
ostendunt; illīc fās rēgna resurgere Troiae. 206
Dūrāte, et vōsmet rēbus servāte secundīs." 207
Tālia vōce refert cūrīsque ingentibus aeger 208
spem vultū simulat, premit altum corde dolōrem. 209

---

accēdō, -ere, -cessī, -cessus: approach, 2
aeger, -gra, -grum: sick, weary, 3
cāsus, -ūs m.: misfortune; chance, 4
Cyclōpius, -a, -um: Cyclopean, of the Cyclopes
discrīmen, -crīminis n.: crisis, peril; difference, 3
dūrō (1): to harden, endure
enim: for, indeed, 4
experior, -īrī, expertus sum: experience, try, test
fās n.: right, righteous; **fās (est)**, it is right, 3
forsan: perhaps, perchance
ignārus, -a, -um: ignorant, inexperienced in (gen)
illīc: there, in that place
iuvō, -āre, iūvī: be pleasing, help, 4
Latium, -ī n: Latium, 4
maestus, -a, -um: sad, mournful, gloomy, 3
malus, -a, -um: bad, wicked, 3
meminī, -isse: remember, recall, 3
mittō, -ere, mīsī, missus: send, dismiss, 4
neque: nor, and not;: neither...nor, 4
ōlim: once, once upon a time, 2
ostendō, -ere, -ī, ntus: show, promise, 2
patior, -ī, passus sum: suffer, endure; allow, 4
penitus: within, deep(ly), wholly, 3
quiētus, -a, -um: calm, peaceful
quoque: also, 2
rābiēs, -ēī f.: rage, madness, fury
resurgō, -ere, -surrēxī, surrectus: rise again
revocō (1): recall, restore
Scyllaeus, -a, -um: of Scylla
secundus, -a, -um: following; favorable, 3
simulō (1): imitate, pretend, feign, 3
sonō (1): resound, roar, 2
timor, -oris m.: fear, dread

198 **Ō sociī**: voc. direct address
neque enim: *indeed...not*; or 'for...not'
malōrum: *of evils, of troubles*; n. substantive
199 **Ō passī**: *(You) having...*; voc. dir. address; a pf. dep. pple: translate as 'having Xed'
graviōra: neut. acc. pl. comparative used as a substantive: supply 'things'
hīs: *to...*: i.e. to these evils; dat. ind. obj.
200 **Vōs et...vōs et...**: *both...and...*; anaphora
penitusque sonantēs scopulōs: *and...*; Scylla lived in a cave over a cliff. In the *Odyssey*, the men could hear the puppy-heads which ringed her waist yelp before she emerged from the cave and grabbed the men from the ship.
201 **acce(ssi)istis**: syncopated 2p pf. accēdō
saxa: There are two rocks in the Cyclops episode of the *Odyssey*: (1) the rock that the Cyclops used to block the entrance of the cave And (2) the rock that the blinded Cyclops threw at Odysseus' ship as Odysseus escaped.
202 **expertī (estis)**: 2p pf. dep.: translate active
animōs: *courage*; common translation in pl.
203 **mittite**: *dismiss, send away*
204 **et haec**: *even these things*; neut. acc. pl.
meminisse: meminī, -isse is a 'defective verb' and found only in the pf. tenses: translate the pf. inf. as a pres. inf.
iuvābit: *it will...*; impersonal
205 **per...(et) per...**: anaphora and asyndeton,
sēdēs...quiētās: *quiet homes*
fāta: i.e. the omens and dreams that Aeneas and the Trojans received along the way
206 **fās (est)**: *it is right*; impersonal
regna resurgere...: *that...*; ind. disc.; regna is poetic pl. and can be translated as regnum
Dūrāte, servāte: pl. imperatives
207 **vōs-met**: *yourselves*; emphatic form of vōs
rēbus secundīs: *for favorable times*; dat. of purpose; secundus derives from sequor
208 **Tālia**: *such things*; marking end of speech

vōce: abl. of manner, i.e. aloud
refert: *says*; 'reports'
cūrīsque ingentibus: *with…*; abl. of cause with aeger; Aeneas hides negative emotions

209 **vultū**: abl. means
(et) premit: asyndeton and iuxtaposition, the arrangment is chiastic (A B B A)
altum (in) corde: *deep in…*; abl. place where

cūra, -ae f.: care, concern; worry, anxiety, 7
fīnis, -is m./f.: end, border; territory, 5
spēs, -eī f.: hope, expectation, 6
varius, -a, -um: various, 5
vultus, -ūs m.: expression, face, 6

Aeneas' 2nd Speech and *Odyssey* Book 12 (3 of 3)

In Book 12 of the *Odyssey*, Odysseus recalls a speech that he delivered to encourage his men near the end of their travels. Notice how Aeneas' speech (I.198-207) is a clear imitation of Odysseus' speech below.

Then I going up and down the ship urged on my companions,
standing beside each man and speaking to him in kind words:
"**Dear friends, surely we are not unlearned in evils.**
This is no greater evil now than it was when the Cyclops
had us cooped in his hollow cave by force and violence,
but even there, by my courage and counsel and my intelligence,
We escaped away. **I think that all this will be remembered**
some day too. Then do as I say, let us all be won over.
Sit well, all of you, to your oarlocks, and dash your oars deep
into the breaking surf of the water, so in that way Zeus
might grant that we get clear of this danger and flee away from it.
… So I spoke, and they quickly obeyed my words. I had not
spoken yet of **Scylla**, a plague that could not be dealt with,
for fear my companions might be terrified and give over their rowing.
Odyssey XII.208-216 (tr. A. T. Murray, 1919)

Originality in Greco-Roman Art: Imitation and Variation

Vergil's imitation of the *Odyssey* is an example of a type of originality in art and literature that was quite common in the Greco-Roman world. Many authors would imitate their predecessors in large and small ways and then offer a variation or twist to distinguish their own work from what came before. This combination of imitation and variation made the originality in the new work intelligible to readers. Audiences could examine both the tradition and the variation and ask themselves why the authors chose to make the changes that they did.

By imitating the *Odyssey* so closely on three occasions (I.92-101, 184-93, 198-207), Vergil cleverly uses the tradition to characterize Aeneas as a Roman Odysseus. As for the variation from tradition, that will come later in the epic. In Book 2, for example, when Aeneas recalls the fall of Troy, Aeneas' *pietās* toward his family, community, and gods is easily contrasted with Odysseus' untrustworthiness in the Sinon episode and impiety in burning and looting the temples. With this variation, Vergil suggests to his Roman audience that Aeneas does not merely rival Odysseus but surpass him.

Aeneas' Leadership (3 of 3)

As a leader, Aeneas is both 'a doer of deeds' and 'a speaker of words,' and the allusion to the Simile of the Pious Orator in l. 197 suggests that Vergil wants us to view Aeneas in light of the orator.

1. The monsters mentioned in lines 200-1 help clarify the *malōrum* and *grāviōra* mentioned in ll. 198-199. Who are these monsters, and which other hero (see the speech above) had met them as well?
2. How do the imperatives in ll. 202-3 and again in 207 reveal that Aeneas' purpose in the speech is similar to that of the pious orator (I.148-153)? What emotional response does Aeneas encourage?
3. What purpose does Aeneas say that fates reveal in 205-6 for their suffering? What will rise again?
4. What words in ll. 208-9 suggest that Aeneas has chosen to restrain his own negative emotions?

Corripuēre viam intereā, quā sēmita mōnstrat.
Iamque ascendēbant collem, quī plūrimus urbī
imminet adversāsque aspectat dēsuper arcēs.
Mīrātur mōlem Aenēās, māgālia quondam,
mīrātur portās strepitumque et strāta viārum.
Īnstant ardentēs Tyriī: pars dūcere mūrōs
mōlīrīque arcem et manibus subvolvere saxa,
pars optāre locum tectō et conclūdere sulcō;
iūra magistrātūsque legunt sānctumque senātum.
Hīc portūs aliī effodiunt; hīc alta theātrīs
fundāmenta locant aliī, immānēsque columnās
rūpibus excīdunt, scaenīs decora alta futūrīs.

---

adversus, -a, -um: facing, opposite, straight on, 5
ascendō, -ere, -ī, -ēnsus: ascend, mount
aspectus, -ūs m.: sight, view, 3
collis, -is m.: hill
columna, -ae f.: column, pillar
conclūdō, -ere, -sī, -sus: close up, enclose
decus, -oris n.: decorations; beauty, grace, glory
dēsuper: from above, 3
effodiō, -ere, -fōdī, -fossus: dig out, excavate
excīdō, -ere, -cīdī, -cīsum: to cut out
fundāmentum, -î n.: foundation, 3
immineō, -ēre: overhang, tower over, 2
īnstō, -āre, -stitī: press on, threatens, 3
iūs, iūris n.: justice, law, right, 2
legō, -ere, lēgī, lectum: to read; pick out, select, 4
locō (1): place, settle, arrange, 2
māgālia, -ium n.: huts (Carthaginian word) 2
magistrātus, -ūs m.: magistrate
mōlior, -īrī, -ītus sum: set in motion, bring about, 4
monstrō (1): show, point out
optō (1): desire, choose, hope (for), 4
plūrimus, a, um: most, very many/full *superl.* multus 4
portus, -ūs m.: port, harbor, 3
quondam: formerly, ever, 4
rūpēs, rūpis f.: rock, cliff, 2
sanctus, -a, -um: consecrated, sacred, hollowed
scaena, -ae f.: background, stage, 2
sēmita, -ae f.: footpath
senātus, -ûs m.; senate, council of elders
sternō, -ere, strāvī, strātum: to lay (low), layer, 4
strepitus, -ūs m.: noise, uproar, 2
subvolvō, -ere, -ī, -volūtus: roll up
sulcus, -ī m.: furrow, trench, ditch
via, -ae f.: way, road, journey, street, 4

Aeneas and faithful companion Achates explore the countryside and stumble upon the building of Carthage. For details, see the summary on pg. 35.

418 **corripuēr(unt)**: syncopated 3p pf.
quā: *where...*; relative adv.

419 **quī plūrimus...**: *which, very large,...*; relative clause; the irreg. superlative of multus modifies nom. sg. quī
urbī: *over...*; dat. of compound verb

421 **Mīrātur...(et) mīrātur**: pres. dep.: translate active; anaphora and asyndeton

422 **māgālia quondam**: in apposition to mōlem
stāta: *pavement*; 'things layered,' PPP sternō; English derives 'street' from this word
ardentēs: i.e. being eager
Tyriī: i.e. Carthaginians, who are colonists from the Phoenician city of Tyre
pars...pars...: *some (men)...others...*; nom. subject, partitive apposition, treat as plural
(Instant) dūcere...mōlīrī: *(press on) to...*; ellipsis: supply the main verb for these complementary infs.
dūcere mūrōs: *to draw up...*; i.e. build

424 **manibus**: abl. means

425 **(instant) optāre...**: *(press on) to...*
tectō: *for...*; dat. of purpose; via synecdoche, tectum means 'house' or 'shelter'
sulcō: *for...*; dat. of purpose

426 **legunt**: *they pick, select*; elsewhere 'read'
aliī...aliī...: *some...others...*; correlatives
alta fundāmenta: acc. obj.
theātrīs: *for...*; dat. of purpose

429 **rūpibus**: *from...*; dat. of compound verb
scaenīs...futūrīs: *for future...*; dat. of purpose and fut. act. pple sum
decora alta: acc. pl. in apposition to columnās

alius, -a, -ud : other, another, else, 9
ardeō, -ēre, arsī, arsus: burn, be eager 8
mīror, -ārī, -ātus sum: wonder, be amazed at, 5
mūrus, ī m.: wall, 8
pars, -tis f.: part, side, direction; some...others, 5
tectum, -ī n.: roof; shelter, house, building, 6

What we missed in ll. 209-417: After Aeneas' speech, Venus approaches Jupiter and laments that Aeneas has not arrived safely in Italy as Jupiter had promised. Jupiter calmly offers a lengthy revelation of the fates that will tie Troy directly to Rome. Jupiter says that after a war in Italy Aeneas will rule Lavinium for 3 years, his son Ascanius will rule nearby Alba Longa for 30 years, and then successive kings will rule Alba Longa for 300 years until Romulus departs and founds Rome. Later, a descendant of Aeneas, 'Troiānus Caesar,' will be born, and a new era of peace will come.

Despite Jupiter's consolations, Venus takes the disguise of a Spartan huntress and greets Aeneas and his comrade Achates as they explore the woods of North Africa. When she encounters her son, she maintains her disguise and explains that the land belongs to the Carthaginians, Phoenician colonists, who had bought the land for their city from the North Africans. The Carthaginian queen Dido had previously lived with her husband Sychaeus in the Phoenician city of Tyre (Lebanon), but Pygmalion, Dido's brother and the current king of Tyre, secretly murdered Sychaeus and hid all evidence of his crime. After Sychaeus revealed to Dido in a dream both the crime and a hidden treasure, Dido found the treasure and left abruptly with her supporters to establish the city of Carthage in North Africa.

When Venus departs, she shrouds the two men in mist so that the Carthaginians cannot see them.

The Romans built cities the way we build Starbucks, Walmarts, and McDonalds. Today, professional teams of itinerant builders travel from town to town to build the exact same structures over and over again. Once they finish a building, they move to the next location, stay in hotels while they work, and repeat the process. By employing the same builders at every location, companies eliminate inefficiencies and create buildings of consistently high quality.

As Aeneas watches the Carthaginians planning and building their entire city from scratch, keep in mind that that, while modern readers may find this process unusual, Roman readers would likely view such large-scale planning and building as common.

Purpose Constructions [25]

Dative of Purpose [13] is the most common purpose construction in the commentary and is found four times on the facing page. Note that purpose clauses with ut are seldom used, and both accusative supines and the prepositions *causā* and *ad* expressing purpose are not found at all in the commentary.

Adverbial purpose [4] (ut/nē + subj.)	ut/nē audīret	*so that he might (not) hear...*	pp. 15, 47
Relative of purpose [3] (quī + subj.)	quī audīret	*who might/would hear...*	pp. 4, 12, 103
Infinitive of purpose [4]	audīre	*(in order) to hear...*	pp. 42, 68
Future participle of purpose [2]	audītūrus	*intending to hear*	p. 52
Dative of Purpose [13]	auxiliō	*for help*	

Synecdoche is a rhetorical device where the part signifies the whole. *Tectum* is the latest example.

tectum 'roof' → *house, shelter* [6]	aes 'bronze' → *bronze beak* [1]	frōns 'forehead'→ *face* [1]
ferrum 'iron' → *sword* [6]	cārīna 'keel' → *ship* [1]	penna 'feather'→ *wing* [1]
ōs 'mouth' → *face* [3]	culmen 'rooftop' → *house* [1]	sāl 'salt' → *salt water* [1]
puppis 'poop deck' → *ship* [2]		

aliī...aliī... and **pars...pars...** are both correlatives which translate as 'some...others...' They occur in pairs only on the facing page (I.423-9) but are critical to interpreting the passage correctly.

Quālis apēs aestāte novā per flōrea rūra 430
exercet sub sōle labor, cum gentis adultōs 431
ēdūcunt fētūs, aut cum līquentia mella 432
stīpant et dulcī distendunt nectare cellās, 433
aut onera accipiunt venientum, aut agmine factō 434
ignāvum fūcōs pecus ā praesēpibus arcent; 435
fervet opus redolentque thymō fragrantia mella. 436
"Ō fortūnātī, quōrum iam moenia surgunt!" 437
Aenēās ait et fastīgia suspicit urbis. 438
Īnfert sē saeptus nebulā (mīrabile dictū) 439
per mediōs, miscetque virīs neque cernitur ūllī. 440

Haec dum Dardaniō Aenēae mīranda videntur, 494
dum stupet obtūtūque haeret dēfīxus in ūnō, 495
rēgīna ad templum, formā pulcherrima Dīdō, 496
incessit magnā iuvenum stīpante catervā. 497

---

adultus, -a, -um: grown up, matured
aestās, aetātis f.: summer, 1
apis, -is f.: bee
arceō, -ēre, -uī: fend or keep off, defend, 2
caterva, -ae f.: retinue, band, troop, 2
cella, -ae f.: cell, storeroom
cernō, -ere, crēvī, crētus: discern, perceive, 3
Dardanius, -a, -um: Dardanian, Trojan, 4
dēfīgō, -ere, -fixī, -fixum: fix, fasten, secure
dīcō (1): to declare, dedicate, consecrate
distendō, -ere, -ī, ntus: distend, stretch
ēdūcō, -ere, -dūxī, -ductus: lead out
exerceō, -ēre, -uī, -ercitum: exercise, busy, 2
fastīgium, -ī: pediment, gable; roof top
ferveō, -ēre, ferbuī: boil, glow
fētus, -ūs m.: offspring
flōreus, -a, -um: flowery
fortūnātus, -a, -um: fortunate, lucky
fūcus, -ī m.: drone (bee)
haereō, -ēre, haesī: cling, stick, hesitate, 2
ignāvus, -a, -um: idle, lazy; cowardly
incēdō, -ere, -cessī: strut; march, proceed, 2
inferō, -ferre, -tulī: carry or bring on, 2
iuvenis, -is m.: youth, young man, 3
liquō, ere: to flow, be clear
mel, mellis n.: honey, 3
mīrābilis, -e: wonderful, marvelous, 2
nebula, -ae f.: cloud, mist, fog, 2
nectar, nectaris n.: nectar
neque: nor, and not;: neither…nor, 4
novus, -a, -um: new, young, strange, 3
obtūtus, -ûs m.: gaze, view
onus, oneris n.: burden, load, freight
opus, -eris n.: work, deed, project, 4
pecus, -oris n.: flock, herd, swarm
praesēpe, -is n.: hive
redoleō, -ēre, -uī: be fragrant, smell (of)
rūs, rūris n.: country
saepiō, -īre, -psī, -ptus: hedge in, enclose, 2
sōl, sōlis m.: sun, 4
stīpō (1): pack, compress, crowd together, 2
stupeō, -ēre: to be stunned, dazed, stupified
suspiciō, ere, suspexī, suspectum: to look up at
thymum, -ī n.: thyme (a fragrant herb)

430 **Quālis…labor**: *Just as work…*; 'which sort of work,' a relative adj. modifying labor and introducing a simile that ends in l. 436
aestāte novā: *at…*; abl. time when; novā here means 'at the beginning of…'
431 **cum…aut cum…**: *when…or when…*; cum + indicative in a temporal clause
adultōs: *matured*
432 **ēdūcunt**: apēs in l. 430 are the subject
433 **dulcī nectāre**: *with…*; abl. of means; 3rd decl. i-stem adj. in the abl.
434 **venientum**: *of (those)…*; i.e. bees, gen. pl. pres. pple veniō;
agmine factō: abl. abs. with PPP faciō; an agmen is a column or formation; see also I.82
435 **ignāvum pecus**: neuter subject
ā praesēpibus: *from…*; abl. of separation
436 **opus**: nom. subject
thymō: abl. means
437 **Ō fortunātī**: *O fortunate ones*; dir. address

439 **infert sē**: i.e. he proceeds
saeptus nebulā: PPP saepiō; Aeneas is shrouded by a cloud of invisibility; When Aeneas and Achates met Venus, disguised as a Spartan huntress, in the woods, she placed a mist of invisibility around both of them so that they could travel undetected.
mīrabile: neut. sg. modifying the clause
dictū: *to speak of*; abl. sg. supine: in the abl. a supine is an abl. of respect, 'in respect to speaking,' translate as an infinitive in English
440 **per mediōs (virōs)**
virīs: *with…*; abl. of association
ūllī: *by…*; dat. of agent

494 **Dardaniō Aenēae**: *to…*; dat. of reference (viewpoint)
miranda: *amazing*; 'worthy to be amazed at,' neut. nom. pred.; common translation for the gerundive ('about/going/worthy to be Xed')
videntur: *seem*; 'are seen (to be),' a common translation for the passive of videō
495 **haeret**: *clings*
formā: *in…*; abl. of respect
pulcherrima: fem. nom. superlative pulcher
496 **incessit**: pf.; note how the same verb is used to describe Juno in l. 46
497 **magnā…stīpante catervā**: abl. abs.
iuvenum: gen. pl.

Dīdō, Dīdōnis f.: Dido, 11
quālis, -e: which/what sort; such as, just as, like, 7
surgō, -ere, -rēxī, -rēctus: raise, rise up, surge, 5
templum, -ī n.: temple, 5

Similes with Quālis[5]: Similes in Latin are subordinate clauses of comparison, and there are nine in the commentary. Two begin with the conjunction *velut,* 'just as/as,' two begin with the relative adv. *quam*, 'than/as, ' and finally five begin with the relative adj. *quālis, -e*, 'which sort/such as.'

Why do we translate *quālis*, 'which sort,' with the words 'such as' or 'just as'?

The adjectives *tālis* and *quālis* are correlatives (demonstrative and relative, respectively), and translate slightly differently when used together than when they are used separately:

tālis *this sort/such* quālis *which sort* tālis…quālis → *this sort which sort* → **such as**

As you see above, when the adj. *tālis* is part of the antecedent in the main clause and *quālis* introduces a relative clause, *tālis* is often translated as 'such' and *quālis* is translated as 'as.' In similes and on other occasions, *tālis* is often missing but understood from context. And so, when we translate the relative *quālis* into English, we assume the antecedent *tālis* in order to make the translation clearer:

quālis → (tālis) quālis → **such as** (or **just as**)

The simile on the facing page (I.430-6), therefore, is one large relative clause of comparison where *tālis* and the main verb are missing but can be understood from context:

(Labor est tālis) Quālis apēs…exercet labor *(the work is this sort) which sort of work busies the bees*
→ *(the work is) such work as busies the bees…*
→ *just as work busies the bees…*

Compare I.498-502 on p. 38, where Vergil offers a similar simile but includes *tālis* and a main clause:

Quālis...exercet Diana chorōs…tālis erat Dīdō *Which sort Diana busies…this sort was Dido*
→ *(just) as Diana busies the chorus…such was Dido*

If you are confused, be patient and reread this note as you encounter more similes. For now, use this rule of thumb: translate *quālis* as 'such as/just as' when alone and as 'as' when accompanied by *tālis*.

1. **Character of the Carthaginians**: What features in Vergil's description of the city of Carthage (I.421-9) would one likely find in Roman cities? Does this description depict the Carthaginians as less civilized than their Roman counterparts? In short, does Vergil portray Carthage positively?
2. **Simile of the Bees** (I.430-44): Similes comparing human activity to nature are common in epics, and in this case we should not assume that every detail about the bees corresponds to an aspect of human activity. How does the simile as a whole contribute to our positive view of Carthaginians?

Quālis in Eurōtae rīpās aut per iuga Cynthī
exercet Dīāna chorōs, quam mīlle secūtae
hinc atque hinc glomerantur Orēades; illa pharetram
fert umerō gradiēnsque deās superēminet omnēs
(Lātōnae tacitum pertemptant gaudia pectus):
tālis erat Dīdō, tālem sē laeta ferēbat
per mediōs instāns operī rēgnīsque futūrīs.
Tum foribus dīvae, mediā testūdine templī,
saepta armīs soliōque altē subnixa resēdit.
iūra dabat lēgēsque virīs, operumque labōrem
partibus aequābat iūstīs aut sorte trahēbat:

---

aequō (1): make equal, 3
chorus, -ī m.: chorus (a group of dancers); a dance
Cynthus, -î m.: Mt. Cynthus
Diana, -ae f.: Diana (Artemis)
Eurōtās, -ae m.: Eurotas river (near Sparta in Greece)
exerceō, -ēre, -uī, -ercitum: exercise, 2
foris, -is f.: door, doorway, entrance
gaudium, -iī n.: gladness, joy
glomerō (1): gather, heap, assemble around, 2
gradior, -ī, gressus sum: step, walk
instō, -āre, -stitī: press on, threaten, 3
iugum, -ī n.: ridge of a mtn., yoke; bench, 2
iūrō (1): to swear, take an oath, 2
iūstus, -a, -um: just, 2
Lātōna, -ae f.: Latona (Gk. Leto, mother of Diana)
lēx, lēgis f.: law, decree, 2
mīlle pl. mīlia, ium n.: thousand, 2
opus, -eris n.: work, deed, project, 4
Orēas, -adis f. (pl. Orēades): mountain-nymph
pertemptō (1): to agitate, thrill
pharetra, -ae f.: quiver, arrow-carrier
resīdō, -ere, -sēdī: sit or settle (down), 2
saepiō, -īre, -psī, -ptus: hedge in, enclose, 2
sequor, -ī, secūtus sum: follow, pursue, 4
solium, -ī n.: throne, seat, 2
subnixus, -a, -um: resting on (*abl.*)
superēmineō, -ēre: tower above, tower over, 2
testūdo, testūdinis f.: tortoise; vault, archway
trahō, -ere, trāxī, tractus: drag (out), draw, 3
umerus, -ī m.: shoulder, 3

498 **Quālis...Dīāna**: *Just as Diana...*; 'which sort Diana,' a relative adj. modifying Dīāna and introducing a <u>simile</u> that lasts through l. 503
500 **quam secūtae ...Orēades**: *whom...*; relative clause, quam is obj. of pf. dep. pple sequor: (translate as 'having Xed'), Orēadēs is subject
hinc atque hinc: *here and there*
illa: *that one*; i.e. Diana
501 **(in) umerō**
502 **tacitum...pectus**: neut. acc.
503 **Talis...**: *such ...*; nom. pred. marking the end of the simile; the relative quālis and demonstrative tālis are correlatives
(et) tālem: *(and) as such...*; acc. pred.; ferēbat here governs a double acc. (obj. and pred.)
laeta: *happily*; nom. adj. as adv.
504 **per mediōs (virōs/hominēs)**: add a noun
instāns: *pressing on*; + dat. of compound verb
505 **(in) foribus**: abl. of place where
dīvae: *of the goddess*; i.e. Juno; gen. sg. substantive from dīvus, -a, -um
(in) mediā testūdine: i.e. an archway or vault
506 **saepta**: fem. nom. PPP, saepiō
armīs: *by armed guards*; <u>synecdoche</u>
soliō: abl. place where with subnīxa
altē: *on high, up high*; 'highly'
507 **virīs**: *to...*; dat. ind. obj.
operumque labōrem: *the labor of the projects*; both opus and labor mean 'work', but labor denotes the toil and sweat while opus denotes the project or completed product
508 **partibus...iūstīs**: *with...*; abl. means; pārs, is 'portion' or 'share;' Dido distributes the work fairly to all
sorte: i.e. randomly, abl. of means; Dido is not playing favorites; she does the equivalent of drawing names from a hat to be fair to all

rīpa, -ae f.: bank, 8
tacitus, -a, -um: silent, speechless, still, 5

Dido's Character and Leadership

Dido is portrayed very positively in Book 1, but readers will see her character decline as she gives in to unrestrained emotions such as love in Book 4 with consequences for both herself and her people. *It is as if Vergil wants to instruct us on the negative effects of love even on those who are virtuous.*

There are three similes in particular that describe the arc of Dido's story in this commentary: first, when Aeneas initially encounters Dido in the facing page, Vergil likens her to the goddess Diana, triumphant among her loyal followers; second, after Dido feels betrayed by Aeneas in Book 4, Vergil likens her to a Bacchante, follower of Bacchus who is frenzied and out of control; and finally, when Aeneas sees Dido in the Underworld, Vergil likens her to a dimly lit moon which does not cast the light that it once had. Here, the connection between the moon and Diana is relevant and important.

Vergil writes with great care, and readers will benefit from paying attention to everything that Dido does and says for the remainder of the book.

Common Adverbs of Place: Note that English often omits 'to' and 'from' in translation.

place where	hīc [13] *here*	illīc [1] *there*	ubi [10] *where*	ibi [2] *there*
place from which	hinc [7] *from here*	illinc [0] *from there*	unde [2] *from where*	inde [2] *from there*
place to which	hūc [5] *to here*	illūc [1] *to there*	quō(nam) [1] *to where*	eō [0] *to there*

dehinc (dē+hinc): *then*; deinde (dē+inde): *next*; adhūc (ad+hūc): *still*; undīque (ubi+dē+que): *from everywhere*

Words easily confused: *solium* (I.506) reminds us that it is good to review words with similar stems.

aura, -ae *breeze*	aestās, -tātis *summer*	labor, -ōris *work*	lātus, -a, -um *wide*
aurum, -ī *gold*	aetās, -tātis *age, time*	labōrō, -āre *work*	latus, lateris *side*
auris, -is *ear*	aestus, -ūs *tide*	lābor, lābī *glide, slip*	lateō, -ēre *lie hidden*
mora, -ae *delay*	opera, -ae *effort*	porta, -ae *gate*	volō, velle *want*
mors, mortis *death*	ops, opis *resources*	portus, -ūs *harbor*	volō, -āre *fly*
mōs, mōris *custom*	opus, operis *work*	portō, -āre *carry*	vultus, -ūs *face, expression*
ōra, -ae *beach*	solus, -a, -um *alone, only*	vīrēs (pl. vīs) *strength*	gēns, gentis *people, race*
ōs, ōris *mouth*	solum, -ī *soil*	vir, -ī, *man*	genus, -eris *kind, birth, race*
ōrō, -āre *beg, plead*	sol, solis *sun*	fatum, -ī *fate*	turbō, turbinis *whirlwind*
os, ossis *bone*	solium, -ī *throne*	for, ārī, fatus *speak*	turba, -ae *crowd,* turbō (1) *confuse*

Dido's Character

1. Readers first learn about Dido when the disguised Venus tells Aeneas how Dido learned about her husband Sychaeus' murder, found treasure, and finally led her follows from Phoenician Tyre to North Africa to establish Carthage. What does this reveal about Dido's character and leadership?
2. How does the **Simile of Diana** (498-502) depict Dido positively? (What does it say about Dido and in particular about the attitude of those under her leadership toward her?)
3. How does Dido's location in front of a newly built **Temple of Juno** depict Dido positively? (What does it say about Dido and the Carthaginians that they build a temple in such a young city?) Note that Romans praetors often presided over courts on the steps of temples in Rome, and so the idea that a leader would conduct public business in such a venue is not at all unusual to Romans.
4. What do the words 'iūra dabat lēgēsque virīs' (I.507) reveal about Dido's strength as a leader?
5. What do the lines 'operumque…trahēbat' (I.507-8) reveal about Dido's fairness toward her people?

cum subitō Aenēas concursū accēdere magnō
Anthea Sergestumque videt fortemque Cloanthum
Teucōrumque aliōs, āter quōs aequore turbō
dispulerat penitusque aliās āvēxerat ōrās.
Obstipuit simul ipse, simul percussus Achātēs
laetitiāque metūque; avidī coniungere dextrās
ardēbant; sed rēs animōs incognita turbat.
Dissimulant et nūbe cavā speculantur amictī
quae fortūna virīs, classem quō lītore linquant,
quid veniant; cūnctīs nam lectī nāvibus ībant
ōrantēs veniam et templum clāmōre petēbant.
Postquam intrōgressī et cōram data cōpia fandī,
maximus Īlioneus placidō sīc pectore coepit:

---

accēdō, -ere, -cessī, -cessus: approach, 2
Achātēs, -ae m.: Achates (companion of Aeneas), 4
amiciō, -īre, -uī, amictum: to wrap, veil, clothe
Antheus, -eī, *acc.* **ea m.**: Antheus (a Trojan leader), 2
āvehō, -ere, -vexī, -vectum: carry away, 2
avidus, -a, -um: eager, greedy
cavus, -a, -um: hollow, 3
Cloanthus, -î m.: Cloanthus (Trojan leader)
coepī, coepisse: to begin
concursus, -ūs m.: gathering, running together, 2
coniungō, -ere: join together
cōpia, -ae f.: abundance, troops; opportunity, 2
cōram: face to face, in person
dispellō, -ere, -pulī, -pulsus: drive apart, scatter, 2
dissimulō (1): hide, disguise, 3
fortūna, -ae f.: fortune, chance, luck
Ilioneus, -î m.: Ilioneus, 3
incognitus, -a, -um: unknown
intrōgredior, -ī, -gressus sum: enter, step in
laetitia, -ae f.: joy, happiness
legō, -ere, lēgī, lectum: to read; pick out, select, 4
linquō, -ere, līquī, lictus: leave, desert, 3
maximus, -a, -um: *superl.* **magnus**
obstipēscō, -ere, sitpuī: stand agape (mouth open), 2
penitus: within, deep(ly), wholly, 3
percutiō, -ere, -cussī, -cussum: strike utterly, strike
placidus, -a, -um: peaceful, calm, 2
postquam: after, 3
Sergestus, -ī m.: Sergestus (Trojan leader), 2
speculor, -ārī, -ātus sum: spy out, watch
subitō: suddenly, 4
turbō (1): confuse, trouble, disturb, 2

509 **cum...videt**: *when...*; temporal clause
concursū...magnō: *with...*; abl. manner
accēdere...Anthea...aliōs: *that Antheus...*; ind. disc. with four acc. subjects governed by videt; Anthea is a Greek acc. sg.
511 **āter quōs turbō...ōrās**: *whom...*; relative clause; āter modifies nom. turbō
(in) aequore
512 **(ad) aliās...ōrās**: acc. place to which
513 **simul...simul...**: *both...and at the same time...*; correlatives
(Aenēas) ipse
percussus (est)
514 **laetitiāque metūque**: *both...and...*; means
avidī: *eagerly, avidly*; nom. adj. as adv.
dextrās (manūs): i.e. in handshakes
515 **rēs incognita**: *unfamiliar circumstances*
516 **nūbe cavā**: abl. means; cloak of invisibility
amictī: PPP amiciō
quae...linquant, quid...veniant: three ind. questions + pres. subj. governed by speculantur
517 **quae fortūna virīs (sint)**: *what fortune...*; dat. of possession; supply subjunctive verb sum
(in) quō lītore: abl. place where
518 **quid**: *why*; 'in respect to what,' acc. respect
cūnctīs navibus: *from...*
lectī: *those chosen/selected...*; PPP lēgō; i.e. leaders from each ship
navibus: *from...*; abl. of source/origin
ībant: impf. eō, īre
519 **clāmōre**: *with...*; abl. of manner
520 **introgressī (sunt)**: 3p pf. dep.: make active
data (est)
cōpia: *an opportunity*
fandī: gen. sg. gerund (-ing) of for, fārī
521 **maximus**: *very mighty*; epithet for Ilioneus
placidō...pectore: *with...*; abl. of manner
coepit: introducing a speech

eō, īre, iī, itus: go, 10 **metus, -ūs f.**: dread, fear, 5

Aeneas and Achates' Veil of Invisibility and *Odyssey* Book 7

Vergil once again is imitating Homer's *Odyssey*. In Book 5, Odyssseus leaves the island of the goddess Calypso after 7 years and suffers a shipwreck in a storm sent by Poseidon. In the *Aeneid*, Aeneas also suffers a shipwreck, but Neptunus does not create the storm but dispels it. In Book 6, Odysseus finds himself on the shore of the island of Phaeacia, where he meets Nausicaa, the young princess of Phaeacia, who directs him to the city and her parents, the king and queen. In the *Aeneid*, Aeneas and Achates meet the disguised Venus, who directs Aeneas to Carthage and Queen Dido. Finally, in Book 7 a disguised Athena veils Odysseus in a mist of invisibility so that he can approach the king and queen unseen. In the *Aeneid*, as we read on the facing page, Aeneas and Achates are safely shrouded in mist as they set to meet Dido and rejoin their comrades from the lost 13 ships.

A **gerund** [3] (stem + nd + 2nd decl. endings) is a verbal noun translated with –ing (e.g. *Running* is fun.) and may have an acc. object. There are only three instances in this book (*fandī*, 'of speaking,' p. 40; *eundō*, 'by going,' p. 76, and *fandō*, 'by speaking,' p. 92). All other -nd- forms are gerundives.

Gen.	fandī	*of speaking*
Dat.	fandō	*for speaking*
Acc.	fandum	*speaking*
Abl.	fandō	*by speaking*

Gerundives [13]

A **gerundive** is a future passive participle (e.g. fandus, -a, -um) and, just as any adjective, agrees with a noun in case, number, and gender. A gerundive can be translated as (a) 'going to be spoken' or (b) 'about to be spoken,' but the most common translations in this commentary are (3) 'worthy to be spoken,' (i.e. speakable) and (4) 'to be spoken.'

(1) **A Gerundive as Adjective** [10] can mean 'worthy to be Xed' or simply 'able to be Xed' or 'Xable'

mīranda	*worthy to be amazed at*	→	*amazing*	p. 36
īnfandōs	*not worthy to be spoken*	→	*unspeakable* (i.e. unrighteous, wrong)	p. 42
fandī	*worthy to be spoken*	→	*speakable* (i.e. righteous, right)	p. 44
nēfandī	*not worthy to be spoken*	→	*unspeakable* (i.e. unrighteous, wrong)	p. 44
horrendōs	*worthy to be shuddered at*	→	*horrible*	p. 56, 76, 104, 108
videndam	*worthy to be seen*	→	*visible, to be seen*	p. 70
arandum	*worthy to be plowed*	→	*plowable*	p. 82

(2) **Passive Periphrastic** [3] **(gerundive + sum)** expresses obligation or necessity and governs a dative of agent. Note the raw and polished (must/has to) translations below:

	raw		**polished**	
simulācrum ducendum est	*the likeness is to be led*	→	*the likeness must be led*	p. 58
nūmina ōranda sunt	*the gods are to be prayed to*	→	*the gods must be prayed to*	p. 58
quae…gerenda sunt	*which are to be waged*	→	*which must be waged*	p. 126

(3) **Gerund-Gerundive flip** [0] is often performed on a **noun + gerundive** (adjective) pair in order to translate the construction into English idiom as a **gerund (-ing) + object**. Although noun + gerundive pairs are common in prose, the construction is surprisingly not used once in this book.

1. How does the use of personal names in I.510 and 521 make Aeneas' reaction more genuine?
2. What mixed feelings do the men have in I.513-5, and why do they not join the others immediately?
3. What are Aeneas and Achates doing in line 516 as the chosen leaders (*lectī*) of the missing Trojans ships approach Dido?
4. What do Aeneas and Achates hope to learn in lines 517-18?

"Ō rēgīna, novam cui condere Iuppiter urbem 522
iūstitiāque dedit gentēs frēnāre superbās, 523
Trōes tē miserī, ventīs maria omnia vectī, 524
ōrāmus, prohibē īnfandōs ā nāvibus ignēs, 525
parce piō generī, et propius rēs aspice nostrās. 526
Nōn nōs aut ferrō Libycōs populāre penātēs 527
vēnimus, aut raptās ad lītora vertere praedās; 528
nōn ea vīs animō nec tanta superbia victīs. 529
Est locus, Hesperiam Graiī cognōmine dīcunt, 530
terra antīqua, potens armīs atque ūbere glaebae; 531
Oenōtrī coluēre virī; nunc fāma minōrēs 532
Ītaliam dīxisse ducis dē nōmine gentem. 533

---

antīquus, -a, -um: ancient, old, 4
cognōmen, -minis n.: nickname
colō, -ere, coluī, cultum: till, farm, cultivate, 3
condō, -ere, condidī, -ditum: found; hide, 4
dux, ducis m./f.: leader, guide, 2
frēnō (1): to bridle, restrain (used with horses), 2
glaeba, -ae f.: soil, clod
Graius, -a, -um: Greek, 2
Hesperia, -ae f.: Hesperia, Italy, 3
īnfandus, -a, -um: unspeakable, accursed (gerundive)
iūstitia, -ae f.: justice, fairness
Libycus, -a, -um: Libyan, of Libya, 3
minor, minus: smaller, less 2
novus, -a, -um: new, young, strange, 3
Oenōtrus, -a, -um: Oenotrian (tribe in toe of Italy)
parcō, -ere, pepercī: spare, refrain (dat), 2
Penātēs, -ium m.: Penates (household gods), 3
pius, -a, -um: unholy, impious
populō (1): ravage, plunder, devastate, 2
potēns, -entis: powerful, 4
praeda, -ae f.: cattle, flocks, loot, spoils
prohibeō, -ēre, -uī, -itus: keep off, prohibit, 2
propius: nearer, closer (*comp.* prope)
superbia, -ae f.: pride, arrogance, hubris
superbus, -a, -um: proud, arrogant, 3
ūber, ūberis: fertile, rich, abundant
vehō, -ere, vēxī, vectum: convey, 4
vertō, -ere, vertī, versum: to turn; overturn, 3

522 **cui...dedit**: *to whom...gave (the power)...*; + inf., i.e. granted; dat. ind. obj. introducing a relative clause
523 **iūstitiā**: *with...*; abl. means
524 **Trōes...miserī**: *We wretched Trojans...*; 1p subject of ōrāmus
maria omnia: *over...*; acc. of extent
vectī: PPP vehō
525 **prohibe, parce**: sg. imperatives
526 **piō generī**: *a pious people*; i.e. the Trojans; dat. obj. of parce;Ilioneus characterizes is own people as pious
proprius: *more closely*; comparative adv.
527 **Nōn...aut...populāre...aut...vertere**: *not either to ravage...or to turn...*; two examples of inf. of purpose governed by vēnimus; the praedās, 'loot' are in fact cattle which one could turn and drive into ships on the shore
ferrō: *by sword*; metonomy, abl. means
529 **nōn ea vīs...victīs (sunt)**: *the conquered do not have this violence and such great arrogance in mind*; 'this violence and such great arrogance are not to the conquered...' victīs is PPP vincō and dat. of possession and animō is abl. place where; ea is demonstrative
530 **(et) Hesperiam**: i.e. Italy; asyndeton
cognōmine: *by...*; abl. of respect
dīcunt: *call (the place)...*; with a double acc.
531 **terra antīqua**: nom. in apposition to locus
armīs atque ūbere: *in...* abl. of respect
coluēr(unt terram): syncopated 3p pf.; add 'terram' as obj.
532 **fāma (est)**: *(there is) a rumor...*
minōrēs dīxisse: *that the descendants...*; ind. disc. with pf. inf. dīcō, which governs a double acc. (obj. and pred.); minōrēs (nātū), 'lesser (by age)' is a comparative adj. and often means 'descendants'
533 **ducis dē nōmine**: *(derived) from...*; i.e. named after a leader named Italus

aspiciō, -ere, spexī, spectus: to look at, see, 9
dē: (down) from; about, concerning, 10
fāma, -ae f.: fame, rumor, reputation, 9
ferrum, -ī n.: iron; sword, weapon, tool, 7
miser, -era, -rum: miserable, wretched, 6
nōmen, -inis n.: name, fame, renown 5
noster, -ra, -rum: our, ours, 10
nunc: now, 15

Ilioneus, Dido, and the Rules of Hospitality

Hospitality is the central theme of the complex exchange between Ilioneus, the Trojan leader speaking on behalf of the 13 lost ships, and queen Dido—even though the word *hospitium* is employed just once in the conversation (I.540) and the word *hospes, hospitis m/f*, 'guest' or 'host,' is not employed at all (Dido will use it later in IV.323). Much of Ilioneus' speech is a plea that Dido abide by the rules of hospitality and a claim that the Trojans come not as enemies but as guests. Dido's speech reveals how responsive she is to Ilioneus' request.

Just as the word *coniunx*, 'spouse,' can refer to a husband or a wife, so the word *hospes, hospitis* m/f can mean 'guest' or 'host.' Scholars often translate *hospes* more generally as 'guest-friend' and *hospitium* as 'the guest-host relationship' in recognition that these terms refer to both 'host' and 'guest' equally. The terms *hospes*, 'guest-friend,' and *hostis*, 'enemy' have a common origin because they both refer to relationships with strangers where there are exchanges with guarded or a complete lack of, trust. (N.B. *Hostis* can mean 'host/guest' but acquired the negative connotation of 'enemy' over time.) *Hospes* and *hospitium* derive from the roots *host-* and *-potis* (cf. potēns, possum, ipse) and mean something like 'a stranger who is respected.'

Jupiter (Zeus) enforces the relationship between guests and hosts among humans. When Paris, for example, visits the house of Menelaus and Helen in Sparta as a guest and steals Menelaus' wife Helen away, Paris acts as an unjust guest, and not surprisingly Jupiter (Zeus) sides with the Greeks during the subsequent Trojan war—in part, to punish Paris and those that protect him. Readers should not be surprised, therefore, that Ilioneus invokes Jupiter's name and the principle of *iūstitia*, 'justice,' in the initial lines of his speech. Jupiter is the god who promotes and enforces *hospitium*.

As you read Ilioneus' speech, note that his purpose is to clarify the relationship between the Trojans and Carthaginians and emphasize that the Trojans do not come as enemies (*hostēs*) but as respectful guests (*hospitēs*) who should be treated accordingly.

Infinitives of purpose [4] are more common in ancient Greek than in Latin, and so Vergil's use of such infinitives in 527-8 may be evidence of the influence of Vergil's knowledge of Greek on his Latin.

populāre *(in order to) plunder*   vertere *(in order) to turn*

N.B. populāre is related to the noun *populus* and means 'to (flood with people and therefore) plunder.'

Hesperia (Grk *hesper*, 'evening') means 'evening land' or 'west land,' because Italy is where the sun sets from the perspective of the Greek mainland. **Oenōtrus** denotes a tribe and area in southern Italy. The name suggests a land fertile in vines that traded wine (Grk. *oenos*) with Greek neighbors.

1. What virtue in 522-3 does Ilioneus claim Jupiter has given to allow Dido to establish a city? (N.B. Ilioneus' words suggest that he knows that the Carthaginans are also new to the land.)

2. In line 526, what adjective does Ilioneus use to characterize his fellow Trojans and their purpose?

3. What does Ilioneus say is NOT their purpose for coming in I.527-9?

4. What land is the Trojans' ultimate destination, according to Ilioneus?

Hic cursus fuit, 534
cum subitō adsurgēns flūctū nimbōsus Orīōn 535
in vada caeca tulit, penitusque procācibus Austrīs 536
perque undās superante salō perque invia saxa 537
dispulit; hūc paucī vestrīs adnāvimus ōrīs. 538
Quod genus hoc hominum? Quaeve hunc tam barbara mōrem 539
permittit patria? Hospitiō prohibēmur harēnae; 540
bella cient prīmāque vetant cōnsistere terrā. 541
Sī genus hūmānum et mortālia temnitis arma, 542
at spērāte deōs memorēs fandī atque nefandī. 543
Rēx erat Aenēās nōbīs, quō iūstior alter 544
nec pietāte fuit, nec bellō maior et armīs. 545

---

adnō (1): swim to, float to
adsurgō, -ere, surrēxī, surrēxtus: rise
alter, -era, -erum: other (of two) 3
Auster, -trī m.: wind; Auster wind, (south) wind, 2
barbarus, -a, -um: foreign, barbaric, hostile
caecus, -a, -um: blind, hidden, 3
cieō, -ēre, cīvī, citus: arouse, stir up, 2
consistō, -ere, -stitī: stop, stand still, 3
dispellō, -ere, -pulī, -pulsus: drive apart, scatter, 2
homō, -inis m./f.: person, people; human, 4
hospitium, -iī n.: hospitality, hospitable reception
hūmānus, -a, -um: human, of men
invius, -a, -um: impassable
iūstus, -a, -um: just, 2
maior, maius: *compar. of* **magnus,** 'great'
memor, -oris: mindful, remembering (*gen*) 4
mortālis, -e: mortal, 4
mōs, mōris m.: custom, law, 2
nefandus, -a, -um: unspeakable, unrighteous
nimbōsus, -a, -um: cloudy, stormy
Orīōn, -ōnis m.: Orion (constellation)
paucī, -ae, -a: little, few, scanty, 3
penitus: within, deep(ly), wholly, 3
permittō, -ere, -mīsī, -missus: allow, grant
procāx, -ācis: wanton, boisterous
prohibeō, -ēre, -uī, -itus: keep off, prohibit, 2
salum, -ī n.: sea, the swelling sea, 2
spērō (1): hope (for), expect, 4
subitō: suddenly, 4
superō (1): surpass, overcome, 4
tam: so, so much, so very, such, 4
temnō, -ere: scorn, despise, disdain
vadum, -ī n.: shallows, shoals, 4
vetō, -āre, -uī, -itus: forbid, prevent, 2

534 **Hic cursus fuit**: hic is nom. subj., and cursus nom. pred.; incomplete lines throughout the epic reveal that the poem was not finished when Vergil died unexpectedly in 19 BC
535 **flūctū**: *on…, from…*; the constellation Orion appears in the horizon over the waves
536 **in vada caeca**: caeca here means 'hidden'
tulit (nāvēs nostrās): pf. ferō; add object
procācibus Austrīs: *with…*; abl. of means
perque…perque…: *both…and…*
537 **superante salō**: abl. abs. with pres. pple
dispulit (nāvēs nostrās): pf. dispellō; add obj.
538 **paucī**: *we few*; 1p nom. subject
vestrīs ōrīs: *to…*; dat. of compound verb, ōra
539 **Quod genus (est)…**: *what race (is)…?*; neut. sg. interrogative adj.
Quaeve…patria: *or what country…?*; fem. sg. interrogative adj.
540 **hospitiō**: *from…*; abl. of separation
cient, vetant: add Carthaginians as subject
(in) prīmā…terrā: *on…*; i.e. the first land available to the Trojans
543 **at**: *at least, still*; 'but,' restrictive
spērāte deōs (esse) memorēs: *expect that…*; i.e. you should expect that…; imperative and ind. disc. with missing inf. sum
fandī atque nefandī: *of what is righteous and unrighteous*; or 'of (anything) speakable or unspeakable;' these gen. sg. gerundives (for, fārī) are often used as the gen. of *fās/nēfās* and are substantives: 'of (anything) worthy to be spoken and (anything) worthy to be unspoken'
544 **nōbīs**: dat. of possession: either 'there was to us' or (2) 'we had'
quō: *than whom…*; abl. of comparison
alter nec…nec (alter): *no other…and no (other)…*
545 **pietāte**: *in…*; abl. of respect
iūstior, maior: comparative adjs., magnus
bellō et armīs: *in…*; abl. of respect

Incomplete lines such as I.534 are found throughout the poem. According to tradition, Vergil was in the process of revising the *Aeneid* and had recently visited Caesar Augustus himself in Athens when the poet took ill and died on his way home in Brundisium on September 21· 19 B.C. Vergil made a request in his will that nothing more be published--including his still unfinished *Aeneid*—but the emperor ordered the epic to be edited and published, contrary to Vergil's wishes.

Incomplete hexameter lines are verses that Vergil intended to complete but never did.

Orion and the Auster Winds

The heliacal rising of Orion occurred in mid-July. At this time, sailors in the Mediterranean would witness the constellation of Orion rise above the horizon at dawn in the east as the sun (Grk. *helios*) was rising. Since this period of the year was associated with the beginning of the storm season, Vergil has Ilioneus describe *Orīōn* as both *adsurgēns* and *nimbōsus* (I.535). This dating is confirmed by the presence of the Auster (Grk. Notus), which brought rain from the south in late-summer and autumn.

Exclusive Aut [31] and Inclusive Vel [8]

Is the light off or (**aut**) on? Do you want lettuce or (**vel**) tomato on your sandwhich?

Both *aut* and *vel (-ve)* mean 'or,' but, when the Romans say 'x aut y', they mean that the option is exclusively x or y (but not both). When they say 'x vel y,' they mean that the option is 'x and/or y' (either or both). Translate *vel* as 'or' but be aware that both options are still possible.

The enclitic *-ve* is just a shortened form of *vel* that behaves like *-que*. We call words *-ve*, *-que*, and *-ne* enclitics because they lose their accent and are pronounced with the preceding word. Vergil often adds *-ve* to questions that do not exclude the previous question: e.g. *quaeve*, 'or what...?' in I.539.

Finally, Dido uses *sīve* (= vel sī) and *seu* (a contracted form of *sīve*) as correlatives: *sīve... sīve...*, which can mean 'if...or if...' or 'whether...or...' This correlative pair is used twice in the commentary and suggests that both options are equally possible.

Interrogative Adjectives

Just a reminder that the interrogative adjectives *quī, quae, quid* have slightly different nominative sg. forms from the interrogative pronoun *quis? quae? quid?* In neut. sg. (nom. and acc.), use *quid* when the interrogative is is a pronoun and *quod* when it is an adjective that agrees with a neut. sg. noun:

Quid est? *What is it?* Quod genus (neut. sg.)...est? *What race of men is this?* (539)

Likewise, use *quis* (m/f) for the pronoun and masc. *quī* or fem. *quae* when the adj. agrees with a noun:

Quis permittit? *Who allows...?* Quae...permittit patria (f. sg.)...? *What country...allows?* (539)

1. How do lines 535-8 support Ilioneus' argument that the Trojans did not come to plunder?
2. Ilioneus claims in 539-40 that a *patria* is 'tam barbara' if it adopts *hunc mōrem*, 'this custom.' To which custom is Ilioneus referring?
3. **Rules of Hospitality**: What right or privilege does Ilioneus claim in 540-41 that the Carthaginians owe to the Trojans in accordance with the rules of *hospitium*?
4. **Trojan View of Aeneas' Leadership, part 1 (544-5)**: What positive qualities does the Trojan Ilioneus attribute to Aeneas? Give the Latin and translation. In short, what do the Trojans think about their own leader? Since Ilioneus says such things while Aeneas is absent, we can assume that this opinion is honest and not mere flattery.

Quem sī fata virum servant, sī vescitur aurā
aetheriā, neque adhūc crūdēlibus occubat umbrīs,
nōn metus; officiō nec tē certāsse priōrem
paeniteat. Sunt et Siculīs regiōnibus urbēs
armaque, Trojānōque ā sanguine clārus Acestēs.
Quassātam ventīs liceat subducere classem,
et silvīs aptāre trabēs et stringere rēmōs:
sī datur Ītaliam, sociīs et rege receptō,
tendere, ut Ītaliam laetī Latiumque petāmus;
sīn absūmpta salūs, et tē, pater optime Teucrum,
pontus habet Libyae, nec spēs iam restat Iūlī,
at freta Sīcaniae saltem sēdēsque parātās,
unde hūc advectī, rēgemque petāmus Acestēn."

---

absūmō, -ere, -mpsī, -mptum: take away
Acestēs, -ae m.: Acestus, from Crete, 4
adhūc: as yet, still, so far, 2
advehō, -ere, -vēxī, -vectus: bear, convey (to)
aetherius, -a, -um: of the upper air, of the upper sky
aptō (1): fit, adapt, 2
certō (1): contend, contest, settle by contest
clārus, a, um: clear; famous, distinguished, 4
fretum, ī n.: strait (narrow waterway)
habeō, -ēre, -uī, -itus: have, hold; consider, 3
Iulus, -ī: Iulus, 3
Latium, -ī n: Latium, 4
licet: it is allowed or permitted, 3
neque: nor, and not;: neither...nor, 4
occubō (1): lie, lie down (in death)
officium, -ī n: service, duty, kindness
optimus, -a, -um: best, noblest
paenitet, -ēre, -uit: it causes (acc) regret (inf.)
parō (1): prepare, make ready, get, 4
quassō (1): shake, shatter
recipiō, -ere, -cēpī, -ceptum: take back, recover, 3
regiō, -ōnis f.: region, district 2
rēmus, -ī m.: oar, 3
restō, -āre, -stiti: remain, survive, 2
saltem: at least, 3
salūs, -ūtis f.: safety, refuge; health
Sīcania, -ae f.: Sicily
Siculus, -a, -um: Sicilian, of Sicily, 2
silva, -ae f.: woods, 4
sīn: but if; if, however
stringō, -ere: to draw out, strip off,
subdūcō, -ere, -dūxī, -ductus: draw up,, 2
trabs, trabis f.: beam (of wood)
Trōiānus, -a, -um: Trojan, 3
unde: whence, from which, 2
vescor, vescī: feed on, eat *(abl.)*

546 **quem...virum**: *this man*; quem is a connective relative adj.: make demonstrative
(et) si vescitur: *(and) if...*; pres. dep. + abl.
547 **(in) crūdēlibus umbrīs:** *among...*; i.e. ghosts
548 **nōn metus (est)**: *(there is)...*; i.e. we Trojans do not fear what comes next
officiō: *in...*; abl. respect, i.e. in hospitality
nec...paeniteat: *let there not be regret*; impersonal jussive pres. subj. + acc. + inf.
tē certā(vi)sse priōrem: *that you compete first*; or 'come in first place,' comparative of prīmus is predicative and modifies acc. subj. tē
549 **et**: *also*
(in) Siculīs regiōnibus
551 **quassātam**: PPP modifies fem. classem
liceat (nōbīs): *let it be...(for us)*; impersonal jussive pres. subj.; add a dat. of interest
552 **silvīs**: *from...*; abl. of source/origin
553 **datur**: *it is granted to, it is allowed to*; + inf.
Ītaliam: *to...*; place to which
sociīs...receptō: abl. abs., PPP recipiō agrees with the closest of the two nouns
554 **ut...petāmus**: *so that...may...;* purpose with 1p pres. subj.
laetī: *happily*; nom. adj. as adv.
555 **Sīn absumpta (est) salūs**: *or if (our) safety...* 3s pf. pass. ab-sumō
pater optime Teucr(ōr)um: i.e. Aeneas
apostrophe: voc. dir. address and gen. pl.,
556 **Libyae**: gen. sg. modifying pontus
at...saltem: *but at least*
558 **advectī (sumus)**: 1p pf. pass.
petāmus: *Let us...*; 1p pres. subj. jussive (hortatory, if he were addressing the Trojans)

crūdēlis, -e: cruel, bloody, 6

Not all of the Trojan survivors followed Aeneas

Vergil mentions several groups of Trojans that settled in different regions of the Mediterranean.

Acestes led Trojan colonists to western Sicily long before the Trojan war. Aeneas and his Trojans are welcomed by Acestes in Sicily at the end of the flashback in Book 3 and are just leaving him when Juno sends a storm in 1.34. In Book 5, Aeneas and the Trojans return to Acestes in order to celebrate funeral games for Anchises, Aeneas' father. It is Acestes' wine that the Trojans drink in I.195-7.

Antenor led Trojan fugitives to found the city of Patavium (Padua) in Northeast Italy after the war. Antenor is mentioned as a counselor to King Priam by Homer. In Book 1 of the *Aeneid*, Venus mentions Antenor when she complains to Jupiter that Antenor is now safely settled with Trojan survivors in Patavium while her own Aeneas remains far from Italy.

Helenus, brother of Hector and twin of Cassandra, ruled the Greek city of Buthrotum (near Actium) after the fall of Troy and married Andromache, the widow of Helenus' brother Hector. Helenus and Andromache were war-captives of Neoptolemus, Achilles' son, and were forced to come with him to Greece. When Neoptolemus was suddenly killed by Orestes, Agamennon's son, Helenus became king of Buthrotum and married Andromache. In a flashback scene in Book 3 of the *Aeneid*, Aeneas and the Trojans visit Helenus, who uses his gift of prophecy to help Aeneas on his journey to Italy.

Jussive Subjunctives [15]

This subjunctive (main verb) is named after the verb *iubeō, iubēre, iussī, iussum: order* and is used to express a type of polite command in 2nd and 3rd person (1s and 1p are usually called 'hortatory'). In the commentary, it occurs in twos or threes and is found in only five speeches. It is usually translated with 'let' or 'should' and governs a *nē* rather than *nōn* in the negative:

liceat	*let it be allowed, it should be allowed*
nē liceat	*let it not be allowed, it should not be allowed*

For readers, the translation is simple; the challenge is recognizing main verbs as present subjunctives. Mnemonics such as 'Let's eat caviar' or 'We beat a liar, friar' are used to help students remember the vowel changes that occur in present subjunctive through the various conjugations:

	dō, dare		videō, vidēre		ducō, -ere		faciō, -ere		audiō, -īre	
1st	dem	dēmus	videam	videāmus	ducam	ducāmus	faciam	faciāmus	audiam	audiāmus
2nd	dēs	dētis	videās	videātis	ducās	ducātis	faciās	faciātis	audiās	audiātis
3rd	det	dent	videam	videant	ducat	ducant	faciat	faciat	audiat	audiant

1. What is the *officiō* in 548 that Ilioneus claims Dido will not regret if she performs first? (note: Hospitium leads to officia, 'duties' or 'obligations,' for both the host and the guest.)

2. Why are jussives (549, 551, 558) more appropriate than imperatives in Ilioneus' speech to Dido? (In short, who has greater power in the conversation and why then are jussives more suitable than imperatives?)

3. **Trojan View of Aeneas' Leadership, part 2 (555)**: What does the direct address "pater optime Teucrum" (1.555) say about Ilioneus' opinion of his leader Aeneas? (N.B. Once again, since Aeneas is absent, readers can assume this is an honest opinion and not mere flattery.)

4. Where does Ilioneus propose to go in I.555-58 if the Trojans do not make it to Italy?

Tālibus Īlioneus; cūnctī simul ōre fremēbant
Dardanidae.
Tum breviter Dīdō, vultum dēmissa, profātur:
"Solvite corde metum, Teucrī, sēclūdite cūrās.
Rēs dūra et regnī novitās mē tālia cōgunt
mōlīrī, et lātē fīnēs custōde tuērī.
Quis genus Aeneadum, quis Troiae nesciat urbem,
virtūtēsque virōsque aut tantī incendia bellī?
Non obtūnsa adeō gestāmus pectora Poenī,
nec tam āversus equōs Tyriā Sōl iungit ab urbe.
Seu vōs Hesperiam magnam Sāturniaque arva,
sīve Erycis fīnēs regemque optātis Acestēn,
auxiliō tūtōs dīmittam opibusque iuvābō.

Acestēs, -ae m.: Acestus, from Crete, 4
adeō: to such a extent or degree, 2
Aeneadēs, -um m.: followers/descendants of Aeneas
arvum, -ī n.: plowed land, field, region, 4
auxilium, -ī n.: help, aid, assistance, 2
āvertō, -ēre, āvertī, āversum: turn away, 4
brevis, -e: short, shallow, 4
cōgō, cōgere, coēgī, coāctum: to collect; compel, 3
custōs, -ōdis m. (f.): guard, guardian, 4
Dardanidēs, -ae m.: Dardanian, Trojan, 2
dīmittō, -ere, -mīsī, -missus: send away, 2
dūrus, -a, -um: hard, harsh, stern, 2
equus, -ī m.: horse, 4
Eryx, -ycis m.: Eryx (city and mtn. in Sicily)
fremō, -ere, -uī, -itus: roar, 3
gestō (1): bear, wear, carry
Hesperia, -ae f.: Hesperia, Italy, 3
Ilioneus, -î m.: Ilioneus, 3
incendium, -(i)î n.: fire, conflagration 2
iungō, -ere, iunxī, -iunctum: to join, 3
iuvō, -āre, iūvī: be pleasing, help, aid, 4
mōlior, -īrī, -ītus sum: set in motion, bring about, 4
nesciō, -īre, -scīvī, -scītum: not know, be ignorant, 2
novitās, -tātis f.: newness,
obtundō, -ere, -tudī, -tū(n)sus: blunt, dull
ops, opis f.: resources, help; power, wealth, 3
optō (1): desire, choose, hope (for), 4
Poenī, -ōrum, m: Phoenician, Carthaginian, 2
profor, -fārī, -fātus sum: speak, say
Sāturnia, -ae f: Saturnian one, Juno, (patronymic), 2
sēclūdō, -ere, -sī, -sus: exclude, shut out
sīve, seu: whether, or (if), 4
sōl, sōlis m.: sun, 4
solvō, -ere, solvī, solūtum: loosen; set sail; pay
tam: so, so much, so very, such, 4
tueor, tuērī, tutus(tuitus) sum: look on, watch, 3
tūtus, -a, -um: safe, secure, 4
virtūs, -ūtis f.: valor, courage

559 **Tālibus (dictīs) Īlioneus (dīxit)**: *with such (words)...*; ellipsis
cunctī Dardanidae: nom. pl., i.e. all the Trojans accompanying Ilioneus before Dido
559 **ōre**: *with...*; abl. manner, i.e. aloud
561 **dēmissa**: *having dropped*; + acc.; PPP dēmittō, here reflexive in sense: 'having been sent down (by herself)'= 'having dropped'
562 **Solvite, sēclūdite**: pl. imperative
corde: *from...*; abl. separation or place where
Teucrī: voc. dir. address
563 **regnī novitās**: i.e. newness of the kingdom of Carthage; Dido and her fellow Phoenicians are colonists from Tyre, just now settling and enforcing their borders against local tribes
mē: obj. of cōgunt, tālia is obj. of mōlīrī
564 **lātē**: i.e. far and wide
custode: *with...*; abl. means
565 **Quis (nesciat)...(et) Quis...nesciat**: *Who does... (and) who does...?*; deliberative pres. subj.: translate pres. subj. as a pres. indicative
Aeneadum: *of the followers of Aeneas*
566 **virtūtēs**: i.e. deeds or feats of valor
567 **obtunsa adeō...tam āversus**: *hearts so dulled...nor Sun, so turned away from...*; i.e. we are not so unfeeling or far from civilization that we are unaware of Trojan suffering
Poenī: *We Phoenicians*; 1p subject
568 **equōs Sōl iungit**: in myth, the god Sun traverses the sky in a horse-drawn chariot
Tyriā ab urbe: i.e. Carthage; Tyrius is an adj.
569 **Seu (optātis)...sīve...optātis**: *if (you hope for) ...or if you hope for...*; ellipsis: seu = sīve
(vōs) tūtōs dīmittam: 1s fut.; supply 'you'

dēmittō, -ere, -mīsī, -missum: drop, let down, sink, 5

Deliberative Subjunctive [7]

This subjunctive is often used in questions to express (1) doubt or (2) the impossibilty of a task. While it often invites the addressee to deliberate over a question, the question is often rhetorical or just exclamatory. It governs a *nōn* in the negative, and, while it is usually translated as 'is she to X?' or 'should she X?' on many occasions the translation is no different from the indicative.

Quid agāmus? *What are we to do? What should we do?*

Juno uses it to express doubt that others will pray to her in the future while Dido uses it in the facing page to express incredulity that there is anyone who does not know about the Trojans and Troy:

quisquam nūmen Iūnōnis adōret...? *Is anyone to pray to the divinity of Juno hereafter?* I.48
Quis genus Aeneadum (nesciat)? *Who does not know the followers of Aeneas?* I.565

Mural of The Trojan War (I.450-493)

Dido's positive reception of the Trojans in 565-6 appears even more genuine in light of the famous mural of the Trojan war that has been omitted from this commentary. Immediately before Aeneas and Achates see Dido ascend the temple of Juno and accept the missing Trojans as guests, Aeneas spots a detailed mural of the events of the Trojan war—on the very walls at the base of the temple of Juno.

The scene is another example of **ecphrasis**, a rhetorical device that includes an unusually detailed description of a scene or work of art. Notably, when Aeneas views the mural he expresses two emotions: grief at the suffering that the scene recalls and joy because the stories of the war and Trojan suffering have reached as far as North Africa. Below are the scenes displayed on the mural:

Atreides (Agamemnon and Menelaus), King Priam of Troy, and Achilles (458)
The Greeks flee the Trojans, and the Greek Achilles chases the Trojans (466-468).
Rhesus loses his famed horses (469-473).
Troilus dies at Achilles' hands (474-478).
The Trojan women worship Athena in vain. (479-482).
Priam ransoms the body of Hector from Achilles (483-487).
Aeneas recognizes himself among the fighters (488-489).
Penthesilea, the Amazon queen, leads the Amazons into war (490-493).

For us, the mural is important because it shows (1) that Dido's empathy toward the Trojans is genuine and (2) that Carthage, under the leadership of Dido, promises to be different. Dido and her people recognize the savageness of war but subordinate these images in order to honor Juno—goddess of marriage and childbirth—and the values of love, family and civilized life.

Dido's hospitality, part 1

1. Does Dido promote retrained or unrestrainted emotion in the first line of her speech (562)? Explain.

2. What reason does Dido offer in 563-4 to defend her show of force against her Trojan guests?

3. In lines 569-71 Dido offers to help the Trojans reach either of two destinations. What two destinations does she mention? (N.B. Dido's attention to detail reveals that she listened very closely to Ilioneus' speech and is very responsive to the Trojans' needs.)

4. How does Vergil use repetition in line 571 to emphasize that Dido will fulfill her obligation of hospitality?

Vultis et hīs mēcum pariter cōnsīdere rēgnīs?
urbem quam statuō vestra est; subdūcite nāvēs;
Trōs Tyriusque mihī nūllō discrīmine agētur.
Atque utinam rēx ipse Notō compulsus eōdem
adforet Aenēās! Equidem per lītora certōs
dīmittam et Libyae lūstrāre extrēma iubēbō,
sī quibus ēiectus silvīs aut urbibus errat."

Prīmus ibi ante omnēs magnā comitante catervā
Lāocoōn ardēns summā dēcurrit ab arce,
et procul: "Ō miserī, quae tanta insānia, cīvēs?
Crēditis āvectōs hostēs? Aut ūlla putātis
dōna carēre dolīs Danaum? Sīc nōtus Ulixēs?

---

adsum, -esse, -fuī: be present, assist (*dat.*), 2
āvehō, -ere, -vexī, -vectum: carry away, 2
careō, -ēre, -uī: be lacking, be without (abl)
caterva, -ae f.: retinue, band, troop, 2
certus, -a, -um: sure, reliable, definite, 4
cīvis, -is m/f: citizen
comitō (1): accompany, attend, 2
compellô (1): address, accost, speak to, 3
cōnsīdō, -ere, -sēdī, -sessus: sit, settle, rest, 2
dēcurrō, -ere, -cururrī: to run down
dīmittō, -ere, -mīsī, -missus: send away, 2
discrīmen, -crīminis n.: crisis, peril; difference, 3
dolus, -ī m.: trick, deceit, 3
ēiciō, -ere, -iēcī, -iectum: throw or cast out
equidem: (I) for my part, (I) indeed, 3
hostis, -is m./f.: enemy, foe, 4
ibi: there, in that place, 2
insānia, -ae f.: insanity, madness
Lāocoön m. acc. **-nta**: Laocoon, 4
lūstrō (1): traverse, survey, 3
Nōtus, -ī m.: Notus wind, South wind (= Auster), 3
pariter: equally, on equal terms, 3
procul: from afar, far, at a distance, 2
putō (1): to think, imagine, 3
silva, -ae f.: woods, 4
statuō, -ere, -uī, -ūtus: establish, build, 2
subdūcō, -ere, -dūxī, -ductus: draw up, 2
Ulixēs, -is m.: Ulysses (Latin name for Odysseus)
utinam: would that! O that!
volō, velle, voluī: will, wish, be willing, 2

572 **vultis**: 2p pres. volō
(in) hīs…rēgnīs
mēcum: cum mē; i.e. as your leader
pariter: adv., i.e. Dido will treat the foreign Trojans and her own people equally
573 **urbem quam**: *the city which*; or 'what city I…' either nom. urbs is attracted into the acc. of quam or quam is a relative adj. with urbem
subdūcite: pl. imperative; ships are pulled onto the beach rather than left at anchor
574 **Trōs Tyriusque**: i.e. both peoples
mihi: *to me*; dat. of reference (viewpoint) with nūllō discrīmine
agētur: *will be led*; fut. but with 3p subject
nūllō discrīmine: *with…*; abl. of manner
575 **utinam…adforet**: *Would that…were present* utinam + subj. of wish; adforet is equiv. to adesset (impf. subj. sum)
Notō eō-dem: abl. means with PPP compellō
576 **certōs (virōs)**: *reliable (men)*; i.e. men to search the shores for signs of Aeneas
577 **dīmittam, iubēbō**: 1s fut.
(certōs virōs) lustrāre
Libyae…extrema: *the farthest (edges)…*; neut. acc. pl.
578 **sī (Aenēās)…errat**
(in) quibus silvīs aut urbibus: *in some…*; quibus is indefinite after sī

Book 2: Aeneas is invited by Dido to a banquet, where he tells her about the fall of Troy. Aeneas recalls how the Trojans found the wooden horse and, as they debated what to do, Laocoon comes. Aeneas is the 1st person narrator in Book 2 and 3.

40 **Prīmus…Lāocoōn…dēcurrit**: i.e. Laocoon is in front of the group ; the adv. prīmum means first in time (e.g. first…then…) while the adj. means that Laocoon was the first to undertake an action
magnā comitāte catervā: abl. abs. pres. pple
42 **procul (clāmat)**
Ō miserī…cīvēs: voc. dir. address
quae tanta insānia (est)?: *what…(is this)?*

42 **Ō miserī...cīvēs**: voc. dir. address
quae tanta insānia (est)?: *what...(is this)?*
43 **Crēditis, putātis**: 2p pres.
āvectōs (esse) hostēs: *that...*; ind. disc. with pf. pass. inf. āvehō
ūlla dona carēre: *that...*; ind. disc., careō governs an abl. of separation as object
Dana(ōr)um: gen. pl. with dōna
44 **nōtus (est)**: *has been known*; Note how negatively Ulysses (Odysseus) is portrayed

crēdō, -ere, -didī: believe, trust, 5
dōnum, -ī n.: gift, offering, prize, 6
extrēmus, -a, -um: farthest, outermost, 5
īdem, eadem, idem: same, the same. 6

Subjunctive of Wish (Optative Subjunctive) [3]

The subjunctive of wish, also called the optative subjunctive (optō, -āre: wish), is often introduced by *utinam*, 'would that,' and is used only three times in the commentary (1.575, 4.678-9). The present subjunctive expresses a wish for the future, while the imperfect and pluperfect subjunctive express an unfulfilled wish (or contrary to fact) in the present and past respectively:

Utinam adsit!	*Would that he be present!* (in a future)
Utinam adesset/adforet!	*Would that he were present!* (but he isn't)
Utinam adfuisset!	*Would that he had been present!* (but he wasn't)

What is adforet? *Fore* is an alternative form for *futūrum esse*, the future infinitive of *sum, esse*. When personal endings are added to the infinitive *fore* (forem, fores, foret...), it becomes an alternative to the imperfect subjunctive of sum, esse (essem, essēs, esset...). And so, *Utinam Aeneas adforet* is equivalent to *Utinam Aeneas adesset*, 'Would that Aeneas were present!'

1. **Dido's hospitality, part 2**: What option does Dido offer in 572-3 and, more importantly, what do the words 'pariter' and 'vestra' indicate about Dido's leadership and regard for *hospitium*?
2. How does 'mihi nūllō discrīmine agetur' in I.574 repeat and reaffirm Dido's promise in 572-3?
3. What does Dido promise to do in 576-7 to find Aeneas?

What Happens at the End of Book 1

After Dido finishes her speech, Aeneas emerges from the mist of invisibility to the amazement of both the Carthaginians and Trojans. After he introduces himself to Dido and reunites with his fellow Trojans, Dido escorts him to the palace for a banquet and arranges to have food sent to the ships.

At this point Aeneas sends Achates back to Aeneas' ship with a dual purpose: (1) to retrieve several gifts for Dido (Helen's clothing, Ilione's scepter and jewels) and (2) to bring Aeneas' son Ascanius to the palace for the evening banquet.

Venus now intervenes with a plan to make Dido more receptive to Aeneas. She puts her grandson Ascanius into a deep sleep and hides him away. We assume that he returns at the end of the banquet in Book 4, but Vergil never tells us. Venus' son Cupid then disguises himself as Ascanius and is sent by Venus to the banquet with the purpose of making Dido fall in love with Aeneas. As Book 1 ends, Dido asks Aeneas to tell of his travels, and, as the disguised Cupid sits on Dido's lap, Vergil says 'unlucky Dido was drinking long draughts of love' (*īnfēlīx Dīdō, longumque bibēbat amōrem*, I.749).

Aeneid Books 2 and 3, therefore, are Aeneas' first person recollection of the fall of Troy (Book 2) and subsequent travels through the Mediterranean (Book 3). In 2.1-39 Aeneas tells Dido and fellow banqueters that in the 10th year of the Trojan war the Greeks mysteriously disappeared with their ships and the Trojans found a wooden horse marked *Minervae*, 'to Minerva,' on the shore. While some argued that the horse should be honored in the center of Troy, others argued that it should be destroyed. At this moment, as the Trojans debate on the shore, the priest Laocoon emerges from the city gates and yells at the Trojans as he runs closer.

Aut hōc inclūsī lignō occultantur Achīvī,
aut haec in nostrōs fabricāta est māchina mūrōs,
inspectūra domōs ventūraque dēsuper urbī,
aut aliquis latet error; equō nē crēdite, Teucrī.
Quidquid id est, timeō Danaōs et dōna ferentēs."
Sīc fātus validīs ingentem vīribus hastam
in latus inque ferī curvam compāgibus alvum
contorsit. Stetit illa tremēns, uterōque recussō
insonuēre cavae gemitumque dedēre cavernae.
Et, sī fāta deum, sī mēns nōn laeva fuisset,
impulerat ferrō Argolicās foedāre latebrās,
Troiaque nunc stāret, Priamīque arx alta manērēs.

Achīvus, -a, -um: Achaean, Greek
aliquis, -qua, -quid: some, any, 2
alvus, -ī f.: belly, womb
Argolicus, -a, -um: Argive, Greek
caverna, -ae f.: cavern, grotto
cavus, -a, -um: hollow, 3
compāgēs, -is f.: seam, joint, 2
contorqueō, -ēre, -torsī, -tortum: hurl violently, whirl
curvus, -a, -um: curved, bent
dēsuper: from above, 3
equus, -ī m.: horse, 4
error, -ōris m.: deception, wandering;
fabricō (1): to build, make, fabricate, engineer
ferus, -a, -um: wild, untamed
foedō (1): defile, befoul, make ugly, 3
hasta, -ae f.: spear, 2
impellō, -ere, -pulī, -pulsus: drive, set into motion, 3
inclūdō, -ere, -clūsī, -clūsum: close in, shut in
insonō, -āre, -uī: resound, make sound
inspiciō, -ere, -spēxī, -spectum: look upon
laevus, -a, -um: left (handed); unfavorable
latebra, -ae f.: lair, hiding-place
lignum, -ī n.: wood
māchina, -ae f.: machine, war engine, 2
maneō, -ēre, mānsī: stay, remain, wait, 4
mēns, mentis f.: mind, intent, purpose, 4
occultō (1): hide, conceal
Priamus, -ī m.: Priam, king of Troy, 4
quisquis, quicquid: whoever, whatever, 2
recutiō, -īre, -cussī, -cussum: reverberate, strike back
timeō, -ēre, timuī: be afraid, fear 2
tremō, -ere, -uī: tremble, quiver, 2
uterus, -ī m.: belly, 2
validus, -a, -um: strong, sturdy, 2

45 **Aut...aut...**: *either...or...*
hōc...lignō: abl. means with PPP inclūsī
Achīvī: *the Greeks*; substantive, nom. subj.
46 **haec...māchina**: nom. subj., i.e. the horse
in nostrōs...mūrōs: *against...*
47 **inspectūra...ventūra**: *intending to...intending to...* ; fut. act. pples expressing purpose, veniō
urbī: *into...*; dat. of direction (~purpose)
48 **nē crēdite**: *Don't...*; neg. imperative employs nē rather than nōn; crēdō governs a dat. ind obj.
Teucrī: voc. dir. address
49 **Quidquid id est**: *whatever...*; parenthetical
et dona ferentēs: *even (while)...*; pres. pple; et is an adv.; Laocoön mistrusts the Greeks, but even more when they offer gifts
50 **fātus**: pf. dep. pple for, fārī: 'having Xed'
validīs vīribus: abl. means; vīrēs, pl. of vīs, means 'strength'
51 **in-que ferī curvam...alvum**: et in curvam alvum ferī; gen. sg. ferī modifies fem. alvum
compagibus: abl. of means with curvam
52 **stetit**: pf. stō; i.e. stuck
illa: i.e. hasta
uterō recussō: abl. abs.
53 **insonuēr(unt)**: syncopated 3p pf.
dedēr(unt): syncopated 3p pf., dō, dare
54 **sī fāta de(ōr)um (et) sī mēns (deōrum)... fuisset, stāret...manērēs**: *if the fates...(and) if the purpose...had, would...would...*; mixed contrary to fact (sī plpf. subj., plpf. subj. and impf. subj.); plpf. subj. sum and impf. subj. stō and maneō; the ellipsis and asyndeton perhaps reflect Aeneas' heightened emotional state
55 **impulerat**: *(the spear) would have struck*; a vivid plpf. indicative where one expects subj.
ferrō: abl. means, i.e. the spearpoint
arx alta Priamī: voc. dir. address and gen.
manērēs: *you would...*; impf subj. in the same condition; apostrophe, a device where a speaker 'turns away' to address someone not present

gemitus, -ūs m.: groan, lament, sob, 5 **stō, -āre, stetī, status:** stand, stop, 6
nē: lest, that not, so that not; no, not, 5

Aeneid Books 2-3 imitate *Odyssey* Books 9-12

Aeneas' recollection of the fall of Troy and his subsequent wanderings at sea in Books 2 and 3 during a banquet with Dido is an imitation of *Odyssey* Books 9-12, where at a banquet of the Phaeacians Odysseus recalls his own travels at sea and encounters with monsters.

Originality in Greco-Roman Art: Imitation and Variation (part 2)

Earlier, it was suggested that Vergil's imitation of the *Odyssey* is an example of originality in art and literature that was quite common in the Greco-Roman world. Many authors would imitate their predecessors in large and small ways and then offer a variation or twist to distinguish their own work from what came before.

Readers who view this imitation as a form of plagiarism or simple laziness in storytelling are missing the point. Vergil wishes to use the imitation not only to embed the *Aeneid* in the tradition of Homer's *Odyssey* and *Iliad* but also to make intelligible how the *Aeneid* rivals and surpasses its predecessors.

In Book 2, Vergil will consistently characterize the Greek people as a whole as untrustworthy and Ulysses (Odysseus) in particular as untrustworthy and impious. And so, as Vergil continues to elevate Aeneas' status as a hero, note how he lowers the reader's opinion of Ulysses and the Greeks.

Contrary to Fact (Contrafactual) Conditions [6]

We identify conditions (if-then clauses) by the tense and mood of the two main verbs. A present contrary to fact condition (*were, would*) has impf. subj. in both the **protasis** (if-clause) and **apodosis** (then-clause). A past contrary to fact (*had, would have*) has plpf. subj. in both parts. See below:

present contrary to fact:	sī audīrēs, scīrēs hoc.	*If you **were** listening, you **would** know this.*
past contrary to fact:	sī audīvissēs, scīvissēs hoc.	*If you **had** listened, you **would have** known this.*

In 2.54-6 the sentence is a mixed contrary to fact condition: the **protasis** is plpf. subj. (*had…*) but the **apodosis** has not only a plpf. (*would have*) but also two impf. subj. verbs (*would*). The sentence is even more complicated because Vergil uses plpf. indicative (*impulerat*) where we expect plpf. subj. (*impulisset*) in order to make the condition even more vivid to readers.

Sī mēns (deōrum)…fuisset, (1) impulerat, (2) stāret, (3) manērēs
If the purpose of the gods had been…,…would have set in motion…would stand…you would remain

Omniscient Narrator vs. Recollection with Hindsight: The muse invoked in Book 1 allows Vergil to be an omniscient narrator and describe events that a human could not know otherwise—the conversations of Juno, Aeolus, and Neptune, for example. In Books 2 and 3 Aeneas is the narrator, and his insight, of course, is that he knows how these events will turn out. Note how often, as in lines 2.54-6, Aeneas uses his knowledge of the outcome to comment on past events.

1. **Character of Ulysses (Odysseus)**: What does Laocoon say about the trustworthiness and of the Greeks and indirectly of Ulysses in 2.43-44?
2. **Character of the Greeks**: How does line 49, 'Quidquid id est, timeō Danaōs et dōna ferentēs,' characterize the Greeks as a people?
3. What violence does Laocoon commit to the horse after he finishes his speech?

Lāocoōn, ductus Neptūnō sorte sacerdōs, 201
sollemnēs taurum ingentem mactābat ad ārās. 202
Ecce autem geminī ā Tenedō tranquilla per alta 203
(horrēscō referēns) immēnsīs orbibus anguēs 204
incumbunt pelagō pariterque ad lītora tendunt; 205
pectora quōrum inter flūctūs arrēcta iubaeque 206
sanguineae superant undās; pars cētera pontum 207
pōne legit sinuatque immēnsa volūmine terga. 208
Fit sonitus spūmante salō; iamque arva tenēbant 209
ardentēs oculōs suffectī sanguine et ignī 210
sībila lambēbant linguīs vibrantibus ōra. 211

---

anguis, -is m. f.: snake
arrigō, -ere, -rēxī, -rectus: raise, prick up, 3
arvum, -ī n.: plowed land, field, region, 4
autem: however, moreover
cēterī, -ae, -a: the remaining, rest, others
ecce: behold!, 2
fīō, fierī, factus sum: be made
geminus, -a, -um: twin, double, two 4
horrescō, -ēre, -uī; begin to bristle, shudder
immensus, -a, -um: immense, vast, boundless, 2
incumbō, -ere, -cubuī,: lie on, 2
iuba, -ae f.: mane, crest
lambō, -ēre, lambī: lick
Lāocoön m. acc. -nta: Laocoon, 4
legō, -ere, lēgī, lectum: to read; pick out; skim, pass, 4
lingua, ae f.: tongue, language, 2
mactō (1): sacrifice, make sacrifice
Neptūnus, -ī m.: Neptune, 3
orbis, -is m.: sphere, coil, circle (of a shield)
pariter: equally, on equal terms, 3
pelagus, -ī n.: sea, 4
pōne: after, behind
sacerdōs, -dōtis m. f.: priest(ess), 2
salum, -ī n.: sea, the swelling sea, 2
sanguineus, a-, um: bloody, blood-red
sībila, -ōrum m.: hissing
sinuō (1): to bend, curve, wind
sollemnis, -e: sollemn, annual
sonitus, -ī m.: sound, noise, clang, 2
spūmō (1): to foam, froth, 3
sufficiō, -ere, -fēcī, -fectum: fill, imbue; supply, 2
superō (1): surpass, overcome, 4
taurus, -ī m.: bull, 2
Tenedus (ōs), -ī m.: island Tenedos
tranquillus, -a, -um: tranquil, calm
vibrō (1): to flap, vibrate, brandish, shake
volūmen, -inis n.: roll,

201 **ductus**: *drawn*; as if from a hat; PPP, dūcō
Neptūnō: *for…*; dat. of interest
sorte: abl. means
sacerdōs: nom. in apposition to Lāocoōn
203 **geminī…anguēs**: nom. subject
ā Tenedō: The 1000-ship Greek fleet is hiding behind the island of Tenedos. Some suggest that the serpents symbolize Agamemnon and Menelaus, the two brothers who led the Greeks to Troy and will capture the city.
alta: *the deep (sea)*; metonomy
203 **horrescō**: Aeneas inserts 1s commentary as he recalls the events
204 **referēns**: *(while) recalling*; i.e. the events
immēnsīs orbibus: *of…*; abl. of quality
205 **pelagō**: *on…*; dat. of compound verb
pariter: *side by side*; 'equally'
206 **pectora quōrum**: *whose chests…*; neut. nom. pl. and gen. pl. relative
arrēcta (sunt): the serpents lift their chests and heads out of the water
pars cētera: i.e. below the serpents' chests
208 **legit**: *skims*; 'traverses'
immēnsa volūmine: *with…*; abl. manner; i.e. in the form of a corkscrew
209 **fit**: 3s pres., serves as the passive of facere
spūmante salō: abl. abs. with pres. pple
tenēbant: i.e. take hold of; i.e. the serpents
210 **ardentēs oculōs suffectī**: *having filled* + acc.; lit. 'having been filled in respect to…' a PPP sufficiō + acc. of respect; this acc. of respect, usually with body parts, is more common in Greek than in Latin; cf. 4.216
sanguine et ignī: abl. of means; abl. ignī is a 3rd decl. i-stem noun
211 **sībila ōra**: neut. nom. pl. subject
linguīs vibrantibus: abl. means

What happens after Laocoon's speech: Sinon's deceit

After Laocoon's speech, a deceitful Greek named Sinon is captured on the shore and brought before King Priam and the Trojans, who are still debating what to do with the horse.

According to the story Sinon tells King Priam, the Greeks were planning to leave Troy and had built the wooden horse in order to honor Minerva on their journey home. When the Greeks were told by an oracle to sacrifice a human before their voyage, Ulysses (Odysseus), who hated his fellow Greek Sinon because of a private dispute, cleverly arranged for Sinon to be chosen as the sacrifice. Sinon says that, when the day of the sacrifice came, he broke free from his captors and remained hidden until all of the Greeks sailed off and the Trojans found him.

Sinon begs for mercy, and King Priam, who trusts Sinon and his story, welcomes him among the Trojans. It is shortly after this acceptance that Laocoon is attacked by the serpents on the facing page.

Themes in Sinon's story

Sinon is actually acting under the instructions of Ulysses and deceiving the Greeks. Sinon persuades the Trojans to accept the horse and will later open the trapdoor and release the men from the horse.

1. **Trojan trustworthiness vs. Greek deceit:** Laocoon warned the Trojans about the tricks of the Greeks and Ulysses, and the account of Sinon confirms Laocoon's view. Sinon takes advantage of the Trojans' willingness to trust others implicitly in order to convince them to accept the horse and allow Sinon—a Greek!—to roam free in the city. Sinon will release the armed men from the horse.
2. **Ulysses (Odysseus) is deceitful and untrustworthy**: Ulysses is the originator not only (a) of the wooden horse but (b) of Sinon's trickery. Ulysses instructed Sinon to play this part. Notably, the deceit relies on Ulysses' poor reputation among the Trojans. Sinon's claim that he was betrayed by Ulysses is immediately accepted by the Trojans and makes Sinon more sympathetic to King Priam.
3. **Trust and Hospitality lead to Troy's downfall**: It is King Priam's willingness to accept Sinon as a suppliant (someone begging for help) and accept an enemy as a guest-friend that leads to the acceptance of the horse and destruction of Troy.
4. **The Serpent Motif**: Sinon's name derives from *sinus*, 'curve' or 'coil,' and highlights how he insinuates (insinuāre, 'twist in') himself into the hearts of the Trojans like a serpent. This wordplay is intentional. In addition to the serpents who kill Laocoon and convince the Trojans to accept the horse, the Trojan horse itself will 'slide' (inlābitur, 2.240) into the city.

The Two Serpents Represent Agamemnon and Menelaus

The Greeks were led to Troy by Agamemnon of Mycenae and his brother, Menelaus of Sparta, who was married to Helen and had invoked the oath of Tyndareus that gathered the Greeks against Troy. All of the Greek ships now lie hidden behind the island of Tenedos. And so, many scholars assume that, when the two serpents come from Tenedos, they symbolize Agamemnon and Menelaus and the destruction that will come from the island of Tenedos to Troy.

fīō, fierī [1] is used just once (2.209) and is commonly used as the passive for **faciō** in primary tenses:

Pres.	facit	*she makes*	fīō, fīs, **fit**, fīmus, fītis, fīunt	*she is made, becomes*
Impf.	faciēbat	*she was making*	fīēbam, fīēbās, **fīēbat**…fīēbant	*she was made, became*
Fut.	faciet	*she will make*	fīam, fīēs, **fīet**…fīent	*she will be made, will become*
Subjunctive				
Pres.	faciat	*she makes*	fīam, fīas, **fīat**…fīant	*she is made, becomes*
Impf.	faceret	*she was making*	fierem, fierēs, **fieret**…fierent	*she was made, became*

Diffugimus vīsū exsanguēs. Illī agmine certō
Lāocoönta petunt; et prīmum parva duōrum
corpora nātōrum serpēns amplexus uterque
implicat et miserōs morsū dēpascitur artūs;
post ipsum auxiliō subeuntem ac tēla ferentem
corripiunt spīrīsque ligant ingentibus; et iam
bis medium amplexī, bis collō squāmea circum
terga datī superant capite et cervīcibus altīs.
Ille simul manibus tendit dīvellere nōdōs
perfūsus saniē vittās ātrōque venēnō,
clāmōrēs simul horrendōs ad sīdera tollit:
quālis mūgitus, fūgit cum saucius āram
taurus et incertam excussit cervīce secūrim.

---

amplector, -ī, -plexus sum: wind around, embrace, 3
artus, -ūs m.: joint, limb, 4
auxilium, -ī n.: help, aid, assistance, 2
bis: twice, 3
certus, -a, -um: sure, reliable, definite, 4
cervīx, -īcis f.: neck, 2
circumdō, -dāre, -dedī, -datum: put around, 2
collum, -ī n.; neck, 3
dēpascor, -ī, pāstus sum: feed or graze from
diffugiō, -ere, -fūgī: flee apart, escape
dīvellō, -ere, -ī, -vulsum: tear apart
duo, duae, duo: two
excutiō, -ere, -cussī, -cussum: strike or shake off, 2
exsanguis, -e: bloodless; pale, 2
horrendus, -a, -um: horrible, to be trembled at, 4
implicō, -āre, -uī, ātum: enfold, mingle, encircle
incertus, -a, -um: unsure, unreliable, uncertain
Lāocoön m. acc. **-nta**: Laocoon, 4
ligō (1): to tie down, fasten
morsus, -ūs m.: bite, 2
mūgitus, -ūs m.: bellowing, mooing
nōdus, -î m.: knot, 2
parvus, -a, -um: small, 3
perfundō, -ere, -fūdī, -fūsum: to pour or shed (over)
saniēs, -ēī f.: blood
saucius, -a, -um: wounded, injured
secūris, -is f.: axe, hachet
serpēns, -ntis f.: serpent
spīra, -ae f.: coil
squāmeus, -a, -um: scaly
superō (1): surpass, overcome, 4
taurus, -ī m.: bull, 2
uterque, utraque, utrumque: each (of two), both, 2
venēnum, -ī n.: poison
vitta, -ae f.: ribbon, fillet, 2

212 **vīsū**: *by...*; 'because of...' abl. of cause
illI: i.e. the serpents, nom. pl.
agmine certō: *in fixed formation*; abl. manner
213 **Lāocoönta**: Grk. acc. sg.
prīmum...post...: *first...afterwards...*; adv.
parva corpora duōrum nātōrum: note the interlocking word word (synchesis), likely reflecting the coiling of the bodies
amplexus: pf. dep. pple: 'having Xed'
215 **morsū**: *with a...*; abl. manner
216 **post**: *afterwards, later*; adv.
(Lāocoönta) ipsum: *(Laocoon) himself*
auxiliō: *for...*; dat. of purpose
subeuntem: pres. pple subeō
217 **corripiunt**: the serpents are subject
spīrīs ingentibus: abl. means
218 **medium**: *his waist*; 'middle of (his body)'
amplexī (sunt): 3p pf. dep.: translate active
collō: *around...*; dat. of compound verb
circum...datī: *having put* (acc) *around* (dat); tmesis for PPP circumdō, 'put around'
capite...altīs: abl. means or absolute
219 **Ille**: i.e. Laocoon
simul...simul: *both...and at the same time*; correlatives
manibus: abl. means
tendit: *strives* + inf., 'stretches'
220 **perfūsus**: *having soaked*; PPP, reflexive in sense; saniē and venēnō are abl. of means
223 **quālis mūgitus**: *just as...*; 'which sort (of) mooing...' relative adj. introducing a simile
fūgit cum: *when...*; cum fūgit + acc. obj. i.e. a sacrificial bull when it flees the altar
224 **excussit**: a sacrificial blow behind the neck that is not fatal stirs the bull to flee the altar
cervīce: *from...*; abl. of separation

fugiō, -ere, fūgī: flee, escape, avoid, 5 **nātus, -ī m.**: son (male having been born), 8

Interlocking Word Order (Synchesis)

Interlocking word order is a rhetorical device where at least two pairs of words are arranged in an A B A B order that must be unteased when interpreted, e.g. Noun$_1$, Noun$_2$, Adjective$_1$ and Adjective$_2$. The initial line of Neptune's speech to the winds contains an famous example of this device:

Tantane vōs generis tenuit **fīdūcia** vestrī? (I.132)

Vergil uses interlocking word order to great effect when he describes how the serpents entwine the limbs of the sons with their coils, and the words themselves reflect the scene that they are describing:

parva duōrum **corpora** nātōrum (2.213-4)

Readers also note that tmesis (circumdātī → circum...dātī) creates a sort of interlocking word order to great effect when Vergil describes how the serpents entwine Laocoon:

squāmea circum **terga** datī... (2.218-9)

Finally, there are two more selections in this passage that are not technically examples of this device but create the same effect with verbs and are noted by readers:

implicat et miserōs morsū **dēpascitur** artūs (2.215)
corripiunt spīrīsque **ligant** ingentibus (2.217)

Subeuntem

The prefix *sub-* often means 'up' (i.e. up from under), and so the participle *subeuntem* means 'coming up to' or 'approaching' as a final translation. The verb *subit* is typically translated 'approaches.' It is worth noting that the adverb *subitō*, 'suddenly' is derived from *eō, īre*, 'go' and means something that 'comes up unexpectedly.'

The present participle of *eō, īre* (iēns, euntis) is used 4 times and the gerund (eundī) is used but once. Note that before the letter 'u,' the stem vowel 'i' becomes 'e.'

iēns	euntēs	*going* (pple)	--	*going* (gerund)
euntis	euntium		eundī	
euntī	euntibus		eundō	
euntem [4]	euntēs		eundum	
euntī/e	euntibus		eundō [1]	

1. **The Two Serpents as a Microcosm of the Trojan War**: The serpents kill the children first and then their father Laocoon. The death of children before the death of their parents is horrible, but it is particularly so when the children die before the eyes of their parents. If we assume that the serpents symbolize the two leaders of the Greeks, Agamemnon and Menelaus, why is it appropriate that the children of Laocoon die in front of Laocoon before he himself is killed? In short, how is this scene a microcosm of what is happening to the Trojans in the war?

2. The **Simile of the Bull** (2.223-4) and **Motif of Human Sacrifice**: One of the motifs of Book 2 that highlights the brutality of the war is human sacrifice and the impious spilling of human blood on altars. Consider the following: (a) Sinon suggested that the Greeks would sacrifice him in place of an animal sacrifice; (b) Aeneas will witness as King Priam is killed by Neoptolemus, son of Achilles, over an altar in Priam's palace; and (c) Aeneas will almost succeed in killing Helen within the Temple of Vesta.

How does the **Simile of the Bull** (2.223-4) suggest that Laocoon is another example in this motif? (Hint: What was Laocoon doing in 201-2, before the serpents arrive? What happens in the simile?)

At geminī lāpsū dēlūbra ad summa dracōnēs
effugiunt saevaeque petunt Trītonidis arcem
sub pedibus deae clipeīque sub orbe teguntur.
Tum vērō tremefacta novus per pectora cūnctīs
insinuat pavor, et scelus expendisse merentem
Lāocoönta ferunt, sacrum quī cuspide rōbur
laeserit et tergō scelerātam intorserit hastam.
Dūcendum ad sēdēs simulācrum ōrandaque dīvae
nūmina conclāmant.
Dīvidimus mūrōs et moenia pandimus urbis.
Accingunt omnēs operī pedibusque rotārum
subiiciunt lāpsūs, et stuppea vincula collō
intendunt: scandit fātālis māchina mūrōs
fēta armīs. Puerī circum innūptaeque puellae
sacra canunt fūnemque manū contingere gaudent:

---

accingō, -ere, -cinxī, cinctum: equip, put on a belt, 2
canō, -ere, cecinī, cantus: sing (about), 3
clipeus, -ī m.: a (round) shield
collum, -ī n.; neck, 3
conclamō (1): cry out together, shout
contingō, -ere, contigī: touch, border; happen, 2
cuspis, -idos f.: point, spearpoint, 2
dēlūbrum, -ī n.: shrine, temple
dīvidō, -ere, -vīsī, -vīsus: divide 3
dracō, -ōnis m.: serpent
effugiō, -ere, -fūgī: flee away, escape
expendō, -ere, -dī: pay, pay for, weigh out
fātālis, -e: deadly, fatal; fated, 3
fetus, -a, -um: teeming, pregnant, 2
fūnis, -is m.: a rope, cord
gaudeō, gaudēre, gāvīsus sum: enjoy, rejoice, 2
geminus, -a, -um: twin, double, two 4
hasta, -ae f.: spear, 2
innūptus, -a, -um: unmarried, 2
insinuō (1): to insinuate, bend in, wind in, curve in
intendō, -ere, -tendī, -tentum: stretch out, aim
intorqueō, -ēre, torsī, tortum: twist around, hurl
laedō, -ere, -sī, -sus: hurt, harm; offend, 2
Lāocoön m. acc. **-nta**: Laocoon, 4
lāpsus, lapsūs m.: gliding, slipping, 2
māchina, -ae f.: machine, war engine, 2
mereō, -ēre, -uī: deserve, merit, earn, 4
novus, -a, -um: new, young, strange, 3
opus, -eris n.: work, deed, project, 4
orbis, -is m.: sphere, coil, circle (of a shield)
pandō, -ere, -ī, passus: spread, 2
pavor, pavōris m.: terror, panic
puella, -ae f.: girl, 2
rōbur, ōris m.: hard wood, oak
rota, -ae f.: wheel, 2
scandō, -ere, scandī: to climb
scelerātus, -a, -um: wicked, profane, 2
scelus, sceleris n.: wickedness, crime
simulācrum, -ī n.: likeness, image; shade, ghost
stuppeus, -a, -um: made of rope
subiciō, -ere, -iēcī, -iectum: throw or place under, 2
tegō, -ere, texī, tectum: cover, protect
tremefaciō, -ere, -fēcī, -factum: cause to tremble, 4
Trītōnis, -idis: Minerva, Athena; daughter of Triton
vērō: in truth, in fact; but (abl. as adv.), 3
vinculum, -ī n.: chain, 4

225 **geminī dracōnēs**: nom. subj.
lapsū: *with...*; abl. of manner
dēlūbra ad: ad dēlūbra summa; anastrophe
226 **saevae Trītonidis**: *of savage Minerva*;; gen. sg. patronymic; in one tradition, Minerva was the daughter of Neptune and Tritonis, who was in turn the daughter of the god Triton
227 **sub pedibus**: on Minerva's statues, serpents are often placed between a shield and legs of the statue to make the base of the statue structurally sound. Vergil takes advantage of this practice by have his serpents assume the same position under the shield of Minerva
228 **cūnctīs**: *for...*; dat. of interest
229 **scelus expendisse...Lāocoönta**: *that Laocoon had paid for...*; ind. disc. with pf. act. inf.; Lāocoönta is Greek acc. subject
merentem: *deservingly*; 'deserving,' the pres. pple here is predicative and behaves as an adv.
230 **ferunt**: *they say*; 'they report'

quī...laeserit...intorserit: *who damaged...*; causal relative clause of characteristic (quī = cum is, 'since he...') with pf. subj.: translate as pf. indicative
cuspide: abl. means
231 **tergō**: *into...*; dat. of compound verb
232 **ducendum (esse)...simulācrum**: *that...must be...*; 'that...is to be led' ind. disc. with pass. periphrastic (gerundive + esse) expressing necessity; all governed by conclāmant
ōranda (esse)...nūmina: *that...must be...*; 'that...are to be prayed to...' ind. disc. with pass. periphrastic (gerundive + esse) expressing necessity or obligation
234 **moenia**: likely refers to 'defenses' in general
235 **accingunt**: *put on their belts*; i.e. prepare themselves by putting on belts
operī: *for...*; dat. of purpose
pedibus: *under...*; dat. of compound verb
236 **lapsūs rōtārum**: acc. pl. obj.; note that the motion of the horse is the same as that of the serpents (serpent motif)
237 **collō**: *on...*; dat. of compound verb
238 **circum (eam)**: *around (it)*; i.e. machina
239 **sacra**: *sacred (songs)*
manū: *with a hand*; abl. means

ōrō (1): plead, beg; pray for, entreat, 8
pēs, pedis m.: foot, 5
puer, -ī m.: boy, child, 6
sacer, -cra, -crum: sacred, holy; rite, ritual, 5

For **Passive Periphrastic constructions** in ll. 232-3, review the discussion of gerundives on pg. 41.

1. **Athena, Goddess of Victory**: Why is significant that the serpents seek refuge (a) in the arx (hilltop fortress and inner sanctum) of Troy and (b) in the temple of the Athena?

2. **Statue of Athena**: Athena is often represented in statues clothed in armor and holding the top edge of a large clipeus (circular shield) in her left hand with the bottom of the shield on the ground. Since the shield is so thin, a serpent is included along the base on the inside of the shield to provide support for the weight of the shield. How does the final resting place of the two serpents in ll 225-7 mimic the representation of Athena in statues?

3. **The Serpent Motif**: As we discussed earlier regarding Sinon, Vergil applies the imagery of serpents—particularly verbs of winding (*sinuāre*) and gliding (*lābor, lābī*)—to a range of factors, large and small, that lead to the fall of Troy. Sinon's name, for example, suggests his role of insinuating himself into the hearts of the Trojans. How do 'insinuat pavor' in 2.228-229 and 'lāpsūs rotārūm' in 2.235-6 each support this motif and contribute to the fall of Troy?

4. **The Trojans' triumphant joy vs. Aeneas' narrative in hindsight**: Throughout Aeneas' narrative of the horse being brought into the city (2.234-49), scenes of Trojan joy are juxtaposed with Aeneas' foreboding doom. Give the Latin and translation in lines 237-9 for foreshadows the impending destruction

illa subit mediaeque mināns inlābitur urbī. 240
Ō patria, Ō dīvum domus Īlium et incluta bellō 241
moenia Dardanidum! Quater ipsō in līmine portae 242
substitit atque uterō sonitum quater arma dedēre; 243
instāmus tamen immemorēs caecīque furōre 244
et mōnstrum īnfēlīx sacrātā sistimus arce. 245
Tunc etiam fātīs aperit Cassandra futūrīs 246
ōra deī iussū nōn umquam crēdita Teucrīs. 247
Nōs dēlūbra deum miserī, quibus ultimus esset 248
ille diēs, festā vēlāmus fronde per urbem. 249

Tempus erat quō prīma quiēs mortālibus aegrīs 268
incipit et dōnō dīvum grātissima serpit. 269

---

aeger, -gra, -grum: sick, weary, 3
caecus, -a, -um: blind, hidden, 3
Cassandra, -ae f.: Cassandra
Dardanidēs, -ae m.: Dardanian, Trojan, 2
dēlūbrum, -ī n.: shrine, temple
diēs, diēī m./f.: day, day(light), 4
festus, -a, -um: festive
frōns, frontis f.: forehead, 2
furor, -ōris m.: rage, fury, madness, 3
grātus, -a, -um: grateful, pleasing
Īlium, -ī n.: Ilium, Troy, 2
immemor, -oris: unmindful, forgetful of (gen) 2
inclutus, -a, -um: celebrated, famous
infēlīx, (īcis): ill-omened, unfortunate, 2
inlābor, -ī, lapsus sum: glide on, slide on
instō, -āre, -stitī: press on, threaten, 3
iussū: by order, by command
minor, -ārī, -ātus sum: threaten, tower, 2
monstrum, -ī n.: monster, 2
mortālis, -e: mortal, 4
quater: four times, 3
quiēs, quiētis f.: rest, repose, sleep
sacrō (1): to consecrate, make holy
serpō, ere, -psī: to creep
sistō, -ere, -stitī: set, make stand; stand, stop, 4
sonitus, -ī m.: sound, noise, clang, 2
substō, -āre, -stitī: to stand firm
tamen: however, nevertheless, 3
tempus, -oris n.: time; occasion, 2
ultimus, -a, -um: farthest, extreme, last
umquam: never, at no time, 2
uterus, -ī m.: belly, 2
velō (1): to veil, cover

240 **illa**: *that one*; i.e. the horse as fem. machīna
mediae...urbī: *into*...; dat. of compound verb
Ō patria, Ō dīv(ōr)um domus...moenia: voc. direct address; apostrophe (turning off to address someone not present); dīvum is gen. pl.; Ilium is an alternative name for Troy and is in apposition to domus
241 **bellō**: *in*...; abl. of respect with incluta
242 **Dardanidum**: gen. pl.
ipso in līmine: in līmine ipsō, i.e. there was a slight rise in the pavement stone as the Trojans pull the wheeled horse from the dirt outside the city over the gateway and into the city
substitit: the horse as subject
243 **(in) uterō**
dedēr(unt): syncopated 3p pf. dō, dare
244 **immemorēs caecīque**: both nom. pl.
245 **mōnstrum īnfēlīx**: neut. acc. sg.
(in) sacrātā...arce
246 **etiam**: *also*
fātīs...futūrīs: *for future*...; dat. of purpose with fut. act. pple sum
247 **ōra**: *her mouth*; the neut. plural suggests repeated action: 'repeatedly opens...'
deī iussū: *by*...; 'because of...' abl. of cause and gen. sg.; Apollo gave Cassandra the gift of prophecy but, when she would not love him in return, he brought it about that no one believed Cassandra's prophecies
crēdita: PPP with ōra
Teucrīs: *for*...; dat. of interest
248 **Nōs...miserī**: nom. pl.; the adj. foreshadows the destruction that Aeneas knows will come
dēlūbra de(ōr)um: acc. obj. of velāmus
quibus...esset: *for whom that day was the last*; causal relative of characteristic + impf. subj. sum (quibus=cum nōbīs, 'since for us...')
festā...fronde: abl. means; i.e. garlands

In the skipped passage, Sinon unlocks the horse and lets the Greeks hidden within come out. As the Trojans sleep, Hector comes to Aeneas in a dream.

268 **Tempus erat**: *it was a time…*
quō (tempore): *in which…*; abl. time when introducing a relative clause
mortālibus aegrīs: *for…*; dat. of interest

269 **donō dīv(ōr)um**: *as a…*; 'for…' dat. of purpose
grātissima: *most pleasingily*; predicative adj. as adv.; grātus has both an active meaning ('grateful') and passive meaning ('pleasant') and here carries the passive meaning

269 **serpit**: *creeps…*; note the serpent motif: the sleep and lack of cautiousness is but one more reason that the Greeks prevail over the Trojans

līmen, -inis n.: threshold, doorway, 5

Cassandra is the daughter of King Priam and Queen Hecuba of Troy. According to tradition, Apollo offered Cassandra the gift of prophecy in exchange for an opportunity to sleep with Cassandra. Once Cassandra received the gift, however, she rejected Apollo's advances. Since Apollo could not take away the gift that he had given, he added a curse so that no one who heard Cassandra's prophecies would believe or trust them.

What Happens in 2.250-267

As the Trojans sleep, the Greek fleet returns from behind the island of Tenedos, and the men disembark and gather outside the gates of Troy. Sinon opens the door to the wooden horse, and armed Greeks descend, including Ulysses, Menelaus, Epeus, the builder of the horse, and Neoptolemus, the son of Achilles. These armed men kill the night-guards and open the gates for the invading army.

The narrative picks up in 268 as the ghost of Hector visits Aeneas in his dreams.

Videor as 'Seem' [5]

The passive videor is often translated as 'seem' in English and governs a predicative nominative. Two of the five instances occur in Lesson 32. Readers can continue to translate it as a normal passive, if they wish, but will need to assume the infinitive *esse* to govern the predicative nominative:

Haec mīranda videntur (esse) → *these things are seen (to be) amazing* (1.494, p. 36)
→ *these things seem amazing*

Other uses: *vīsus est*, 'seemed,' *vidēbar*, 'I seemed,' (p. 62); *vidērī*, 'to seem,' (p. 70); *vīsa est*, 'seemed,' (p. 86)

1. **The Serpent Motif**: How do 'mediaeque minās inlābitur urbī' in 2.240 and 'quiēs…grātissima serpit' in 2.268-9 each support the view that Vergil consistently uses the imagery of a serpent to describe the various factors that contribute to the fall of Troy?

2. **Apostrophe** is the rhetorical device of turning off and addressing someone is is not present. What does Aeneas address in 2.241-2?

3. **Narrative in Hindsight**: What words in particular does Aeneas us in 242-5 to foreshadow the real purpose of the horse that was overlooked by the Trojans?

4. **Narrative in Hindsight**: How does Aeneas juxtapose Trojan joy and his own dread in 248-9?

In somnīs, ecce, ante oculōs maestissimus Hector
vīsus adesse mihī largōsque effundere flētūs,
raptātus bīgīs ut quondam, āterque cruentō
pulvere perque pedēs trāiectus lōra tumentēs.
Ei mihi, quālis erat, quantum mūtātus ab illō
Hectore quī rediit exuviās indūtus Achillī,
vel Danaum Phrygiōs iaculātus puppibus ignēs;
squālentem barbam et concrētōs sanguine crīnēs
vulneraque illa gerēns, quae circum plūrima mūrōs
accēpit patriōs. Ultrō flēns ipse vidēbar
compellāre virum et maestās exprōmere vōcēs;
"Ō lūx Dardaniae, spēs Ō fīdissima Teucrum,
quae tantae tenuēre morae? Quibus Hector ab ōrīs
expectāte venīs? Ut tē post multa tuōrum
fūnera, post variōs hominumque urbisque labōrēs
dēfessī aspicimus? Quae causa indigna serēnōs
foedāvit vultūs? Aut cūr haec vulnera cernō?"

Achillēs, -is (ī) m.: Achilles, 2
adsum, -esse, -fuī: be present, assist (*dat.*), 2
barba, -ae f.: beard
bīgae, -ārum f.: chariot drawn by a pair of horses
cernō, -ere, crēvī, crētus: discern, perceive, 3
compellō (1): address, accost, speak to, 3
concrescō, -ere, -crēvī, -crētum: clot, matt, thicken
crīnis, -is m.: locks, hair, 4
cruentus, -a, -um: bloody, cruel
cūr: why
Dardanius, -a, -um: Dardanian, Trojan, 4
dēfessus, -a, -um: wearied, exhausted, worn out, 3
ecce: behold!, 2
effundō, -ere, -fūdī, -fūsum: pour out, 3
Eī: ouch, ow; woe to + dat.! (exclamation)
expectō (1): look out for, await
exprōmō, -ere, -psī, -ptum: to bring forth, produce
exuviae, -ārum f.: skin, armor
fīdus, -a, -um: faithful, trustworthy, 3
fleō, -ēre, flēvī, flētum: weep, bewail
flētus, -ūs m.: weeping, wailing
foedō (1): defile, befoul, make ugly, 3
fūnus, fūneris n.: burial; death, 4
Hector, -oris m.: Hector, 4
homō, -inis m./f.: person, people; human, 4
iaculor, -ārī, iaculātus sum: throw, hurl, 2
indignus, -a, -um: unworthy
induō, -ere, -duī, -dūtum: put on, clothe
largus, -a, -um: copious, generous
lōrum, -ī n.: rein, leather strap, 2
maestus, -a, -um: gloomy, sad, mournful, 3
mora, -ae f: delay, hesitation
mūtō (1): to change
patrius, -a, -um: paternal, ancestral, 3
Phrygius, -a, -um: Phrygian, Trojan, 3
plūrimus, a, um: most, very many/full *superl.* multus 4
pulvis, pulveris m.: dust, dirt, 2
quantus, -a, -um: how great, much, many, 4
quondam: formerly, ever, 4
raptō (1): drag, snatch, seize
redeō, -īre, -īvī: go back, return, come back
serēnus, -a, -um: fair, serene
squāleō, -ēre: be rough, be stiff
trāiciō, -ere, -iēcī, -iectum: pierce, throw across, 2
tumō, -ere: to swell, puff up
ultrō: voluntarily, on his/her/my own, 3

270 **ante oculōs (meōs)**: This is Aeneas' dream.
vīsus (est): *seemed* + inf.; 'was seen,' pf. pass.
mihī: *before...*; dat. of compound verb adesse

271 **raptātus...āter...trāiectus**: see notes on facing page; nom. sg. modifying Hector within the ut clause of comparison
ut quondam (vīsus est): *as (he seemed)...*; ut introduces a clause of comparison, which omits the verb repeated from the main clause
raptātus bīgīs: *(after)...*; PPP and abl. means; Hector's corpse was dragged behind Achilles' chariot daily in the *Iliad* Books 22-24.
cruentō pulvere: *with...*; abl. of cause

273 **per pedēs tumentēs**: see note on facing page
trāiectus: PPP; see p. 63 for explanation
lōra: *with...;* 'in respect to...,' acc. of respect

274 **Ei mihi**: *Alas for me*; Ei is an exclamation
Quālis (Hector) erat: *what sort...!*; exclamatory sentence
Quantum mūtātus: *How much changed...!*; exclamatory sentence; inner acc. and PPP
ab īllō Hectore: i.e. from the younger Hector
275 **exuviās indūtus Achillī**: *having put on...*; + acc. obj.; PPP, reflexive in sense; <u>see note below regarding the description of Hector</u>
276 **Dana(ōr)um**: gen. pl. with puppibus
iaculātus: pf. dep. pple: 'having Xed' see explanation below
277 **barbam...gerēns**: pres. pple gerō, 'wear'
278 **quae plūrima**: *which, very many,...*; vulnera is antecedent; superlative of multus
circum mūrōs patriōs: see explanation below
279 **(ego) ipse**
flēns: pres. pple
vidēbar: *seemed* + inf.; 'I was seen,' 1s impf. pass. videō; Aeneas, of course, is dreaming
280 **vōcēs**: i.e. words;
281 **Ō lūx**: voc. direct address; i.e. Hector
Dardaniae: *of Troy*; gen. sg.
Ō spēs fīdissima: voc. direct address, superlative adj.; again referring to Hector
Teucr(ōr)um: gen. pl.
282 **Quae tantae tenuēr(unt) morae**: *what...?*; interrogative adj.; syncopated 3p pf.
ab quibus ōrīs...: *from...*; ōra, -ae f.: shore
Hector...expectāte: *Hector having been waited for*; voc. direct address and voc. of the PPP expectō (expectātus → expectāte)
283 **venīs**: 2s pres. venīo
Ut...post multa...funera ...aspicimus: *after how many...after...*; ut, 'how,' is here an interrogative adv. modifying multa
285 **Quae causa indigna...?**: *what....*; nom. sg. interrogative adj.

lux, lūcis f.: light, daylight; life, 5 **somnus, -ī m.**: sleep; dream 5

Hector's Ghost: Allusions to Homer's *Iliad*

Hector was the clear favorite of his father King Priam and the foremost fighter of the Trojans. This encounter between Hector's ghost and Aeneas in a dream alludes to several episodes in Homer's *Iliad* that are worth noting.

Danaum Phrygiōs iaculātus puppibus ignēs (276): In Book 8 of the *Iliad*, Hector leads a successful attack on all the Greek ships drawn up on the shore near Troy and almost succeeds in burning the entire fleet and leaving the Greeks destitute.

quī rediit exuviās indūtus Achillī (275): In Book 16, Hector kills the Greek Patroclus, who happened to be wearing Achilles' armor. Achilles had withdrawn from battle after a quarrel with the Greek king Agamemnon in Book 1. When Patroclus could not persuade Achilles to fight, Patroclus put on Achilles' armor as a disguise to encourage the Greeks but ended up dying in a duel with Hector. Hector strips off Achilles' armor and wears it into battle when he is killed by Achilles himself.

sī Pergama dextrā dēfendī possent, etiam hāc dēfēnsa fuissent (290-1): In Book 18, Achilles learns about Patroclus' death and vows to kill Hector. Thetis, Achilles' mother and sea goddess, warns Achilles (a) that the death of Hector will lead to the fall of Troy and (b) that Achilles will die soon after Hector dies. Thetis then has Hephaestus make Achilles divine armor to fight against Hector.

squālentem barbam...gerēns quae circum plūrima mūrōs accēpit patriōs (277-9): In Book 22 Achilles challenges Hector to a duel and kills him, as King Priam and the Trojans watch from the wall. Achilles then pierces Hector's ankles (**pedēs tumentēs**, 273) to thread a leather strap through them and drags Hector's body behind his chariot (**raptātus bīgīs**, 272) around the walls to disfigure the corpse and deny Hector a beautiful death. In Book 24 Priam recovers Hector and buries him.

Ut [11] is used 3 times with subjunctive and 8 times with the indicative. <u>When in doubt, translate as 'as.'</u>

Purpose [3] (so that)	**ut...exigat**	*so that she may...*	pp.14, 46, 100
Temporal [4] (as, when)	**ut prīmum**	*as/when first, as soon as...*	66, 82, 110, 116
Clause of Comparison [1] (as, just as)	**ut quondam**	*just as once...*	62
Parenthetical [1] (as)	**ut perhibent**	*as they report*	76
Interrogative adverb [2] (how)	**Ut multa...**	*how many...!*	62, 120

Ille nihil, nec mē quaerentem vāna morātur, 286
Sed graviter gemitūs īmō dē pectore dūcēns, 287
"Heu fuge, nāte deā, tēque hīs" ait "ēripe flammīs. 289
Hostis habet mūrōs; ruit altō ā culmine Troia. 290
Sat patriae Priamōque datum: sī Pergama dextrā 291
dēfendī possent, etiam hāc dēfēnsa fuissent. 292
Sacra suōsque tibī commendat Troia Penātēs; 293
hōs cape fātōrum comitēs, hīs moenia quaere 294
magna, pererrātō statuēs quae dēnique pontō." 295
Sīc ait et manibus vittās Vestamque potentem 296
aeternumque adytīs effert penetrālibus ignem. 297

---

adytum, ī n.: inner shrine, sanctuary
aeternus, -a, -um: eternal, everlasting, 4
commendō (1): entrust, commend
culmen, -minis n.: rooftop; peak, summit, 4
dēfendō, -ere, -nsī, -nsum: to defend, 2
dēnique: lastly, finally
efferō, -ferre, -tulī, ēlātus: raise, lift up 2
ēripiō, -ere, -uī, -reptus: rescue, snatch from, 4
habeō, -ēre, -uī, -itus: have, hold; consider, 3
hostis, -is m./f.: enemy, foe, 4
moror, -ārī, -ātus sum: delay, linger, 2
nihil: nothing, 2
Penātēs, -ium m.: Penates (household gods), 3
penetrālis, -e: inner, internal
pererrō (1): wander through or over
Pergama, -ōrum n.: citadel of Troy, 3
potēns, -entis: powerful, 4
Priamus, -ī m.: Priam, king of Troy, 4
sat (satis): enough
statuō, -ere, -uī, -ūtus: establish, build, 2
suus, -a, -um: his, her, its, their own, 2
vānus, -a, -um: empty, vain, worthless
Vesta, -ae f.: Vesta (goddess of the hearth), 2
vitta, -ae f.: ribbon, fillet, 2

286 **Ille nihil (respondet)**: i.e. Hector, ellipsis
vāna: *empty things*; 'worthless,' substantive
morātur: *linger for, delay for* + acc.
287 **dūcēns (dīcit)**: *(he) drawing...(says)*; ellipsis
289 **heu**: *hey*; interjection to call attention
nāte deā: voc. direct address and PPP of nascor with abl. of source (*from*...)
hīs...flammīs: *from*...; abl. separation
291 **sat...datum (est)**: neut. subject and 3s pf. pass.; Aeneas has fulfilled his obligations
patriae Priamōque: *to*...; dat. ind. obj.
sī...possent,...defensa fuissent: *if...were.., would have been*...; Hector indicates that he alone could have saved Troy; a mixed contrary to fact condition (sī impf. subj., plpf. subj.), possum, defendō; defensa fuissent is equiv. to plpf. pass. dēfēnsa essent but fuissent (plpf. sum) emphasizes the finality of the action: 'would (already) have been...'
dextrā (manū): *by (any)*...; abl. of mean
292 **dēfendī**: pres. pass. inf.
hāc (dextrā meā): *by this*...; abl. of means; in the *Iliad*, the fall of Troy is said to follow directly from Hector's death; Hector here suggests that he alone could have saved Troy
293 **sacra**: *sacred rites, sacraments*; neut. pl.
Penātēs: These are represented as figurines that people can carry. Every household had them to protect its own food stores, and the city possessed its own Penates to protect the city. Hector is referring to the city's Penates.
294 **hōs**: i.e. Penates
cape: sg. imperative, capiō
fātōrum comitēs: *as*...; predicative acc.
hīs: *for these*; i.e. for Penātēs; dat. of interest
quaere: sg. imperative
295 **pererrātō...pontō**: abl. abl.
quae dēnique statuēs: 2s fut., moenia is the antecedent
296 **ait**: dīcit
manibus: abl. of means
vittās: acc. obj., worn by priets and sacrifices
Vestamque...ignem: hendiadys (two terms describing the same object): translate Vestam potentem as possessive gen. after ignem
adytīs penetrālibus: *from*...; place from which

capiō, -ere, -cēpī, captus: take, seize, catch, 5
comes, -itis m/f: companion; comrade, 5
heu: alas! ah! ah me!, 7
quaerō, -ere, quaesīvī, -sītus: search for, ask, 5

Aeneas, *Piētās*, and the Traditional Epic Hero

Aeneas is not consistently heroic in Book 2. Instead, he wavers—often frantically—between fight and flight. Some scholars believe that he is making a transition in Book 2 from a traditional Homeric epic hero, who strives though deeds to achieve immortal glory, to Vergil's ideal of the Roman epic hero, who embodies *pietās*, devotion to family, community, and the gods. Notice how again and again Aeneas is urged to protect the gods and his family and yet impulsively rushes off to fight to his death:

Roman heroic ideal (*pietas*)		**Traditional epic ideal (*gloria*)**
1. Hector offers Penates in dream, urges flight (289-95)	→	Aeneas 'mindlessly' rushes to fight (298-317)
2. Panthus offers real Penates, urges flight (318-335)	→	Aeneas rushes to fight: 'Let us die' (336-437)
3. Priam's death reminds Aeneas of family (438-566)	→	Sight of Helen incites Aeneas to kill her (567-87)
4. Venus reveals gods' roles, urges flight (588-633)	→	Anchises refuses to leave, Aeneas obeys (634-78)
5. Ascanius' flame and comet urge flight (679-704)	→	Aeneas frantically returns to find Creusa (735-74)
6. Creusa's ghost urges flight, Aeneas obeys (775-94)		

It is hard to find fault with Aeneas' wavering. If Hector came to us in a dream, would we accept what he says? It is only when his divine mother reveals the gods' roles, that he chooses to leave. And, it is his father Anchises' reluctance to leave and Aeneas' dutiful decision to obey that makes Aeneas stay. Faced with imperfect understanding, Aeneas and his wavering seem reasonable in war.

Originality in Greco-Roman Art (part 3)

We do not have to accept the interpretation of Book 2 above, but it leads to attractive conclusions: (1) Vergil's hero develops over time. While literature and film often depict heroes who unrealistically do not learn and change, Vergil presents an imperfect hero who is still struggling to find the best course of action. (2) The contrast between traditional hero and Roman hero allows Vergil to make intelligible to his audience just how his ideal differs from previous epic ideals. While Vergil continues to imitate the *Odyssey* in Book 1-6 and the *Iliad* in Books 7-12 and rely on his audience's knowledge of the tradition, he hints that *pietās* will allow Aeneas not merely to rival but surpass his predecessors.

Odysseus' Impiety

When Aeneas returns to the city late in Book 2 to find his missing wife Creusa, he spots Ulysses guarding the treasure 'plundered from the burned temples' (incensīs ērepta adȳtīs, 2.762-7). The scene is brief but very important. Ulysses not only takes part in the burning of the temples but also carries away the offerings made to the gods. At the very moment that Aeneas shows increasing devotion to his family, community and gods, Ulysses is engaging in impieties against the gods.

Hector's Speech

1. What does Hector reveal to Aeneas in 2.289-90?

2. What does Hector say about Aeneas' prior obligations:'Sat patriae Priamōque datum (est)' (291)?

3. What does Hector entrust to Aeneas in line 293?

4. What, according to Hector, must Aeneas do for with these objects in 294-5?
   (N.B. This is the first revelation of Aeneas' purpose when he leaves Troy.)

5. What physical items does Hector offer to Aeneas from the temple in 296-7?

At mē tum prīmum saevus circumstetit horror.
Obstipuī; subiit cārī genitōris imāgō,
ut rēgem aequaevum crūdēlī vulnere vīdī
vītam exhālantem; subiit dēserta Creūsa
et dīrepta domus et parvī cāsus Iūlī.
Respiciō et quae sit mē circum cōpia lūstrō.
Dēseruēre omnēs dēfessī, et corpora saltū
ad terram mīsēre aut ignibus aegra dedēre.
Iamque adeō super ūnus eram, cum līmina Vestae
servantem et tacitam sēcrētā in sēde latentem
Tyndarida aspiciō; dant clāram incendia lūcem
errantī passimque oculōs per cūncta ferentī.
Illa sibi infestōs ēversa ob Pergama Teucrōs
et poenās Danaum et dēsertī coniugis īrās
praemetuēns, Troiae et patriae commūnis Erīnys,
abdiderat sēsē atque ārīs invīsa sedēbat.

---

abdō, -ere, -didī, -ditus: hide, put away, 2
adeō: to such a extent or degree, 2
aeger, -gra, -grum: sick, weary, 3
aequaevus, -a, -um: equal-lived
cārus, -a, -um: dear, 3
cāsus, -ūs m.: fortune; misfortune, chance, 4
circumstō, -āre, -stetī: stand around, beset
clārus, a, um: clear; famous, 4
commūnis, -e: common
cōpia, -ae f.: abundance, troops; opportunity, 2
Creūsa, -ae f.: Creusa, 2
dēfessus, -a, -um: wearied, exhausted, worn out, 3
dīripiō, -ere, -uī, -reptum: to ransack, snatch apart
Erīnys, -yos m.: Erinyes, Fury (avenging spirit); curse
ēvertō, -ere, -vertī: overturn, turn over, 3
exhālō (1): exhale, breathe, out
genitor, -ōris m.: begetter, father, 4
horror, -ōris m.: bristling, shuddering, dread, 2
imāgō, -inis f.: image, likeness, ghost, 3
incendium, -ī n.: fire, conflagration 2
infestus, -a, -um: hostile, aggressive
Iulus, -ī: Iulus, 3
lūstrō (1): traverse, survey, 3
mittō, -ere, mīsī, missus: send, dismiss, 4
ob: on account of, because of (*acc.*), 3
obstipēscō, -ere, obsitpuī: stand agape, 2
parvus, -a, -um: small, 3
passim: here and there, to and fro, 4
Pergama, -ôrum n.: citadel of Troy, 3
praemetuō, -ere: fear or dread beforehand
respiciō, -ere, -spexī: to look back (at), respect, 3
rēx, rēgis m.: king, 4
saltus, -ūs m.: leap up, jump, spring
sēcrētus, -a, -um: set apart, separated
sedeō, -ēre, sēdī, sessum: sit, 4
supersum, -esse: survive, be over and above
Tyndaridēs, -ae: Helen, daughter of Tyndareus, 2
Vesta, -ae f.: Vesta (goddess of the hearth), 2
vīta, -ae f.: life, soul, spirit, 4

See note on facing page

560 **subiit**: 3s pf. subeō, imāgō is subject
cārī genitōris: i.e. of Anchises, gen. sg.

561 **Obstipuī**: 1s pf., Aeneas is talking in 1s
ut…vīdī: *when I…, as I…;* temporal clause
rēgem aequaevum: i.e. Priam of equal age to Aeneas' father Anchises
crūdēlī vulnere: *by*...; abl. cause; i-stem abl. Aeneas saw Priam killed by sword on an altar

562 **exhālantem**: pres. pple modifying rēgem
subiit: 3s pf. subeō with 3p subject

563 **dīrepta**: PPP with fem. domus
parvī…Iūlī: i.e. Ascanius, Aeneas' son

564 **quae sit...cōpia**: *what troops...;* ind. question with 3s pres. subj. sum, all governed by lūstrō; Aeneas led troops to a rooftop, but while watching the death of Priam, he did not pay attention to his own men as they perished
mē circum: circum mē; anastrophe

565 **Dēseruēr(unt)**: syncopated 3p pf.
corpora (sua): *(their own) bodies*
saltū: *with…*; abl. means

566 **mīsēr(unt)**: i.e jumped off the roof; the men are on a high rooftop

ignibus: *to…*; dat. ind. obj.
(corpora) aegra dedēr(unt): syncopated 3p
567 **super…eram**: tmesis for impf. supersum
ūnus: *alone*
cum…aspiciō: *when…*; temporal clause
līmina Vestae servantem: *protecting…*; pres. pple and the next acc. modify Tyndarida
569 **Tyndarida**: Grk. acc., fem. sg.; a patronymic referring to Helen, daughter of Tyndareus
tacitam: translate adj. as an adv.
in sēde: i.e. in templō Vestae
570 **errantī…ferrentī**: *to (the one)…*; i.e. to Helen; dat. ind. obj. following dant
per: *over…*

571 **illa…praemetuēns**: *that one…*; i.e. Helen; with pres. pple praemetuō two lines below
sibi: dat. with infestōs
ēversa ob Pergama: *on account of…* PPP modifies neut. acc. pl. Pergama
572 **Dana(ōr)um**: gen. pl.
dēsertī coniugis: gen. sg., i.e. Menelaus, Grk. king of Sparta and husband of Helen, who came to Troy to recover Helen
573 **commūnis Erīnys**: *a common curse*; in apposition to illa
sēsē: reflexive, emphatic form of acc. sg. sē
574 **(in) ārīs**; abl. āra, 'altar'

dēsero, -ere, -ruī: desert, forsake, abandon, 6

What Happens in 2.298-558

After Aeneas awakes from his dream, he rushes outside, where **Panthus**, priest of Apollo, rushes to him, bringing the physical **Penates**, presumably from the Temple of Vesta, across Aeneas' threshhold (2.318-21). Aeneas rushes off to fight and eventually finds himself with his men on a rooftop near the palace of Priam, since the streets are overrun with Greeks.

From this rooftop, Aeneas looks down in the courtyards of the palace and watches as Queen **Hecuba**, King **Priam**, and their daughters-in-law find refuge at an altar. Pyrrhus, otherwise known as Neoptolemus, the son of the deceased hero Achilles, breaks down the door and chases down Polites, a son of Priam, and kills him in front of Priam and Hecuba. When Priam chastises **Pyrrhus** and claims that Achilles never showed such a lack of respect, Pyrrhus slaughters Priam on the altar—a very impious act. The scene highlights the increasing savageness of the war.

It is at this point on the facing page that Aeneas thinks about his father Anchises, son Ascanius, and wife Creusa. He turns away from the palace scene and notices that his men have abandoned the rooftop. Alone, he sets out back home when he notices Helen seeking refuge in the Temple of Vesta.

Iulus [3], Ascanius [3], and Political Propaganda

Iūlus is just an alternative name for Aeneas' son Ascanius. The Julian clan, *gēns Iūlia*, which included **Gaius Julius Caesar** and his adopted grand-nephew, the emperor **Augustus Caesar**, claimed that Iulius was their ancestor (Iūlius means 'son or descendant of Iūlus') and therefore that the family descended from Aeneas and ultimately from Venus. When Vergil uses the name Iūlus, he offers readers an opportunity to connect Aeneas directly with the emperor and his family.

Patronymics such as *Tyndarides* are common epic conventions, but this one has added significance. Before Tyndareus chose Helen's husband, all the Greek suitors swore an oath to come to her aid if she were harmed. This oath explains why the Greeks agree to fight against Troy. And so, when Aeneas uses this patronymic, he reminds readers that the oath of Tyndareus is one reason for Troy's ruin.

1. After Aeneas witnesses Priam's death, what three people come to Aeneas' mind in 2.559-63?
2. What two courses of action did his men take on the rooftop (563-4), and what does this suggest about the hopelessness of the Trojan cause?
3. **Helen's Fear**: What three groups does Helen fear in 2.571-3 as she waits in the Temple of Vesta?

Exarsēre ignēs animō; subit īra cadentem
ulciscī patriam et scelerātās sūmere poenās.
"Scīlicet haec Spartam incolumis patriāsque Mycēnās
aspiciet, partōque ībit rēgīna triumphō,
coniugiumque domumque patris nātōsque vidēbit
Īliadum turbā et Phrygiīs comitāta ministrīs?
occiderit ferrō Priamus? Troia arserit ignī?
Dardanium totiēns sūdārit sanguine lītus?
Nōn ita. namque etsī nūllum memorābile nōmen
fēmineā in poenā est, habet haec victōria laudem;
exstīnxisse nefās tamen et sūmpsisse merentēs
laudābor poenās, animumque explēsse iuvābit
ultrīcis flammae et cinerēs satiāsse meōrum."

---

cadō, cadere, cecidī: to fall, 3
cinis, cineris m.: ashes
comitō (1): accompany, attend, 2
coniugium, -ī n.: marriage, 2
Dardanius, -a, -um: Dardanian, Trojan, 4
etsī: even if, although, though, 2
exardescō, -ere, -arsī: catch fire, begin to burn up
expleō, -ēre, -plēvī, -plētum: fill (acc) up of (gen)
exstinguō, -ere, -stinxī, -stinctum: put out, 4
fēmineus, -a, -um: womanly, of a woman, 2
habeō, -ēre, -uī, -itus: have, hold; consider, 3
Īlias, -adis f.: Trojan
incolumis, -e: unscathed, safe, 2
ita: so, thus
iuvō, -āre, iūvī: be pleasing, help, 4
laudō (1): to praise
laus, laudis f.: praise, adulation, 2
memorābilis, -e: memorable, remarkable
mereō, -ēre, -uī: deserve, merit, earn, 4
minister, -trī m.: attendant, assistant
Mycēnae, -ārum f.: Mycenae
nefās n.: unrighteous(ness), sacrilege, forbidden act, 3
occidō, -ere, -cidī, -cāsum m.: fall, die, perish
pariō, -ere, peperī, partum: gain; bear, produce
patrius, -a, -um: paternal, ancestral, 3
Phrygius, -a, -um: Phrygian, Trojan, 3
Priamus, -ī m.: Priam, king of Troy, 4
satiō (1): to satisfy, sate
scelerātus, -a, -um: wicked, profane, 2
scīlicet (scīre licet): of course, evidently, clearly
Sparta, -ae f.: Sparta
sūdō (1): sweat, perspire
sūmō, -ere, sumpsī, sumptum: take, spend; exact, 3
tamen: however, nevertheless, 3
totiēns: so often, so many times
triumphus, -ī m.: triumph
turba, -ae f.: crowd, mob, 4
ulciscor, -ī, ultus sum: avenge, take vengeance
ultrix, ultrīcis (adj.): avenging
victōria, -ae f.: victory

575 **Exarsēr(unt)**: syncopated 3p pf.
(in) animō (meō)
cadentem...patriam: acc. obj.
576 **ulciscī...sūmere**: *to...and to...;* dep. and active infs. of purpose
577 **haec...incolumnis**: *this one...*; i.e. Helen
Mycēnās: *Maecenae*; home of Agamemnon and Menelaus, the Greek leaders
578 **aspiciet, ībit**: 3s fut. aspiciō, eō; Aeneas imagines Helen's life after the war
partō triumphō: abl. abs.
rēgīna: *as...*
579 **domum patris**: i.e. in Sparta, Helen's father Tyndareus ruled Sparta before Menelaus
580 **Īliadum**: fem. gen. pl, i.e. female slaves
comitāta: PPP, nom. fem. sg.
581 **occiderit... arserit... sudā(ve)rit...**: *Will...have...? Will...have...? Will...have...?*; or '(After)...has...?' 3s fut. pf. of occidō, ardeō and sūdō: questions without an interrogative indicate shock or bewilderment
ferrō: *by sword*; metonomy, abl. means
ignī: abl. means; 3rd decl. i-stem
582 **Dardarnium lītus**: neut. nom. subj.
Nōn ita: Aeneas answers his own question
583 **Etsī...**: *even if...*; or 'although...'
584 **laudem**: *its own reward, its own praise*
585 **exstīnxisse...sūmpisse...laudābor**: *I will be praised to...*; fut. pass. + complementary pf. inf.
exstīnxisse: i.e. kill
nefās: i.e. Helen; neut. acc. sg.
merentēs: pres. pple with poenās

586 **animum explē(vi)sse...utrīcis flammae**: pf. inf.+ acc. + partitive gen.; governed by iuvābit
iuvābit: *it will...*; impersonal

587 **satiā(vi)sse**: pf. inf.; i.e. appease
meōrum: *of my own (people)*

Infinitives of purpose [4] are used twice in 2.576. See pp. 42-3 for the other uses of this construction.

Questions Expressing Surprise or Indignation in 2.577-82

Questions in Latin that lack an introductory interrogative express surprise or bewilderment. The same can be true for questions in English: e.g. 'You are dropping out of school? You plan to live off of you YouTube channel?' In lines 2.577-82, a series of such questions allow Aeneas to express incredulity and anger that Helen will live a full life, while the Trojans suffer certain ruin. Translate the questions (a) as regular sentences with a question mark at the end or (2) as yes/no questions introduced by -ne.

Future Perfect [3] in 2.581-2

Future Perfect, found only 3 times in this commentary, is used in Latin to express actions completed (*perfectum*) in the future before another action in the future. Most often, future perfect is translated into English as (a) a present with future sense or (b) a present perfect ('has/have Xed'):

Future more vivid	sī hoc **audīveris**, sciēs.	*If **you hear** this, you will know.*
Temporal clause	Cum hoc **audīveris**, sciēs	*When **you have heard** this, you will know.*

In 2.577-80 Aeneas uses the future tense to describe the good life that Helen will enjoy after the war and the future perfect (2.581-2) to describe actions that will be completed (perfectum) before Helen will return to the good life. Translate the three fut. pf. verbs simply with 'will have Xed' or as present perfect with '(After)...has Xed.'

occiderit?	→	*Will...have fallen...?*	*(After)...has fallen?*
arserit?	→	*Will...have burned...?*	*(After)...has burned?*
sūdā(ve)rit?	→	*Will...have sweated...?*	*(After)...has sweated?*

Unrestrained Anger as Fire

Aeneas uses the words *ignēs* (575) and *flammae* (587) to describe the changes to his *animus* as he becomes enraged. For some in the ancient world, the physiological changes that we associate with anger, such as increased heart rate, irregular breathing, and sweating (e.g. My blood is boiling!) are caused by the primary element of fire in the body. The fire is the cause of anger (or is anger itself), and these bodily changes are evidence of fire. Note the juxtaposition of fire and anger in 2.575:

Exarsēre ignēs animō; subit īra cadentem — *Fires began to burn in my soul; anger comes up*

These are not two separate activities: the *ignēs* and *īra* are two sides of the same coin in the body.

1. **Aeneas and unrestrained emotion**: What in brief is Aeneas' state of mind in 2.577-82 as he offers a series of rhetorical questions in the future and future perfect without the usual enclitic -ne introducing the yes/no questions?
2. What role does Aeneas predict the surviving Trojans will serve in 2.580?
3. **Aeneas' test of piety**: What does Aeneas plan to do in 2.583-87—in the Temple of Vesta, no less? (Note that Aeneas was given the responsibility of protecting Vesta by Hector in a dream.)
4. Vergil often includes language in the introduction of a speech that is reinforced in the speech itself. The repetition is intended to draw the audience's attention to important details in the narrative. In what two ways do Aeneas' words in 2.585-7 repeat what Vergil said above in 2.575-6?

Tālia iactābam et furiātā mente ferēbar,
cum mihi sē, nōn ante oculīs tam clāra, videndam
obtulit et pūrā per noctem in lūce refulsit
alma parēns, confessa deam quālisque vidērī
caelicolīs et quanta solet, dextrāque prehēnsum
continuit roseōque haec insuper addidit ōre:
"Nāte, quis indomitās tantus dolor excitat īrās?
Quid furis aut quōnam nostrī tibi cūra recessit?
Nōn prius aspiciēs ubi fessum aetāte parentem
līqueris Anchīsēn, superet coniūnxne Creūsa
Ascaniusque puer? Quōs omnēs undique Grajae
circum errant aciēs et, nī mea cūra resistat,
iam flammae tulerint inimīcus et hauserit ensis.

---

aciēs, -ēī f.: edge, battle line 2
addō, -ere, -didī, -ditum: to bring to, add, 4
aetās, aetātis f.: age, time
almus, -a, -um: nourishing, kind
Ascānius, -ī m.: Ascanius, 3
caelicolus, -a, -um: heaven-dwelling
clārus, a, um: clear; famous, 4
confiteor, -ērī, -fessus sum: acknowledge, confess
contineō, -ēre, -nuī: hold back, keep together
Creūsa, -ae f.: Creusa, 2
ensis, -is m.: sword, 3
excitō (1): rouse up, raise, 2
fessus, -a, -um: tired, weary, worn, 3
furiō, -āre,: to make furious, drive mad
Graius, -a, -um: Greek, 2
hauriō, haurīre, hausī: take in, drain, exhaust, 3
indomitus, -a, -um: untamed, uncontrollable, wild
inimīcus, -a, -um: unfriendly, 4
insuper: on top; in addition, 2
linquō, -ere, līquī, lictus: leave, desert, 3
mēns, mentis f.: mind, intent, purpose, 4
nī, nisī: if not, unless 2
offerō, -ferre, obtulī, oblātum: offer, show
prehendō, -ere, -dī, -ēnsus: grasp, catch
pūrus, -a, -um: pure, clean
quantus, -a, -um: how great, much, many, 4
quōnam: to where then?
recēdō, -ere, -cessī: go back, withdraw, recede, 2
refulgeō, -ēre, -fulsī: flash back, shine
resistō, -ere, -stitī: stand still, stop; oppose (dat)
roseus, -a, -um: rosy, pink
soleō, -ēre, solitus sum: be accustomed
superō (1): surpass, overcome, 4
tam: so, so much, so very, such, 4
undīque: from all sides

588 **tālia**: *such things*; marks the end of soliloquy
iactābam: *I was pondering*; 'I was tossing around (in my mind),' impf. act. iactō
furiātā mente: abl. means or absolute
ferēbar: 1s impf. pass.; the emotion rather than Aeneas is in control
589 **cum...sē...obtulit...videndam**: *when...*; pf. offerō governs a double acc. sē and videndam (obj., pred.); alma parēns (Venus) is subject
mihi: *to...*; dat. ind. obj. of obtulit
nōn...tam clāra: modifies alma parēns
oculīs (meīs): *to...*; dat. of reference; ante is an adverb
videndam: *visible*; 'worthy/going to be seen' gerundive (fut. pass. pple) and acc. pred.
590 **confessa**: pf. dep. participle: translate as 'having Xed'
591 **(sē) deam (esse)**: *that (she was)...*; ind. disc., deam is predicative acc., add a linking verb
quālisque et quanta caelicolīs vidērī solet: *both what sort and how large she was accustomed to seem to the heaven-dwelling (gods)*; relative with deam as antecedent; dat. of reference and pass. inf. videō, which is often translated as 'seem' or 'appear'
592 **(mē) prehēnsum**: *(me)...*; add mē as acc. obj.; as often, Latin uses a PPP and finite verb where English prefers two finite verbs: 'grabbed and held'
roseō...ōre: *from...*; abl. means or source
593 **haec (verba)**
594 **Nāte**: *son*; voc. dir. address, PPP nascor
quis tantus dolor: *what...?*; interrogative adj. note that Aeneas' emotions are 'indomitās'

595 **Quid**: *Why...?*
quō-nam: *to where, then...?*
nostrī: *for me*; objective gen. of nōs with cūra; Venus uses 1p to describe herself (the royal we, see p. 99)
tibi: *your*; dat. of possession
596 **prius**: comparative adv. prīmus, 'early'
aspiciēs: 2s fut.
ubi...līqueris: *where...*; ind. question with 2s pf. subj. linquō (translate as pf.), governed by aspiciēs
(et) superet coniūnxne: *(and) whether...*; ind. question (-ne introduces the question) with 3s pres. subj. but 3p subject

598 **quōs...circum**: *around whom*; anastrophe; antecedents: Anchises, Creusa, and Ascanius
nī...resistat, tulerint...hauserit: *if my care should not stop (them), by now the flames would have carried (them) off and an unfriendly sword would have consumed (their blood)*; not contrary to fact but a fut. less vivid should-would condition (sī pres. subj., pf. subj.) with pf. subj. of ferō and hauriō; the pf. subj. ('would have') is used in place of the present subj. ('would') to emphasize the completion and certainty of the action. Venus is talking about the future, not the past.

Anchīsēs, -ae, acc. ēn m.: Anchises, 8

Furor vs. Pietās

Furor is an unrestrained emotion and opposing force to *pietās*. And just as we saw in Book 1 that *pietās* leads to order—in the individual, in society, and in nature—so *furor* is associated with disorder. So far, we have seen *furor* and its cognates used to describe (a) Juno, (b) the winds, (c) Ajax, (d) the storm at sea, (e) a riotous crowd, and finally (f) the Trojans conveying the horse into their walls:

Ajax in Athena's temple	*ob...**furiās** Aiācis* , 'because of...the madness of Ajax, 1.41
the winds	*loca fēta **furentibus** Austrīs*, 'places pregnant with furious winds' 1.51
the riotious crowd	***furor** arma ministrat*, 'Fury supplies its own weapons.' 1.150
the storm	***furit** aestus harēnis*, 'the tide rages with the sands, 1.107
the unaware Trojans	*immemorēs caecīque **furōre***, 'unmindful and blind with fury' 2.244
Juno, inciting the Greeks	*Iūnō...**furēns***, 'Juno, raging...' 2.612

Both Vergil and Venus use the same word on the facing page to describe Aeneas' state of mind as he approaches Helen: (a) *furiātā mente ferēbar* in 2.588 and (b) *Quid furis?* in 2.595. And so, the central question in this passage is the following:

> Will Aeneas submit to *furor* and commit an impiety by killing Helen in the temple or will he restrain his emotion and preserve the ideal of *pietās*?

Hector commended not only the Penates but also the eternal fire of Vesta to Aeneas' protection. If Aeneas does not restrain his *furor*, he risks dishonoring the very god that he was entrusted to protect.

Furor vs. Pietas

1. How do the verb form and type of ablative in the clause 'furiātā mente ferēbar' (588) show that Aeneas is not in control of his emotions?

2. What specifically does Venus say about Aeneas' emotional state in 594-5? (What does the word 'indomitās' say about Aeneas' self-control and self-restraint?)

3. In response to these emotions, Venus appeals to Aeneas' *pietās*. What four (4) family members does Venus refer to in lines 595-8?

4. What would happen to them if Venus should to remove her protection in 598-600?

nōn tibi Tyndaridis faciēs invīsa Lacaenae
culpātusve Paris, dīvum inclēmentia, dīvum
hās ēvertit opēs sternitque ā culmine Troiam.
Aspice (namque omnem, quae nunc obducta tuentī
mortālēs hebetat vīsūs tibi et ūmida circum
cālīgat, nūbem ēripiam; tū nē qua parentis
iussa timē neu praeceptīs pārēre recūsā):
hīc, ubi disiectās mōlēs āvulsaque saxīs
saxa vidēs, mixtōque undantem pulvere fūmum,
Neptūnus mūrōs magnōque ēmōta tridentī
fundāmenta quatit tōtamque ā sedibus urbem
ēruit. Hīc Iūnō Scaeās saevissima portās
prīma tenet sociumque furēns ā nāvibus agmen
ferrō accīncta vocat.

---

accingō, -ere, -cinxī, cinctum: equip, put on a belt, 2
āvellō, -ere, -vellī, -vulsum: tear apart or away
cālīgō (1): to cover with dark mist; be misty
culmen, -minis n.: rooftop; peak, summit, 4
culpō (1): blame
disiciō, -ere, -iēcī, -iectum: scatter, throw apart, 4
ēmoveō, -ēre, -mōvī: move out, remove
ēripiō, -ere, -uī, -reptus: rescue, snatch from, 4
ēruō, -ere, -uī, -utus: overwhelm, overturn
ēvertō, -ere, -vertī: overturn, turn over, 3
faciēs, -ēī f.: face, countenance; appearance
fūmus, -ī m.: smoke, vapor
fundāmentum, -î n.: foundation, 3
hebetō (1): to make dull, blunt
inclēmentia -ae f.: harshness, lack of mercy,
Lacaena, -ae f.: Spartan woman
mortālis, -e: mortal, 4
Neptūnus, -ī m.: Neptune, 3
neu (nēve = vel nē): nor, or lest, or don't
obdūcō, -ere, -duxī, -ductum: draw over, cover
ops, opis f.: resources, power, wealth, 3
pāreō, -ēre, paruī: obey, 3
Paris, -idis m.: Paris, 3
praecipiō, -ere, -cēpī, -ceptum: instruct, admonish
pulvis, pulveris m.: dust, dirt, 2
quatiō, -īre, quassī: to shake, brandish
recūsō (1): refuse, object to, protest, against
Scaeus, -a, -um: Scaean (name of the set of gates)
sternō, -ere, strāvī, strātum: to lay (low), layer, 4
timeō, -ēre, timuī: be afraid, fear 2
tridēns, -ntis m.: trident, 3
tueor, tuērī, tutus(tuitus) sum: look on, watch, 3
Tyndaridēs, -ae: Helen, daughter of Tyndareus, 2
ūmidus, -a, -um: wet, moist, damp
undō (1): billow, undulate, wave, surge,
vīsus, -ūs m.: vision, sight, 2

601 **nōn faciēs...-ve Paris...(sed) inclēmentia... ēvertit**: *not the appearance...or Paris but the harshness...*; ellipsis; all three are subjects of 3s ēvertit
tibi: *to you*; dat. of reference or ethical dat. equiv. in sense to 'you know' or 'you should know'
Tyndaridis Lacaenae: *of the Spartan woman, daughter of Tyndareus*; gen. sg. in apposition
602 **dīv(ōr)um...dīv(ōr)um**: deōrum...deōrum; gen. pl. repeated for emphasis
603 **hās opēs**: *this power, these resources*
604 **Aspice**: sg. imperative
omnem...nūbem: obj. of ēripiam, 1s fut.
quae...hebetat...et calīgat: *which...*; relative: the antecedent is fem. sg. nūbem
obducta: PPP modifying quae, i.e. the cloud
tuentī...tibi: *for you...*; dat. of interest and pres. pple tueor
606 **ēripiam**: 1s fut.
nē...timē: *Don't...*; neg. imperative
qua...iussa: *any orders...*; quis is indef. after sī, nisi, num, and nē; 'things ordered'
neu...recūsā: *or don't...*; neu = nē-ve; neg. imperative
praeceptīs: *instructions*; 'things instructed, substantive from the PPP, dat. obj. of pārēre
Venus reveals the gods hidden from human vision
608 **hīc**: *here*; Venus points as she talks
disiectās, āvulsa: PPP
saxīs: *from...*; abl. pl. of separation
609 **mixtō...pulvere**: abl. abs., PPP misceō

undantem fūmum: pres. pple; obj. of vīdēs
610 **magnō...tridentī**: abl. means, i-stem 3rd decl.
ēmōtā: *dislodged*; PPP
611 **ā sēdibus**: i.e. foundations
612 **Scaeās portās**: *Scaean gates*; famous set of gates in the city walls of Troy
613 **prīma**: *as a leader*; 'foremost,' the adv. prīmum means 'first in time'
tenet: i.e takes position on, takes possession of
socium: *allied*; modifies agmen; i.e. Greek
614 **ferrō**: *by sword*; metonomy
accincta: *equipped*; 'belted'
vocat: i.e. summons; Juno calls the Greeks from their ships to enter through the gates

Helen: Innocent Victim or Complicit Adulterer?

The debate over whether Helen is an innocent victim of a kidnapping or a willing adulteress is as old as the epics themselves. Perhaps the most clever presentation of this dispute is found in Book 4 of the *Odyssey*, when Odysseus' son Telemachus comes to Sparta almost ten years after the war and visits King Menelaus and Queen Helen, who had reunited after the war and returned to Sparta.

Menelaus and Helen present themselves to Telemachus as the perfect couple and never give any indication of past marital strife. When Telemachus, who has no memory of Odysseus, asks about his father, Helen recalls how she alone recognized Odysseus walking in disguise as a beggar in the streets of Troy. After she swore an oath not to reveal him, he divulged the plans of the Greeks discretely to her and then killed many Trojans before he returned to the Greek camp. (4.240-65). After Helen finishes her story, Menelaus responds by stating that he remembers a different account and relates how Odysseus, Menelaus, and other Greeks hid quietly in the wooden horse as Helen approached the structure, assumed the voices of various Greek wives, and called out to the Greek men in the hopes of persuading them to reply to their wives' voices and reveal their hiding places. Odysseus showed great restraint, Menelaus adds, and was able to keep the men disciplined and avoid detection (4.266-90).

Ostensibly, both Helen and Menelaus present Telemachus with flattering portrayals of Odysseus during the war, but perceptive readers will notice that each story depicts Helen in a very different light. While Helen's story suggests that she was loyal to the Greek cause during the war and hopeful that the Greeks would succeed, Menelaus' story indicates that even on the night before the fall of Troy Helen was willing to betray the Greeks for the Trojans.

While both Menelaus and Helen continued to play the part of the perfect couple for the duration of Telemachus' visit, their accounts of Odysseus reveal that even ten years after the end of the war questions about Helen's role in the war and loyalty to the Greeks and Trojans remained unresolved.

1. After appealing to Aeneas' devotion to his family, what does Venus say is the true cause of the overthrow of Troy in 2.601-3?

2. When Venus reveals the role of the gods in the overthrow of the city, she does not say that the gods are invisibile. Why, according to Venus, can the gods not be seen by mortals in 2.604-6?

3. Who is the god in 608-11 and what is he doing?

4. Where is Juno standing in 2.612-614 and what is she doing?

Iam summās arcēs Trītōnia, respice, Pallas
insēdit limbō effulgēns et Gorgone saevā.
Ipse pater Danaīs animōs vīrēsque secundās
sufficit, ipse deōs in Dardana suscitat arma.
Ēripe, nāte, fugam fīnemque impōne labōrī.
Nūsquam aberō et tūtum patriō tē līmine sistam."

Intereā magnō miscērī murmure caelum
incipit, insequitur commixtā grandine nimbus,
et Tyriī comitēs passim et Troiāna iuventūs
Dardaniusque nepōs Veneris dīversa per agrōs
tēcta metū petiēre; ruunt dē montibus amnēs.
Spēluncam Dīdō dux et Troiānus eandem
dēveniunt. Prīma et Tellūs et prōnuba Iūnō
dant signum; fulsēre ignēs et cōnscius aethēr
cōnūbiīs, summōque ululārunt vertice nymphae.

---

absum, -esse, āfuī: be absent, 2
aether, -eris m.: aether, (upper) sky, 3
ager, agrī m.: field, land; farm
amnis, -is m: stream; river, 2
commisceō, -ēre, -cuī, -mixtum: mix up, mix together
conscius, -ī m.: participant, witness
cōnūbium, -iī n.: marriage, wedlock, 4
Dardanius, -a, -um: Dardanian, Trojan, 4
Dardanus, -a, -um: Trojan, 2
dēveniō, -īre, -vēnī, -ventus: arrive at, come to
dīversus, -a, -um: in different directions, apart, 2
dux, ducis m./f.: leader, guide, 2
effulgeō, -ēre, -lsī: shine out, gleam
ēripiō, -ere, -uī, -reptus: rescue, snatch from, 4
fulgeō, -ēre, -fulsī: flash, shine, 2
Gorgō, -onis f.: Gorgon
grando, -dinis f.: hail
insequor, -sequī, -secūtus sum: follow, ensue, 3
insideō, -ēre, -sēdī, sessum: sit on
iuventūs, -ūtis f.: youth, young man
limbus, -ī m.: border, hem, fringe
murmur, -uris n.: murmur, rumble, 4
nepōs, nepōtis m.: grandson, decendent, 3
nimbus, -ī m.: (storm) cloud, rain/dark cloud 3
nūsquam: nowhere
nympha, -ae f.: nymph, 4
Pallas, -adis f.: Pallas (Minerva), 2
passim: here and there, to and fro, 4
patrius, -a, -um: paternal, ancestral, 3
prōnuba, -ae f.: bridesmaid, attending the bride
respiciō, -ere, -spexī: to look back (at), respect, 3
secundus, -a, -um: following; favorable, 3
signum -ī, n.: signal, gesture
sistō, -ere, -stitī: set, make stand; stand, stop, 4
spēlunca, -ae f.: cave, 2
sufficiō, -ere, -fēcī, -fectum: fill, imbue; supply, 2
suscitō (1): stir up, rouse, excite
Trītōnius, -a, -um: Tritonian, child of Triton
tūtus, -a, -um: safe, secure, 4
ululō (1): to howl, ululate
Venus, -eris f.: Venus

615 **Trītōnia**: *Tritonian one*; i.e. Minerva, child of Triton; patronymic, see note on 2.226
respice: sg. imperative
limbō...et Gorgone saevā: *with..*; abl. means; Athena wore an aegis, a goat-skin mantle over her shoulders with a border made of serpents and the head of the Gorgon Medusa. See p, 75.
617 **ipse pater**: i.e. Jupiter
Danaīs: *to the Greeks*; dat. ind. obj.
animōs: *courage*; acc. pl.
vīrēs: *strength*; fem. acc. pl. vīs
618 **(et) ipse**: *(and) he himself...*; asyndeton
in Dardana arma: *against...*
619 **Ēripe, impone**: sg. imperatives
nāte: *son*; voc. dir. address; nātus, PPP nāscor
labōrī: *on...*; dat. of compound verb
620 **aberō**: 1s fut. absum
sistam: 1s fut. + double acc. (obj. and pred.)
(in) patriō...līmine: *on...*

A storm drives Dido and Aeneas to the same cave

160 **magnō...murmure**: abl. of manner; alliteration and onomatopoeia

miscērī: complementary pass. inf. of incipit
161 **(et) insequitur**: pres. dep.: translate as active
commixtā grandine: abl. abs.
163 **Dardaniusque nepōs Veneris**: i.e. Ascanius
tēcta: *shelters*; synecdoche; perhaps man-made and natural, such as caves, tree covers
164 **metū**: *because of...*; 'out of...' abl. of cause
petiēr(unt): syncopated 3p pf.
165 **eandem**: acc. sg. īdem modifying spēluncam
166 **Prīma Tellūs**: *First Earth*; i.e. primeval earth
fulsēr(unt): syncopated 3p pf. fulgeō
ignēs: i.e. lightning
cōnscius (erat): nom. pred., supply verb
168 **conūbiīs**: *for...*; dat. of purpose or dat. of special adj.
ululā(vē)runt: syncopated 3p pf.
summō vertice: *from...*; abl. of place where or place from which; i.e. hilltops

The Aegis of Athena in 2.616-7

Athena wears around her neck and draped over her shoulders, chest, and back a goatskin (*aegis*) covering—a circular piece of goat hide with a hole in the center for the head. This goatskin has a fringed border (*limbus*) of living snakes, and, even stranger, the decapitated head of Medusa (one of three Gorgon sisters) is attached and displayed in front. Surprisingly, Athena never complains about wearing a decapitated head all day long. It is actually Jupiter's *aegis*, but Athena wears it.

Athena is the goddess of victory in war. When she shakes the *aegis*, she instills fear in the enemy. The head of Medusa is believed to be *apotropaic*, i.e. something that turns (Grk. *tropos*) away (Grk. *apo*) evil, and therefore effective in turning away the attack of an enemy.

1. Translate and explain the significance of 'limbō effulgēns et Gorgone saevā' (616).
2. Who is "ipse pater' and what does he provide to the Greeks in 2.617-8?
3. Where does Venus direct Aeneas to flee in 2.619-20?

What Happened at the end of Book 2

Readers are encouraged to review p. 65. After Aeneas leaves Venus and flees to his father Anchises' house, he is joined by his son Ascanius, his wife Creusa, and the Penates. When Aeneas urges them to flee, the aged Anchises refuses, and Aeneas obeys and plans to stay. Then, Anchises witnesses two omens: (1) Ascanius' head catches fire and is exstinguished with no harm to Ascanius, and (2) a comet appears in the sky. These omens convince Anchises to depart, and Aeneas flees, carrying Anchises, who holds the Penates, over his shoulder and leading Ascanius by the hand. Creusa trails behind and is lost before they find refuge outside the city. When Aeneas returns to look for her, she appears as a ghost, tells him that she is already dead, and urges him to leave and take care of their son.

Book 3

Aeneas now proceeds to tell Dido and the banqueters an account of the seven years that he and the Trojans wandered the eastern Mediterraean, where he frequently settled in one place only to receive a omen that he must keep moving. Eventually, the destination of Italy is revealed by the gods. It is worth noting that Dido is told repeatedly that Aeneas believes that he is on a divine mission to Italy.

Book 4

After the banquet ends, Dido reveals to her sister Anna that she is falling in love with Aeneas. When Anna advises Dido to seek the gods' approval, Dido renews animal sacrifices all day long—evidence that the gods do not give her the approval that she seeks. When Juno notices that Dido is distraught with love, she proposes to Venus an alliance of marriage and peace between Dido and Aeneas. Venus agrees—as long as Juno seeks Jupiter's approval—but Juno does not seek him out. Instead, while the Trojans and Carthaginians participate in a hunt, Juno sends a storm and sets her plan into motion.

Ille diēs prīmus lētī prīmusque malōrum
causa fuit; neque enim speciē fāmāve movētur
nec iam furtīvum Dīdō meditātur amōrem:
coniugium vocat, hōc praetexit nōmine culpam.
  Extemplō Libyae magnās it Fāma per urbēs,
Fāma, malum quā nōn aliud vēlōcius ūllum:
mōbilitāte viget vīrēsque adquīrit eundō,
parva metū prīmō, mox sēsē attollit in aurās
ingrediturque solō et caput inter nūbila condit.
Illam Terra parēns īrā inrītāta deōrum
extrēmum, ut perhibent, Coeō Enceladōque sorōrem
prōgenuit pedibus celerem et pernīcibus ālīs,
monstrum horrendum, ingēns, cui quot sunt corpore plūmae,
tot vigilēs oculī subter (mīrabile dictū),
tot linguae, totidem ōra sonant, tot subrigit aurēs.

---

adquīrō, -ere, -quīsīvī, -quīsītum: to acquire
āla, -ae f.: wing
attollō, -tolle, attulī, allātum: to raise, lift up, 3
auris, -is: **f.**: ear, 3
Coeus, -ī m.: Coeus, Titan father of Latona
condō, -ere, condidī, -ditum: found; hide, 4
coniugium, -ī n.: marriage, 2
culpa, -ae m: blame, fault; cause
diēs, diēī m./f.: day, day(light), 4
Enceladus, -ī m.: Enceladus
enim: for, indeed, 4
extemplō: immediately, forthwith, 2
furtīvus, -a, -um: hidden, secret, concealed
horrendus, -a, -um: horrible, to be trembled at, 4
ingredior, -ī, -gressus sum: step in, enter; begin, 3
inrītō (1): incite, stir up
lētum, -ī n.: death, destruction
lingua, ae f.: tongue, language, 2
malus, -a, -um: bad, wicked, 3
meditor, -ārī, meditātus sum: ponder, consider, reflect
mīrābilis, -e: wonderful, marvelous, 2
mōbilitās, -tātis f.: mobility
monstrum, -ī n.: monster, 2
mox: soon
neque: nor, and not;: neither...nor, 4
nūbilus, ī (pl. nūbila): cloud, rain-cloud
parvus, -a, -um: small, 3
perhibeō, -ēre, -uī: assert, say; hold out, bring forward
pernix, -īcis: nimble, swift, quick
plūma, -ae f.: feather
praetegō, -ere, -xī, -ctum: to cover over
prōgignō, -ere, -genuī: bring forth
quot: as many as, how many
solum, -ī n.: soil; ground, 3
sonō (1): resound, roar, 2
species, -ēi f.: sight, appearance, aspect
subrigō, -ere, -rēxī: to raise, lift up
subter: beneath, below
totidem: just so many, just as many
vēlox, vēlocis: swift, rapid, fast
vigeō, -ēre: to grow vigorous, thrive, flourish
vigil, -vigilis: watchful; *subj.* watchman, 2

168 **ille diēs (fuit) ~~prīmus~~ prīma (causa) lētī et ~~prīmus~~ prīma causa malōrum fuit**: prīmus should logically agree with fem. causa but is attracted into the masc. by masc. diēs: translate as prīma causa (predicative nom.) **malōrum**: *of evils*, *of troubles*; substantive
170 **neque enim**: *for...not...*; or 'indeed not' **fāmā**: *reputation*
171 **meditātur**: pres. dep. governing a double acc. (obj. and pred.)
172 **vocat**: *calls it (y)*; governs a double acc.; 'it' refers to 'amōrem' above **(et) hōc...nōmine**: *and...*; asyndeton; abl. of means: this comment is Vergil's own opinion
173 **Fāma**: *Rumor*; personification; Rumor is personified as a flying monster.
174 **Quā nōn ūllum aliud malum (est) velōcius**: *than which not any other evil is faster*; ellipsis; the relative pronoun is an abl. of comparison; neut. malum, 'evil,' is a substantive; velōcius is a neut. nom. sg. comparative of velōx
175 **vīrēs**: *strength*; acc. pl. vīs

eundō: abl. means, gerund (-ing) for eō, īre
176 **parva (est)**: *(it is)...*
metū: *because of...*; abl. of cause
prīmō...mōx: *at first...(but) soon*; abl. as adv.
177 **ingreditur**: pres. dep.
solō: *on...*; dat. of compound or abl. place where, solum, -ī n.
178 **Illam**: *that one*; i.e. Fāma; lines 178-80 explain the mythological origins of Fama
Terra parēns...prōgenuit
extrēmum...sorōrem: in apposition to illam
ut perhibent: *as they say*; i.e. as people say
Coeō Enceladōque: *to...*; dat. of interest
pedibus...et pernīcibus ālīs: *in...*; abl. of respect
celerem: modifies illam
181 **monstrum**: in apposition to illam in l. 178
cui...sunt: *who has...*; 'to whom are...' dat. of possession
quot...tot...tot...totidem: *as many...so many ...so many...just as many...*; demonstrative tot and relative quot are correlatives; the monster has as many as the people who spread rumors
181 **(in) corpore**
182 **mīrabile**: neut. sg. modifying the entire passage
dictū: *to speak of*; a supine; in the abl. a supine behaves as an abl. of respect: 'in respect to speaking'

Traditional Wedding Procession

A traditional Roman wedding procession (*deductio*) began after a short ceremony in the house of the bride and the lighting of the wedding torch (*spina alba*, 'white thorn'). The bride was pulled from the embrace of her mother and, while veiled, escorted by three boys, one of whom carried the torch, from her house to the house of the groom. Along the way, participants would sing traditional bridal songs—some invoking the god Hymen Hymenaeus, others quite risqué—and tell jokes. When the bride arrived, she would be lifted over the threshold and entered the house of the groom. The bride and groom would then consummate their relationship as the processsion sang songs outside the home.

One popular explanation for this procession is the belief that the bride was moving from the protection of her family's household gods to those of her husband, and the procession itself occurred at a vulnerable time when the bride was protected by neither set of gods. Once she is separated from her mother's embrace, the veil, escort, torch, and songs served as protection from curses and physical harm until she was carried over the threshold and accepted by the groom's gods.

The marriage torch (*taeda*) held the symbolic signficance similar to wedding rings today.

Aeneas and Dido in the Cave

1. How could each aspect of the narrative in 4.165-8 correspond to a traditional wedding procession?
   a. Spēluncam Dīdō dux et Troiānus eandem dēveniunt.
   b. Prīma et Tellūs et prōnuba Iūnō signum dant
   c. fulsēre ignēs
   d. cōnscius aethēr (est) cōnūbiīs
   e. The *nymphae ululārunt* likely corresponds to songs sung by processioners as the marriage is consummated. Readers can therefore assume that Aeneas and Dido were intimate in the cave.
2. What two things in 4.170 no longer motivate Dido?
3. What does Dido call her love in 172? What does Vergil say that she is covering up with that word?

Fama Personified

4. Explain how the description of the monster Fama in 174-7 corresponds to how rumors are spread.
5. Explain once again how the description of Fama in 181-183 corresponds to how rumors are spread.

Nocte volat caelī mediō terraeque per umbram
strīdēns, nec dulcī dēclīnat lūmina somnō;
lūce sedet custōs aut summī culmine tectī
turribus aut altīs, et magnās territat urbēs,
tam fictī prāvīque tenāx quam nuntia vērī.
Haec tum multiplicī populōs sermōne replēbat
gaudēns, et pariter facta atque infecta canēbat:
vēnisse Aenēān Troiānō sanguine crētum,
cui sē pulchra virō dignētur iungere Dīdō;
nunc hiemem inter sē luxū, quam longa, fovēre
rēgnōrum immemorēs turpīque cupīdine captōs.
Haec passim dea foeda virum diffundit in ōra.
Prōtinus ad rēgem cursūs dētorquet Iarbān
incenditque animum dictīs atque aggerat īrās.

---

aggerō (1).: to heap up, pile up
canō, -ere, cecinī, cantus: sing (about), 3
crescō, -ere, -crēvī, crētum: grow, arise, spring forth
culmen, -minis n.: rooftop; peak, summit, 4
cupīdō, -dinis f.: desire, longing
custōs, -ōdis m. (f.): guard, guardian, 4
dēclīnō (1): turn away, bend aside
dētorqueō, -ēre, -rsī, -rtus: turn off or from, twist
dictum, -ī n.: word, speech, 4
diffundō, -ere, -fūdī, -fūsum: pour or spread out
dignor, -āre, -ātus: deem worthy
fingō, -ere, finxī, fictum: make up, imagine, 3
foedus, -a, -um: foul, horrible, abominable
foveō, -ēre, fōvī, fōtus: nuture, foster; caress, 4
gaudeō, gaudēre, gāvīsus sum: enjoy, rejoice, 2
hiems, hiemis f.: winter, storm, 3
Iarbās, -ae, m.: Iarbas, 2
immemor, -oris: unmindful, forgetful of (gen) 2
incendō, -ere, -ī, -ēnsus: kindle, burn, 4
infectus, -a, -um: not done
iungō, -ere, iunxī, -iunctum: to join, 3
luxus, -ūs m.: luxury, extravagance
multiplex, multiplicis: multiple
nuntia, -ae f.: messenger
pariter: equally, on equal terms, 3
passim: here and there, to and fro, 4
prāvus, -a, -um: deformed, irregular, crooked
prōtinus: *adv.* immediately, continuously, further on
repleō, -ēre: fill up, fill again
rēx, rēgis m.: king, 4
sedeō, -ēre, sēdī, sessum: sit, 4
sermo, -mōnis m.: conversation, discourse, 3
strīd(e)ō, -ēre, -dī: rustle, whir, hiss, screech, creak, 3
tam: so, such, 4
tenāx, tenācis: tenacious, steadfast, persistent
territō (1): to frighten, keep terrifying
turpis, -e: ugly, shameful
turris, turris f.: tower
vērus, -a, -um: true, real, 2
volō (1): to fly, 3

184 **nocte**: *at...*; abl. time when
caelī (in) mediō terraeque
strīdēns: *screeching*; as a bird; pres. pple; the same verb is used to describe whistling wind (I.102) and hissing air leaving Dido's lungs (IV.689)
lūmina: *eyes*; 'lights,' metonomy

185 **lūce**: *in...*; abl. time when, in contrast to nocte above
custōs: *as...*; in apposition to the subject

186 **aut (in) culmine...aut (in) turribus**: *either...or...*; abl. place where

188 **tam...tenāx quam nuntia**: *as tenacious a messenger of...as of...*; tam...quam are correlatives and quam introduces a clause of comparison; nuntia, 'messenger,' is fem. sg.

189 **haec**: *this one*; i.e. Fama
multiplicī sermōne: *with...*; abl. means, abl. sg. of a 3rd decl. i-stem adj.; i.e. different versions of the same event

190 **facta**: *things...*; neut. PPP as substantive
infecta: *things...*; i.e. nōn facta, see above

191 **vēnisse Aenēān...**: *that...*; ind. disc. in apposition to facta above; -ān is Grk acc. sg.
crētum: PPP crescō

192 **cui...virō**: *to whom, as a husband*; or 'to which man,' dat. of interest with iungere and dat. apposition or just dat. of interest

dignētur: 3s pres. dep. subj. of subordinate verb (relative clause) in ind. disc.: make active
193 **hiemem…(eōs) fovēre**: *that (they)…*; add an acc. subj.
hiemem: *for…*; acc. duration of time
inter sē: *one another*; 'between themselves,' a common reflexive
(tam longam) quam longa (hiems est): *as long as (the winter is)*; '(as long) as (the winter is) long' clause of comparison as often with heavy ellipsis; see note on quam below
194 **immemorēs…captōs**: acc. modifying the understood acc. subj. of fovēre (eōs)
turpī cupīdine: abl. of means; 3rd decl i-stem
195 **haec…dea foeda**: nom. subj., i.e. Fama
vir(ōr)um: gen. pl. with ōra
ōra: acc. pl. ōs
196 **ad rēgem Iarbān**: Grk. acc. Iarbas
197 **animum**: i.e. of Iarbas
dictīs: *with…*; abl. means, substantive

lūmen, -inis n.: light, lamp; eye; life, 5

The Steady Progression of Cause and Effect in Book 4

Most events in Book 4 follow from the preceding event. Our passages are highlighted in boldface.

1-30	Dido confides to Anna after the banquet that she feels the spark of old flame
31-55	Anna supports such a marriage, but Dido must first consult the gods; the spark is now a fire
56-89	Dido renews sacrifices all day. She is engulfed by love and relaxes her sense of *pudor*.
90-128	Juno proposes an alliance of marriage and plans storm; Venus agrees, if Jupiter approves.
160-72	**Dido and Aeneas in the cave. Dido is not motivated by rumor (fama) or appearance.**
173-197	**Rumor (Fama) personified spreads like a monster**
198-218	**Iarbas, a North African king, hears the rumor and prays to father Jupiter to intercede**
219-258	Jupiter takes note and sends Mercury to tell Aeneas to depart for Italy.
259-278	**Mercury visits Aeneas and repeats Jupiter's command.**
279-295	**Aeneas plans to depart with his men but delays telling Dido.**
296-330	**Dido realizes Aeneas' plans, confronts him about the secrecy and betrayal of marriage**
331-361	**Aeneas defends himself, appeals to family and gods, argues that it was not a marriage**
362-387	Dido angrily replies and rejects Aeneas' claim that the gods pursue this course
388-650	As Aeneid prepares to depart, Anna and Dido build a pyre to burn his belongings.
651-671	**Dido climbs on top of the pyre and falls on Aeneas' sword, while Anna is away**
672-685	**Anna arrives and comforts the dying Dido.**
686-705	**Juno sends Iris, who releases Dido's soul from her body.**

The **Relative Adverb Quam** [8] (***as, than***) introduces a clause of comparison (e.g. longior quam…, 'longer than...'). Together, adverbs *tam* and *quam* are correlatives (demonstrative and relative, respectively), and translate slightly differently when used together than when they are used separately:

tam *so* quam *as/than* tam tenāx quam → *so tenacious as (tenacious)*→ **as tenacious as** (4.188)

On 3 occasions, *tam* is omitted via ellipsis, but we supply it in English to make the translation clearer:

Quam longa…	→	(tam longam) quam longa	*as long as*	4.193
Quam multa…	→	(tam multī) quam multa	*as many as*	6.309
Quam multae…	→	(tam multī) quam multae	*as many as*	6.311

Fama Personified (cont.)

4. How does Fama's behavior at night and in daylight 184-7 correspond to how rumors are spread?

5. What distinction is Vergil making between *fictī* and *vērī* in 188 (and *facta* and *infecta* in 190)?

6. What moral blame does Fama assert that Dido and Aeneas deserve in 2.194?

Hic Hammōne satus raptā Garamantide nymphā
templa Iovī centum lātīs immānia rēgnīs,
centum ārās posuit vigilemque sacrāverat ignem,
excubiās dīvum aeternās, pecudumque cruōre
pingue solum et variīs flōrentia līmina sertīs.
Isque āmēns animī et rūmōre accēnsus amārō
dīcitur ante ārās media inter nūmina dīvum
multa Iovem manibus supplex ōrāsse supīnīs:
"Iuppiter omnipotēns, cui nunc Maurūsia pictīs
gēns epulāta torīs Lēnaeum lībat honōrem,
aspicis haec? An tē, genitor, cum fulmina torquēs,
nēquīquam horrēmus, caecīque in nūbibus ignēs
terrificant animōs et inānia murmura miscent?

---

accendō, -ere, -ī, ēnsus: kindle, enflame, enrage, 3
aeternus, -a, -um: eternal, everlasting, 4
amārus, -a, -um: bitter
āmēns, -entis: out of one's mind; frantic, senseless, 2
an: or (in questions), 3
caecus, -a, -um: blind, hidden, 3
centum: one hundred, 3
cruor, -ōris m.: gore, blood, 3
epulor, -ārī, epulātus sum: to feast together, feast on
excubiae, -ārum f.: watchfires, guard
flōrēns, -entis: flowering
flūmen, -inis n.: river, stream, 2
Garamantis, -idis (fem. adj.): Garamantian, of the Garamantes (North African tribe)
genitor, -ōris m.: begetter, father, 4
Hammōn, -ōnis m.: Hammon (Jupiter). Ammon
honor, -ōris m.: honor; offering, sacrifice, 3
horreō, -ēre, -uī; bristle at, shudder at; fear, dread, 3
inānis, -e: empty, fruitless, meaningless, 3
Lēnaeus, -a, -um: Bacchic, of wine
lībō (1): pour (as an offering)
Maurūsius, -a, -um: Mauritanian
murmur, -uris n.: murmur, rumble, 4
nēquīquam: in vain, to no purpose
nympha, -ae f.: nymph, 4
omnipotēns, -entis: all-powerful, 3
pecus, pecudis f.: cattle, herd of cattle
pingō, -ere, pīnxī, pictus: paint, embroider, 2
pinguis, -e: rich, sleek, fat
rūmor, -ōris f.: rumor, hearsay, 2
sacrō (1): to consecrate, make holy
serō, -ere, sēvī, satum: sow, plant, 2
serta, -ōrum n.: garlands
solum, -ī n.: soil; ground, 3
supīnus, -a, -um: supine, flat, on the back
supplex, -icis: suppliant, 3
terrificō (1): frighten, terrify
torus, -ī m.: (banqueting) couch, 3
vigil, vigilis: watchful; *subj.* watchman, 2

198 **hic**: *this one*; i.e. Iarbas
satus: PPP serō; i.e. be born
Hammōne: *from…*; abl. of source; Romans identified the god (H)ammon with Jupiter
raptā…nymphā: abl. abs.; Iarbas is the son of Jupiter and a nymph who had been kidnapped
199 **templa centum immania (et) centum ārās**: asyndeton; acc. obj. of pf. pōnō
Iovī: *for…*; dat. of interest, Iuppiter
(in) lātīs…rēgnīs
excubiās…solum…līmina: all acc. objects of posuit
201 **dīv(ōr)um**: gen. pl.
pecudum cruōre: *with…*; abl. of cause
202 **pingue solum**: neut. acc. sg.; i.e. the grease from the burning sacrifices saturate the soil around the altars: sacrifices are very frequent
flōrentia līmina: neut. pl. pres. pple; i.e. the entrances to the temples
203 **Isque**: *and he…*; et is; i.e. Iarbas.
āmēns animī: *mindless in his mind*; pleonasm (more words than necessary) describing an excess of emotion; animī is an old locative
204 **dīcitur**: *is said*; + inf.
inter media nūmina: *between the middle of…* i.e. statues of the gods
dīv(ōr)um: gen. pl.
205 **multa**: *many things*; substantive
supplex: *as a suppliant*; nom. apposition
ōrā(vi)sse: pf. inf. ōrō, 'pray to (acc) for (acc)'
206 **cui**: *for whom…*; dat. of interest
Maurūsia…gēns: *the Mauritanian race*

(in) pictīs...torīs: PPP, 'embroidered'
207 **epulāta**: PPP with fem. sg. gēns
Lenaeum honōrem: i.e. a libation, a wine offering to the gods
208 **aspicis haec?**: *Do you...?*; neut. acc. pl.; The lack of an interrogative -ne indicates shock or bewilderment
tē...nēquīquam horrēmus: *Do we...*; Iarbas asks why humans should fear the gods' wrath, if a pious man such as Iarbas cannot expect their rewards
209 **cum fulmina torquēs...caecīque...miscent**: *when...*; an extended cum-clause; the words "nēquīquam horrēmus" belong outside the cum-clause as the main verb
caecī: *hidden*; elsewhere 'blind;' modifies ignēs
210 **inānia murmura**: neut. nom. pl.

Roman Religion as a Business Exchange

The Romans viewed religion as transactional, i.e. a business exchange. If the Romans prayed and sacrificed in honor to the appropriate gods in the proper way, they expected to be rewarded with a proportionate amount of success by those same gods. If, on the other hand, Romans failed to honor the appropriate gods in the proper way, they expected to suffer as a result. And so, when Vergil poses the central question of the epic in Book 1.8-11, 'Why must this pious man suffer?' the poet is asking why the gods are not fulfilling their own obligations in the relationship.

Iarbas poses the same question to Jupiter, his father, and thus calls into question the purpose of Roman religion. The passage that precedes the speech is important because it offers objective confirmation that Iarbas is pious toward the gods and Jupiter, his father, in particular. When Iarbas then questions the benefit of honoring or fearing the gods, his words become more meaningful because readers realize that they come from a man who has made every effort to honor the gods.

Roman Religion after 100 years of Civil Wars

There is good reason to believe that Vergil's question, 'Why must the pious suffer?,' would have been relevant and meaningful to his contemporary readers. The period known as the Fall of the Republic (133-31 BC) was marked by political upheaval and multiple civil wars. Scholars widely believe that the Romans questioned how the same religious practices that helped them achieve so much success for most of the Roman Republic (509-31 BC) failed them in the last 100 years.

Iarbas' piety and subsequent complaints would likely have resonated with many readers.

Evidence of Iarbas' Piety

1. Who is Iarbas' father (4.198)? Do we normally expect father's to favor their children over others?
2. What three tasks has Iarbas completed in 199-200 to honor the god?
3. What does the line 'pecudumque cruōre pingue solum' (201-2) suggest about the frequency of Iarbas' animal sacrifices to the god?
4. What does 'variīs flōrentia līmina sertīs' (202) suggest about Iarbas' maintenance of the temples?
5. What does 'media inter nūmina dīvum multa' (204-5) suggest that Iarbas has placed near the altars? Are these a great or small expense?
6. What final activity does Iarbas engage in to show his piety with the words 'Iovem manibus supplex ōrāsse supīnīs' (205)? (Recall that Aeneas displays the same behavior when readers first meet him.)
7. What additonal offering does Iarbas make to Jupiter in 206-7?

A Reward for Piety?

8. When Iarbas asks the question 'Do you see these things? (aspicis haec?, 208), what is the *haec*?
9. What does Iarbas mean when he asks the question 'tē nēquiquam horrēmus?' (208-9)?

Fēmina, quae nostrīs errāns in fīnibus urbem
exiguam pretiō posuit, cui lītus arandum
cuique locī lēgēs dedimus, cōnūbia nostra
reppulit ac dominum Aenēān in rēgna recēpit.
Et nunc ille Paris cum sēmivirō comitātū,
Maeoniā mentum mitrā crīnemque madentem
subnexus, raptō potitur: nōs mūnera templīs
quippe tuīs ferimus fāmamque fovēmus inānem."

Ut prīmum ālātīs tetigit māgālia plantīs
Aenēān fundantem arcēs ac tecta novantem
cōnspicit. Atque illī stellātus iaspide fulvā
ēnsis erat Tyriōque ardēbat mūrice laena
dēmissa ex umerīs, dīves quae mūnera Dīdō
fēcerat, et tenuī tēlās discrēverat aurō.

ālātus, -a, -um: winged
arō, arāre, -āvī: plow
aurum, -ī n.: gold
comitātūs, -ūs m.: retinue, train of followers
conspiciō, -ere, spexī, spectus: see, behold 2
cōnūbium, -iī n.: marriage, wedlock, 4
crīnis, -is m.: locks, hair, 4
discernō, -ere, crēvī, crētus: separate, distinguish, discern
dīves, dīvitis: rich, wealthy in (gen), 2
dominus, -ī m.: master
ensis, -is m.: sword, 3
exiguus, -a, -um: small, scanty
fēmina, -ae f.: woman
foveō, -ēre, fōvī, fōtus: nuture, foster; caress, 4
fulvus, -a, -um: tawny, yellow
fundō (1): to found, lay (a foundation), begin
iaspis,, -idis m.: jasper
inānis, -e: empty, fruitless, meaningless, 3
laena, -ae f.: cloak, upper garment
lēx, lēgis f.: law, decree, 2
madeō, -ēre: to be wet, moist, drip
Maeonius, -a, -um: Maeonian
māgālia, -ium n.: huts (Punic word) 2
mentum, ī n.: chin, 2
mitra, -ae f.: miter (type of head-dress)
mūnus, -eris n.: gift, duty; function 3
mūrex, mūricis m.: purple (from murex shell)
novō (1): renew, make new, build, 2
Paris, -idis m.: Paris, 3
planta, -ae f.: sole of a foot
potior, -īrī, -ītus: possess, take possession of (*abl.*), 2
pretium, iī n.: price, value
quippe: of course, truly; surely, 3
recipiō, -ere, -cēpī, -ceptum: take back, recover, 3
repellō, -ere, -pulī, -pulsum: drive back, repulse
sēmivir, -ī m.: half-man
stellātus, -a, -um: starred; studded
subnectō, -ere, -x(u)ī, -xus: fasten up
tangō, -ere, tetigī, tactum: to touch
tēla, -ae f.: thread, (horizontal) thread, web
tenuis, -e: thin, 2
umerus, -ī m.: shoulder, 3

211 **Fēmina**: i.e. Dido; note the prominent position of fēmina in the four-line sentence.
pretiō: *for a price*; abl. of price; Dido and the Tyrians bought the land from North African tribes. The money came mainly from a treasure that Sychaeus, Dido's late husband, revealed to Dido in a dream.

212 **cui...cuique**: *to whom...and to whom...*; dat. ind. obj.
arandum: *plowable, arable*; 'worthy to be plowed,' gerundive modifying neut. lītus

213 **lōcī**: gen. sg. with lēgēs

214 **dominum**: *as master*; Iarbas assumes that Dido and Aeneas will not rule as equals but Dido will be submissive to Aeneas. This view that a woman holds lower status than the man may explain why he calls the queen 'fēmina' but never by her personal name Dīdo.

215 **ille Paris**: i.e. Aeneas; Iarbas contemptuously likens Aeneas to Paris, who stole Helen from the Spartan Menelaus. Iarbas implies that Aeneas is stealing Dido from Iarbas

216 **Maeoniā...mitrā**: abl. means; A cylinder-shaped hat that resembles a fez.

mentum...crīnemque madentem...
subnexus: *having fastened up* + acc.; lit. 'having been fastened in respect to...' a PPP + acc. of respect; this construction is more common in Greek than in Latin, cf. 2.210; the hair is anointed with olive oil, a popular hair treatment in the Mediterranean
217 **raptō**: *(something) stolen*; PPP substantive; i.e. Dido, who is not treated as an equal but as a prize or possession to be owned
potitur: pres. deponent + abl. obj.
218 **ferimus**: 1p pres. ferō
fāmam inānem: i.e. meaningless because Jupiter does not reward those who honor him.
259 **ut prīmum...(Mecūrius) tetigit**: *as soon as (Mercury)...*; 'when first Mercury...' pf. tangō
ālātīs plantīs: abl. means
261 **illī...erat**: *that one had...*; 'to that one was;' dat. of possession
iaspide fulvā: *with...*; abl. means
262 **Tyriō mūrice**: *with...*; the highly valued purple dye produced by the murex seashell near Phoenician cities in modern Lebanon
263 **dēmissa**: *draped, dropped*; 'cast down,' PPP
quae mūnera...fēcerat: *which gifts...*; relative adj. introducing a relative clause; dīves Dīdō is the subject
264 **tenuī aurō**: i.e. gold threading in the cloak; abl. means, 3rd decl. i-stem abl.

Iarbas' Speech (cont.)

1. **Iarbas' view of Dido**: What does Iarbas claim he gave to Dido in 212-3? What did she reject in return (213-4)?
2. What does the word 'dominum' (4.214) suggest about Iarbas' view of the relationship between Dido and Aeneas?
3. **Iarbas' view of Aeneas**: As a guest, Paris took Helen from his host, King Menelaus of Sparta, (and with Helen the right to rule Sparta) and set in motion the Trojan war. When Iarbas calls Aeneas 'Paris' (4.215) and suggests that Aeneas 'takes possession of something stolen' (raptō potitur, 4.217) what role does Iarbas think that he and Dido play in the analogy? What role should Jupiter, enforcer of the guest-host relationship play?
4. Some Romans perceived eastern Mediterraneans as more luxuriant and less austere—in dress and tastes—than western Mediterraneans. How does Iarbas' description of Aeneas in 4.215-6 fit this stereotype of eastern Mediterraneans?
5. **The Rewards of Piety**: How do the words 'mūnera' and 'fāmam inānem' (217-8) suggest that Jupiter is not fulfilling his part in the relationship between the pious and the gods?

Mercury Arrives

6. What is Aeneas doing when the god Mercury arrives in 4.259-60?
7. How do the descriptions of Aeneas' sword and cloak (261-64) suggest that Aeneas has changed during his stay with Dido in Carthage?

Continuō invādit: "Tū nunc Karthāginis altae
fundāmenta locās pulchramque uxōrius urbem
exstruis? Heu, rēgnī rērumque oblīte tuārum!
Ipse deum tibi mē clārō dēmittit Olympō
rēgnātor, caelum ac terrās quī nūmine torquet:
ipse haec ferre iubet celerēs mandāta per aurās:
Quid struis? Aut quā spē Libycīs teris ōtia terrīs?
Sī tē nūlla movet tantārum glōria rērum
[nec super ipse tuā mōlīris laude labōrem,]
Ascanium surgentem et spēs hērēdis Iūlī
respice, cui rēgnum Ītaliae Rōmānaque tellūs
dēbētur." Tālī Cyllēnius ōre locūtus
mortālis vīsūs mediō sermōne relīquit
et procul in tenuem ex oculīs ēvānuit auram.
    At vērō Aenēās aspectū obmūtuit āmēns,
arrēctaeque horrōre comae et vōx faucibus haesit.

āmēns, -entis: mindless, senseless, 2
arrigō, -ere, -rēxī, -rectus: raise, prick up, 3
Ascānius, -ī m.: Ascanius, 3
aspectus, -ūs m.: sight, view, 3
clārus, a, um: clear; famous, 4
coma, -ae f.: hair
continuō: immediately, at once
Cyllēnius, -a, -um: Cyllenian (offspring of Mercury)
dēbeō, -ēre, dēbuī: ought, owe
ēvanescō, -ēre, -uī: vanish
exstruō, -ere, -struxī, -structum: build up
faucēs, -ium f.: throat, gullet
fundāmentum, -ī n.: foundation, 3
glōria, -ae, f.: glory, fame
haereō, -ēre, haesī: cling, stick, hesitate, 2
hērēs, hērēdis: heir, heiress
horror, -ōris m.: bristling, shuddering, dread, 2
invādō, -ere, -vāsī, -vāsum to go in, enter; attack
Iulus, -ī: Iulus, 3
Karthāgō, -inis f.: Carthage, 4
laus, laudis f.: praise, adulation, 2
Libycus, -a, -um: Libyan, of Libya, 3
locō (1): place, settle, arrange, 2
loquor, -ī, locūtus sum: speak, say, 2
mandō (1): order, command 2
mōlior, -īrī, -ītus sum: set in motion, bring about, 4
mortālis, -e: mortal, 4
oblītus, -a, -um: forgetful, unmindful (of), 2
obmūtescō, -ere, -mutuī: to become speechless
Olympus, -ī m.: Mt. Olympus, 2
ōtium, -iī n.: leisure, free time, peace
procul: from afar, far, at a distance, 2
rēgnātor, -ōris m.: ruler
relinquō, -ere, -līquī, -lictus: leave, abandon, 3
respiciō, -ere, -spexī: to look back (at), respect, 3
sermo, -mōnis m.: conversation, discourse, 3
struō, -ere, strūxī, structum: build, draw up, 2
super: above, beyond (*acc.*); *adv.* in addition, 3
tenuis, -e: thin, 2
terō, -ere, trīvī, trītum: wear away, rub
uxōrius, -a, -um: submissive, uxorious
vērō: in truth, in fact; but (abl. as adv.), 3
vīsus, -ūs m.: vision, sight, 2

265 **continuō**: *immediately*
invādit: i.e. begins to speak, assails
266 **uxōrius**: nom. adj.: translate as an adv.
oblīte: *(you) ...*; voc. dir. address + gen.
rēgnī rērumque...tuārum: i.e. both his leadership of the Trojans and of his household
267 **ipse**: *He himself*; i.e. Jupiter
de(ōr)um: gen. pl. with rēgnātor
tibi: dat. ind. obj.
clārō Olympō: *from...*; abl. place from which
270 **ipse**: *he himself*; i.e. Jupiter
(mē) ferre iubet: ellipsis: add 'mē;' inf. ferō
mandāta: *orders*; 'things ordered,' neut. PPP
271 **Quid...?**: *Why...?*; 'in respect to what?'
Quā spē: *With what expectation...?*
(in) Libycīs terrīs
273 **[nec...labōrem]**: omit the line as spurious
274 **Ascanium...et spēs**: acc. objs.; Ascanius and Iulus refer to the same person: son of Aeneas
275 **cui**: *to whom...*; dat. ind. obj.

276 **dēbētur**: 3s pres. pass. with 3p subject
Tālī...ōre: *with such an utterance*; metonomy
locūtus: pf. dep. pple: translate 'having Xed'
277 **mortālis**: *of the mortal one*; i.e. of Aeneas
(in) mediō sermōne: abl. place where or time when
279 **At vērō**: *but in truth*
aspectū: *at...*; 'because of...' abl. of cause
280 **arrēctae (sunt)**: 3p pf. pass.
(in) faucibus

What Jupiter Really Said

In 4.271-6 Mercury does not repeat verbatim what Jupiter commands. Below is the original message that Jupiter ordered Mercury to convey to Aeneas in 233-8. The few words that Mercury repeats verbatim are boldfaced, the words that Mercury rephrases are italicized, and the words that Mercury chooses not to repeat in his own speech are in regular type:

Si nulla accendit **tantarum gloria rerum**,
nec super ipse sua molitur laude laborem,
*Ascanio*ne pater Romanas invidet arces?
Quid struit, **aut qua spe** inimica in gente moratur,
nec prolem Ausoniam et *Lavinia respicit arva*?
Naviget: haec summa est; hic nostri nuntius esto."

Vergil could easily have had Mercury repeat the message verbatim, and it certainly would have saved the poet time. But, such repetition would have portrayed Mercury as nothing more than a mindless voice recorder. Instead, Mercury's ability to rephrase Jupiter's message and offer context (265-70) reminds readers that Mercury is just as independent as the other gods that we have encountered.

Homer's oral culture vs. Vergil's Literary culture: Homer often repeats entire passages large and small and likely would have had Mercury repeat Jupiter's speech verbatim. For many years, readers though Vergil was the better poet because he avoided these repetitions, but scholars now realize that Homer was part of an oral tradition where singers sang epic songs extemporaneously and repetition was common. Vergil, on the other hand, came from a literary culture where he did not compose the poem extemporaneously and therefore had time to prepare and differentiate his verses.

What the Square Brackets Indicate in 273

Square brackets indicate that the words enclosed are part of the manuscript tradition, but the editor believes that they are spurious, i.e. not genuine. In this case, line 273 is a repetition of line 234 in Jupiter's speech, and Mercury does not otherwise repeat lines from Jupiter's speech:

nec super ipse sua molitur laude laborem, 234 Jupiter's speech

[**nec super ipse** *tuā mōlīris* **laude labōrem**,] 273 Mercury's speech

While the editor's reasoning is undoubtedly more nuanced, what likely happened is that, while someone was copying by hand Mercury's speech from an older manuscript into a new one, the copyist inadvertedly looked up at Jupiter's lines in the original manuscript and copied it into Mercury's lines in the new copy. Then, the copyist's attention was directed back to Mercury's speech, and the mistake was not corrected. Either the same copyist or a later copyist modified 'sua molitur' to 'tua moliris.'

1. What criticism does Mercury offer with the words 'Heu, rēgnī rērumque oblīte tuārum!' (267)?

2. What is Aeneas doing in 265-7 instead of what he ought to do, and how is the word 'uxōrius' significant? (Is it a figure of speech or does it express Mercury's view of the relationship?)

3. What does Mercury claim is owed to Ascanius (also called 'Iūlus') in 274-6?

4. Give the Latin and translation for two of Aeneas' physical reactions to Mercury in 279-80.

Ardet abīre fugā dulcēsque relinquere terrās,
attonitus tantō monitū imperiōque deōrum.
Heu quid agat? Quō nunc rēgīnam ambīre furentem
audeat adfātū? Quae prīma exordia sūmat?
Atque animum nunc hūc celerem nunc dīvidit illūc
in partēsque rapit variās perque omnia versat.
Haec alternantī potior sententia vīsa est:
Mnēsthea Sergestumque vocat fortemque Serestum,
classem aptent tacitī sociōsque ad lītora cōgant.
arma parent et quae rēbus sit causa novandīs
dissimulent; sēsē intereā, quandō optima Dīdō
nesciat et tantōs rumpī nōn spēret amōrēs,
temptātūrum aditūs et quae mollissima fandī
tempora, quis rēbus dexter modus. Ōcius omnēs
imperiō laetī pārent et iussa facessunt.

---

abeō, -īre, -ivī, itus: go away, 2
adfātus, -ūs m.: address, speech
aditus, -ūs m.: approach, entrance, access, 2
alternō (1): change; hesitate
ambeō, -īre, -iī, -ītum: to petition, solicit, go around
aptō (1): fit, adapt, 2
attonitus, -a, -um: thunder-struck, stunned
audeō, -ēre, ausus sum: dare (+ inf.), 2
cōgō, cōgere, coēgī, coāctum: to collect; compel, 3
dissimulō (1): hide, disguise, 3
dīvidō, -ere, -vīsī, -vīsus: divide 3
exordium, -iī n.: introduction, beginning (of a speech)
facessō, -ere, -ī: perform, fulfill, accomplish
illūc: to there, to that place
Mnēstheus, -ī acc. -a: Mnestheus
modus, ī n.: manner, form, 2
mollis, -e: soft, gentle, tender
monitus, -ūs m.: admonish, warning
nesciō, -īre, -scīvī, -scītum: not know, be ignorant, 2
novō (1): renew, make new, change, 2
ōcior, ōcius f.: swifter, faster; *adv.* ōcius, rather swiftly
optimus, -a, -um: best, noblest
pāreō, -ēre, paruī: obey, 3
parō (1): prepare, make (ready), get, 4
potior, -ius: preferable, better (comparative potis, -e)
quandō: when, since, 2
relinquō, -ere, -līquī, -lictus: leave, abandon, 3
rumpō, -ere, -rūpī, -ruptum: burst, break through, 2
sententia, -ae f.: decision; opinion, thought, judgment,
Serestus, -ī m.: Serestus (Trojan leader)
Sergestus, -ī m.: Sergestus (Trojan leader), 2
spērō (1): hope (for), expect, 4
sūmō, -ere, sumpsī, sumptum: take, spend; exact, 3
temptō (1): to attempt, try
tempus, -oris n.: time; occasion, 2
versō (1): keep turning, revolve

281 **fugā**: *in...*; abl. manner
agat: *is he to do?*; 'should he do,' deliberative pres. subj.; Aeneas debates in his mind
Quō...adfātū: *With what address...?*;
284 **audeat**: *is he to dare...?*; deliberative subj.
sūmat: *is he to take...?*; deliberative subj.
nunc hūc...nunc illūc
286 **in partēs variās**: i.e. 'directions'
rapit: *seizes*; choosing one path, then another
287 **alternantī**: *to (the one)...*; dat. of reference, pres. pple + neut. pl. object
vīsa est: *seemed*; + nom.
289 **aptent...cōgant...parent...dissimulent**: *Let them fit out...let them...let them...*; or 'they should,' jussive subj: Aeneas orders his men
tacitī: *silently*; nom. adj. as adv.
290 **quae...sit**: *what...*; ind. question with 3s pres. subj. sum governed by dissimulent
rēbus novandīs: *for changing things*; dat. purpose; flip and make a gerund (-ing) + obj.
291 **(et dīcit) sēsē...temptātūrum (esse) aditūs...**: *(and says) that he will...*; ellipsis; ind. disc. with fut. inf. tempō; add a main verb
quandō...nesciat...spēret: *since...*; cause clause with pres. subj. of subordinate verb in ind. disc.; spērō means 'expect'
292 **tantōs rumpī...amōrēs**: *that...*; ind. disc. with pres. pass. inf. governed by spēret
quae tempora (sint): *what times...(are)...*; ellipsis, ind. question: add 3p pres. subj. sum

fandī: *for speaking*; gen. sg. gerund (-ing)
294 **(et) quis...modus (sit)**: *(and) what manner (is)…*; ind. questions; dexter, 'favorable,' is nom. pred.; ellipsis; supply pres. subj. sum
rēbus: *for…*; dat. of purpose

Ōcius: comparative adv.
295 **laetī**: *happily*; predicative adj. as adv.
pārent: *obey*; 3p pres. pāreō + dat.
iussa: *orders*; 'things ordered,' neut. PPP

Mnestheus and Sergestus as Ancesters of Aristocratic Roman Families

We have already mentioned how, even before Vergil wrote the *Aeneid*, the Julian clan, *gēns Iūlia*, claimed Aeneas' son Ascanius (Iulus)) and therefore Aeneas and Venus as illustrious ancestors. The Trojan captains Mnestheus and Sergestus are two more examples. Members of the Roman aristocratic clan Memmius, *gēns Memmia,* claimed Mnestheus as an ancestor, and members of the clan Sergius, *gēns Sergia*—which included Catiline himself—claimed Sergestus as an ancestor.

And so, these names were significant not only to Aeneas but to Vergil's contemporaries, who likely promoted the connection between these ancestors and some of the leading families in the Republic.

Antony and Cleopatra

44 BC	Julius Caesar is assassinated.
43	**Second Triumvirate** (Octavian, Marcus Antonius, Lepidus)
40	Marcus Antonius and Octavia, Octavian's sister, marry, have two daughters
36	Second Triumvirate dissolves, Lepidus is forced to retire
	Octavian oversees western Mediterranean; Antonius, the eastern Mediterranean
33	Marcus Antonius divorces Octavia
32-31	**Marcus Antonius and Cleopatra marry, have two children**
Sept. 31	**Battle of Actium**, Greece; Octavian wins naval battle; Antonius and Cleopatra flee
30	Marcus Antony and Cleopatra commit suicide, Octavian captures Egypt

Both the love affair between Aeneas and Dido and the entire account of Dido's life appears to have been made up by Vergil alone and are not found in any historical record. Many readers assume that Vergil based this relationship in part on the well-known and tragic relationship between Cleopatra and Marcus Antonius, whom we call Mark Antony today.

After the death of Julius Caesar, power in Rome was divided among three men, who formed what we call the second Triumvirate: Marc Antony, Octavian, and Lepidus. Julius Caesar had adopted his grand-nephew Gaius Octavius, in his will, and so the nephew was thereafter called Gaius Julius Caesar Octavianus, or just Octavian by modern readers. We will later know him as Caesar Augustus, the first emperor. Over time, Octavian consolidated power in the western Roman Empire, while Marc Antony did the same in the east. Marc Antony even married Octavia, the sister of Octavian, in 40 BC to reaffirm the second Triumvirate. Finally, as tensions continued to rise, Mark Antony divorced Octavia and married Cleopatra, the Queen of Egypt, with whom he had two children.

On the 2nd of September 31 BC at Actium, off the western coast of Greece, Octavian and his forces defeated the fleet of Marc Antony and Cleoptra, and the latter two fled to Alexandria, Egypt, where nearly one year later they committed suicide as Octavian's naval fleet approached.

What is relevant for our current lesson is that Octavian was careful to avoid the view that he and Marc Antony were engaged in a civil war. Instead, Octavian's supporters asserted (a) that Rome was fighting against Cleopatra and the Egyptians, and (b) that Marc Antony had betrayed his duty toward Rome to join Cleopatra's cause. Aeneas' dilemma is similar to Antony's—Aeneas must choose between (a) building the kingdom of his new love or (2) fulfilling his obligation to Italy and the future of Rome. While Octavian's version of Antony chose love, Vergil's Aeneas decisively chooses duty.

At rēgīna dolōs (quis fallere possit amantem?)
praesēnsit, mōtūsque excēpit prīma futūrōs
omnia tūta timēns. Eadem impia Fāma furentī
dētulit armārī classem cursumque parārī.
Saevit inops animī totamque incensa per urbem
bacchātur, quālis commōtīs excita sacrīs
Thȳias, ubi audītō stimulant trietērica Bacchō
orgia nocturnusque vocat clāmōre Cithearōn.
Tandem hīs Aenēān compellat vōcibus ultrō:
"Dissimulāre etiam spērāstī, perfide, tantum
posse nefās tacitusque meā dēcēdere terrā?
Nec tē noster amor nec tē data dextera quondam
nec moritūra tenet crūdēlī fūnere Dīdō?

---

amō (1): to love, like
armō (1): to arm, 3
audiō, -īre, -ivī, -ītus: hear, listen to, 3
Bacchus, -î m.: (god of) wine, 2
baccor, -ārī, -ātus sum: rave, rage (like a Bacchante)
Cithearōn, -ōnis f.: Mt. Cithaeron (north of Athens)
commoveō, -ēre, -mōvī: upset, trouble, set in motion, 2
compellō (1): address, accost, speak to, 3
dēcēdō, -ere, -cessī, -cessum: depart, withdraw, die, 4
dēferō, -ferre, -tulī, -lātum: report, offer, 2
dissimulō (1): hide, disguise, 3
dolus, -ī m.: trick, deceit, 3
excipiō, -ere, -cēpī, -ceptum: take out; catch, perceive
excitō (1): rouse up, raise, 2
fallō, -ere, fefellī, falsum: deceive, 3
fūnus, fūneris n.: death; burial, 4
impius, -a, -um: unholy, impious
incendō, -ere, -ī, -ēnsus: kindle, burn, 4
inops, -opis: lacking of, destitute of, needy, (gen), 2
mōtus, -ūs m.: change, movement
nefās n.: unrighteous(ness), sacrilege, forbidden act, 3
nocturnus, -a, -um: nocturnal, nightly
orgia, -ōrum n.: orgies, (Bacchic) festivals
parō (1): prepare, make (ready), get, 4
perfidus, -a, --um: disloyal, traitor(ous), faithless,
praesentiō, -īre, -sī: feel before, realize before
quondam: formerly, ever, 4
saeviō, -īre, -īvī (iī), -ītus: rage, be fierce or savage, 2
spērō (1): hope (for), expect, 4
stimulō: to excite, rouse
Thȳias, -adis f.: Bacchante, Thyiad
timeō, -ēre, timuī: be afraid, fear 2
trietēricus, -a, -um: every third year, trienniel
tūtus, -a, -um: safe, secure, 4
ultrō: voluntarily, on his/her own, 3

296 **Quis...possit**: *Who is able...*; deliberative subj. with pres. subj. (translate as pres. ind.)
amantem: *a lover*
297 **prīma...excēpit**: *was the first to perceive*
futūrōs: fut. act. pple
298 **tūta**: *(however) safe*; i.e. although being safe
timēns: pres. pple with rēgīna
furentī: *(the one)...*; dat. ind. obj., pres. pple
299 **dētulit**: pf. dēferō
armārī classem: *that...*; ind. disc., pass. inf.
cursumque parārī: *that...*; ind. disc., pres. pass. inf.
300 **inops animī**: *lacking of sense*; partitive gen. or animī is an old locative; 'lacking in mind'
301 **quālis...Thȳias**: *just as a Bacchante...*; 'which sort of Bacchante;' a simile which ends in l. 303; i.e. a follower of the god Bacchus
commōtīs excita sacrīs: *excited by the sacred objects having been set in motion*; PPP and abl. means; a neut. pl. substantive from sacer
302 **ubi**: *when...*
audītō...Bacchō: *(the word) 'Bacchus'...*; abl. abs., Bacchus' name is called out in the rites
trierērica orgia: *orgies every third year*; this festival occurs every two years (biennial), but Vergil is counting inclusively
303 **Cithearōn**: *Mount Cithearon*; the cult center for Bacchus where the festival occurs
hīs...vōcibus: *with these words*
305 **spērā(vi)stī...posse**: *Did you...?*; 2s pf. spērō and inf. possum; dissimulāre is a complementary inf. governed by posse
perfide: voc. dir. address
tantum nefās: neut. obj. of dissimulāre

306 **tacitus**: nom. adj.: translate as an adv.
meā...terrā: *from*...; abl. of separation
307 **Nec tē...nec tē...nec (tē)**: *Neither...nor... nor*...; anaphora
dextera: *pledges*; neut. nom. ; metonymy: marriages pledges given with the right hand
308 **moritūra...Dīdō**: fut. act. pple morior
tenet: 3s verb of all three subjects
crūdēlī fūnere: *with*...; abl. of manner; 3rd decl. i-stem adj.

morior, morī, mortuus sum: die, 5
tandem: finally, at length, pray, 5

Similes with Quālis: See p. 37 for a fuller explanation. Recall that *tālis* is omitted in the main clause via ellipsis but is supplied in English translation to make the translation clearer:

tālis *this sort/such* quālis *which sort* (tālis) quālis → *this sort which sort* → **such as**

Thyias / Bacchante / Maenad

A female follower of Bacchus (Grk Dionysus) is called a Bacchante (baccha, -ae f.), a Thyias (Thȳias, -adis f.), or a Maenad (Maenas, -adis f.). All three terms are Greek, and Maenad is the most common word used in English. The words 'bacchant' and 'bacchante' refer to masculine and feminine followers respectively and are substantives formed from the present participle of the verb bacchor, bacchārī: 'the one following Bacchus' or 'the one raving.'

Mount Cithearon, located in central Greece around 75 km northwest of Athens and 30 km south of Thebes, was sacred to Bacchus and the site of the orgies (orgia, -ōrum n.), the nocturnal festival in honor of Bacchus. The orgia took place every other year (biennial), but because Vergil was counting inclusively, he referred to it as *trierērica orgia*, 'orgies every third year' (302-3).

Part of the festival involved the revelation of *sacra*, 'sacred objects' (301), which were shaken to encourage the participants to enter into a state of ecstatic frenzy. Participants dressed in animal skins, danced, and often called out the name 'Bacchus' during the festival.

In Euripides' famous Greek tragedy the *Bacchae* (405 BC), the maenads reach such an ecstatic state that when they discover King Pentheus of Thebes attempting to disguise himself as a woman and witness the *orgia*, they envision him as a wild animal and tear him apart alive. Pentheus' own mother Agave participates, unaware that the head that she carries is not that of a wild animal but of her son.

For our interpretation, the bacchante represents someone who submits to **unrestrained emotion**.

Dido's Character and Leadership (part 2)

As noted on p. 39, Dido is portrayed positively in Book 1, but readers see her character degenerate as she gives in to unrestrained emotion such as love in Book 4. The simile of the Bacchante is the second of three similes describing Dido in the commentary. The first one in Book 1.498-502 likened Dido to Diana, and the third one in the Underworld in Book 6.452-5 will liken her to a dimly lit moon.

1. **Dido's reaction**: How does Dido learn about Aeneas' departure in 296-9? Does Aeneas tell her?

2. What three words in 4.300 describe Dido's state of unrestrained emotion?

3. **Simile of a Bacchante (4.301-3)**: The details in the simile do not correspond directly to Dido's actions. Instead, it is the description of Dido as a Bacchante which is important. How in general does the simile emphasize that Dido is out of control? Did the **Simile of Diana** give the same impression?

4. How is Dido's accusation that Aeneas is 'perfide,' (305) critical of the view that Aeneas is pious?

5. What relationship does Dido claim that she has with Aeneas with the words 'data dextera' (307)?

6. **Foreshadowing**: What two words in line 308 foreshadow Dido's suicide?

Quīn etiam hībernō mōlīris sīdere classem 309
et mediīs properās Aquilōnibus īre per altum, 310
crūdēlis? Quid, sī nōn arva aliēna domōsque 311
ignōtās peterēs et Troia antīqua manēret, 312
Troia per undōsum peterētur classibus aequor? 313
Mēne fugis? Per ego hās lacrimās dextramque tuam tē 314
(quandō aliud mihi iam miserae nihil ipsa relīquī), 315
per cōnūbia nostra, per inceptōs hymenaeōs, 316
sī bene quid dē tē meruī, fuit aut tibi quicquam 317
dulce meum, miserēre domūs lābentis et istam, 318
ōrō, sī quis adhūc precibus locus, exue mentem. 319
Tē propter Libycae gentēs Nomadumque tyrannī 320
ōdēre, infensī Tyriī; tē propter eundem 321
exstīnctus pudor et, quā sōlā sīdera adībam, 322
fāma prior. Cui mē moribundam dēseris,—hospes 323

---

adeō, -īre, i(v)ī, itus: go to, approach, 2
adhūc: as yet, still, so far, 2
antīquus, -a, -um: ancient, old, 4
Aquilō, -ōnis m.: Aquilo wind, north wind, 2
arvum, -ī n.: plowed land, field, region, 4
bene: well
cōnūbium, -iī n.: marriage, wedlock, 4
exstinguō, -ere, -stinxī, -stinctum: put out, 4
exuō, -ere, -uī, -ūtum: take off, put off
hibernus, -a, -um: of winter, wintry
hospes, -itis m.: guest, host, stranger
hymenaeus, -ī m.: wedding
ignōtus, -a, -um: unknown
infensus, -a, -um: hostile, aggressive
iste, ista, istum: that (of yours, near you), those, 3
lābor, -ī, lapsus sum: glide, slide, slip, fall, 2
Libycus, -a, -um: Libyan, of Libya, 3
maneō, -ēre, mānsī: stay, remain, wait, 4
mēns, mentis f.: mind, intent, purpose, 4
mereō, -ēre, -uī: deserve, merit, earn, 4
misereor, -ērī: have pity/compassion for (gen.)
mōlior, -īrī, -ītus sum: set in motion, bring about, 4
moribundus, -a, -um: dying, deadly
nihil: nothing, 2
Nomas, Nomadis n/f/: Nomads; Numidians
ōdī, -isse: to hate
precēs, -um: prayer, entreaty
properō (1): hasten, hurry (+ inf.)
propter: on account of, because of, 2
pudor, -oris m: sense of shame (a positive quality)
quandō: when, since, 2
quīn: nay (rather), but rather (following a neg. clause)
quisquam, quae-, quicquam: any(one), any(thing), 4
relinquō, -ere, -līquī, -lictus: leave, abandon, 3
tyrannus, -ī m.: tyrant, ruler
undōsus, -a, -um: full of waves, wavy, stormy

309 **Quīn etiam**: *Nay...even, but rather...even*
hībernō sīdere: *in...*; abl. time when; Dido says that it is the winter/storm season, when it is too dangerous to sail safely.
mōlīris: 2s pres. dep.: translate as active
310 **(in) mediīs Aquilōnibus**
īre: complementary inf. eō with properās
per altum: *through the deep sea*; metonomy
311 **crūdēlis**: either voc. direct address, 'cruel one' or nom. predicative adj. "cruelly"
312 **Quid**: *Why?*
Sī...peterēs...et...manēret...peterētur: *if you were...and...were..., ...would be...*; a pres. contrary to fact. condition (sī impf. subj., impf. subj.); all three verbs are impf. subj.
313 **per undōsum aequor**: *over...*
classibus: abl. means
314 **Mē-ne fugis?**: -ne introduces a yes/no question
per...tē...(et) per...(et) per...ōrō: *I beg you by... and by...and by...*; hyperbaton (distortion of normal word order) likely reflecting Dido's emotional state; translate ōrō (l. 319) first; per 'by' + acc. marks the reasons for the begging
315 **quando...ipsa relīquī**: *since I myself...*; 1s
aliud...nihil: acc. obj.
mihi iam miserae: *for...*; dat. of interest
317 **sī bene...meruī, (aut) fuit...meum...**: *if I...* the protasis (if-clause) of a mixed condition
quid: *anything*; indefinite after sī

fuit aut: *or was…*; aut fuit
quicquam…meum: *anything of mine*; subject
318 **miserēre**: imperative sg. dep. governs a gen.
lābentis: *collapsing*; pres. pple
istam…mentem: *that purpose of yours*; 'that thought of yours,' obj. of imperative exue
319 **sī quis…locus (est)**: *if any…*; ellipsis: supply a linking verb; quis is an indef. adj.
precibus: *for…*; dat. of purpose
exue: sg. imperative
320 **Tē propter…Tē propter**: *because of… because of…*; propter tē…propter tē…; anastrophe (inverted order) and anaphora
321 **ōdēr(unt mē)**: syncopated 3p pf.; add obj. ōdī is a defective pf.: translate as present
Tyriī (sunt)
eundem: acc. sg. īdem modifying tē
exstīnctus (est): 3s pf. pass. with 3p subject
322 **pudor (meus)**: *my sense of shame*
quā…adībam: *by which…*; the antecedent is fāma; abl. means, 1s impf. adeō
(ad) sīdera
323 **fāma prior**: *my earlier reputation…*; second subject of 3s exstīnctus est
Cui: *for…?*; dat. of interest
hospes: voc. direct address

lacrima, -ae f.: tear, 5
sōlus, -a, -um: alone, only, sole, 5

How long did Aeneas stay in Carthage?

The answer to this question is still debated among scholars. Some argue that Aeneas stays almost a year, while others argue that Aeneas remains for several months. The crux of the problem are the words *hiems* and *hībernus*, which can refer to 'winter' or more generally 'storm season.'

We know from Ilioneus' mention of *adsurgēns Oriōn* in I.535 (see p. 45) that the Trojans arrived in mid-June, when the storm season begins. If Dido's mention of 'hībernō sīdere' in 4.309 refers to the storm season, Aeneas may be leaving no later than September or October in the same year. If Dido's 'hībernō sīdere' refers to the winter, then Aeneas may be leaving in early spring of the following year.

Contrary to Fact (Contrafactual) Conditions [6] (part 2)

As we saw on p. 53, we identify conditions (if-then clauses) by the tense and mood of the two main verbs. A present contrary to fact (*were, would*) has impf. subj. in both the **protasis** (if-clause) and **apodosis** (then-clause). A past contrary to fact (*had, would have*) has plpf. subj. in both parts.

present contrary to fact	sī audīrēs, scīrēs hoc.	*If you **were** listening, you **would** know this.*
past contrary to fact	sī audīvissēs, scīvissēs hoc.	*If you **had** listened, you **would have** known this.*

The sentence in 4.311-4 is a present contrary to fact condition:

sī…peterēs et Troia antīqua manēret, Troia…peterētur?
If you were seeking…were remaining/remained…, would Troy be sought…?

Dido's disordered speech reflects a disordered mind: This speech is difficult to read precisely because it reflects Dido's agitated state. Note how Vergil uses rhetorical questions, anaphora, anastrophe (usual word order), and ellipsis to show how emotion prevents Dido from thinking clearly. (Compare, for example, Dido's measured response to Ilioneus.)

1. What 3 phrases does Dido use in 314-6 to suggest that he is bound in marriage to her?

2. What in 317-9 does Dido ask in return for favors that she has given Aeneas in the past?

3. How do North Africans and Carthaginians feel toward Dido because of Aeneas (320-21)?

4. What happened to her 'pudor et…fāma priōr' because of Aeneas?

5. How is line 323 and example of foreshadowing?

6. What is the significance of addressing Aeneas as a mere 'hospes' (323)?

(hoc solum nōmen quoniam dē coniuge restat)?
Quid moror? An mea Pygmaliōn dum moenia frāter
dēstruat aut captam dūcat Gaetūlus Iarbās?
saltem sī qua mihī dē tē suscepta fuisset
ante fugam subolēs, sī quis mihi parvulus aulā
lūderet Aenēās, quī tē tamen ōre referret,
nōn equidem omnīnō capta ac dēserta vidērer."
 Dīxerat. Ille Iovis monitīs immōta tenēbat
lūmina et obnixus cūram sub corde premēbat.
Tandem pauca refert: "Ego tē, quae plūrima fandō
ēnumerāre valēs, numquam, rēgīna, negābō
prōmeritam; nec mē meminisse pigēbit Elissae
dum memor ipse meī, dum spīritus hōs regit artūs.

---

an: or (in questions), 3
artus, -ūs m.: joint, limb, 4
aula, -ae f.: hall, palace, 2
dēstruō, -ere, -uī: pull down, dismantle, destroy
Elissa, -ae f.: Elissa (another name for Dido)
ēnumerō (1): reckon, count up, enumerate
equidem: (I) for my part, (I) indeed, 3
frāter, -tris m.: brother, 2
Gaetūlus, -ī m.: Gaetulian (a North African tribe)
Iarbās, -ae, m.: Iarbas, 2
immōtus, -a, -um: motionless, unmoved
lūdō, -ere, -sī, -sus: sport, mock, 3
meminī, -isse (imper. **memento**): remember, recall, 3
memor, -oris: mindful, remembering (*gen*) 4
monita, -ōrum n.: warnings
moror, -ārī, -ātus sum: delay, linger, 2
negō (1): to deny, say that...not
numquam: never, 4
obnitor, -nitī -nixus sume: struggle, strive, resist
omnīnō: altogether, wholely, entirely
parvulus, -a, -um: very small, small
paucī, -ae, -a: little, few, scanty, 3
piget, -ēre, -guit: it causes (acc) regret, it disgusts,
plūrimus, a, um: most, very many/full *superl.* multus 4
prōmereor, -ērī, prōmeritus sum: deserve, merit
Pygmaliōn, -ōnis m.: Pygmalion
quoniam: seeing that
restō, -āre, -stiti: remain, survive, 2
saltem: at least, 3
spīritus, -ūs m.: breath, spirit
subolēs, is f.: offspring
suscipiō, -ere, -cēpī, -ceptum: undertake, take up, 2
tamen: however, nevertheless, 3
valeō, -ēre, -uī: prevail, be able (inf.); be strong

324 **hoc solum nōmen quoniam...**: *since...*
dē : *from...*; he is not a coniunx but hospes
325 **Quid**: *Why...?*
An...dum...dēstruat...dūcat: *or (do I delay) until...?* dum + pres. anticipatory subj.; Dido answers her own question: she fears that her brother Pygmalion or Iarbas will attack.
326 **(mē) captam**: *(me)...*; PPP capiō
dūcat: i.e. lead away to execution or slavery
327 **sī...suscepta fuisset (et) sī...lūderet,... vidērer**: *If...had been taken up, if...were..., I would seem...*; mixed contrary to fact (sī plpf. subj., impf. subj.); suscepta fuisset is equiv. to plpf. suscepta esset but stresses the completion of the action; impf. subj. videor, 'seem'
qua...subolēs: *some offspring...*; nom. subject qua becomes indefinite following sī
mihi: *for...*; dat. of interest
dē tē: *from...*
328 **quis...parvulus...Aenēās**: *some very small Aeneas*; i.e. a child; quis is indefinite after sī
329 **quī...referrent**: *who would recall...*; impf. subj in a relative clause of characteristic
ōre: *in appearance*; 'in face,' abl. of respect
330 **capta ac deserta**: i.e. by love; PPP and nom. pred. after vidērer (see note l. 327)
331 **Ille**: i.e. Aeneas
Iovis monitīs: *because of...*; abl. of cause and gen. sg. Iuppiter
332 **lūmina**: *eyes*; 'lights,' metonomy
obnixus: *struggling*; dep. 'having struggled,'
333 **pauca**: *a few things/words*; neut. substantive
refert: *says*; 'reports'
quae plūrima ...valēs: *very many things which you...*; obj. of prōmeritam (esse); plūrima is neut. pl. antecedent; valēs = 2s pres.

fandō: *by...*; abl. means, gerund (-ing) for, fārī
335 **tē...prōmeritam (esse)**: *that you have...*; ind. disc. translate the pf. dep. inf. as active; 'plūrima quae...vālēs' is the object
meminisse: *to recall*; defective pf. and logical subject of pigēbit: translate as pres. + gen.
pigēbit: *it will...*; impersonal fut.

Elissae: another name for Dido; Aeneas talks about Dido here in the 3rd person, not 2nd
336 **dum (sum) memor...**: *While (I) myself (am)*
meī: *of myself*; i.e. conscious; partitive gen. sg. of ego (not from meus) governed by memor
(et) dum: *(and) while...*

Pygmalion's history with Dido is explained on p. 35.

Dum [6] (while, until)

Dum + indicative [4] denotes an actual event.

dum memor ipse meī (sum), dum spīritus hōs regit artūs.	*while (I am)..., while...rules*	4.336

Dum + subjunctive [2] denotes an anticipated or intended event.

dum moenia frāter dēstruat aut captam dūcat	*until...destroys...or...leads*	4.325-6
dum conderet urbem inferretque deōs Latiō	*until...might found...and bring*	1.5-6

The present anticipatory subj. is often translated as present with future sense, while the imperfect anticipatory subj. is translated with modal 'would,' 'might,' or 'could.'

Dido's Unfulfilled Wish (Contrary to fact): When a speaker uses a contrary to fact condition, just as in 4.327-30 on the facing page, to convey a wish about the past that did not come true, she expresses an 'unfulfilled wish.' Note how Dido's wish emphasizes her vulnerability and lack of control.

Sī...suscepta fuisset (et) sī...lūderet,	*If (only)...had been undertaken...and if...were playing...*
nōn vidērer	*I would not seem...*

Relative Clause of Characteristic [3] is common in Caesar and Cicero but occurs rarely in this book. This relative + subjunctive occurs when the antecedent of the relative is particularly vague:

(1) the antecendent is a vague demonstrative such as is, ea, id
vīdī eum quī tē ōre referret — *I saw that one who would recall you in appearance*

(2) the antecedent is nēmō, nihil, or nūllus
videō nēminem quī tē ōre referret — *I saw no one who would recall you in appearance*

(3) the antecedent is indefinite (e.g. quisquam) or missing
erat quī tē ōre referret — *There was (someone) who would recall you in appearance*

The purpose of a relative of characteristic is to clarify *what sort of person* or *thing* the vague antecedent is. In 4.328-9, it clarifies what sort of person the offspring of Aeneas and Dido would be.

1. **Dido faces dual threats**: What two threats does Dido say that she faces in 325-6?

2. **Dido's unfulfilled wish:** What in 327-330 does Dido wish she had since Aeneas is leaving?

Aeneas responds directly to Dido's concerns

3. What in particular in 4.331-2 makes Aeneas restrain his physical and emotional response to Dido?

4. What does Aeneas say in 333-5 in response to Dido's claim that she is deserving (sī...meruī, 317)?

5. What does Aeneas say in 335-6 in response to Dido's wish to have a child to remind her of Aeneas?

Prō rē pauca loquar. Neque ego hanc abscondere furtō
spērāvī (nē finge) fugam, nec coniugis umquam
praetendī taedās aut haec in foedera vēnī.
Mē sī fāta meīs paterentur dūcere vītam
auspiciīs et sponte meā compōnere cūrās,
urbem Troiānam prīmum dulcēsque meōrum
relliquiās colerem, Priamī tecta alta manērent,
et recidīva manū posuissem Pergama victīs.
Sed nunc Ītaliam magnam Grȳnēus Apollō,
Ītaliam Lyciae iussēre capessere sortēs;
hic amor, haec patria est. Sī tē Karthāginis arcēs
Phoenissam Libycaeque aspectus dētinet urbis,
quae tandem Ausoniā Teucrōs cōnsidere terrā
invidia est? Et nōs fās extera quaerere rēgna.

---

abscondō, -ere, -ī, -itus: hide away, conceal
Apollo, Apollinis m.: Apollo, 2
aspectus, -ūs m.: sight, view, 3
Ausonia, -ae f.: Ausonia, lower Italy
auspicium, ī n.: auspices
capessō, -ere, -īvī, -ītus: to take; carry out, execute, 2
colō, -ere, coluī, cultum: till, farm, cultivate, 3
compōnō, -ere, -suī, -situs: compose, arrange, calm, 2
cōnsīdō, -ere, -sēdī, -sessus: sit, settle, rest, 2
dētineō, -ēre, -uī: hold back, detain
exterus, -a, -um: outward; foreign, strange
fās n.: right, righteous; **fās (est)**, it is right, 3
fingō, -ere, finxī, fictum: make up, imagine, 3
foedus, -eris n.: treaty, agreement, 2
furtō: in secret, in secrecy
Grȳnēus, -a, -um.: Grynean, of Grynion (a site in Asia Minor sacred to Apollo)
invidia, -ae f.: envy, ill-will, grudging
Karthāgō, -inis f.: Carthage, 4
Libycus, -a, -um: Libyan, of Libya, 3
loquor, -ī, locūtus sum: speak, say, 2
Lycius, -a, -um: Lycian, of Lycia, (in Asia Minor), 2
maneō, -ēre, mānsī: stay, remain, wait, 4
neque: nor, and not;: neither...nor, 4
patior, -ī, passus sum: suffer, endure; allow, 4
paucī, -ae, -a: little, few, scanty, 3
Pergama, -ōrum n.: citadel of Troy, 3
Phoenissa, -ae f.: Phoenician (woman), 2
praetendō, -ere, tetendī, tentus: stretch out, hold out
Priamus, -ī m.: Priam, king of Troy, 4
prō: before; for, in behalf of (*abl.*), 3
recidīvus, -a, -um: restored, rebuilt
relliquiae, -ārum f.: survivors, remains, 2
spērō (1): hope (for), expect, 4
sponte: *abl.* by...own will, willingly, 2
taeda, -ae f.: torch, wedding/marriage torch
umquam: never, at no time, 2
vīta, -ae f.: life, soul, spirit, 4

337 **prō rē**: *for (on behalf of) this matter*
pauca: *a few things/words*; ironically, Aeneas has many things to say
loquar: 1s fut. dep.
hanc...fugam: acc.
338 **nē finge**: *Don't...*; neg. imperative
339 **taedas coniugis**: i.e. marriage-torches, symbolizing the wedding and marriage in the same way wedding rings do today; see p. 77 for their role in the processsion
aut: *nor...*; include the negative from nec
in haec foedera: *into...*; i.e. marriage pacts
340 **sī...paterentur,...colerem...manērent... posuissem**: *if...allowed...,...would...would... would have...*; mixed contrary to fact condition (sī impf. subj., impf/impf/plpf. subj.)
meīs...auspiciīs: *by my own auspices...*; i.e. by my own wishes or power; abl. of manner
paterentur: *allowed* + inf.; impf. patior; neut. pl. fātum is subject
342 **prīmum**: *first (of all)*; adv.
meōrum: *of my own (people)*
343 **colerem**: *I would...*; 1s impf. subj. apodosis
(et)...manērent: *(and)...would...*; impf subj.
344 **manū (meā)**: abl. means
posuissem: *I would have...*; plpf. subj. pōnō
victīs: *for (those)...*; i.e. for the Trojans; dat. interest; PPP vincō
345 **Gryneus Apollō (iussit mē capessere)**: ellipsis; pf. iubeō

346 **Lyciae sortēs**: *Lycian oracles*; i.e. the oracles of Lycian Apollo. Recall that an oracle can denote (a) a place for prophecy and (b) the prophecy itself. In Book 3, where Aeneas recalls his journey from Troy to Sicily, Aeneas receives many omens, including one from Apollo himself on the island of Delos, sacred to Apollo.
iussēr(unt mē): syncopated 3p pf.
347 **Hic (est) amor (meus)**
Haec patria (mea) est: add possessive

Sī...dētinet, quae....invidia est?: *if..., what envy is there...?*; simple present condition (sī pres. ind. pres. ind.) Aeneas draws attention to how the Trojans and Phoenicians share a similar history
arcēs...aspectus: two subjects of 3s verb
(in) Ausoniā terrā: i.e. in Italy
Teucrōs cōnsidere: *that...*; ind. disc.
350 **fās (est)**: *it is right* + inf.; impersonal verb
nōs...quaerere: *that...*; ind. disc.

Negative Imperatives [6]

Vergil uses ***nē*** **+ imperative** rather than ***nōlī/nōlīte*** **+ infinitive** to express a negative command.

nē crēdite	*Don't trust*	(2.48)	nē finge	*Don't make it up*	(4.338) ← on facing page
nē timē	*Don't fear*	(2.606-7)	nē subtrahe	*Don't withdraw*	(6.465)
nē recūsā	*Don't refuse*	(2.607)	nē quaere	*Don't ask*	(6.868)

Contrary to Fact (Contrafactual) Conditions [6] **(part 3)**

Once again, we identify conditions (if-then clauses) by the tense and mood of the two main verbs. A present contrary to fact (*were, would*) has impf. subj. in both the **protasis** (if-clause) and **apodosis** (then-clause). A past contrary to fact (*had, would have*) has plpf. subj. in both parts.

present contrary to fact	sī audīrēs, scīrēs hoc.	*If you* ***were*** *listening, you* ***would*** *know this.*
past contrary to fact	sī audīvissēs, scīvissēs hoc.	*If you* ***had*** *listened, you* ***would have*** *known this.*

Aeneas' Unfulfilled Wish: The sentence in 4.311-4 is a mixed contrary to fact condition:

sī...paterentur...et...,	colerem (et)...tecta manērent, et...posuissem
If...allowed (were allowing)...	*I would....would...would have been...*

Aeneas responds directly to Dido's concerns

1. What does Aeneas say in 337-8 in response to Dido's claim at the beginning of her speech that 'you hoped to be able to hide so great a unrighteous act' (dissimulāre etiam spērāstī... nefās, 305-6)?
2. What does Aeneas say in 338-9 in response to Dido's claim that they are bound by marriage?
3. While Dido expresses an unfulfilled wish that she had a child with Aeneas, what unfulfilled wish does Aeneas express in 340-4 if the fates had allowed him?
4. What two groups in 345-6 urge Aeneas to seek Italy?
5. How does Aeneas suggest that by the Carthaginians' own example the Trojans are right to pursue Italy? (348-50).

Mē patris Anchīsae, quotiēns ūmentibus umbrīs
nox operit terrās, quotiēns astra ignea surgunt,
admonet in somnīs et turbida terret imāgō;
mē puer Ascanius capitisque iniūria cārī,
quem rēgnō Hesperiae fraudō et fātālibus arvīs.
Nunc etiam interpres dīvum Iove missus ab ipsō
(testor utrumque caput) celerēs mandāta per aurās
dētulit: ipse deum manifestō in lūmine vīdī
intrantem mūrōs vōcemque hīs auribus hausī.
Dēsine mēque tuīs incendere tēque querēlīs;
Ītaliam nōn sponte sequor."

---

admoneō, -ēre, -uī, -itum: warn, advise
arvum, -ī n.: plowed land, field, region, 4
Ascānius, -ī m.: Ascanius, 3
astrum, ī n.: star, constellation
auris, -is: **f.**: ear, 3
cārus, -a, -um: dear, 3
dēferō, -ferre, -tulī, -lātum: report, offer, 2
dēsinō, -ere: cease, leave off
fātālis, -e: deadly, fatal; fated, 3
fraudō (1): defraud, cheat, deceive, swindle
hauriō, haurīre, hausī: take in, drain, exhaust, 3
Hesperia, -ae f.: Hesperia, Italy, 3
igneus, -a, -um: fiery, burning
imāgō, -inis f.: image, likeness, ghost, 3
incendō, -ere, -ī, -ēnsus: kindle, burn, 4
iniūria, -ae f.: injury, insult, injustice, 2
interpres, -pretis m/f: messenger
intrō (1): go into, enter
mandō (1): order, command 2
manifestus, -a, -um: clear, visible, palpable
mittō, -ere, mīsī, missus: send, dismiss, 4
operiō, -īre, -uī: cover, conceal, overwhelm
querēla, -ae f.: complaint, complaining
quotiēns: as often as, 2
sequor, -ī, secūtus sum: follow, pursue, 4
sponte: *abl.* by...own will, willingly, 2
terreō, -ēre, -uī, -itum: terrify, 2
testor, -ārī, testātus sum: bear witness, attest, swear
turbidus, -a, -um: cloudy, muddy, 2
ūmens, ūmentis: moist
uterque, utraque, utrumque: each (of two), both, 2

351 **patris Anchīsae...turbida imāgō**: hyperbaton (distortion of normal word order for emphasis); turbida imāgō patris Anchīsae is the subject of two verbs
quotiēns...(et) quotiēns...: anaphora and asyndeton; these are relative advs. introducing relative clauses
ūmentibus umbrīs: abl. means; i.e. dew
353 **in somnīs**: *in dreams*
354 **mē puer Ascanius -que iniūria capitis cārī (mōvērunt)**: ellipsis and metonomy; caput Here refers to 'life' (e.g. per capita); gen. sg.
regnō Hesperiae...et fātālibus arvīs: *from...*; abl. of separation governed by verb fraudō
356 **dīv(ōr)um**: i.e. deōrum, gen. pl.
Iove...ab ipsō: *by...*; abl. of agent, Iuppiter
357 **utrumque caput**: *on both of our heads*; 'on each head (of ours)' i.e. lives, metonomy
mandāta: *orders*; 'things ordered,' PPP as substantive
358 **dētulit**: pf. dēferō
(ego) ipse: *I myself*
359 **intrantem mūrōs**: pres. pple
360 **Dēsine**: *Cease to...*; imperative + inf.
mēque...tēque...: *both...and...*
tuīs querēlīs: abl. means
361 **sponte (meā)**: *by my own will, willingly* ; a common expression, often with a possessive adj. (meus, tuus, etc.); abl. of manner that can often be translated as an adv.; Note that the end of the line is missing because Vergil died before he could finish the poem.

Aeneas appeals to his obligations

1. Aeneas' father Anchises died in Sicily at the end of Book 3. His funeral games will be celebrated in Book 5 when Aeneas returns to Sicily.
   In what form does Anchises now advise Aeneas in 4.351-3?
2. What does Aeneas think that he owes his son Ascanius in 4.354-5?
3. Who is the *interpres* in line 356, who sent him, and what did he bring to Aeneas in 357-8?
4. In the final line, Aeneas summarizes the speech and says "Ītaliam nōn sponte sequor." Name all the individuals in the speech that make Aeneas feel obligated to go to Italy.

What happens next in 4.362-659

After Aeneas admits that he sails to Italy unwillingly, Dido offers her final words to the Trojan leader, in which she accuses him of being unfeeling, argues that the gods would not disturb their own tranquility and be concerned with Aeneas' endeavors, and finally curses Aeneas as she sends him off.

After Dido sends Anna to convince Aeneas to stay and Aeneas refuses, Dido tells Anna that she plans to bring closure to the relationship by building a pyre and burning all of Aeneas' possessions, including his *lectus* and *gladius*. Anna, unaware of Dido's plan to commit suicide, agrees to help and arranges the pyre. While Anna is way, Dido sees Aeneas' ships set sail and offers a final curse that there will be no peace between the Carthaginians and the descendants of Aeneas. Then, she ascends the pyre.

Below is part of the outline of Book 4 from p. 79. The passages in this commentary are boldfaced.

296-330 **Dido realizes Aeneas' plans, confronts him about the secrecy and betrayal of marriage**
331-361 **Aeneas defends himself, appeals to family and gods, argues that it was not a marriage**
362-387 Dido angrily replies and rejects Aeneas' claim that the gods pursue this course
388-650 As Aeneid prepares to depart, Anna and Dido build a pyre to burn his belongings.
651-671 **Dido climbs on top of the pyre and falls on Aeneas' sword, while Anna is away**
672-685 **Anna arrives and comforts the dying Dido.**
686-705 **Juno sends Iris, who releases Dido's soul from her body.**

Dīxit, et ōs impressa torō "Moriēmur inultae,
sed moriāmur" ait. "Sīc, sīc iuvat īre sub umbrās.
Hauriat hunc oculīs ignem crūdēlis ab altō
Dardanus, et nostrae sēcum ferat ōmina mortis."
Dīxerat, atque illam media inter tālia ferrō
conlāpsam aspiciunt comitēs, ensemque cruōre
spūmantem sparsāsque manūs. It clāmor ad alta
ātria: concussam bacchātur Fāma per urbem.
lāmentīs gemitūque et fēmineō ululātū
tecta fremunt, resonat magnīs plangōribus aether,
nōn aliter quam sī immissīs ruat hostibus omnis
Karthāgō aut antīqua Tyros, flammaeque furentēs
culmina perque hominum volvantur perque deōrum.
audiit exanimis trepidōque exterrita cursū
unguibus ōra soror foedāns et pectora pugnīs
per mediōs ruit, ac morientem nōmine clāmat:

---

aether, -eris m.: aether, (upper) sky, 3
aliter: otherwise
antīquus, -a, -um: ancient, old, 4
ātrium, -(i)ī n.: great hall, atrium
audiō, -īre, -ivī, -ītus: hear, listen to, 3
bacchor, -ārī, -ātus sum: rave, rage (like a Bacchante)
clāmō (1): shout, cry out
concutiō, -ere, -cussī, -cussus: shake, strike 2
conlābor, -lābī, -lapsus sum: collapse, slide down
cruor, -ōris m.: gore, blood, 3
culmen, -minis n.: rooftop; peak, summit, 4
Dardanus, -a, -um: Trojan, 2
dīcō (1): to declare, dedicate, consecrate
ensis, -is m.: sword, 3
exanimis, -e: breathless; lifeless, dead
exterreō, -ēre, -uī, -itum: to frighten bady, terrify
fēmineus, -a, -um: womanly, of a woman, 2
foedō (1): defile, befoul, make ugly, 3
fremō, -ere, -uī, -itus: roar, 3
hauriō, haurīre, hausī: take in, drain, exhaust, 3
homō, -inis m./f.: person, people; human, 4
hostis, -is m./f.: enemy, foe, 4
immittō, -ere, -mīsī, -missum: send into, 2
imprimō, -ere, impressī, -ssum: press into, imprint
inultus, -a, -um: unavenged
iuvō, -āre, iūvī: be pleasing, help, 4
Karthāgō, -inis f.: Carthage, 4
lāmenta, -ōrum n.: wailing, weeping
mors, -rtis f.: death, 3
ōmen, -inis n.: omen, auspices
plangor, -ōris m.: wailing, beating
pugnus, -ī m.: fist
resonō (1): to resound, echo
spargō, -ere, -rsī, -rsus: scatter, disperse, 2
spūmō (1): to foam, froth, 3
torus, -ī m.: (banqueting) couch, 3
trepidus, -a, -um: trembling, agitated, alarmed
Tyros (-us), ī f.: Tyre (Phoenician city)
ululātus, -ūs m.: howling, wailing
unguis, -is: nail, finger-nail

Anna and Dido had planned to burn a wooden pyre (bonfire) with all of the possessions that Aeneas left behind so that Dido might have a fresh start; but, while Anna is away, Dido climbs on the pyre, delivers the speech above, and falls on Aeneas' sword to commit suicide. The pyre is located in a courtyard in Dido's palace.

659 **impressa**: *having pressed*; PPP imprimō, reflexive in sense
torō: *on...*; dat. of compound verb or abl. p.w.
moriēmur: 1p fut. dep.: a 'Royal We,' translate as 1s, same below (see note on p. 99)
moriāmur: *let...*; 1p hortatory pres. dep. subj.; a 'Royal We': translate as 1s
iuvat: *it is...*; impersonal

661 **hauriat**: *let...*; 3s jussive pres. subj.
crūdēlis...Dardanus: i.e. Aeneas
ab altō: *from the deep sea*; i.e. Aeneas will see her pyre burn as his ships leave the harbor

662 **sēcum**: cum sē
ferat: *let...*; 3s jussive pres. subj.

663 **illam...conlāpsam**: *that one...*; pf. dep. pple ('having Xed'); Dido falls onto the sword with the swordpoint up and the handle on the bed

inter media tālia: *in…*; the pyre is located in the middle of a courtyard in Dido's palace
(in) ferrō: i.e. sword given to Aeneas by Dido
665 **sparsās**: *blood-splattered*; PPP
668 **tecta**: *the halls*; synecdoche; neut. nom. pl. the pyre is in the courtyard of Dido's palace
669 **nōn aliter quam sī... ruat**: *not otherwise than if...should fall*; clause of comparison, introducing a simile; ruat is pres. subj. in a fut. less vivid (should-would) condition (sī pres. subj., pres. subj.) with omitted apodosis (then-clause)
immissīs hostibus: abl. abs.
Tyros: *Tyre*; nom. fem. sg.
671 **per(que) culmina hominum...perque (culmina) deōrum**: *both through...and through...*; use culmina twice; via synecdoche culmina refers to houses and temples
volvantur: *should be..., were to be...*; pres subj. in same fut. less vivid condition
audi(v)it: 3s pf.; soror below is subject
trepidō...cursū: *with...*; abl. of manner
673 **ōra**: *her face*; 'mouths,' synecdoche; the pl. suggests repetition: 'repeatedly scratching...'
pugnīs: abl. of means from pugnus, 'fist,' not pugna
per mediōs (hominēs)
674 **morientem**: *(the one)...*; i.e. Dido, pres. pple morior
nōmine clāmat: *shouts by name*

The 'Royal We' or **'Majestic We'** is often employed by gods and royalty and is a 1p pronoun or verb where one expects 1s. Some readers retain the 1p in translation while others revert to 1s.

moriēmur	*We will die* → *I will die*	4.659
moriāmur	*Let us die* → *let me die*	4.660

While an impersonal verb or subject, for example, tries not to focus on any particular person (e.g. 'one should floss daily'), the royal we places extra emphasis on the subject above all others.

Hortatory Subjunctive[1] (main verb) is named after the verb *hortor, -ārī, hortātus sum: encourage, urge* and is used to express a polite command or exhortation in 1st singular and plural. Hortatory and jussive subjunctives are very similar and are together called volitive subjunctives (*volō*, 'want,' 'wish'). It is usually translated with 'let' or 'should' and governs a *nē* rather than *nōn* in the negative.

moriāmur	*let us die! we should die!* (4.660)
nē eam audiāmus	*let us not listen to her, we should not listen to her*

A Simile Foreshadowing the Fall of Carthage

The simile in 4.669-70 which foreshadows the fall of Carthage is appropriate when we consider that Juno had heard that the Trojan offspring 'would one day overturn the Tyrian citadels' (Tyriās ōlim quae verteret arcēs 1.20), an allusion to the three Punic Wars fought between Roman and Carthage. The relationship between Aeneas and Dido was Juno's attempt to avoid that future and redirect the Trojans to Carthage rather than Italy. Since Dido's death and Aeneas' departure mark the failure of Juno's attempt, readers know that the fall of Carthage will proceed as planned.

Dido's Suicide

1. What does Dido expect Aeneas to see in 661-2 as he sets sail with the Trojans from Carthage?

2. What specifically does Dido do in 663-5?

3. Name three ways the Carthaginians lament Dido's actions in 665-8.

4. What catastrophic event does Vergil liken to Dido's death in 669-71?

5. In what two ways does the sister Anna show grief in 673?

"Hoc illud, germāna, fuit? Mē fraude petēbās?
Hoc rogus iste mihi, hoc ignēs āraeque parābant?
Quid prīmum dēserta querar? Comitemne sorōrem
sprēvistī moriēns? Eadem mē ad fāta vocāssēs:
īdem ambās ferrō dolor atque eadem hōra tulisset.
Hīs etiam strūxī manibus patriōsque vocāvī
vōce deōs, sīc tē ut positā crūdēlis abessem?
Exstīnxtī tē mēque, soror, populumque patrēsque
Sīdoniōs urbemque tuam. Date, vulnera lymphīs
abluam et, extrēmus sī quis super hālitus errat,
ōre legam." Sīc fāta gradūs ēvāserat altōs
sēmianimemque sinū germānam amplexa fovēbat
cum gemitū atque ātrōs siccābat veste cruōrēs.
Illa gravēs oculōs cōnāta attollere rursus
dēficit; infīxum strīdit sub pectore vulnus.

---

abluō, -ere, -luī, -lutum: wash away, clean, purify
absum, -esse, āfuī: be absent, 2
ambō, -ae, -ō: both, two together
amplector, -ī, -plexus sum: wind around, embrace, 3
attollō, -tolle, attulī, allātum: to raise, lift up, 3
cōnor, cōnārī, cōnātus sum: to try
cruor, -ōris m.: gore, blood, 3
dēficiō, -ere, -fēcī, -fectum: fail, fall short
ēvadō, -ere, ēvāsī, ēvāsum: to go out, escape, 2
exstinguō, -ere, -stinxī, -stinctum: put out, 4
foveō, -ēre, fōvī, fōtus: nuture, foster; caress, 4
fraus, -dis f.: fraud, deceit
germāna, -ae: sister, 2
gradus, -ûs m.: step, stide, gait, 2
hālitus, -ūs m.s: exhalation, breath
hōra, -ae f.: hour
infīgō, -ere, -fīxī, -fīxus: fix, pierce, fasten on, 2
iste, ista, istum: that (of yours, near you), those, 3
legō, -ere, lēgī, lectum: to read; pick out, select, 4
lympha, -ae f.; water
parō (1): prepare, make (ready), get, 4
patrius, -a, -um: paternal, ancestral, 3
queror, querī, questus sum: complain, lament
rogus, -ī m.: pyre, 2
rursus: again, back
sēmianimis, -is: half-alive, half-dead
siccō (1): to dry, make dry
Sīdōnius, -a, -um: Sidonian, of Sidon (Phoenician city)
sinus, -ūs m.: curve; bosom, lap, 2
spernō, -ere, sprēvī, sprētum: spurn, scorn, reject, 2
strīd(e)ō, -ēre, -dī: rustle, whir, hiss, screech, creak, 3
struō, -ere, strūxī, structum: build, draw up, 2
super: above, beyond (*acc.*); *adv.* in addition, 3
vestis, -is f.: clothing, 2

675 **hoc fuit illud?**: *This was that?*; At Dido's request, Anna had built the pyre to burn Aeneas' belongings and did not realize that Dido planned to commit suicide and be burned on the same pyre. Anaphora (hoc… hoc…hoc) and the use of questions without interrogatives reflect her shock and surprise.
germāna: voc. dir. address
fraude: *because of…*; 'out of…' abl. of cause
676 **hoc iste rogus mihi (parābat)**: hoc is acc. obj. and refers to Dido's death
677 **querar**: *am I to...?*; *should I...?*; deliberative subj. or 1s fut. dep.
comitem: *as...*; Anna suggests joining Dido
678 **moriēns**: pres. pple morior
ad fāta eadem: acc. place to which, īdem
vocā(vi)ssēs: *You should have...*; '(would that) you had…' 2s plpf. subj. of wish (unfulfilled wish); Anna wishes that she had died along with her sister—a very disturbing confession that is amplified even more in the next line.
679 **īdem dolor atque eadem hōra**: nom. subj.
(nōs) ambās: *(us) two, (us) both*; acc. obj.
ferrō: *with a sword*; metonomy
tulisset: *should have…*; 'would that…had' plpf. subj. of wish (unfulfilled wish) ferō
680 **(rogum) strūxī**: ellipsis; 1s pf.
681 **vōce**: abl. of means; i.e. aloud
ut...abessem: *so that...might...*; purpose clause with 1s impf. subj. ab-sum
sīc tē...positā: i.e. on the pyre; abl. abs., pōnō
crūdēlis: *cruelly*; translate adj. as an adv.

682 **Exstīnx(is)tī**: 2s pf.
patrēs: i.e. senators or elder leaders
Sīdoniōs: i.e. Carthaginian; Phoenician Sidon and Tyre are the cities that colonized Carthage
683 **Date**: *Grant that…*; 'give (the power),' as if addressing the gods in prayer; this pl. imper. governs the noun result clause below
lymphīs: abl. means; a synonym for aquīs
684 **(ut) abluam et…legam**: *that I…*; noun result clause with 1s pres. subj.
quis extrēmus hālitus: *any…*; indefinite quis following sī, nisi, num, and nē; Anna attempts to catch the last breath of Dido with her mouth. The soul is identified with the breath.
super: *above*; adv.
686 **fāta**: pf. dep. pple *for, fārī*: 'having Xed'
amplexa: pf. dep. pple: translate 'having Xed'
veste: abl. means
688 **illa**: i.e. Dido, illa marks a change of subject
conāta: pf. dep. pple: translate 'having Xed'
689 **infixum…vulnus**: neut. nom. sg. and PPP
strīdit: *hisses*; a pierced lung produces a hissing sound as the air travels through the open wound rather than through the mouth.

Anna's Unfulfilled Wish: Recall from p. 51 that a subjunctive of wish [3] (optative subj.) in the present tense expresses a wish for the future and in the past tense expresses an unfulfilled wish (i.e. a wish that did not come true). In 1.575-6 it was introduced by *utinam*, 'would that,' but in 4.678-9, as often, there is no *utinam*, and so you may add 'would that' or simply use modal verbs 'may' or 'should.'

(Utinam) vocēs .	*Would that you may call me*	*May you/you should call me* (in a future)/
(Utinam) vocārēs	*Would that you were calling me you*	*should be calling me* (but you aren't)
(Utinam) **vocāvissēs**	***Would that you had called me***	***you should have called me*** (but you didn't)
(Utinam) ferat .	*Would that…may carry us both off*	*May…carry/…should carry us both* (in a future)/
(Utinam) ferret	*Would that…were carrying us both off*	*should be carrying us both off* (but it isn't)
(Utinam) **tulisset**	***Would that...had carried us both off***	***should have carried us both off*** (but it didn't)

This construction is unusual in this book, but so is the content of the wish itself.

The gods intervened for Aeneas but not for Dido

If Venus had not intervened in Book 2, Aeneas would have killed Helen in the Temple of Vesta and committed a great impiety. If Mercury had not intervened in Book 4, Aeneas likely would never have sailed to Italy. In both cases, the gods stopped Aeneas from acting dishonorably, and yet Juno does not stop Dido from committing suicide and acting impiously toward her family and her people, as Anna notes in 6.682-3. For readers, divine intervention seems arbitrary. While Aeneas maintains his reputation for piety *with the help of the gods,* Dido faces death and her betrayal of her city all alone.

Noun Result Clauses (ut/ut nōn) [1] There are two types of result clauses: (1) adverbial and (2) noun. Noun result clauses are (a) the objects of verbs that express *doing*, *effort*, or *occurrence* where (b) the main verb is vague and does not express the specific action that causes the result:

Dīdō effēcit ut sē occīderet.	*Dido brought it about that that she killed herself.*
Accidit ut sē occīderet.	*It happened that she killed herself.*

Lines 4.683-5 is a noun result clause with *dō, dāre*, 'give (the power)' or 'grant.' Anna appears to call the gods in prayer that they bring about the result. Translate the present subj. as a present indicative:

Date (ut) abluam et…legam *(O gods), grant that I wash away…and I take…* (4.683-5)

1. Give examples of how rhetorical questions, anaphora, and ellipsis reflect Anna's state of mind.
2. What does Anna suggest in 677-9 would happen if Dido had confided her plan to Anna?
3. What had Anna done unawares in 680-1 to help Dido carry out her plan?
4. Who, in Anna's final words to Dido in 682-3, has been harmed by Dido's actions?
5. What does Anna hope to do in 683-5?

Ter sēsē attollēns cubitōque adnixa levāvit,
ter revolūta torō est oculīsque errantibus altō
quaesīvit caelō lūcem ingemuitque reperta.
Tum Iūnō omnipotēns longum miserāta dolōrem
difficilēsque obitūs Īrim dēmīsit Olympō
quae luctantem animam nexōsque resolveret artūs.
Nam quia nec fātō meritā nec morte perībat,
Sed misera ante diem subitōque accēnsa furōre,
nōndum illī flāvum Prōserpina vertice crīnem
abstulerat Stygiōque caput damnāverat Orcō.
Ergō Īris croceīs per caelum rōscida pennīs
mīlle trahēns variōs adversō sōle colōrēs
dēvolat et suprā caput astitit. "Hunc ego Dītī
sacrum iussa ferō tēque istō corpore solvō."
Sīc ait et dextrā crīnem secat: omnis et ūnā
dīlāpsus calor atque in ventōs vīta recessit.

---

auferō, auferre, abstulī, ablātus: take or carry away
accendō, -ere, -ī, ēnsus: kindle, enflame, enrage, 3
adnixus, -a, -um: leaning upon
adversus, -a, -um: facing, opposite, straight on, 5
artus, -ūs m.: joint, limb, 4
astō, -āre, abstiti: stand by or near, 2
attollō, -tolle, attulī, allātum: to raise, lift up, 3
calor, -ōris m.: heat, glow
color, colōris m.: color
crīnis, -is m.: locks, hair, 4
croceus, -a, -um: yellow, saffron
cubitum, -ī n.: elbow
damnō (1): condemn, convict
dēvolō (1): fly down, fly from
diēs, diēī m./f.: day, day(light), 4
difficilis, difficile: hard, difficult
dīlābor, -ī, lapsus sum: glide apart
Dīs, Dītis m.: Dis, Pluto, 2
ergō: therefore, then, 3
flāvus, -a, -um: blonde; tawny, yellow
furor, -ōris m.: rage, fury, madness, 3
ingemō, -ere, -uī: groan, sigh
Īris, -ridis, f.: Iris, 2
iste, ista, istum: that (of yours, near you), those, 3
levō (1): lift up, raise; relieve, 2
luctor, -ārī, -ātus sum: wrestle, struggle, 2
mereō, -ēre, -uī: deserve, merit, earn, 4
mīlle pl. mīlia, ium n.: thousand, 2
miseror, -ārī, -ātus sum: pity, 4
mors, -rtis f.: death, 3
nectō, -ere, -uī, nexum: connect, tie, join
nōndum: not yet
obitus, -ūs m.: death, destructon
Olympus, -î m.: Mt. Olympus, 2
omnipotēns, -entis: all-powerful, 3
Orcus, -ī m.: Orcus, underworld
penna, -ae f.: feather; wing
pereō, -perīre, periī: to pass away, perish
Prōserpina, -ae f.: Proserpina, 2
quia: because
recēdō, -ere, -cessī: go back, withdraw, recede, 2
reperiō, -īre, -ivī, repertum: found, discovered
resolvō, -ere, -ī, -solūtum: loosen, set loose; relax, 2
revolvō, -ere, -ī, -volūtus: roll back
rōscidus, -a, -um: dewy, moistened
secō, -āre, -uī, sectus: cut, divide, 2
sōl, sōlis m.: sun, 4
solvō, -ere, solvī, solūtum: loosen; set sail; pay
Stygius, -a, -um: Stygian, of the river Styx, 4
subitō: suddenly, 4
suprā: above, over, on the top
ter: thrice, three times, 4
torus, -ī m.: (banqueting) couch, 3
trahō, -ere, trāxī, tractus: drag (out), draw, 3
vīta, -ae f.: life, soul, spirit, 4

690 **(Dīdō) attolēns**: sēsē (emphatic sē) is obj. of both the pres. pple attolēns and levāvit
cubitō: *on...*; dat. of compound adnixa
691 **revolūta...est**: pf. pass.
(in) torō
oculīs errantibus: abl. means or abs.
(in) altō caelō
692 **reperta**: *at the things found*; acc. pl. PPP

693 **miserāta**: fem. pf. dep. pple: 'having Xed'
694 **difficilēs obitūs**: poetic acc. pl.: translate. sg.
Olympō: *from...*
695 **quae...resolveret**: *who would...*; relative clause of purpose (quae = ut ea), impf. subj.
luctantem: pres. pple
nexōs...artūs: PPP, nectō
696 **nec fātō...nec meritā morte**: *neither... nor...*; abl. cause
697 **misera**: *love-sick*; Dido is subject
ante diem: *before her time*; i.e. before Dido was supposed to die naturally
698 **illī**: *of that one*; dat. of possession or interest
vertice: *from...*; i.e. capite; abl. separation
699 **abstulerat**: plpf. au-ferō
Stygiō Orcō: *to...*; dat. ind. obj. or direction
700 **pennīs**: *wings*; 'feathers,' synecdoche
701 **trahēns mīlle variōs colōrēs**: pres. pple
(in) adversō sole
702 **Hunc...sacrum**: *this sacred (gift)*; or 'this sacred rite'
Dītī: dat. ind. obj. Dīs, another name for Pluto
iussa: fem. sg. PPP iubeō; i.e. by Juno
703 **istō corpore**: *from...*; abl. of separation
704 **dextrā (manū)**: abl. of means
omnis et ūnā: *all and together*; ūnā is an adv.
705 **dīlāpsus (est)**: 3s pf. dep.: translate active

Furor vs. Pietās (part 2)

On p. 71 we discussed how *furor* is an unrestrained emotion and opposing force to *pietās*. As we saw, the cognate verbs *furō* and *furiō* were both used in 2.588 and 2.595 to describe Aeneas' state of mind as he set out to kill Helen impulsively, and it appears that he would have committed that impiety in the temple of Vesta—the very goddess Hector commended him to protect—had Venus not intervened.

Furor and its cognates are used four times in the Book 4 selections, and three of those instances describe Dido. The final occurrence in 4.697 is offered as the cause of Dido's premature death:

...rēgīnam ambīre furentem audeat	*he should dare to approach the raving queen*	4.283-4
Eadem impia fāma furentī dētulit	*the same impious rumor reported to the one raving...*	4.298-9
Flammae furentēs...volvantur	*raging flames were churning up through the rooftops...*	4.670-1
perībat...misera...accēnsa furōre,	*she was perishing, lovesick and enflamed by madness...*	4.697

Not surprisingly, in Dido's final moments Vergil again contrasts *furor* with *pietās*. In 697-8 the poet states that being 'lovesick' (*misera*) and 'enflamed by madness' (*accēnsa furōre*) were the reasons that Dido was perishing 'before her time and suddenly' (*ante diem subitōque*). While Vergil as narrator does not allude to Dido's *pietās*, Anna does. In 682-3, Anna's final words to Dido are 'Sister, you have snuffed out yourself and me and the people and the Sidonian senators and your city' (*exstīnxtī... urbemque tuam*, 4.682-3). And so, we observe that the same unrestrained *furor* that caused Dido to kill herself led her to harm the very people that *pietās* would have urged her to protect.

Dido's Death

1. What did Dido attempt and fail to do three times in 690-1? Why did she groan in 693?
2. What in particular in 4.696-7 caused Dido to die prematurely?
3. What is Proserpina supposed to do under normal circumstances in 698-9?
4. Give the Latin and translation for the one verse that describes the messenger Iris as the goddess of rainbows. How does Iris travel from Mt. Olympus?
5. What exactly descends to the underworld?
   a. How do the words 'tēque istō corpore solvō' (703) suggest that Dido's self is distinct from her body? (N.B. Many cultures do not make such a distinction.)
   b. What part of Dido is struggling to free itself in line 695?
   c. What in 704-5 leaves from Dido's body once Iris has cut her hair?

Hinc via Tartareī quae fert Acherontis ad undās.
Turbidus hīc caenō vastāque vorāgine gurges
aestuat atque omnem Cocytō ēructat harēnam.
Portitor hās horrendus aquās et flūmina servat
terribilī squālōre Charōn, cui plūrima mentō
cānitiēs inculta iacet, stant lūmina flammā,
sordidus ex umerīs nōdō dēpendet amictus.
Ipse ratem contō subigit vēlīsque ministrat
et ferrūgineā subvectat corpora cumbā,
iam senior, sed crūda deō viridisque senectus.
hūc omnis turba ad rīpās effūsa ruēbat,
matrēs atque virī dēfūnctaque corpora vītā
magnanimum hērōum, puerī innūptaeque puellae,
impositīque rogīs iuvenēs ante ōra parentum:

Acheron, ontis m.: Acheron river
aestuō (1): seethe, surge, boil over
amictus, -ûs m.: wrap, cover, robe
aqua, -ae f.: water, 3
caenum, -ī n.:, mud, mire
cānitiēs, -is f.: grey-white hair
Charōn, -ontis m.: Charon, 2
Cōcȳtus, -ī m.: Cocytus river, 2
contus, -ī m.: pole (used to push a boat)
crūdus, -a, -um: fresh, immature; crude
cumba, -ae f.: skiff, small boat, 2
dēfungor, -ī, dēfunctus sum: finish; die; perform (abl.)
dēpendeō, -ere: hang down (from)
effundō, -ere, -fūdī, -fūsum: pour out, 3
ēructō (1): throw up, vomit up, belchs up
ferrūgineus, -a, -um: rust-colored
flūmen, -inis n.: river, stream, 2
gurges, -itis m.: whirl (of water), whirlpool, 3
hērōs, -hērōis m.: hero, 3
horrendus, -a, -um: horrible, to be trembled at, 4
iaceō, iacēre, iacuī: lie, 2
incultus, -a, -um: uncultivated, ungroomed, unkempt
innūptus, -a, -um: unmarried, 2
iuvenis, -is m.: youth, young man, 3
magnanimus, -a, -um: great-souled
mater, matris f.: mother
mentum, ī n.: chin, 2
ministrō (1): assist; supply, manage, 2
nōdus, -î m.: knot, 2
plūrimus, a, um: most, very many/full *superl.*multus 4
portitor, -ōris m.: carrier, boatman, ferryman, 2
puella, -ae f.: girl, 2
ratis, -is f.: raft, boat, ship, 2
rogus, -ī m.: pyre, 2
senectus, -ūs f.: old age
senior: older (comp. of senex)
sordidus, -a, -um: dirty, shabby
squālor, -ōris m.: dirt, filth
subigō (sub-agō), -ere, -ēgī, -actus: drive up/forward
subvectō (1): to convey up, carry forward
Tartareus, -ī m.: of Tartarus, Tartarean, 2
terribilis, -e: terrible, dreadful
turba, -ae f.: crowd, mob, 4
turbidus, -a, -um: cloudy, muddy, troubled, 2
umerus, -ī m.: shoulder, 3
vēlum, -ī n.: sail, 2
via, -ae f.: way, road, journey, street, 4
viridis, -e: green; lively, vigorous
vīta, -ae f.: life, soul, spirit, 4
vorāgo, -inis f.: abyss, watery depth

295 **hinc (est)**: *From here (there is)...*; add a verb The Sibyl, priestess of Apollo, leads Aeneas underground in Cumae, Italy and guides him now on a path (*via*) through the underworld.
Tartareī Acherontis: *of the Tartarean Acheron River*; with ad undās; Tartarus can refer to the entire Underworld or where souls are punished
fert: *carries along*; i.e. the road leads to...

296 **turbidus...gurges**: nom. sg. subj.
caenō...vorāgine: *with...*; abl. cause + turbidus

297 **omnem harēnam**: i.e. silt from Acheron R.
(in) Cocytō: *in...*; abl. place where; the Acheron feeds its silt into the Cocytus river.

298 **Portitor...horrendus...Charōn**: nom. subj.
servat: *protects*

299 **terribilī squālōre**: *with/of...*; abl. of quality
cui: *whose...*; dat. of possession
plūrima...cānitiēs inculta
(in) mentō

300 **stant**: i.e. stand fixed

lūmina: *eyes*; metonomy; nom. subj.
flammā: *of*...; abl. of quality with lūmina
301 **nōdō**: *with..., on...*; abl. of means
302 **Ipse**: *He himself*
contō, velīs: abl. means
303 **(in) ferrūgineā...cumbā**: or abl. means
304 **iam senior**: *already too old*; comparative often suggests excess: 'too/excessively old'
(sed est) crūda...senectūs: *(but it is) the fresh and lively old age of a god*; dat. possession
305 **omnis**: *entire*
effūsa: PPP, effundō; reflexive in sense: translated as 'having Xed'
306 **dēfuncta...vītā**: *dead, having died*; 'having finished from life,' pf. dep. pple (translate 'having Xed') + abl. of separation; dēfungor vītā is a common euphemism for 'to die'
vitā: *from...*; abl. separation with dēfuncta
307 **magnanim(ōr)um hērōum**: gen. pl.
308 **impositī**: PPP
rogīs: *on...*; dat. of compound verb impositī
ōra: *faces*; 'mouths,' synecdoche

What Happened in 6.1-294

When the Trojans arrive in Italy, Aeneas and Achates go to the Temple of Apollo at Cumae, where they meet the Sibyl, a priestess of Apollo. Aeneas requests to see Anchises in Hades, and Apollo, speaking through Sibyl, tells him that he must first bring a golden bough (a tree branch) and bury a comrade. With the help of Venus and her doves, Aeneas recovers the bough, and, when told that his comrade Misenus had drowned, Aeneas buries him. Having paid respects to the dead and found the golden bough, Aeneas enters the underworld with Sibyl as guide.

Overview of Book 6

Trojans arrive at **Cumae** in Italy (6.1-32)
Aeneas, Achates visit **Sibyl**, priestess of Apollo (33-97)
Aeneas requests to see Anchises (98-123)
Sibyl requests Aeneas complete two tasks: (124-235)
Retrieval of the **Golden Bough**
Burial of companion **Misenus**
Aeneas is led by Sibyl into the Underworld (236-267)
Death-Bringing Powers and Monsters (268-94)
Charon by the **River Styx** (295-336)
Palinurus and unburied dead by the river, (337-383)
Charon sees Bough, leads Aeneas over Styx (384-416)
Cerberus (417-425)
King Minos judges; Untimely Dead (426-547)
Dido, untimely dead because of love (450-476)
Deiphobus, last Trojan husband to Helen (477-547)
Tartarus on the left (548-627)
House of **Dis** and **Proserpina** (628-636)
Elysium (**Elysian Fields**) on the Right (637-665)
Anchises reveals destiny of Rome (666-892)
Future heroes of Rome wait along the river **Lethe**
Romulus and **Augustus**
Rome will spare the weak and war down the proud
Marcellus, heir to Augustus
Gate of Ivory and **Gate of Horn** (893-901)

Relevant Vocabulary in the Charon Passage

Many of these words occur just once on pp. 104-14 but are more memorable when reviewed together.

Charōn, -ontis m.: Charon, 2
portitor, -ōris m.: carrier, boatman, ferryman, 2
nāvita, -ae m.: sailor (nauta), boatman, 2

harēna, -ae f.: sand, 6
rīpa, -ae f.: bank, 8
lītus, -oris n.: shore, coast, beach, 15

ratis, -is f.: raft, boat, ship, 2
cumba, -ae f.: skiff, small boat, 2
alveus, -ī m.: vessel, small boat
carīna, -ae f.: ship, keel (of a ship)
puppis, -is f.: deck, ship, boat, 5
contus, -ī m.: pole (used to push the boat)
vēlum, -ī n.: sail, 2
rēmus, -ī m.: oar, 3

Acheron, -ontis m.: Acheron river
Cōcȳtus, -ī m.: Cocytus river, 2
Stygius, -a, -um: Stygian, of the river Styx, 4

flūmen, -inis n.: river, stream, 2
fluvius, -iī m.: river, stream, 2
fluentum, -ī n.: flow; river, stream

gurges, -itis m.: whirl (of water), whirlpool, 3
stagnum, -ī n.: pool, standing water, 3
vadum, -ī n.: shallows, shoals, 4
lacus, -ūs m.: lake
palūs, palūdis f.: swamp, marsh, 2
caenum, -ī n.: mud, mire
līmus, -ī m.: mud, filth, mire

quam multa in silvīs autumnī frīgōre prīmō 309
lāpsa cadunt folia, aut ad terram gurgite ab altō 310
quam multae glomerantur avēs, ubi frigidus annus 311
trāns pontum fugat et terrīs immittit aprīcīs. 312
Stābant ōrantēs prīmī trānsmittere cursum 313
tendēbantque manūs rīpae ulteriōris amōre. 314
Nāvita sed trīstis nunc hōs nunc accipit illōs, 315
ast aliōs longē summōtōs arcet harēnā. 316
Aenēās mīrātus enim mōtusque tumultū 317
"Dīc," ait, "Ō virgō, quid vult concursus ad amnem? 318
Quidve petunt animae? Vel quō discrīmine rīpās 319
hae linquunt, illae rēmīs vada līvida verrunt?" 320
Ollī sīc breviter fāta est longaeva sacerdōs: 321

---

amnis, -is m: stream; river, 2
aprīcus, -a, -um: sunny, open to the sun (~aperiō)
arceō, -ēre, -uī: fend or keep off, defend, 2
autumnus, -ī n.: autumn
avis, avis f.: bird
brevis, -e: short, shallow, 4
cadō, cadere, cecidī: to fall, 3
concursus, -ūs m.: gathering, running together, 2
discrīmen, -crīminis n.: crisis, peril; difference, 3
enim: for, indeed, 4
folium, -ī n.: leaf, foliage, 2
frigidus, -a, -um: chilly, cold
frīgus, -ōris n.: cold, chill, 2
fugō (1): put to flight, 2
glomerō (1): gather, heap, assemble around, 2
gurges, -itis m.: whirl (of water), whirlpool, 3
immittō, -ere, -mīsī, -missum: send into, 2
lābor, -ī, lapsus sum: glide, slide, slip, fall, 2
linquō, -ere, līquī, lictus: leave, desert, quit, 3
līvidus, -a, -um: blue, black and blue
longaevus, -a, -um: long-lived, aged
nāvita, -ae m.: sailor (nauta), boatman, 2
rēmus, -ī m.: oar, 3
sacerdōs, -dōtis m. f.: priest(ess), 2
silva, -ae f.: woods, 4
submoveō, -ēre, -mōvī: move up; remove
trāns; over, across (+ acc.), 2
trānsmittō, -ere, -mīsī: cross (over), pass; send across
trīstis, -e: sad, sullen, dreary, grim, 2
tumultus, -ūs m.: tumult, commotion, 2
ulterior, -ius: farther
vadum, -ī n.: shallows, shoals, 4
verrō, -ere, -ī, -rsus: sweep, 2
virgō, virginis f.: maiden, unmarried young woman
volō, velle, voluī: will, wish, be willing, 2

309 **quam multa...folia**: *as many as the...*; simile; quam begins a clause of comparison (equiv. to *tam multī quam*, 'as many as')
autumnī frīgōre prīmō: *at...*; abl. time when
310 **lāpsa**: pf. dep. pple: translate as 'having Xed'
aut...quam multae...avēs: *or as many as the...;* simile and clause of comparison (= *tam multī quam multae*, 'as many as')
ad terram gurgite ab altō: i.e. whirling flocks of birds come from the sea to the shore; part of the comparison that follows in 311
311 **ubi**: *when*
frigidus annus: *cold (part of) the year*
312 **fugat (avēs)...immittit**: add avēs as acc. obj.
terrīs...aprīcīs: *to...*; dat. of compound verb
313 **ōrantēs**: pres. pple
primī: *the first ones*; nom. subj., i.e. those souls at the front of the crowd; or '(to be) the first to cross...'
(sē) transmittere cursum: *that (they) cross the course*; ind. disc. governed by ōrō where one expects an ind. command (ut cursum transmittant); cursum may refer to the stream of water or the journey itself
314 **rīpae ulteriōris**: *for...*; objective gen.
amōre: *with...*; 'because of...' abl. cause
315 **navita trīstis**: i.e. Charon, nom. sg.
nunc hōs...nunc illōs: *now...now...*; i.e. animōs, 'souls'
316 **longē**: *far*
harēnā: *from...*; abl. of separation
317 **mirātus**: pf. dep. pple: translate 'having Xed'
mōtus: PPP moveō, i.e. emotionally moved
Dīc: sg. imperative, dīcō

318 **Ō virgō**: voc. dir. address; i.e. the Sibyl is indeed unmarried and perhaps young when compared to Charon, but she is over 700 years old and Vergil describes her as *longaeva* in 6.321 below; the Sibyl is the priestess of Apollo who guides Aeneas
vult: 3s volō
ad: *near..., at...*
319 **-ve...Vel**: *Or...Or...* ; vel and enclitic -ve are inclusive and can mean 'and/or' Aeneas wants at least one of the questions answered.
quō discrīmine: *because of what difference..?* or 'by what distinction,' abl. of cause and interrogative adj.
320 **hae (animae)...(sed) illae (animae)**: i.e. shades or ghosts ; nom. subj.
linquunt: i.e. walk away without crossing
rēmīs: abl. means
321 **Ollī**: *to that one*; i.e. to Aeneas; dat. ind. obj.: ollī is an archaic form for illī
fāta est: pf. dep. for, fārī
sacerdōs: i.e. Sibyl, priestess of Apollo

Aeneid Book 6 and *Odyssey* Book 11

The *Aeneid* Book 6 is an imitation of *Odyssey* Book 11, where Odysseus, seated at a banquet of the Phaeacians, gives an account of his own journey to the Underworld. And, just as Odysseus goes to the Underworld to seek the advice of the prophet Tiresias, so pious Aeneas goes to the Underworld to seek advice from his deceased father Anchises.

The Traditional Epic Hero and the Underworld

Recall that a traditional epic hero strives though deeds to achieve immortal glory. One motif that is common among all these heroes is a journey to the Underworld and back. Since the dead are not allowed to come back to the living, the return of the hero alive from the Underworld symbolizes the hero's ability to cheat death and achieve a form of immortality.

Aeneas, therefore, follows a long tradition of heroes travelling to the Underworld. **Orpheus** descended into Hades in order to retrieve his wife Eurydice and, although his wife could not join him, he returned home alive. **Theseus** and **Pirithous** attempted to kidnap Proserpina, but, when they were caught, both were condemned to spend an eternity stuck motionless in chairs in the Underworld. **Hercules**, however, descended into Hades during his 12th labor to retrieve the dog Cerberus. He not only returned above ground to complete his last labor but descended once more to return the guard dog. While there, the hero spotted Theseus, freed him from the chair, and escorted him out of the Underworld. (Vergil still has Theseus stuck in the Underworld.) **Odysseus** famously set out and returned from Hades in the *Odyssey* Book 11, and finally, while **Achilles** did not undertake a physical journey to the Underworld, scholars note that especially in *Iliad* 18-24 Achilles made a symbolic journey to the realm of the dead where he separated himself from the living, was mourned as if dead, and finally returned to commune with the living in the final book.

Similes introduced by Quam Multa/Multae – *as many as*

The quam clauses in 6.309 and 311 are clauses of comparison that introduce two distinct similes. As we mentioned on p. 79, quam ('as,' 'than') is a relative adverb [8] introducing a clause of comparison (e.g. longior quam, 'longer than...'). Here, the correlative *tam* is missing but must be added from context (quam = tam...quam). The missing *tam multī* modifies the undead along the beach in 305-8:

(tam multī) quam multa	→ (so many dead) as many... →	*as many as*	6.309
(tam multī) quam multae	→ (so many dead) as many... →	*as many as*	6.311

In short, *quam multa* and *quam multae* are equivalent to *tam multī quam*, but while Latin regularly leaves out the second *multa*/*multae* in the comparison, here it retains those words and omits *tam multī*.

"Anchīsā generāte, deum certissima prōlēs,
Cōcytī stagna alta vidēs Stygiamque palūdem,
dī cuius iūrāre timent et fallere nūmen.
Haec omnis, quam cernis, inops inhumātaque turba est;
portitor ille Charōn; hī, quōs vehit unda, sepultī.
nec rīpās datur horrendās et rauca fluenta
trānsportare prius quam sēdibus ossa quiērunt.
Centum errant annōs volitantque haec lītora circum;
tum dēmum admissī stagna exoptāta revīsunt."
Constitit Anchīsā satus et vestīgia pressit
multa putāns sortemque animō miserātus inīquam.

---

admittō, -ere, mīsī, missum: admit, allow
centum: one hundred, 3
cernō, -ere, crēvī, crētus: discern, perceive, 3
certus, -a, -um: sure, reliable, definite, 4
Charōn, -ontis m.: Charon, 2
Cōcȳtus, -ī m.: Cocytus river, 2
consistō, -ere, -stitī: stop, stand still, 3
dēmum: at length, finally
exoptō (1): to long for, desire eagerly
fallō, -ere, fefellī, falsum: deceive, 3
fluentum, -ī n.: flow; river, stream
generō (1): to beget, create, generate
horrendus, -a, -um: horrible, to be trembled at, 4
inhumātus, -a, -um: unburied
inīquus, -a, -um: unjust, unfair, 2
inops, -opis: lacking, destitute of, needy, (gen), 2
iūrō (1): to swear, take an oath, 2
miseror, -ārī, -ātus sum: pity, 4
os, ossis, n.: bone
palūs, palūdis f.: swamp, marsh, 2
portitor, -ōris m.: carrier, boatman, ferryman, 2
prōlēs, -is f.: offspring, 2
putō (1): to think, imagine, 3
quiēscō, -ere, -ēvī, -ētus: rest, be peaceful
raucus, -a, -um: hoarse, harsh-sounding
revīsō, -ere: revisit, 2
sepeliō, -īre, -īvī, sepultum: to bury, 2
serō, -ere, sēvī, satum: sow, plant, 2
stagnum, -ī n.: pool, standing water, 3
Stygius, -a, -um: Stygian, of the river Styx, 4
timeō, -ēre, timuī: be afraid, fear 2
trānsportō (1): carry over, take across
turba, -ae f.: crowd, mob, 4
vehō, -ere, vēxī, vectum: convey, 4
vestīgium, -iī n.: foot-print, footstep; traces
volitō (1): flitter, flutter, fly

322 **Anchīsā**: *from Anchises*; abl. of source or origin, 1st decl. masc.
generāte: *(you)...*; i.e. Aeneas; vocative dir. address of PPP generātus; Since Aeneas is in the Underworld to visit his deceased father, this address is particularly appropriate
de(ōr)um: gen. pl.
certissima prōlēs: vocative dir. address, recognizing Venus as Aeneas' divine mother and Anchises' more distant lineage as descendant of Dardanus, son of Jupiter
323 **dī**: deī, subject of timent in the cuius clause
cuius...nūmen: *whose divine power...*; relative clause, the antecedent is the river Styx (Stygiampalūdem); gods swear oaths to Styx
324 **haec omnis...turba**: nom. subject
326 **portitor ille (est)**
hī (animī): nom. subj. i.e. souls
sepultī (sunt): 3p pf. pass.
327 **nec...datur (Charontī)**: *it is not allowed (for Charon)*; 'it is not granted to Charon'
328 **trānsportāre (hās animās)**: *to carry (these souls) across (acc)*
prius quam: *before...*; 'earlier than' often one word, priusquam, 'before;' comparative adv.
(in) sēdibus: *in resting places*; i.e. in graves
329 **centum...annōs**: *for...*; acc. duration of time
haec lītora circum: circum haec lītora; anastrophe
330 **(hī) admissī**: *(these)...*; PPP is nom. pl. i.e those unburied who must wait 100 years
331 **Anchīsā**: *from...*; abl. of source
satus: *(the one)...*;; i.e. Aeneas; PPP serō;
vestīgia pressit: pf. premō; an unusual event since most souls are weightless and do not leave footprints in the sand on the shore
332 **multa**: *many things*
miserātus: pf. dep. pple: translate as 'having Xed'
(in) animō

Three Evolving Views of the Underworld

There was no monolithic view of the afterlife accepted by all Greeks or all Romans. For this reason, it is important that we never generalize and say 'the Romans believed this' or 'the Greeks believed that.' Instead, it is better to limit our comments to the evidence before us and say that 'this Roman author depicts the Underworld this way' or 'the *Aeneid* portrays the afterlife in that way.' Consider how different the three literary depictions of the Underworld are below. Each in its own way influences Vergil's Underworld in Book 6.

Homer's *Odyssey* Book 11 (720 BC): According to Odysseus, the hero visits a beachhead, likely on the Atlantic coast of Hispania, where he sacrifices a black sheep on the shore, and various souls approach. Since these souls are too weak to speak, he allows chosen spirits to drink the blood of the sacrifice and gather enough energy to answer his questions. His aim is to seek the advice of the prophet Tiresias, who advises Odysseus not to harm the cattle of Helius and warns him about the suitors that have gathered in his house. More generally, Odysseus explains that all souls—good and bad—go to the same dreary place, and, as Achilles famously swears to Odysseus, it is better to be a serf among the living than king among the dead (11.488-91). Although Odysseus sees figures such as Tantalus being punished in the distance, these souls are punished for crimes against the gods. No one is rewarded or punished for their behavior toward other humans, and while King Minos does serve as judge, he does not judge the moral lives of the dead but merely settles minor quarrels that arise among the souls.

***Hymn to Demeter* (600s BC):** This Greek epic poem explains how Proserpina (Grk. Persephone) became the queen of the Underworld and offers humans the possibility of changing their afterlife. While young Proserpina is picking flowers in a field, the god Pluto with the permission of Proserpina's father Jupiter kidnaps the young goddess and carries her into the Underworld as his bride. Proserpina's mother Ceres (Grk. Demeter), who was not consulted about Jupiter's arrangement with Pluto, goes in search of her daughter and becomes so despondent that grain no longer grows for humans. When the grain fails to grow, farmers fail to make sacrifices to the gods, and Jupiter finally intervenes when he realizes the role that Ceres plays in allowing humans to honor the gods. When Pluto is told to return Proserpina, he persuades her to eat pomegranate seeds, which ensures that Proserpina will spend part of the year in the Underworld with Pluto and the remainder of the year above ground with Ceres.

An important consequence of this account is that, while humans cannot honor Pluto (sacrificial smoke goes to Olympus, not to Hades), they can now sacrifice to Proserpina while she is above ground in the hopes that she will descend and improve their lot in the afterlife. Proserpina can be honored and persuaded in a way Pluto cannot.

The Myth of Er in Plato's *Republic* (380s BC): In the *Republic*, a philosophical dialogue on justice, the Athenian Plato has Socrates tell the tale of Er, a man who died and then came back several days later to relate his account of the Underworld. According to Er, souls first encounter the brothers Minos, Rhadamanthus, and Aeacus, who do not adjudicate disputes among the dead as they did in the *Odyssey* but judge the entire moral life of the soul and assign the soul either to Elysium or to Tartarus. If the soul is in Elysium, it will be rewarded tenfold during the course of 1000 years. If the soul is in Tartarus, it will be punished tenfold during the course of 1000 years. Once the time has passed, all souls—good and bad—are reincarnated. A choice of lives is set out in front of all, and the souls are allowed to examine and choose their next life. Souls that are thoughtful and observant choose wisely and avoid superficial happiness that conceals underlying pain or depravity, while less thoughtful souls choose poorly. Once the choice is made, the souls are reborn, and the cycle repeats itself.

Plato's Myth of Er includes a number of novel views: (1) that souls are reincarnated, (2) that souls are rewarded or punished for their behavior toward other people, and (3) that there is so sharp a division between Tartarus and Elysium. None of these views are expressed in the *Odyssey* or *Hymn to Demeter* but all will find their way into Vergil's *Aeneid* 400 years later.

1. What, according to the Sibyl, do gods fear to do in 6.324?
2. What distinction does Sibyl make between 'haec omnis turba' and 'hī' in 325-6? What happens to each group?
3. How long do the souls wait in 329-30 until they are allowed to cross?

Ergō iter inceptum peragunt fluviōque propinquant.
Nāvita quōs iam inde ut Stygiā prōspexit ab undā
per tacitum nemus īre pedemque advertere rīpae,
sīc prior adgreditur dictīs atque increpat ultrō:
"Quisquis es, armātus quī nostra ad flūmina tendis,
fāre age quid veniās iam istinc, et comprime gressum.
Umbrārum hic locus est, somnī noctisque sopōrae:
corpora vīva nefās Stygiā vectāre carīnā.
nec vērō Alcīdēn mē sum laetātus euntem
accēpisse lacū, nec Thēsea Pīrithoümque,
dīs quamquam genitī atque invictī vīribus essent.
Tartareum ille manū custōdem in vincla petīvit
ipsius ā soliō rēgis traxitque trementem;
hī dominam Dītis thalamō dēdūcere adortī."

---

adgredior, -ī, aggressus sum: attack
adorior, -īrī, -ortus sum: attack; undertake + inf.
advertō, -ere, advertī, adversum: to turn (to), 2
Alcīdēs, -is m.: Heracles, descendant of Alceus
armō (1): to arm, 3
carīna, -ae f.: keel (of a ship)
comprimō, -ere, -pressī: hold back, check; press
custōs, -ōdis m. (f.): guard, guardian, 4
dēdūcō, -ere: draw down, lead
dictum, -ī n.: word, speech, 4
Dīs, Dītis m.: Dis, Pluto, 2
domina, -ae f.: master, mistress
ergō: therefore, then, 3
flūmen, -inis n.: river, stream, 2
fluvius, -iī m.: river, stream, 2
gignō, -ere, -genuī, genitum: to beget, bear
gressus, -ūs m.: a step
increpō (1): utter aloud; chide, rebuke
inde: from there, then, 2
invictus, -a, -um: invincible, 2
istinc: from that place, thence
iter, itineris n.: way, road, journey
lacus, -ūs m.: lake
laetor, -ārī, -ātus sum: rejoice, exult
nāvita, -ae m.: sailor (nauta), boatman, 2
nefās n.: unrighteous(ness), sacrilege, forbidden act, 3
nemus, -oris n.: wood, forest, grove, 4
peragō, -ere, -ēgī, -actum: to pass or drive through
Pīrithous, -ī m.: Pirithous
propinquō (1): approach, draw near (dat) 2
prōspiciō, -ere, -spexī, -spectus: look out on, survey, 4
quamquam: although, 4
quisquis, quicquid: whoever, whatever, 2
rēx, rēgis m.: king, 4
solium, -ī n.: throne, seat, 2
sopōrus, -a, -um: sleep-bringing
Stygius, -a, -um: Stygian, of the river Styx, 4
Tartareus, -ī m.: of Tartarus, 2
thalamus, -ī m.: bedchamber
Thēseus, -eōs acc. **-a m.**: Theseus
trahō, -ere, trāxī, tractus: drag (out), draw, 3
tremō, -ere, -uī: tremble, quiver, 2
ultrō: voluntarily, on his/her own, 3
vectō (1): to convey, carry
vērō: in truth, in fact; but (abl. as adv.), 3
vinculum, -ī n.: chain, 4
vīvus, -a, -um: living, alive, 3

384 **iter inceptum**: neut. PPP incipiō
peragunt: i.e. Sibyl and Aeneas, subjects
385 **Nāvita quōs...ut prōspexit...īre...**: *when the boatman saw these go...*; ut (when/as) + ind. is temporal; quōs is connective relative and acc. subj.: translate quōs as demonstrative
ab undā: i.e. from Charon's perspective on the river Styx
386 **īre...advertere**: ind. disc. eō, īre; quōs, 'these' is acc. subject
rīpae: *to..*; dat. of compound
387 **prior**: *first*; i.e. earlier than the Sibyl
dictīs: *with...*; abl. means, substantive, dictum
388 **es**: 2s pres. sum
quī armātus...tendis: *you who...*; 2s relative
389 **fāre**: sg. imperative dep. for, fārī
age: *come!*; a sg. imperative often used to draw attention: translate before fāre
quid veniās: *why...*; ind. question, pres. subj.
comprime: sg. imperative
391 **nefās (est)**: *it is not right* + inf.; impersonal
carīnā: *by ship*; 'by keel,' synecdoche

vērō: *in truth*; common abl. as adv..

392 **Alcīdēn mē...accēpisse**: *that I*...; ind. disc. with pf. inf.; the patronymic Alcīdēn (Grk. acc. obj.) refers to Heracles, whose mortal grandfather was Alceus. Heracles came to the underworld to complete his 12th labor and kidnap Cerberus, the three-headed dog. After completing the labor, he returned the dog.

laetātus sum: 1s pf. dep.: translate active: Charon unhappily led Heracles, Theseus, and Pirithous across the river Styx

euntem: pres. pple eō, īre modifying Alcīdēn

393 **(in) lacū**

Thēsea Pīrithoümque: *Theseus and Pirithous*; Grk acc. Thēsea; These men came to kidnap Proserpina and, when caught, were forced to sit on chairs in the underworld from which they could not get up. When Heracles returned Cerberus, he picked Theseus from his chair and returned him to the world above. In Vergil's account, however, Theseus still sits.

394 **dīs**: *from*...; abl. of source, deus with genitī

genitī (essent): *had been*...; plpf. pass. subj. (subj. of subordinate verb in ind. disc.) Heracles and Pirithous are sons of Jupiter; Theseus is said to be the son of King Aegeus by some and son of Neptune by others.

invictī...essent: *they were*...; impf. subj. of a subordinate verb in ind. disc. + nom. pred.

vīribus: *in strength*; abl. of respect, vīs

395 **ille**: i.e. Heracles

Tartareum monstrum: i.e. Cerberus, whom Heracles kidnapped and later returned

manū: abl. means

396 **ipsius...regis**: i.e. of Pluto, gen. sg.

traxit (custōdem): pf. trahō

trementem: pres. pple modifying custōdem

397 **hī**: *these men*; i.e. Theseus and Pirithous

dominam Dītis: i.e. Proserpina, Pluto's wife, whom they tried to kidnap; gen. sg. Dīs

thalamō: *from*...; dat. of compound verb or abl. place from which

adortī (sunt): *rose up to* + inf.; i.e. attempted; 3p pf. dep.

Hercules (Alcides), Theseus, and Pirithous

Just as Vergil's previous imitations of the *Odyssey* make Aeneas a rival of equal or greater status to Odysseus, so these allusions to Hercules, Theseus and Pirithous in 6.392-7 remind readers that Aeneas is of equal status to Hercules, Theseus, and Pirithous. Charon's complaint that the theft of Cerberus and kidnapping of Proserpina were mischievous acts highlights that, while Aeneas follows in their footsteps, his purpose in the Underworld in far nobler.

Hercules, Aeneas, and Caesar Augustus

In the second half of the *Aeneid*, the relationship between these three figures will become much more prominent. Aeneas, for example, will arrive at the site of Rome in Book 7 just as the Greek King Evander is performing sacrifices on August 12th to honor Hercules for the time when the god first arrived at the site of Rome with cattle many years earlier and freed the people from the terror of the monster Cacus. Many years later, Caesar Augustus will arrive on August 13th, 29 BC to celebrate a triple triumph over his enemies and ceremoniously close the gates of Janus and usher in a new age of peace. Vergil famously alludes to this triple triumph by depicting it in the center of the shield that Aeneas will receive from Venus in Book 8.

This and other details suggest that Vergil wants readers to identify all three as similarly heroic. Just as Hercules killed the monster Cacus and made Rome more inhabitable, so Aeneas and later Caesar Augustus will overcome their own enemies and make the world more inhabitable for Rome and its descendants. This allusion to Hercules in Book 6, therefore, is just a first step in the identification of Aeneas and Hercules.

1. What is Charon's specific complaint in 390-1?

2. Who does the patronymic Alcīdēs refer to and what did he do in 395?

3. What did Theseus and Pirithous attempt to do in 396-7?

Quae contrā breviter fāta est Amphrȳsia vātēs:
"Nūllae hīc īnsidiae tālēs (absiste movērī),
nec vim tēla ferunt; licet ingens iānitor antrō
aeternum lātrāns exsanguēs terreat umbrās,
casta licet patruī servet Prōserpina līmen.
Trōius Aenēās, pietāte insignis et armīs,
ad genitōrem īmās Erebī dēscendit ad umbrās.
sī tē nūlla movet tantae pietātis imāgō,
at rāmum hunc (aperit rāmum quī veste latēbat)
agnōscās." Tumida ex īrā tum corda resīdunt;
nec plūra hīs. ille admīrāns venerābile dōnum
fātālis virgae longō post tempore vīsum
caeruleam advertit puppim rīpaeque propinquat.

---

absistō, -ere, -stitī: cease, stop, 2
admīror, -ārī, admīrātus sum: admire, wonder at
advertō, -ere, advertī, adversum: to turn (to), 2
aeternus, -a, -um: eternal, everlasting, 4
agnoscō, -ere, -nōvī, -nōtum: to recognize, 2
Amphrȳsius, -a, -um: Amphrisian (epithet of Apollo)
brevis, -e: short, shallow, 4
caeruleus, -a, -um: blue, sky-blue
castus, -a, -um: clean, pure
contrā: opposite, facing (*acc.*), 3
dēscendō, ere, ī, ēnsus: descend
Erebus, -ī n.: Erebus, underworld
exsanguis, -e: bloodless; pale, 2
fātālis, -e: deadly, fatal; fated, 3
genitor, -ōris m.: begetter, father, 4
iānitor, -ōris m.: door-keeper
imāgō, -inis f.: image, likeness, ghost, 3
īnsidiae, -ārum f.: ambush, trap
insignis, -e: distinguished, marked, 3
lātrō (1): to bark, bay
licet: it is allowed or permitted, 3
patruus, -ī m.: father's brother, uncle
piūs, plūris: more, *compar.* multus
propinquō (1): approach, draw near (dat) 2
Prōserpina, -ae f.: Proserpina, 2
rāmus, -ī m.: branch, 2
resīdō, -ere, -sēdī: sit or settle (down), 2
tempus, -oris n.: time; occasion, 2
terreō, -ēre, -uī, -itum: terrify, 2
tumidus, -a, -um: swelling, swollen, 2
vātēs, -is m/f: prophet, seer, bard, 3
venerābilis, -e: venerable, revered
vestis, -is f.: clothing, 2
virga, -ae f.: branch, bough

398 **quae contrā**: *in response to these things*; 'in response to which,' a connective relative: translate as a demonstrative
fāta est: pf. dep. for, fārī: translate active
Amphrȳsia vātēs: i.e. Sibyl; Amphrysus is a river associated with Apollo, and so translate adj. Amphrȳsia merely as 'Apollonian'
399 **(Sunt) nūllae īnsidae tālēs**: *(There are)...*
absiste: sg. imperative
400 **vim**: *violence*; i.e. there is no intent to harm
licet (ut) terreat: *it is allowed that...terrorize* Translate this construction as if licet governs an ind. command with missing ut
ingens iānitor: i.e. Cerberus
(in) antrō
401 **aeternum (tempus)**: *for...*; acc. duration
402 **licet...servet**: *it is allowed (that)...*; see note for line 400; pres. subj. servō, 'protect'
patruī: *of (her) uncle*; i.e. Pluto, brother to Proserpina's father, Jupiter
403 **insignis**: nom. sg. modifying Aenēās
pietāte et armīs: *in...and in...;* abl. of respect; note how Sibyl chooses to characterize Aeneas
404 **ad genitōrem**: i.e. to Anchises
īmās Erebī...ad umbrās
406 **at**: *at least*; or simple adversative 'but'
ramum hunc...agnōscās: *you should recognize...*; 2s potential pres. subj.
aperit: *reveals*
(in) veste
407 **tumida corda**: poetic nom. pl.: translate sg.
408 **nec plūra hīs (dicit)**: *and (he does not say)...*; ellipsis; plūra is comparative of multus and neut. acc. substantive (add 'things')
hīs: *to these*; i.e. to Sibyl and Aeneas
ille: i.e. Charon

fatālis virgae: *of…*; appositional gen.: clarifying what the dōnum is

409 **longō post tempore**: *a long time afterwards*; 'afterwards by a long time,' abl. of degree of difference with adv. post, 'afterwards

visum: PPP videō modifying dōnum

410 **puppim**: *boat*; 'deck,' synecdoche

rīpae: *to…*; dat. obj. of propinquat

The Underworld as a Metaphor for Aeneas' Past Sufferings and Future Reward

Readers note that, while Vergil depicts Book 6 as a physical journey to the Underworld, it is also a metaphysical one where Aeneas relives his past sufferings and learns about future rewards. In short, it answers the question posed in the invocation of the poem: Why must the pious suffer? Aeneas encounters four people in the Underworld whom he knew during his lifetime, and each person symbolizes a different aspect of his life:

Palinurus	suffering at sea	6.337-383
Dido	suffering at Carthage	6.450-76
Deiphobus	suffering in war at Troy	6.477-547
Anchises	the reward for piety	6.666-892

We will read about Aeneas' encounters with Dido and Anchises soon, but it worth mentioning the encounters with Palinurus and Deiphobus, which this commentary omits. Aeneas meets **Palinurus**, the helmsman of one of Aeneas' ships, before the crossing of the river Styx and learns that Palinurus fell overboard and drowned unburied as the Trojans skirted the coast of Italy. Palinurus pleads for Aeneas to arrange his burial, but the Sibyl intervenes and says that Palinurus' body will be found along the coastline by natives and properly buried.

After Aeneas later encounters Dido, he travels through the area of the Underworld reserved for warriors who died before their time and meets **Deiphobus**, whose face is horribly mutilated. Deiphobus was a son of Priam who married Helen after the death of Paris but before the fall of Troy. According to Deiphobus, when the Greeks descended from the horse, they straightaway tortured, mutilated, and killed him for his relationship with Helen. After Deiphobus finishes his account, Sibyl again intervenes and urges Aeneas to continue his journey.

Through these encounters with Palinurus, Deiphobus, and Dido not only Aeneas but also the readers relive Aeneas' suffering at sea (Book 1, 3), at Troy (Book 2), and finally in Carthage (Book 1, 4). It is only when Aeneas meets his father Anchises, who was the reason for the funeral games in Book 5 and the inspiration for Aeneas' journey to the Underworld, that the suffering of the pious is justified.

Note how the Sibyl's responses regarding Hercules, Theseus, and Pirithous provide another opportunity for readers to view Aeneas as a hero of equal status to those heroes who had travelled to the Underworld in the past.

1. What does the Sibyl say in 399-401 in reply to Charon's complaint that Hercules took Cerberus?

2. What does the Sibyl say reply to Charon's complaint that Theseus and Pirithous attempted to kidnap Proserpina?

3. What about Aeneas does Sibyl claim in 6.403-5 should motivate Charon to assist them?

4. What does Sibyl reveal in 6.406-9 to convince Charon to let Aeneas onto the boat?

Inde aliās animās, quae per iuga longa sedēbant,
dēturbat laxatque forōs; simul accipit alveō
ingentem Aenean. Gemuit sub pondere cumba
sūtilis et multam accepit rīmōsa palūdem.
Tandem trāns fluvium incolumēs vātemque virumque
informī līmō glaucāque expōnit in ulvā.
  Cerberus haec ingēns latrātū rēgna trifaucī
personat adversō recubāns immānis in antrō.
Cui vātēs horrēre vidēns iam colla colubrīs
melle sopōrātam et medicātīs frūgibus offam
obicit. ille famē rabidā tria guttura pandēns
corripit obiectam, atque immānia terga resolvit
fūsus humī tōtōque ingēns extenditur antrō.
Occupat Aenēās aditum custōde sepultō
ēvāditque celer rīpam inremeābilis undae.

---

aditus, -ūs m.: entrance, access, 2
adversus, -a, -um: facing, opposite, straight on, 5
alveus, -ī m.: vessel, small boat; hull
Cerberus, -ī m.: Cerberus
collum, -ī n.; neck, 3
coluber, -brī m.: snake, serpent
cumba, -ae f.: skiff, small boat, 2
custōs, -ōdis m. (f.): guard, guardian, 4
dēturbō (1): dislodge, drive off
ēvadō, -ere, ēvāsī, ēvāsum: to go out, escape, 2
expōnō, -ere, -posuī, -positum: set forth, explain
extendō, -ere, -ī: to stretch out, expand
famēs, -is f.: hunger
fluvius, -iī m.: river, stream, 2
forus, -ī m.: gangway, walkway (of the ship)
frūx, frūgis f.: grain, 2
fundō, -ere, -fūdī, fūsus: pour (out), lay low, 2
gemō, -ere, -uī: to groan
glaucus, -a, -um: grey, bluish-grey
guttur, gutturis n.: windpipe, throat
horreō, -ēre, -uī; bristle at, shudder at; fear, dread, 3
humus, -ī m.: ground; **humī**, on the ground, 2
incolumis, -e: unscathed, safe, 2
inde: from there, then, 2
informis, -e: formless, shapeless
inremeābilis, -e: of no return
iugum, -ī n.: bench; ridge of a mtn., yoke, 2
lātrātus, -ūs m.: barking
laxō (1): to loosen, set free
līmus, -ī m.: mud, filth, mire
medicō (1): to medicate, drug
mel, mellis n.: honey, 3
obiciō, -ere, -iēcī, obiectum: toss, throw forth, 2
occupō (1): seize, occupy
offa, -ae f.: lump of dough, mass
palūs, palūdis f.: swamp, marsh, 2
pandō, -ere, -ī, passus: spread, 2
personō, -āre, -uī: sound through, fill with sound
pondus, ponderis n.: weight
rabidus, -a, -um: raging, mad
recumbō, -ere, uī: lie back, recline
resolvō, -ere, -ī, -solūtum: loosen, set loose; relax, 2
rīmōsus, -a, -um: full of cracks
sedeō, -ēre, sēdī, sessum: sit, 4
sepeliō, -īre, -īvī, sepultum: to bury, 2
sopōrō (1): to make sleep-inducing, put to sleep
sūtilis, -e: sewn together, fastened together
trāns; over, across (+ acc.), 2
trēs, tria: three, 4
trifaux, trifaucis: having three throats
ulva, -ae f.: sedge
vātēs, -is m/f: prophet, seer, bard, 3

411 **per iuga longa**: *along the long benches*
412 **(in) alveō**
415 **cumba sūtilis...et rīmōsa**: The boat appears to have been made from animal hides that are stitched together on a wooden frame
415 **que...que...**: *both...and*
416 **(in) informī līmō**: i-stem abl. place where **glaucāque...in ulvā**
417 **haec...rēgna**: neut. acc.
latrātū trifaucī: abl. means 3rd decl. i-stem
419 **cui**: *to this one*; 'to whom' a connective relative (translate as demonstrative); dat. obj. of compound verb obicit
vātēs: i.e. the Sibyl; nom. subject

horrēre...colla colubrēs: *that serpents…*; ind. disc. governed by pple vidēns
420 **melle...et medicātīs frūgibus**: abl. means
sopōrātam: *made sleep-inducing*; PPP
421 **ille**: i.e. Cerberus
famē rabidā: *with…*; abl. of cause
obiectam (offam): PPP; add object
423 **fūsus**: *having spread out*; PPP reflexive in sense: 'having been spread out (by himself)'
humī: *on…*; locative case, place where
(in) tōtō...antrō
424 **custōde sepultō**: i.e. in sleep; abl. abs.
celer: *quickly*; nom. adj. as adv.
425 **undae**: *of the river*; 'wave,' synecdoche

Uses of the Ablative in the Commentary

construction	example	translation
Ablative Absolute	agmine factō	*a formation having been made*
Ablative of Means	hīs accēnsa	*enflamed by these things*
Ablative of Agent	missus ab Iove	*having been sent by Jupiter*
Ablative of Separation (includes From Which)	exciderat animō	*had slipped from her mind*
Ablative of Manner	magnō amōre	*with great love*
Ablative of Accompaniment	cum tē	*with you*
Ablative of Place Where	in altō	*on the deep sea*
Ablative of Place From Which	ē nubibus	*out from the clouds*
Ablative of Time When	nocte	*at night*
Ablative of Respect (Specification)	insignem pietāte	*distinguished in piety*
Ablative of Quality (Description)	praestantī corpore	*(nymphs) of outstanding body*
Ablative of Cause	fātō profugus	*a fugitive by (because of) fate*
Ablative of Comparison	dictō citius	*faster than said*
Ablative of Degree of Difference	longō post tempore	*afterwards by a long time*
w/ verbs: *potior*, *utor*, *fungor*, *fruor*, *vescor*	hīs vocibus ūsa est	*employed these words*

Uses of the Dative in the Commentary

construction	example	translation
Dative of Indirect Object	dīcite regī vestrō	*say **to your king***
Dative of Compound Verbs	ārīs imponet	*will place (on) the altar*
Dative of Purpose	excidiō Libyae	*for the destruction of Libya*
Dative of Possession + sum	sunt mihi	*there are to me (I have)*
Dative of Interest (Advantage)	mihi…fas est	*it is right for me*
Dative of Reference	Aenēae…videntur	*seemed to Aeneas*
Dative of Special Adjectives	inimīca mihi	*unfriendly to me*
Dative of Agent	cenitur ūllī	*is seen by any one*

Uses of the Genitive in the Commentary

construction	example	translation
Genitive of Possession	Iovis rapidum ignem	*the rapid fire of Jupiter*
Genitive of the Whole (Partitive)	regīna deōrum	*queen of the gods*
Genitive of Description (Quality)	tantae mōlis erat	*it was (of) so great a burden*
Objective Genitive	magnō amōre tellūris	*with great love for the land*
Subjective Genitive	iudicium Paridis	*the judgment of Paris*
Genitive of Special Adjectives	memor veteris bellī	*mindful of the old war*
Gen. of Verbs of Remembering/Forgetting	meminisse Elissae	*to recall Elissa*

1. Why does the boat groan and take in water in 6.413-4?
2. Where is Cerberus lying and what precisely does the Sibyl throw before him?
3. What happened to Cerberus in 6.422-3?

Inter quās Phoenissa recēns ā vulnere Dīdō
errābat silvā in magnā; quam Trōius hērōs
ut prīmum iuxtā stetit agnōvitque per umbrās
obscūram, quālem prīmō quī surgere mense
aut videt aut vīdisse putat per nūbila lūnam,
dēmisit lacrimās dulcīque adfātus amōre est
"Īnfēlīx Dīdō, vērus mihi nuntius ergō
vēnerat exstinctam ferrōque extrēma secūtam?
Fūneris heu tibi causa fuī? Per sīdera iūrō,
per superōs et sī qua fidēs tellūre sub īmā est,
invītus, rēgīna, tuō dē lītore cessī.
Sed mē iussa deum, quae nunc hās īre per umbrās,
per loca senta sitū cōgunt noctemque profundam,
imperiīs ēgēre suīs; nec crēdere quīvī
hunc tantum tibi mē discessū ferre dolōrem.

---

adfor, -fārī, -fātus sum: address, speak to
agnoscō, -ere, -nōvī, -nōtum: to recognize, 2
cēdō, -ere, -cessī, -cessus: withdraw, go
cōgō, cōgere, coēgī, coāctum: to collect; compel, 3
discessus, -ūs m.: departure, exit
ergō: therefore, then, 3
exstinguō, -ere, -stinxī, -stinctum: put out, 4
fidēs, eī f.: faith, honor, 2
fūnus, fūneris n.: burial; death, 4
hērōs, -hērōis m.: hero, 3
infēlīx, (īcis): ill-omened, unfortunate, 2
invītus, -a, -um: unwilling
iūrō (1): to swear, take an oath, 2
iuxtā: close by, next
lūna, -ae f.: moon
mensis, -is m.: month
nūbilus, ī (pl. nūbila): cloud, rain-cloud
nuntius, -iī m.: messenger, message
obscūrus, -a, -um: dim, obscure
Phoenissa, -ae f.: Phoenician (woman), 2
profundus, -a, -um: deep, vast, 2
putō (1): to think, imagine, 3
queō, quīre, quīvī: to be able
recēns, -ntis: fresh, recent, 2
sentus, -a, -um: thorny, rough, rugged
sequor, -ī, secūtus sum: follow, pursue, 4
silva, -ae f.: woods, 4
situs, -ūs m.: neglect, idleness; dust, dirt
superus, -a, -um: above, higher; *subst.* god above, 3
suus, -a, -um: his, her, its, their own, 2
Trōius, -a, -um: Trojan
vērus, -a, -um: true, real, 2

450 **inter quās**: *among these*; 'among whom,' a connective relative is often translated as a demonstrative; the quās refers to souls who have committed suicide out of love
quam Trōius hērōs...ut prīmum...: *whom as soon as...*; 'whom when first...' ut introduces a temporal clause and prīmum is an adv.; quam is within this temporal clause

453 **obscūram**: modifies acc. quam
quālem surgere ...lūnam: *just as a moon someone sees...*; 'which sort of moon...,' simile; ind. disc. with videt and vīdisse putat
prīmō...mense: *at the first of...*; abl. time when; the first of the month is a new moon, when the moon does not reflect any light
quī: *someone*; indefinite (ali)quī

454 **vīdisse**: *to...*; object of putat or ind. disc. with missing acc. subject sē: 'that (one) has seen...'

455 **dulcī...amōre**: *with...*; abl. of manner; 3rd decl. i-stem adj.
adfātus est: 3s pf. adfor: translate active

456 **nūntius**: *message*; elsewhere 'messenger'

457 **(tē) exstinctam (esse)...secūtam (esse)**: *that (you)...*; ind. disc. with pf. pass. inf. and pf. dep. inf., in apposition to vērus nūntius
ferrō: *by sword*; synecdoche
extrēma: *extreme ends*; i.e. death, neut. pl.

458 **fuī?**: *Was I...?*; pf. sum; a question without an interrogative often indicates surprise
tibi: *for...*; dat. of interest

459 **Per...Per...**: *by...by...*; per + acc. is used to mark the reason for swearing an oath
sī qua...est: *if there is any...*; qua is indefinite after sī, nisi, num, and nē

460 **invītus**: *unwillingly*; nom. adj. as adv.
cessī: *I departed*; 'went (away),' pf. cēdō
461 **iussa**: *orders*; 'things ordered,' PPP
de(ōr)um: gen. pl.
quae...(mē) īre...cogunt: *which compel...*; relative; supply mē as acc. object of cogunt
has...per umbrās: per hās umbrās
462 **(et) per loca**
senta sitū: *thorny with neglect*; 'because of neglect,' abl. of cause
463 **ēgēr(unt)**: *drove*; iussa de(ōr)um is subject
imperiīs suīs: abl. means
quīvī: *I was able*; 1s pf. queō, = potuī
464 **hunc...mē...ferre**: *that I...*; ind. disc. with mē as acc. subject; irreg. inf. ferō, 'bring'
tibi: *to...*; dat. ind. obj.
discessū: *because of...*; abl. of cause

The Untimely Dead between Tartarus and Elysium

Vergil's Underworld is by far the most detailed treatment in the Greco-Roman world. One development that is not found in the depictions of the Underworld from the *Odyssey*, *Hymn to Demeter,* or the Myth of Er in Plato's *Republic* (see p. 109) is an intermediary realm for souls before the path splits to Tartarus, where souls are punished, or to Elysium, where souls are rewarded.

In 6.426-49, immediately after passing Cerberus, Aeneas sees Minos, who judges the entire lives of souls and assigns them to Tartarus, Elysium, or the realm of untimely dead. Among the untimely dead are (a) infants, (b) suicides, especially those who die because of love, and (c) heroes cut down prematurely in battle. Aeneas has just entered the woods where those who committed suicide because of love dwell when he spots Dido in lines 450.

Dido as a Dimly Lit Moon

This simile in 453-4 that likens Dido to a dimly lit moon is the third that readers encounter involving Dido in this commentary. When Aeneas first sees Dido as a strong and just leader, she is likened to the goddess Diana surrounded by a throng of supporters (1.498-502, p. 38). Later in Book 4.301-3, when Dido first learns that Aeneas is leaving, Dido is likened to a Bacchante, overcome with raving and out of control.

Vergil's decision to describe Dido as a dimly lit moon may seem to be a poor choice when compared to previous similes, but in fact the moon is sacred to Diana just as the sun is sacred to her brother Apollo. This third simile, therefore, invites readers to revisit the simile of Diana in Book 1 and witness how much Dido has changed between then and now as a result of love: what once was bright is now a shadow of its former self.

1. Where is Dido wandering when Aeneas first sees her in 4.450-1?

2. How is Dido's appearance likened to a moon in 452-4? What specifically is the same?

3. What emotion does Vergil, our objective narrator, ascribe to Aeneas in 455?

4. What rumor had Aeneas heard in 456-7?

5. The anaphora in 6.458-9 'per sīdera iūrō...per superōs' is very similar to the anaphora expressed by Dido in Book 4 as she pleads for Aeneas to stay: 'per...lacrimās dextramque tuam...per cōnūbia...per inceptōs hymenaeōs...ōrō.' If we assume that this similarity is intentional, why is it appropriate for Vergil to compare Aeneas's speech here to Dido's speech when Aeneas was departing from Carthage?

6. What keywords in 460-3 suggest that Aeneas did not leave voluntarily but was compelled to do so?

Siste gradum tēque aspectū nē subtrahe nostrō.
Quem fugis? Extrēmum fātō quod tē adloquor hoc est.”
Tālibus Aenēās ardentem et torva tuentem
lēnībat dictīs animum lacrimāsque ciēbat.
Illa solō fīxōs oculōs āversa tenēbat
nec magis inceptō vultum sermōne movētur
quam sī dūra silex aut stet Marpēsia cautēs.
Tandem corripuit sēsē atque inimīca refūgit
in nemus umbriferum, coniūnx ubi prīstinus illī
respondet cūrīs aequatque Sychaeus amōrem.
Nec minus Aenēās cāsū concussus inīquō
prōsequitur lacrimīs longē et miserātur euntem.

---

adloquor, -ī, -locūtus sum: address, speak to
aequō (1): make equal, requites, 3
aspectus, -ūs m.: sight, view, 3
āvertō, -ēre, āvertī, āversum: turn away, 4
cāsus, -ūs m.: misfortune; chance, 4
cautēs, -is m.: rock, sharp rock
cieō, -ēre, cīvī, citus: arouse, stir up, 2
concutiō, -ere, -cussī, -cussus: shake, strike 2
dictum, -ī n.: word, speech, 4
dūrus, -a, -um: hard, harsh, stern, 2
fīgō, -ere, fīxī, fīxus: fix, fasten
gradus, -ûs m.: step, stide, gait, 2
inimīcus, -a, -um: unfriendly, hostile, 4
inīquus, -a, -um: unjust, unfair, 2
lēniō, -īre, -īvī (iī), -ītus: soothe, soften
magis: more, rather, 2
Marpēsius, -a, -um: of Mt. Marpesus, Marpesian,
minor, minus: smaller, less 2
miseror, -ārī, -ātus sum: pity, 4
nemus, -oris n.: wood, 4
prīstinus, -a, -um: former
prōsequor, sequī, secūtus: follow, pursue, escort, 2
refugiō, -ere, -fūgī: flee back
respondeō, -ēre, -dī, -ōnsum: to answer
sermo, -mōnis m.: conversation, discourse, 3
silex, -icis m./f.: flint
sistō, -ere, -stitī: set, make stand; stand, stop, 4
solum, -ī n.: soil; ground, 3
subtrahō, -ere, -trāxī: to draw away, withdraw
Sychaeus, -ī m.: Sychaeus, 3
torvus, -a, -um: grim, fierce, gloomy
tueor, tuērī, tutus(tuitus) sum: look on, watch, 3
umbrifer, -a, -um: shady

465 **Siste**: imperative + acc.
aspectū nostrō: *from...*; abl. of separation;
nē...subtrahe: *Don't...*; neg. imperative
466 **Extrēmum...hoc est**: *this is the last (time)*
fātō: *by...*; ‘because of...’ abl. cause
quod tē adloquor: *that...*; relative clause with neut. inner acc.
467 **Tālibus...dictīs**: *with...*; abl. of means; marking the end of the speech
ardentem et torva tuentem...animum: *the spirit (of Dido)...*; pres. pples with animum
torva: *grimly, fiercely*; nom. adj. as adv.
468 **lēni(e)bat...ciēbat**: *tried to...and tried to...*; conative impf.; Aeneas tries but does not succeed at these tasks
469 **Illa**: i.e. Dido
(in) solō
tenēbat: *was holding* (x) (y); governs a double acc. (obj. and pred.)
470 **nec magis...quam**: *and not more...than...*; quam introduces a clause of comparison
inceptō...sermōne: abl. abs., PPP incipiō
vultum: *in...*; acc. of respect
471 **sī...stet**: *if...should stand there*; pres. subj.; The Greek Mt. Marpesus was known for its quarries of marble, a hard and durable stone
472 **corripuit sēsē**: i.e. moved abruptly; Dido is the subject; sēsē is an emphatic form for sē
inimīca: nom. adj.: translate as an adv.
473 **ubi coniūnx prīstinus**: *where...*; i.e. Sychaeus, Dido’s previous husband
illī: *that one's*; i.e. Dido’s; dat. of possession modifying cūrīs
474 **cūrīs**: dat. ind. obj. of respondet
Nec minus: *and no less*; comparative adv.
cāsū...iniquō: abl. means
concussus: PPP concutiō
476 **prōsequitur**: pf. dep. pple: translate active
lacrimīs: *with...*; abl. of manner
longē: *far*; adv.
miserātur: pf. dep. pple: translate active
euntem: *(the one)...*; pres. pple eō, īre

Conative Imperfect

This type of imperfect is named after the verb *cōnor, cōnārī: to attempt, try*. Imperfect verbs express actions that are not (*im-*) completed (*perfectum*), but while most imperfects are actions that are not yet completed but eventually will be, a conative imperfect is an action that is not yet completed and will likely fail. It is suitably translated as 'attempted/tried to X' or 'was attempting/trying to X,' in 6.468:

lēnībat dictīs animum	*he tried to soothe her spirit with such words*
lacrimāsque ciēbat.	*and he tried to incite tears*

Unresolved Questions

Is *Amor* an Evil or a Good? Frequently, we are told in the modern world that love is a virtue which makes us better human beings and allows us to live more fulfilling lives. In the Christian church, for example, 'faith, hope, and love (charity)' are promoted as primary virtues. But, Greco-Roman writers such as Plato, Aristotle, and Cicero spend considerable time outlining the moral and intellectual virtues, and *amor* is conspicuously absent. In addition, poets such as Catullus, Vergil, and Ovid highlight how *amor* often gives rise to a lack of self control and tragic outcomes.

As readers, we witnessed the role of *amor* in Dido's precipitous decline from a strong, just, and hospitable leader to a woman who lacked personal control, neglected her people, and finally commited suicide. Now in the Underworld, we find that Dido dwells among the untimely dead, where 'unforgiving love consumes souls with a cruel wasting sickness' (durus amor crudeli tabe peredit, 6.442). This love is seemingly destructive and unending. Dido and the others will not forget their past grief and move on but continue to pine away for the objects of their love for eternity. What then is Vergil saying about *amor* in our lives? Is 'romantic love' or 'obsessive love' perhaps a better translation for *amor* in this case than 'love' in general?

Throughout this commentary we have highlighted a contrast between unrestrained emotions and *pietās*, proper devotion. Is this distinction helpful in understanding the *amor* between Dido and Aeneas and its consequences both for themselves and for their descendants?

1. What do Aeneas' words reveal about Dido's physical behavior in 6.465?

2. Aeneas' question 'Quem fugis?' in 6.466 recalls Dido's question 'Mēne fugis?' in 4.314. If the similarity is intentional, why is it appropriate?

3. After Dido's plea in Book 4, Aeneas 'held his eyes unmoved' (immota tenebat lumina, 4.331-2, p. 92), with what words does Dido behave in a similar fashion in 6.467-71?

4. In Book 4, after Aeneas tells Dido that Anchises, Ascanius, and the gods compel him to go, Dido delivers a final speech, omitted from this commentary, where she claims that Aeneas is so unfeeling in his betrayal that he was born not from a goddess but from the harsh Caucasus mountains or from Hyrcanian Tigers (4.365-7). What similar comparison does Vergil make in 6.469-71 to show that Dido is now as unfeeling and unresponsive to Aeneas' pleas?

5. Dido reunites with Sychaeus in the woods in 6.471-4. Who is Sychaeus? (For summary, see p. 35.)

6. **Empathy**: If empathy is the ability to acknowledge and share the thoughts and feelings of another person, how does Vergil's seemingly conscious decision to have Aeneas' speech imitate Dido's pleas in Book 4 show that Aeneas is empathic and not as unfeeling as Dido claimed that he was in Book 4? Did Aeneas display empathy in his response to Dido's pleas in Book 4?

7. What is Aeneas doing physically in 6.476 as Dido walks off with Sychaeus?

Excūdent aliī spīrantia mollius aera
(crēdō equidem), vīvōs dūcent dē marmore vultūs,
ōrābunt causās melius, caelīque meātūs
dēscribent radiō et surgentia sīdera dīcent:
tū regere imperiō populōs, Rōmāne, mementō
(hae tibi erunt artēs), pācisque impōnere mōrem,
parcere subiectīs et dēbellāre superbōs."
Sīc pater Anchīsēs atque haec mīrantibus addit:
"Aspice, ut īnsignis spoliīs Mārcellus opīmīs
ingreditur victorque virōs superēminet omnēs.
Hic rem Rōmānam magnō turbante tumultū
sistet, eques sternet Poenōs Gallumque rebellem,
tertiaque arma patrī suspendet capta Quirīnō."

---

addō, -ere, -didī, -ditum: to bring to, add, 4
aes, aeris n.: bronze, 2
ars, artis f.: art
dēbellō (1): wage war, , fight out, conquer
dēscribō, -ere, -psī, -ptum: describe, draw/mark out
eques, equitis m.: equestrian
equidem: (I) for my part, (I) indeed, 3
excūdō, -ere: strike out, hammer out, 2
Gallus, -a, -um: Gaul
ingredior, -ī, -gressus sum: step in, enter; begin, 3
insignis, -e: distinguished, marked, 3
Marcellus, -ī m.: Marcellus, 2
marmor, -oris n.: marble
meātus, -ūs m.: motion, course
melior melius: better, superior
meminī, -isse (imper. **memento)**: remember, recall, 3
mollis, -e: soft, gentle, tender
mōs, mōris m.: custom, law, 2
opīmus, -a, -um: rich, fertile
parcō, -ere, pepercī: spare, refrain (dat), 2
pāx, pācis f.: peace,1
Poenī, -ōrum, m: Phoenician, Carthaginian, 2
Quirīnus, -ī m.: Quirinus (deified Romulus)
radius, -ī m.: measuring-rod
rebellis, -e: renewing a war; rebel
sistō, -ere, -stitī: make stand, set up; stop, 4
spīrō (1): to breathe
spolium, -ī n.: spoils, plunder
sternō, -ere, strāvī, strātum: to lay (low), layer, 4
subiciō, -ere, -iēcī, -iectum: throw under, subject, 2
superbus, -a, -um: proud, arrogant, 3
superēmineō, -ēre: tower above, tower over; surpass, 2
suspendō, -ere, -pendī, -pensum: hang up
tertius, -a, -um: third
tumultus, -ūs m.: tumult, commotion, 2
turbō (1): confuse, trouble, disturb, 2
victor, -ōris m.: victor, 2
vīvus, -a, -um: living, alive, 3

847 **excūdent**: 3p fut., Anchises is describing the future to Aeneas and uses many future verbs
aliī: *some, others*; i.e. the Greeks
spīrantia...aera: i.e. lifelike bronze statues; neut. acc. pl., pres. pple
mollius: *more...*; comparative adv.
848 **dūcent**: *will draw out*; 3p fut.
vīvōs vultūs: again, in statues
849 **ōrābunt causās**: *will plead cases*; an idiom, Anchises refers to the Greek art of oratory
melius: comparative adv. bonus
850 **dēscribent...dīcent**: 3p fut.
radiō: abl. of means; a radius is here a mechanical compass used to draw circles
surgentia sīdera: neut. acc. pl. and pres. pple
dīcent: *will predict*
851 **tū...Rōmāne**: voc. direct address; Anchises addresses his son Aeneas as a Roman
imperiō: abl. of means
mementō: *remember to...!* fut. sg. imperative meminī + four infinitives
852 **tibi**: *your*; dat. of possession
erunt: 3p fut. sum
impōnere: governed by mementō
853 **parcere...superbōs**: governed by mementō
subiectīs: *the subjected*; i.e. those conquered by Rome; PPP and dat. obj. of parcere
854 **haec**: *these things*; neut. acc. pl.
mīrantibus: *to (those)...*; i.e. to Aeneas and Sibyl; dat. ind. obj. pres. obj.
855 **Aspice**: sg. imperative
ut insignis...: *how distinguished...!* ;
ut is an interrogative adv. modifying nom. sg. insignis in an exclamatory sentence

spoliīs...opīmīs: *in rich spoils*; abl. of respect; neut. pl. 'spolia opimia' is a technical term for the weapons and armor a Roman general strips from a enemy commander after single combat.
Marcellus: The elder Marcellus (268-208 BC) led the Romans against against the Gauls and then Carthaginians in the 2nd Punic War
856 **ingreditur**: pres. dep.
victorque: *and as victor*
857 **Hic**: *this one*; i.e. Marcellus
rem Rōmānam: *the Roman state*
magnō turbante tumultū: abl. abs.
858 **sistet, sternet**: 3s fut.
eques: *as equestrian, he...*; i.e. Marcellus
859 **tertia arma capta**: neut. acc.; According to tradition, the victor nails *spolia opimia* to the trunk of an oak tree, a tree sacred to Jupiter. For more, see the note in the box below
patrī...Quirīnō: *for...*; dat. of interest; Quirinus is the name of Romulus once he died and was deified.
suspendet: 3s fut.

What Happened in 6.477-846

After Aeneas leaves Dido, he walks among heroes who have died before their time and encounters **Deiphobus**, who, as noted on p. 113, was a son of Priam and last Trojan husband to Helen. Deiphobus recognizes Aeneas and explains how he was mutilated and killed by Menelaus and Ulysses at the fall of Troy. After the Sibyl urges Aeneas to press on, the two pass Tartarus on their left side, where the Sibyl describes the horrors suffered by those who have commited crimes against the gods or against other humans. From there, the two proceed to the house of Proserpina and Dis, where Aeneas leaves the golden bough by the doorway as a gift to Proserpina.

At last, Aeneas arrives in Elysium, where he sees souls enjoy doing whatever each soul enjoyed while living. He then reunites with Anchises, who takes Aeneas and the Sibyl to the river Lethe, the river of forgetfulness, where souls after 1000 years wait in a line to drink the water of the river, forget their past lives, and be reborn. Here, Anchises points out the figures that will give rise to Rome: the Alban kings, the kings of Rome, many of Rome's famous generals, and Augustus Caesar himself, who shall extend his power to the ends of the world.

Beginning at line 847 on the facing page, Anchises contrasts the excellence of others, i.e. the Greeks, with the excellence of the Romans and offers a detailed description of the first of three Romans named Marcellus.

Rōmāne in line 851 may refer to Aeneas as well the reader. It would not be unusual for Anchises to refer to his son as a Roman. In Book 1 when Jupiter foretells the future for Venus and connects Aeneas to the future fo Rome, he refers to Caesar as 'Trōiānus Caesar' (1.283) in a clear attempt to connect Caesar with his Trojan ancestry. It would not, therefore, be strange for Vergil to identify Aeneas by the name of his descendants—even if Aeneas does not know what *Rōmāne* means.

Of course, readers could also view Anchises as speaking to them directly and not to Aeneas alone.

Spolia opima were arms that a Roman general stripped from the body of an enemy leader in single combat. The victor would fasten the spoils to an oak trunk and dedicate them to Jupiter on the Capitoline Hill (Vergil has them dedicated to Quirinus, Romulus' name once deified). This dedication occurred only three times: (1) Romulus stripped King Acron in 752 BC, (2) Cossus stripped Lar Tolumnius in 5th c., and (3) Marcellus stripped the Gallic Viridomarus of the Gaesatae in 222 BC.

1. Name five (5) ways the Greeks will excel in 6.847-50.

2. Name four (4) ways that the Romans will excel in 851-3.

3. What two foes will Marcellus (discussed in the next page) defeat in line 858?

Atque hīc Aenēās (ūnā namque īre vidēbat
ēgregium formā iuvenem et fulgentibus armīs,
sed frōns laeta parum et dēiectō lūmina vultū.)
"Quis, pater, ille virum quī sīc comitātur euntem?
Fīlius, anne aliquis magnā dē stirpe nepōtum?
Quī strepitus circā comitum! Quantum instar in ipsō!
Sed nox ātra caput trīstī circumvolat umbrā."
Tum pater Anchīsēs lacrimīs ingressus obortīs:
"Ō nāte, ingentem lūctum nē quaere tuōrum;
ostendent terrīs hunc tantum fāta neque ultrā
esse sinent. Nimium vōbīs Rōmāna propāgo
vīsa potēns, superī, propria haec sī dōna fuissent.

---

an: or (in questions), 3
circā: around, around about
circumvolō (1): fly around
comitor, -ārī, comitātus sum: accompany, attend
dēiciō, -ere, -iēcī, -iectum: cast down
ēgregius, -a, -um: remarkable, distinguished
fīlius, -iī m.: son
frōns, frontis f.: forehead, brow, 2
fulgeō, -ēre, -fulsī: flash, shine, 2
ingredior, -ī, -gressus sum: step in, enter; begin, 3
instar n.: image, likeness; figure, bearing
iuvenis, -is m.: youth, young man, 3
luctus, -ūs m.: grief, lamentation
nepōs, nepōtis m.: grandson, decendent, 3
neque: nor, and not;: neither…nor, 4
nimium: too much, exceedingly
oborior, -orīrī, -ortus sum: rise up, appear
ostendō, -ere, -ī, ntus: show, promise, 2
parum: not enough, too little
potēns, -entis: powerful, 4
propāgo, -īnis f.: descendants, posterity, offspring
proprius: its own, their own, one's own, 2
quantus, -a, -um: how great, much, many, 4
sinō, -ere, sīvī, situs: allow, permit, 2
stirps, stirpis f.: stock, shoot
strepitus, -ūs m.: noise, uproar, 2
superus, -a, -um: above, higher; *subst.* god above, 3
trīstis, -e: sad, sullen, dreary, 2
ultrā: beyond, more, besides

860 **Aenēās (dīxit)**
ūnā: *together*; adv.; with the elder Marcellus
īre….iuvenem: *that…*; ind. disc. eō, īre; this young man is Marcellus (3) (42-23 BC)
formā et fulgentibus armīs: *in…and in…*; abl. respect with ēgregium
862 **frōns (erat) laeta parum**: *his face (was)…*; 'his brow' synecdoche and litotes
dēiectō lumina vultū: *his eyes were cast down on his face*; 'his face cast down in respect to his eyes' abl. abs., acc. of respect
863 **Quis (est) ille…quī…**
virum…euntem: obj. of comitātur and pres. pple eō, īre; i.e. elder Marcellus (1)
864 **(Estne) Fīlius an-ne (est)…**: *(Is he)….or (is he)…?*; add linking verbs
865 **Quī strepitus (est)**: *What…(there is)…!*; interrogative adj. in an exclamatory sentence
circā: *around (him)*
comitum: gen. pl. comes
Quantum instar (habet)…: *How great…*; interrogative adj. in exclamatory sentence
in (eō) ipsō: *in him himself*; i.e. Marcellus (3)
866 **trīstī…umbrā**: abl. means; 3rd decl i-stem
867 **lacrimīs…obortīs**: abl. abs.
ingressus (est): i.e. to speak; 3s pf. dep.
868 **Ō nāte**: voc. dir. address, nātus
nē quaere: *Don't…*; neg. imperative
tuōrum: *of your own (people)*
869 **ostendent**: fut.; neut, fāta is the subject
terrīs: dat. ind. obj.
tantum (tempus): *for so much (time)*; or 'only so long,' acc. of duration or just adverbial acc.
ultrā…(eum) esse: *that (he) exist more*
870 **sinent**: fut.
nimium: adv. with nom. pred. potēns
Rōmāna propāgō: *Roman descendants*
vōbīs: i.e. to the gods, dat. pl. of reference, vōs
871 **vīsa (esset), sī…fuisset**: *would have seemed…, if…had been…*; past. contrary to fact (sī plpf. subj. of sum, plpf. pass. subj.);
superī: *(the gods) above*; voc. dir. address

Three Men named Marcellus

In 6.860-2 Aeneas notices a young Marcellus (3) walking alongside Marcellus (1).

Marcus Claudius Marcellus (1) 268-208 BC
held consulship five (5) times
consul during Gallic War of 225 BC
earned *Spolia Opima* in hand-to-hand combat with the Gaul Viridomarus in 222 BC
proconsul/consul during 2nd Punic War (216-11 BC)
famously captured the city of Syracuse in Sicily

Gaius Claudius Marcellus (2) 88-40 BC
descendant of Marcellus (1) and father to Marcellus (3)
married Augustus' sister Octavia (69-11 BC) in 54 BC
had three children with Octavia: two daughters and Marcus
elected consul in 50 BC
opposed Julius Caesar during the Civil war but was later pardoned
died in 40 BC (Octavia then married Marcus Antonius)

Marcus Claudius Marcellus (3) 42-23 BC
son of Marcellus (2) and Octavia, Augustus' sister who will later marry Antony
heir apparent to his uncle, Caesar Augustus, who had no male heirs
married Julia, his cousin and Augustus' sole daughter, in 25 BC
died of illness in Baiae, near Mr. Vesuvius, in 23 BC
buried in Mausoleum of Augustus still extant in the Campus Martius

Political Propaganda and Marcellus (3)

Before the premature death at 19 years old in 23 BC, Marcellus (3) was supposed to be the heir to Caesar Augustus' power in Rome and become the second emperor of Rome. He had already married Julia, Caesar Augustus's daughter and Marcellus' own cousin, which reaffirmed the political alliance and communicated to others that Marcellus was the heir apparent to his uncle's wealth and power.

By including this laudatory tribute, Vergil suggests that both the gods and fates approved and promoted Marcellus' rise to power in the same way they promoted Augustus' own rise to power.

Why Include the Elder Marcellus (1)?

The mention of Marcellus (1) in 855-859 serves at least three purposes: (a) he is a natural part of the procession of Roman figures along the riverbank, (b) his mention ennobles Marcellus (3) and reminds readers that Augustus' heir had a distinguished aristocratic pedigree just as Augustus himself, and (c) the praise lavished on Marcellus (3) while he walks beside Marcellus (1) emphasizes that the young man would have surpassed his famous ancestor in accomplishments.

1. What do 8.860 and 863 indicate that Marcellus (1) and Marcellus (3) are doing as Aeneas watches?
2. How do lines 862 and 866 foreshadow the premature death of Marcellus (3)?
3. What is Anchises' physical reaction in 867 when Aeneas asks about young Marcellus (3)?
4. Why, according to Anchises in 6.868-71, do the gods cut short the life of Marcellus, who was so full of promise?

Quantōs ille virum magnam Māvortis ad urbem
campus aget gemitūs! Vel quae, Tiberīne, vidēbis
fūnera, cum tumulum praeterlābēre recentem!
Nec puer Īliacā quisquam dē gente Latīnōs
in tantum spē tollet avōs, nec Rōmula quondam
ūllō sē tantum tellūs iactābit alumnō.
Heu pietās, heu prīsca fidēs invictaque bellō
dextera! Nōn illī sē quisquam impūne tulisset
obvius armātō, seu cum pedes īret in hostem
seu spūmantis equī foderet calcāribus armōs.
Heu, miserande puer, sī quā fāta aspera rumpās,
tū Mārcellus eris. Manibus date līlia plēnīs,
purpureōs spargam flōrēs animamque nepōtis
hīc saltem accumulem dōnīs, et fungar inānī
mūnere." Sīc tōtā passim regiōne vagantur

---

accumulō (1): heap upon, pile upon
alumnus, -a, -um: nurtured; nutured one, offspring
armō (1): to arm, 3
armus, -ī m.: shoulder, flank (side)
asper, aspera, asperum: harsh, rough, 2
avus, -sī m.: forefather, grandfather
calcār, -āris m.: spur (on a boot)
campus, -ī m.: field, 3
equus, -ī m.: horse, 4
fidēs, eī f.: faith, honor, 2
flōs, flōris m.: flower
fodiō, -ere, fōdī, fossum: dig, stab
fungor, -ī, functus sum: perform, execute (abl.)
fūnus, fūneris n.: burial, burial rites, death, 4
hostis, -is m./f.: enemy, foe, 4
Īliacus, -a, -um: of Ilium, Trojan, 2
impūnē: *adv.* with impunity, without punishment
inānis, -e: empty, fruitless, meaningless, 3
invictus, -a, -um: invincible, 2
Latīnus, -a, -um: Latin, of Latin, 2
līlium, -ī n.: lily (flower)
Marcellus, -ī m.: Marcellus, 2
Māvors, Māvortis, m.: Mars
miseror, -ārī, -ātus sum: pity, 4
mūnus, -eris n.: gift, duty; function 3
nepōs, nepōtis m.: grandson, decendent, 3
obvius, -a –um: in the way, to meet (dat.)
passim: here and there, to and fro, 4
pedes, peditis m.: on foot; foot-soldier
plēnus, -a, -um: full, complete
praeterlābor, -ī, lapsus sum: glide past, slide past
prīscus, -a, -um: ancient, old, venerable
purpureus, -a, -um: crimson, purple
quantus, -a, -um: how great, much, many, 4
quisquam, quae-, quic-: any(one), any(thing), 4
quondam: formerly, ever, 4
recēns, -ntis: fresh, recent, 2
regiō, -ōnis f.: region, district 2
Rōmulus, -a, -um: of Romulus
rumpō, -ere, -rūpī, -ruptum: burst, break through, 2
saltem: at least, 3
sīve, seu: whether, or (if), 4
spargō, -ere, -rsī, -rsus: scatter, disperse, 2
spūmō (1): to foam, froth, 3
Tiberīnus, -a, -um: of the Tiber river, Tiber river's, 2
tumulus, -ī m.: mound, hill
vagor, -ārī, vagātus sum: wander, roam

872 **Quantōs...gemitūs**: *How many...*; yet more exclamatory sentences;
ille Marvortis campus: *that (famous) Campus Martius*; NW Rome where Marcellus is buried
vir(ōr)um: gen. pl.
873 **aget**: *will drive*
Vel: *or...*; inclusive disjunctive (= and)
Quae...funera...!: *What funerals...!*; in an exclamatory sentence
Tiberīne: voc. dir. address; apostrophe, He addresses the Tiber river, which flows nearby
vidēbis: 2s fut.
874 **cum...praeterlābēr(is)**: 2s fut. dep.: translate as present active with fut. sense
875 **Nec puer...quisquam**: *not any boy...*
876 **in tantum**: *so much*; 'to so much'
spē: *in expectation/hope;* abl. of respect
Rōmula...tellūs: nom. fem. sg. subject

877 **tantum...iactābit**: *will boast...so much*; tantum is an inner acc. ('make so great a boast'); sē is acc. obj.
ūllō...alumnō: *for any offspring*; dat. of interest
878 **Heu**: *Hail!*
pietās...fīdes...dextera (manus): qualities of the young Marcellus (3)
(in) bellō
879 **Nōn...quisquam...tulisset**: *not anyone would have carried...away*; i.e. an enemy; plpf. subj. ferō, contrary to fact (past potential)
illī...armātō: *that one (when) armed*; dat. of compound adj. obvius
880 **seu cum...iret...seu (cum)...foderet...**: *whether when...or (when)...*; seu = sī-ve; cum-clauses with impf. subj. eō and fodiō
pedes: *as a foot-soldier*; or 'on foot'
in hostem: *against...*
881 **foderet...armōs**: i.e. fighting on horseback
calcāribus: abl. means
882 **miserande**: *pitable*; 'worthy to be pitied,' gerundive, voc. dir. address
sī quā...rumpās,...eris: *if in any way...you should..., you will be...*; a mixed condition (sī pres. subj., fut. ind.); quā is an interrogative adv. and indefinite before sī, nisi, num and nē
883 **tū Mārcellus eris**: Vergil has Anchises give his name at the end for dramatic effect. The younger Marcellus is Caesar Augustus's nephew, who was supposed to be Augustus' heir before his untimely death in 23 BC.
manibus...plēnīs: abl. means
date: pl. imperative
884 **spargam**: *Let me...*; 1s jussive pres. subj.
nepōtis: *of (my) descendant*; with animam
885 **accumulem**: *let me...*+ acc.; 1s jussive pres. subj.; as if commemorating a gravesite
dōnīs: abl. means
fungar: *let me...*; + abl.; 1s jussive subj.; dep. fungor governs an abl. object
inānī mūnere: abl. obj.; 3rd decl. i-stem abl.
886 **(in) tōtā regiōne**
vagantur: pres. dep.; Aeneas and the Sibyl are the 3p subject

Octavia's Reaction to Hearing Vergil's Tribute to Marcellus

The historian Suetonius (AD 69 –122) offers the following account of what happened when Vergil first recited the passage about Marcellus in Book 6 in front of Augustus and his sister Octavia:

> But it was not until long afterwards, when the material was at last in shape, that Vergil read to him three books in all, the second, fourth, and sixth. The last of these produced a remarkable effect on Octavia, who was present at the reading; for it is said that when he reached the verses about her son, "Thou shalt be Marcellus," she fainted and was with difficulty revived.
>
> (Trans. J.C. Rolfe, Suetonius' *Vita Vergilii* 32)

This account, perhaps fictional, reminds us of two points: (1) that Vergil was under the patronage of Augustus and his supporters and the epic is in part a work of political propaganda, and (2) that Vergil postpones the naming of young Marcellus for 24 lines in order to maximize the dramatic effect and emotional impact on his contemporary readers.

Exclamatory Sentences [8] are often introduced by interrogatives. Three are used when Aeneas encounters Hector, and five are used in the Marcellus episode.

ut īnsignis...ingreditur!	*How distinguished...!*	6.855	p. 120
Quī strepitus circā comitum!	*What a noise...!*	6.865	p. 122
Quantum instar in ipsō!	*How great an image...!*	6.865	p. 122
Quantōs...campus aget gemitūs!	*How many...!*	6.872	p. 124
Quae...vidēbis fūnera	*What funerals...!*	6.873	p. 124

1. What is the reaction to Marcellus' death in the Campus Martius along the Tiber river?
N.B. Marcellus was buried in the Mausoleum Of Augustus in the Campus Martius.

2. What does Anchises say about Marcellus' promise among the Romans in 875-7?

3. What moral excellence in 6.878 does Marcellus share with Aeneas?

4. What ritual is Anchises observing in 883-6, even though Marcellus will not be born for 1000 years?

āeris in campīs lātīs atque omnia lūstrant.
Quae postquam Anchīsēs nātum per singula dūxit
incenditque animum fāmae venientis amōre,
exim bella virō memorat quae deinde gerenda,
Laurentēsque docet populōs urbemque Latīnī,
et quō quemque modō fugiatque feratque labōrem
   Sunt geminae Somnī portae, quārum altera fertur
cornea, quā vērīs facilis datur exitus umbrīs,
altera candentī perfecta nitēns elephantō,
sed falsa ad caelum mittunt insomnia mānēs.
Hīs ibi tum nātum Anchīsēs ūnāque Sibyllam
prōsequitur dictīs portāque ēmittit eburnā;
ille viam secat ad nāvēs sociōsque revīsit.

āēr, āeris n.: air, mist
alter, -era, -erum: other (of two), 3
campus, -ī m.: field, 3
candeō, -ere, -uī: be shiny white, glow
cornū, -ūs n.: horn, 2
deinde: then, next, 2
doceō, -ēre, -uī, -ctus: teach, tell, instruct
eburnus, -a, -um: ivory, made of ivory
elephantus, -ī m.: ivory; elephant
ēmittō, -ere, -mīsī, -missum: send away 2
exim: from there, thence, (exinde),
exitus, -ūs m.: result exit
facilis, -e: easy
fallō, -ere, fefellī, falsum: deceive, 3
geminus, -a, -um: twin, double, two 4
ibi: there, in that place, 2
incendō, -ere, -ī, -ēnsus: kindle, burn, 4
insomnium, -ī n.: dream
Latīnus, -ī m.: Latinus (king of the Latins)
Laurentes, -um m.: Laurentians
lūstrō (1): traverse, survey, 3
mānēs, -ium m.: spirits (of the dead), shades,
memorō (1): recall, recount, 2
mittō, -ere, mīsī, missus: send, dismiss, 4
modus, ī n.: manner, form, 2
nitēns, -entis: bright, shining
perficiō, -ere, -fēcī, -fectum: complete, polish, refine
postquam: after, 3
prōsequor, sequī, secūtus: follow, pursue, escort, 2
quisque, quaeque, quodque: each, every
revīsō, -ere: revisit, 2
secō, -āre, -uī, sectus: cut, divide, 2
Sibylla, -ae f.: Sibyl
singulī, -ae, -a: one-by-one; *subst.* details
vērus, -a, -um: true, real, 2
via, -ae f.: way, road, journey, street, 4

887 **āeris**: *of mist*; with campīs
888 **Quae...per singula**: *through which one by one*; or connective relative: 'through these one by one'
889 **animum**: i.e. Aeneas'
fāmae venientis: *for...*; objective gen. following amōre; pres. pple veniō
890 **virō**: i.e. for Aeneas; dat. of interest
quae...gerenda (sunt): *which must be...*; 'which (are) to be...' a passive periphrastic (gerundive + sum) expressing necessity
891 **Latīnī**: *of Latinus*; i.e. Laurentum, the coastal city of King Latinus and the Latins in Latium
892 **quō...modō**: *in what way...*; ind. question with pres. subj. fugiō and ferō, 'carry out'
quemque labōrem: *each...*; obj. of both verbs
893 **Sunt**: *There are...*
altera...(et) altera: *one...another...*; i.e. gates correlatives
fertur (esse): *is said (to be)*; 'is reported to be'
894 **quā**: *by which...*; relative, abl. of means
vērīs...umbrīs: *to...*; dat. ind. obj.
895 **altera (porta)**
(fertur esse) perfecta nitēns: *(is said to be)...*
candentī...elephantō: *with...*; abl. means or quality; 3rd decl. i-stem abl.
896 **ad caelum**: i.e. to the upperworld of humans
mānēs: subject of mittunt
897 **Hīs...dīctīs**: *with these things said*; abl. abs.
ūnā: *together*; adv.
prōsequitur: *escorts*; 'follows in front'
898 **portā...eburnā**: *from...*; 'by means of...'
899 **ille**: i.e. Aeneas
viam secat: i.e. proceeds quickly; an idiom

Does the Gate of Ivory Subvert the Political Message of Book 6?

Does Aeneas' exit through the Gate of Ivory subvert the political propaganda of Book 6? More specifically, does Aeneas' exit call into question Anchises' revelation of a divine plan that connects Aeneas with Rome, Augustus, and Marcellus? Some readers see controversy where others do not.

The problem lies in Vergil's description of the gates, where readers are asked to compare the 'true shades' that exit through the Gate of Horn to the 'false dreams' that exit from the Gate of Ivory. The 'shades' (*umbrae*) and 'dreams' (*insomnia*) do not seem as comparable as readers would like:

Gate of Horn (Porta Cornea)	vērīs umbrīs (= vēra insomnia?)
Gate of Ivory (Porta Eburna)	falsa insomnia (= falsīs umbrīs?)

Some readers see no controversy and argue that Aeneas exits through the Gate of Ivory because he is not a 'true shade' (vēra umbra) as required by the Gate of Horn. Other readers, however, find significance in the fact that the Gate of Ivory is reserved for 'false dreams' and argue that Aeneas' exit through the gate of falsehoods suggests that the propaganda in Anchises' speech is less than truthful.

Finally, still other readers suggest that Vergil intended for there to be ambiguity and wrote an ending that could be acceptable to Augustus and his political supporters and at the same time cast lingering doubt that the propaganda was true.

Vergil's Gates of Ivory and Horn and *Odyssey* 19

In the following speech from *Odyssey* Book 19, Odysseus' wife Penelope reveals to the disguised Odysseus a dream that she had about Odysseus' return to Ithaca but then offers the following explanation for why such a dream may not come true. Vergil imitates this same description of the gates in the closing of Book 6:

"Stranger, dreams verily are baffling and unclear of meaning,
and in no wise do they find fulfillment in all things for men.
For two are the gates of shadowy dreams,
and one is fashioned of horn and one of ivory.
Those dreams that pass through **the gate of sawn ivory**
deceive men, **bringing words that find no fulfillment**.
But those that come forth through **the gate of polished horn**
bring true issues to pass, when any mortal sees them.
But in my case it was not from thence, methinks,
that my strange dream came.

Odyssey XIX.559-69 (tr. A. T. Murray, 1919)

Vergil does not copy Homer's words verbatim, but the imitation is clear: (1) Vergil expects his readers to have read the *Odyssey* in Greek and to recognize the imitation. (2) Since Vergil imitates the *Odyssey* regularly in Books 1-6, this final imitation is intentional. Finally, (3) Penelope makes it very clear that the Gate of Ivory brings false and deceptive dreams, while the Gate of Horn brings the truth. The imitation seems to support the view that Aeneas' exit through the Gate of Ivory casts Anchises' account in doubt.

1. How does Aeneas respond to what he sees and hears from Anchises in 889?

2. What exits through the Gate of Horn in 894?

3. What is sent through the Gate of Ivory in line 896?

4. Which gate does Aeneas pass through in 898?

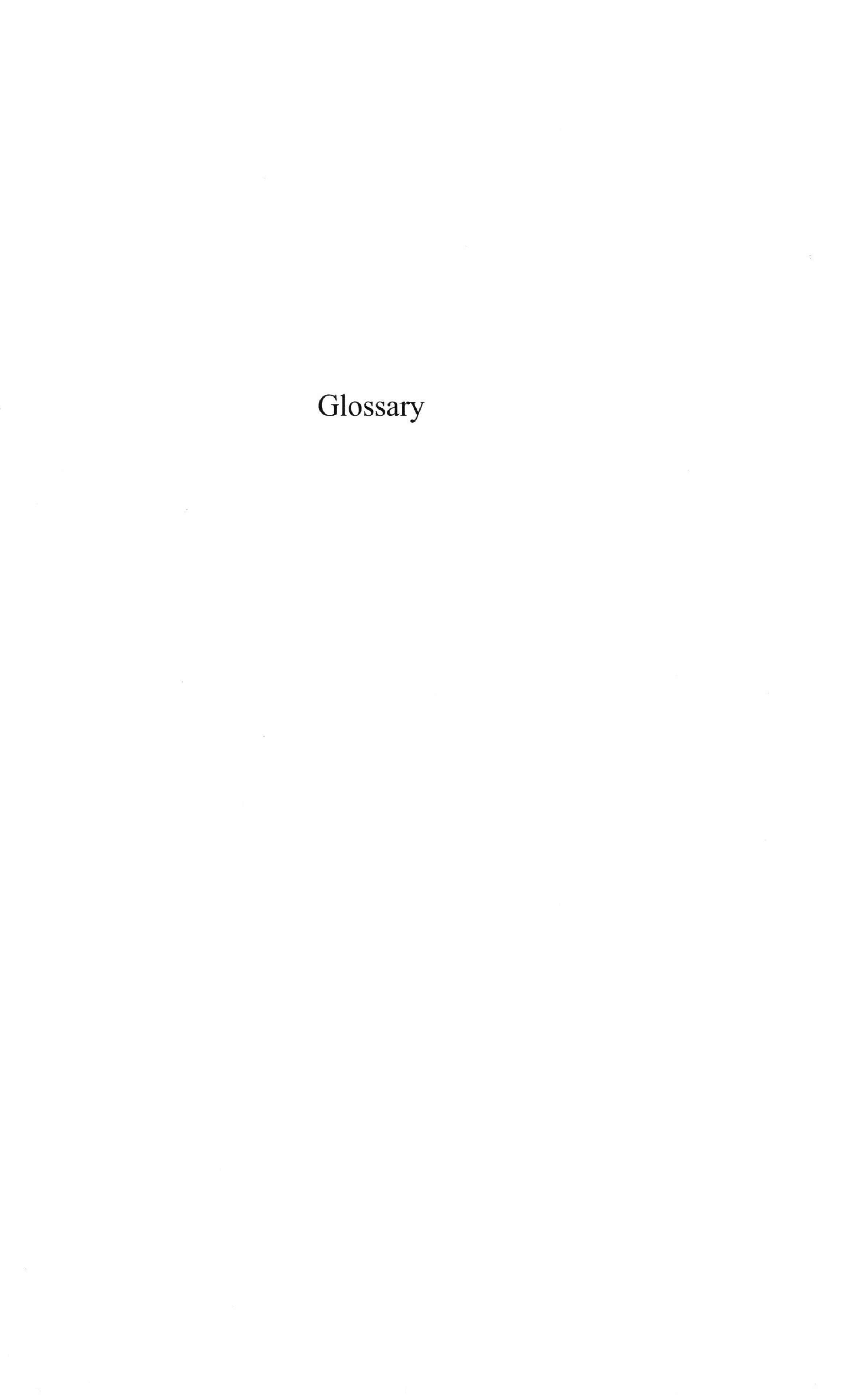

Glossary

	1st Declension		2nd Declension (m.)		2nd Declension (n.)	
Nom.	copi**a**	copi**ae**	legat**us**	legat**ī**	proeli**um**	proeli**a**
Gen.	copi**ae**	copi**ārum**	legat**ī**	legat**ōrum**	proeli**ī**	proeli**ōrum**
Dat.	copi**ae**	copi**īs**	legat**ō**	legat**īs**	proeli**ō**	proeli**īs**
Acc.	copi**am**	copi**ās**	legat**um**	legat**ōs**	proeli**um**	proeli**a**
Abl.	copi**ā**	copi**īs**	legat**ō**	legat**īs**	proeli**ō**	proeli**īs**

	3rd Declension (m/f)		3rd Declension (n.)	
Nom.	mīles	mīlit**es**	iter	itiner**a**
Gen.	mīlit**is**	mīlit**um**	itiner**is**	itiner**um**
Dat.	mīlit**ī**	mīlit**ibus**	itiner**ī**	itiner**ibus**
Acc.	mīlit**em**	mīlit**ēs**	iter	itiner**a**
Abl.	mīlit**e**	mīlit**ibus**	itiner**e**	itiner**ibus**

	4th Declension (m/f)		4th Declension (n.)	
Nom.	man**us**	man**ūs**	corn**ū**	corn**ua**
Gen.	man**ūs**	man**uum**	corn**ūs**	corn**uum**
Dat.	man**uī**	man**ibus**	corn**ū**	corn**uibus**
Acc.	man**um**	man**ūs**	corn**ū**	corn**ua**
Abl.	man**ū**	man**ibus**	corn**ū**	corn**uibus**

	5th Declension (m/f)	
Nom.	r**ēs**	r**ēs**
Gen.	r**ēī**	r**ērum**
Dat.	r**ēī**	r**ēbus**
Acc.	r**em**	r**ēs**
Abl.	r**ē**	r**ēbus**

Selected Pronouns

Nom.	is	*he*	ea	*she*	id	*it*
Gen.	eius	*his*	eius	*her*	eius	*its*
Dat.	eī	*to/for him*	eī	*to/for her*	eī	*to/for it*
Acc.	eum	*him*	eam	*her*	id	*it*
Abl.	eō	*with/from him*	eā	*with/from her*	eō	*with/from it*
Nom.	eī	*they*	eae	*they*	ea	*they*
Gen .	eōrum	*their*	eārum	*their*	eōrum	*their*
Dat.	eīs	*to/for them*	eīs	*to/for them*	eīs	*to/for them*
Acc.	eōs	*them*	eās	*them*	ea	*them*
Abl.	eīs	*with/from them*	eīs	*with/from them*	eīs	*with/from them*

**is, ea, id* is a demonstrative and in Caesar is often translated as "this/that" in the singular and "these/those" in the plural.

Nom.	quī	quae	quod	quī	quae	quae	*who, which, that*
Gen.	cuius	cuius	cuius	quōrum	quārum	quōrum	*whose, of whom/which*
Dat.	cuī	cuī	cuī	quibus	quibus	quibus	*to whom/which*
Acc.	quem	quam	quod	quōs	quās	quae	*whom, which, that*
Abl.	quō	quā	quō	quibus	quibus	quibus	*by/with/from whom/which*

Nom.	ille	illa	illud	*that*	hic	haec	hoc	*this*
Gen.	illīus	illīus	illīus	*of that*	huius	huius	huius	*of this*
Dat.	illī	illī	illī	*to/for that*	huic	huic	huic	*to/for this*
Acc.	illum	illam	illud	*that*	hunc	hanc	hoc	*this*
Abl.	illō	illā	illō	*with/from that*	hōc	hāc	hōc	*with/from this*
Nom.	illī	illae	illa	*those*	hī	hae	haec	*these*
Gen.	illōrum	illārum	illōrum	*of those*	hōrum	hārum	hōrum	*of these*
Dat.	illīs	illīs	illīs	*to those*	hīs	hīs	hīs	*to these*
Acc.	illōs	illās	illa	*those*	hōs	hās	haec	*these*
Abl.	illīs	illīs	illīs	*with/from those*	hīs	hīs	hīs	*with/from these*

	reflexive pronoun	possessive reflexive adjective					
Nom.	---	suus	sua	suum	suī	suae	sua
Gen.	suī	suī	suae	suī	suōrum	suārum	suōrum
Dat.	sibi	suō	suae	suō	suīs	suīs	suīs
Acc.	sē	suum	suam	suum	suōs	suās	sua
Abl.	sē	suō	suā	suō	suīs	suīs	suīs

Adjectives and Adverbs

Decl.	Positive	Comparative	Superlative
1st/2nd	altus, -a, -um *high (deep)*	altior, altius *higher (deeper)*	altissimus, -a, -um *highest, very high (deepest)*
3rd	fortis, forte *brave*	fortior, fortius *braver, more brave*	fortissimus, -a, -um *bravest, most brave, very brave*
1st/2nd	altē *deeply*	altius *more deeply*	altissimē *very deeply*
3rd	fortiter *bravely*	fortius *more bravely*	fortissimē *very bravely*

Irregular Adjectives and Adverbs

Positive	Comparative	Superlative
bonus, -a, -um *good*	melior, melius *better*	optimus, -a, -um *best*
magnus, -a, -um *great*	maior, maius *greater*	maximus, -a, -um *greatest*
parvus, -a, -um *small*	minor, minus *smaller*	minimus, -a, -um *smallest*
multus, -a, -um *much*	---, plus *more*	plurimus, -a, -um *most*

amō, amāre, amāvī, amātum: to love

	active		translation	passive		translation
Indicative						
Pres.	amō	amāmus	*I love*	amor	amāmur	*I am (being) loved*
	amās	amātis		amāris	amāminī	
	amat	amant		amātur	amantur	
Impf.	amābam	amābāmus	*I was loving*	amābar	amābāmur	*I was (being) loved*
	amābās	amābātis		amābāris	amābāminī	
	amābat	amābant		amābātur	amābantur	
Fut.	amābō	amābimus	*I will love*	amābor	amābimur	*I will be loved*
	amābis	amābitis		amāberis	amābiminī	
	amābit	amābunt		amābitur	amābuntur	
Perf.	amāvī	amāvimus	*I have loved*	amāta sum	amātae sumus	*I have been loved*
	amāvistī	amāvistis		amāta es	amātae estis	*was loved*
	amāvit	amāvērunt		amāta est	amātae sunt	
Plpf.	amāveram	amāverāmus	*I had loved*	amāta eram	amātae erāmus	*I had been loved*
	amāverās	amāverātis		amāta erās	amātae erātis	
	amāverat	amāverant		amāta erat	amātae erant	
Fut. Pf	amāverō	amāverimus	*I will have loved*	amāta erō	amātae erimus	*I will have been loved*
	amāveris	amāveritis		amāta eris	amātae eritis	
	amāverit	amāverint		amāta erit	amātae erunt	
Subjunctive						
Pres.	amem	amēmus	same as indicative	amer	amēmur	same as indicative
	amēs	amētis		amēris	amēminī	
	amet	ament		ametur	amentur	
Impf.	amārem	amārēmus		amārer	amārēmur	
	amārēs	amārētis		amārēris	amārēminī	
	amāret	amārent		amāretur	amārentur	
Perf.	amāverim	amāverīmus		amāta sim	amātae sīmus	
	amāverīs	amāverītis		amāta sīs	amātae sītis	
	amāverit	amāverint		amāta sit	amātae sint	
Plpf.	amāvissem	amāvissēmus		amāta essem	amātae essēmus	
	amāvissēs	amāvissētis		amāta essēs	amātae essētis	
	amāvisset	amāvissent		amāta esset	amātae essent	
Imperative						
	amā	amāte	*love!*			

Participle	active	translation	passive	translation
Pres.	amāns (*gen.* amantis)	*loving*		
Perf.			amātus, -a, -um	*having been loved*
Fut.	amātūrus, -a, -um	*going to love*	amandus, -a, -um	*going to be loved*

Infinitive	active	translation	passive	translation
Pres.	amāre	*to love*	amārī	*to be love*
Perf.	amāvisse	*to have loved*	amātum esse	*to have been loved*
Fut.	amātūrum esse	*to be going to loved*		

teneō, tenēre, tenuī, tentum: to hold

	active		translation	passive		translation
Indicative						
Pres.	teneō	tenēmus	*I hold*	teneor	tenēmur	*I am (being) held*
	tenēs	tenētis		tenēris	tenēminī	
	tenet	tenent		tenētur	tenentur	
Impf.	tenēbam	tenēbāmus	*I was holding*	tenēbar	tenēbāmur	*I was (being) held*
	tenēbās	tenēbātis		tenēbāris	tenēbāminī	
	tenēbat	tenēbant		tenēbātur	tenēbantur	
Fut.	tenēbō	tenēbimus	*I will hold*	tenēbor	tenēbimur	*I will be held*
	tenēbis	tenēbitis		tenēberis	tenēbiminī	
	tenēbit	tenēbunt		tenēbitur	tenēbuntur	
Perf.	tenuī	tenuimus	*I have held*	tenta sum	tentae sumus	*I have been held*
	tenuistī	tenuistis		tenta es	tentae estis	*was held*
	tenuit	tenuērunt		tenta est	tentae sunt	
Plpf.	tenueram	tenuerāmus	*I had held*	tenta eram	tentae erāmus	*I had been held*
	tenuerās	tenuerātis		tenta erās	tentae erātis	
	tenuerat	tenuerant		tenta erat	tentae erant	
Fut. Pf.	tenuerō	tenuerimus	*I will have held*	tenta erō	tentae erimus	*I will have been held*
	tenueris	tenueritis		tenta eris	tentae eritis	
	tenuerit	tenuerint		tenta erit	tentae erunt	
Subjunctive						
Pres.	teneam	teneāmus	same as	tenear	teneāmur	same as indicative
	teneās	teneātis		teneāris	teneāminī	
	teneat	teneant		teneatur	teneantur	
Impf.	tenērem	tenērēmus		tenērer	tenērēmur	
	tenērēs	tenērētis		tenērēris	tenērēminī	
	tenēret	tenērent		tenērētur	tenērentur	
Perf.	tenuerim	tenuerīmus		tenta sim	tentae sīmus	
	tenuerīs	tenuerītis		tenta sīs	tentae sītis	
	tenuerit	tenuerint		tenta sit	tentae sint	
Plpf.	tenuissem	tenuissēmus		tenta essem	tentae essēmus	
	tenuissēs	tenuissētis		tenta essēs	tentae essētis	
	tenuisset	tenuissent		tenta esset	tentae essent	
Imperative						
	tenē	tenēte	*hold!*			

Participle

	active	translation	passive	translation
Pres.	tenēns (*gen.* tenentis)	*holding*		
Perf.			tentus, -a, -um	*having been held*
Fut.	tentūrus, -a, -um	*going to hold*	tenendus, -a, -um	*going to be held*

Infinitive

	active	translation	passive	translation
Pres.	tenēre	*to hold*	tenērī	*to be held*
Perf.	tenuisse	*to have held*	tentum esse	*to have been held*
Fut.	tentūrum esse	*to be going to hold*		

dūcō, dūcere, dūxī, ductum: to lead

	active		translation	passive		translation
Indicative						
Pres.	dūcō	dūcimus	*I lead*	dūcor	dūcimur	*I am (being) led*
	dūcis	dūcitis		dūceris	dūciminī	
	dūcit	dūcunt		dūcitur	dūcuntur	
Impf.	dūcēbam	dūcēbāmus	*I was leading*	dūcēbar	dūcēbāmur	*I was (being) led*
	dūcēbās	dūcēbātis		dūcēbāris	dūcēbāminī	
	dūcēbat	dūcēbant		dūcēbātur	dūcēbantur	
Fut.	dūcam	dūcēmus	*I will lead*	dūcar	dūcēmur	*I will be led*
	dūcēs	dūcētis		dūcēris	dūcēminī	
	dūcet	dūcent		dūcētur	dūcentur	
Perf.	dūxī	dūximus	*I have led*	ducta sum	ductae sumus	*I have been led*
	dūxistī	dūxistis		ducta es	ductae estis	
	dūxit	dūxērunt		ducta est	ductae sunt	
Plpf.	dūxeram	dūxerāmus	*I had led*	ducta eram	ductae erāmus	*I had been led*
	dūxerās	dūxerātis		ducta erās	ductae erātis	
	dūxerat	dūxerant		ducta erat	ductae erant	
Fut.. Pf.	dūxerō	dūxerimus	*I will have led*	ducta erō	ductae erimus	*I will have been led*
	dūxeris	dūxeritis		ducta eris	ductae eritis	
	dūxerit	dūxerint		ducta erit	ductae erunt	
Subjunctive						
Pres.	dūcam	dūcāmus	same as indicative	dūcar	dūcāmur	same as indicative
	dūcās	dūcātis		dūcāris	dūcāminī	
	dūcat	dūcant		dūcātur	dūcantur	
Impf.	dūcerem	dūcerēmus		dūcerer	dūcerēmur	
	dūcerēs	dūcerētis		dūcerēris	dūcerēminī	
	dūceret	dūcerent		dūcerētur	dūcerentur	
Perf.	dūxerim	dūxerīmus		ducta sim	ductae sīmus	
	dūxerīs	dūxerītis		ducta sīs	ductae sītis	
	dūxerit	dūxerint		ducta sit	ductae sint	
Plpf.	dūxissem	dūxissēmus		ducta essem	ductae essēmus	
	dūxissēs	dūxissētis		ducta essēs	ductae essētis	
	dūxisset	dūxissent		ducta esset	ductae essent	
Imperative						
	dūc(e)	dūcite	*lead!*			

Participle

	active	translation	passive	translation
Pres.	dūcēns (*gen.* dūcentis)	*leading*		
Perf.			ductus, -a, -um	*having been led*
Fut.	ductūrus, -a, -um	*going to lead*	dūcendus, -a, -um	*going to be led*

Infinitive

	active	translation	passive	translation
Pres.	dūcere	*to lead*	dūcī	*to be led*
Perf.	dūxisse	*to have led*	ductum esse	*to have been led*
Fut.	ductūrum esse	*to be going to lead*		

capiō, capere, cēpī, captum: to take, seize

	active		translation	passive		translation
Indicative						
Pres.	capiō	capimus	*I take*	capior	capimur	*I am (being) taken*
	capis	capitis		caperis	capiminī	
	capit	capiunt		capitur	capiuntur	
Impf.	capiēbam	capēbāmus	*I was taking*	capiēbar	capiēbāmur	*I was (being) taken*
	capiēbās	capiēbātis		capiēbāris	capiēbāminī	
	capiēbat	capiēbant		capiēbātur	capiēbantur	
Fut.	capiam	capiēmus	*I will take*	capiar	capiēmur	*I will be taken*
	capiēs	capiētis		capiēris	capiēminī	
	capiet	capient		capiētur	capientur	
Perf.	cēpī	cēpimus	*I have taken*	capta sum	captae sumus	*I have been taken*
	cēpistī	cēpistis		capta es	captae estis	*was taken*
	cēpit	cēpērunt		capta est	captae sunt	
Plpf.	cēperam	cēperāmus	*I had taken*	capta eram	captae erāmus	*I had been taken*
	cēperās	cēperātis		capta erās	captae erātis	
	cēperat	cēperant		capta erat	captae erant	
Fut. Pf.	cēperō	cēperimus	*I will have taken*	capta erō	captae erimus	*I will have been*
	cēperis	cēperitis		capta eris	captae eritis	*taken*
	cēperit	cēperint		capta erit	captae erunt	
Subjunctive						
Pres.	capiam	capāmus	same as	capiar	capiāmur	same as indicative
	capiās	capiātis		capiāris	capiāminī	
	capiat	capiant		capiātur	capiantur	
Impf.	caperem	caperēmus		caperer	caperēmur	
	caperēs	caperētis		caperēris	caperēminī	
	caperet	caperent		caperētur	caperentur	
Perf.	cēperim	cēperīmus		capta sim	captae sīmus	
	cēperīs	cēperītis		capta sīs	captae sītis	
	cēperit	cēperint		capta sit	captae sint	
Plpf.	cēpissem	cēpissēmus		capta essem	captae essēmus	
	cēpissēs	cēpissētis		capta essēs	captae essētis	
	cēpisset	cēpissent		capta esset	captae essent	
Imperative						
	cape	capite	*take!*			

Participle

	active	translation	passive	translation
Pres.	capiēns (*gen.* capientis)	*taking*		
Perf.			captus, -a, -um	*having been taken*
Fut.	captūrus, -a, -um	*going to take*	capiendus, -a, -um	*going to be taken*

Infinitive

	active	translation	passive	translation
Pres.	capere	*to take*	capī	*to be taken*
Perf.	cēpisse	*to have taken*	captum esse	*to have been taken*
Fut.	captūrum esse	*to be going to taken*		

sciō, scīre, scīvī, scītum: to know

	active		translation	passive		translation
Indicative						
Pres.	sciō	scīmus	*I know*	scior	scīmur	*I am (being) known*
	scīs	scītis		scīris	scīminī	
	scit	sciunt		scītur	sciuntur	
Impf.	sciēbam	sciēbāmus	*I was knowing*	sciēbar	sciēbāmur	*I was (being) known*
	sciēbās	sciēbātis		sciēbāris	sciēbāminī	
	sciēbat	sciēbant		sciēbātur	sciēbantur	
Fut.	sciam	sciēmus	*I will know*	sciar	sciēmur	*I will be known*
	sciēs	sciētis		sciēris	sciēminī	
	sciet	scient		sciētur	scientur	
Perf.	scīvi	scīvimus	*I have known*	scīta sum	scītae sumus	*I have been known*
	scīvistī	scīvistis		scīta es	scītae estis	
	scīvit	scīvērunt		scīta est	scītae sunt	
Plpf.	scīveram	scīverāmus	*I had known*	scīta eram	scītae erāmus	*I had been known*
	scīverās	scīverātis		scīta erās	scītae erātis	
	scīverat	scīverant		scīta erat	scītae erant	
Fut. Pf.	scīverō	scīverimus	*I will have*	scīta erō	scītae erimus	*I will have been*
	scīveris	scīveritis	*known*	scīta eris	scītae eritis	*known*
	scīverit	scīverint		scīta erit	scītae erunt	
Subjunctive						
Pres.	sciam	sciāmus	same as	sciar	sciāmur	same as indicative
	sciās	sciātis	indicative	sciāris	sciāminī	
	sciat	sciant		sciātur	sciantur	
Impf.	scīrem	scīrēmus		scīrer	scīrēmur	
	scīrēs	scīrētis		scīrēris	scīrēminī	
	scīret	scīrent		scīrētur	scīrentur	
Perf.	scīverim	scīverīmus		scīta sim	scītae sīmus	
	scīverīs	scīverītis		scīta sīs	scītae sītis	
	scīverit	scīverint		scīta sit	scītae sint	
Plpf.	scīvissem	scīvissēmus		scīta essem	scītae essēmus	
	scīvissēs	scīvissētis		scīta essēs	scītae essētis	
	scīvisset	scīvissent		scīta esset	scītae essent	
Imperative						
	scī	scīte	*know!*			

Participle				
Pres.	sciēns (gen. scientis)	*knowing*		
Perf.			scītus, -a, -um	*having been known*
Fut.	scītūrus, -a, -um	*going to know*	sciendus, -a, -um	*going to be known*
Infinitive				
Pres.	scīre	*to know*	scīrī	*to be known*
Perf.	scīvisse	*to have known*	scītum esse	*to have been known*
Fut.	scītūrum esse	to *be going to know*		

	Sum, esse, fuī, futūrum: to be		translation	**possum, posse, potuī, -- : to be able, can**		translation
Indicative						
Pres.	sum	sumus	*I am*	possum	possumus	*I am able, can*
	es	estis		potes	potestis	
	est	sunt		potest	possunt	
Impf.	eram	erāmus	*I was*	poteram	poterāmus	*I was able, could*
	erās	erātis		poterās	poterātis	
	erat	erant		poterat	poterant	
Fut.	erō	erimus	*I will be*	poterō	poterimus	*I will be able*
	eris	eritis		poteris	poteritis	
	erit	erunt		poterit	poterunt	
Perf.	fuī	fuimus	*I have been, I was*	potuī	potuimus	*I have been able, I was able, could*
	fuistī	fuistis		potuistī	potuistis	
	fuit	fuērunt		potuit	potuērunt	
Plpf.	fueram	fuerāmus	*I had been*	potueram	potuerāmus	*I had been able*
	fuerās	fuerātis		potuerās	potuerātis	
	fuerat	fuerant		potuerat	potuerant	
Fut. Pf.	fuerō	fuerimus	*I will have been*	potuerō	potuerimus	*I will have been able*
	fueris	fueritis		potueris	potueritis	
	fuerit	fuerint		potuerit	potuerint	
Subjunctive						
Pres.	sim	sīmus	same as indicative	possim	possīmus	same as indicative
	sīs	sītis		possīs	possītis	
	sit	sint		possit	possint	
Impf.	essem	essēmus		possem	possēmus	
	essēs	essētis		possēs	possētis	
	esset	essent		posset	possent	
Perf.	fuerim	fuerīmus		potuerim	potuerīmus	
	fuerīs	fuerītis		potuerīs	potuerītis	
	fuerit	fuerint		potuerit	potuerint	
Plpf.	fuissem	fuissēmus		potuissem	potuissēmus	
	fuissēs	fuissētis		potuissēs	potuissētis	
	fuisset	fuissent		potuisset	potuissent	
Imperative						
	xxx			xxx		
Infinitive						
Pres.	esse		*to be*	posse		*to be able*
Perf.	fuisse		*to have been*	potuisse		*to have been heard*
Fut.	futūrum esse*		*to be going to be*	----		

* alternative = fore

sum, esse, fuī, futūrum: to be, 165

adsum, -esse, -fuī: be present, assist, 3
dēsum, -esse, -fuī: be lacking, lack, fail, 6
intersum, -esse, -fuī: take part in, engage in, 1
possum, posse, potuī: be able, can, avail, 40
praesum, -esse, -fuī: be over, preside over, 2
subsum, -esse, -fuī: be near, close at hand, 1

eō, īre, i(v)ī, itūrum: to go

	active		translation
Indicative			
Pres.	eō	īmus	*I go*
	īs	ītis	
	it	eunt	
Impf.	ībam	ībāmus	*I was going*
	ībās	ībātis	
	ībat	ībant	
Fut.	ībō	ībimus	*I will go*
	ībis	ībitis	
	ībit	ībunt	
Perf.	iī	iimus	*I went, have gone*
	īstī	īstis	
	iit	iērunt	
Plpf.	ieram	ierāmus	*I had gone*
	ierās	ierātis	
	ierat	ierant	
Fut. Pf.	ierō	ierimus	*I will have gone*
	ieris	ieritis	
	ierit	ierint	
Subjunctive			
Pres.	eam	eāmus	same as indicative
	eās	eātis	
	eat	eant	
Impf.	īrem	īrēmus	
	īrēs	īrētis	
	īret	īrent	
Perf.	ierim	ierimus	
	ieris	ieritis	
	ierit	ierunt	
Plpf.	īssem	īssēmus	
	īssēs	īssētis	
	īsset	īssent	
Imperative			
	ī	īte	
Participle			
Pres.	iēns (euntis)		*going*
Perf.	---		
Fut.	itūrus, -a, -um		*going to go*
Infinitive			
Pres.	īre		*to go*
Perf.	īsse		*to have gone*
Fut.	ītūrum esse		*to be going to go*

Compound verbs

adeō, -īre, iī, itus: go to, approach, 2
eō, īre, iī, itum: to go, come, 10
abeō, -īre, -iī, -itus: go away, 2
redeō, -īre, -īvī: go back, return, 1
subeō, -īre, -iī, -itum: approach, undergo, 6

Popular Uses of the Subjunctive Identified in *College Vergil*

	How to identify	special translation	example
1. Purpose, adverbial [4]	ut/nē + pres./impf.	may/might	ut Catilīna mitteret *so that Catiline might send*
Purpose, relative [3]	quī, quae, quod + pres./impf.	may/might would	quī mitteret *who would send*
2. Result, adverbial [1] or noun clause	**tam, tantus, sīc, ita** + ut/ut nōn	none	ut Catilīna mitteret *that Catiline sent*
3. Cum-Clauses [1]	cum + subjunctive	none	Cum Catilīna mitteret *When Catiline sent*
4. Indirect Question [9]	interrogatives: e.g. quis, cūr	none	nōvit quōs Catilīna mitteret *he learned whom Catiline sent*
5. Indirect Command [0]	verb of commanding + ut/nē	none	persuāsit ut Catilīna mitteret *he persuaded that Catiline send*
6. Relative Clause of Characteristic [3]	quī, quae, quod + subj.	none/would	quōs Catilīna mitteret *the sort whom Cicero would send*
7. Subordinate Verb in Ind. Disc. [6]	quī, quae, quod in an acc. + inf. or ut clause	none	eōs, sī id mitteret, lēgere *that they read it, if he sent it*
8. Deliberative Subj.[7]	main verb (interrogative) often in 1s or 1p	am I to X are we to X	Quid mittam? *What am I to send? What should...?*
8. Anticipatory Subj. [2]	dum + subj.	none	dum mitteret... *until he might send...*
9. Subj. of Wish [3] (Optative subj.)	often utinam/ut + main verb (neg. nē)	Would that...	Utinam eōs mittat? *Would that he may see*
10. Jussive Subj.[15]	main verb (neg. nē) often in 3s or 3p	let/should	Catilīna mittat *Let Catiline send...*
11. Future Less Vivid [3]	sī pres. subj., pres. subj.	should/would	sī sit, mittat *if he should be...he would send*
12. Pres. Contrary to Fact [1] Condition	sī impf. subj., impf. subj.	were/would	sī esset, mitteret *if he were.. he would send*
13. Past Contrary to Fact [1] Condition	sī plpf. subj., plpf. subj.	had/would have	sī fuisset, mīsisset *if he had been.. he would have*
14. Mixed Contrary to Fact [4] Condition	sī impf. or plpf. subj impf. or plpf. subj	if were/had would/would have	sī esset/ fuisset, mitteret/mīsisset
15. Past (unreal) Potential [1] not a condition	plpf. subj.	would have	mīsisset *he would have sent it*

Rhetorical Devices

Below is a list of the rhetorical devices, otherwise known as "rhetorical figures" or "stylistic devices," readers will discover in the text and commentary. As you encounter these devices in the readings, consider how each one enhances the poetry and what would be lost if the device were removed.

allegory: an extended metaphor, prolonged use of an image to express meaning

alliteration: repetition of consonant sounds at the beginning of a series of words
Peter Piper picked a peck of pickled peppers.
vastōs volvunt ad lītora flūctūs (I.86)

anaphora: repetition of a word or words at the beginning of successive clauses
We shall go on to the end. We shall fight in France, we shall fight on the seas.... (Winston Churchill)
Mīrātur mōlem Aenēās...mīrātur portās (I.421)

anastrophe: inversion of usual word order (i.e. prepositions and objects)
Up the hill went Jack and Jill.
maria omnia circum. "around all seas" (I.32)

aposiopesis: breaking off in the middle of a sentence
I am so angry. Oh, you can go to...
Quos ego ---! Sed motos praestat componere fluctus. (Aeneid I.135)

apostrophe: sudden turn to address a person or object who is present or absent
Twinkle, twinkle, little star. How I wonder what you are.
O patria, O divum domus Ilium! (Aeneid 2.241)

asyndeton: omission of conjunctions
But in a larger sense, we cannot dedicate, we cannot consecrate, we cannot hallow this ground...(Lincoln)
saevus ubi Aeacidae tēlō iacet Hector, (et) ubi ingēns Sarpedon, (et) ubi tot Simoīs... (I.99-101)

chiasmus: an "a-b-b-a" arrangement of words, often used with pairs of nouns and adjectives
Ask not what your country can do for you, ask what you can do for your country
Nāvem in cōnspectū nūllam, trēs lītore cervōs (noun, adj., adj. noun) I.184)

ecphrasis: extended description of a work of art or scene of nature

ellipsis: omission of words easily understood in context
She is enrolled in Latin; he, in Spanish.
Haec sēcum (dīxit)... "(she said) these things with herself" (I.37)

enjambment: continuation of a clause beyond the end of one line and into the beginning of the next
litora, multum ille et terris iactatus et alto
vi superum, (I.3-4)

golden line: synchesis (interlocking word order) with a verb in the middle
***Tanta**ne vos generis tenuit **fīducia** vestri?* (I.132)

hendiadys: expressing a single idea with two nouns joined by a conjunction
It sure is nice and cool today! (for "nicely cool")
Molemque et montes (for "mass of mountains") (Aeneid I.61)

hyperbaton: distortion of normal word order (e.g. separation of words meant to be together)
This I must see!
Omnem miscet agēns tēlīs nemora inter frondea turbam (I.190-1)

hyperbole: exaggeration
I must have translated a million lines today.
clamores simul horrendos ad sidera tollit "he raised horrible shouts to the stars" (2.222)

hysteron proteron: reversal of the natural order of events
Put your shoes and socks on!
summersāsque obrue puppēs "rush over the sunken ships" (I.69)

interlocking word order (synchesis): ABAB order often used with pairs of nouns and adjectives
saevae memorem ***Iunonis*** *ob* *iram* *(Adj.1 – Adj.2 – Noun1 –Noun2)* (I.4)

litotes: use of a negative (often, a double negative) to express something positive
She is not a bad singer. (i.e. She's a good singer.)
Neque enim ignari sumus., "We are not ignorant of evils..." (1.198)

metaphor: expression of meaning through another image
Don't count your chickens before they're hatched!
spumas salis aere ruebant "they turned over the foam of the sea with bronze" (i.e. ships are plows, I.35)

metonymy: the use of one noun or image to suggest another
The pen is mightier than the sword. (the pen suggests discourse; the sword suggests violence.)
Arma virumque cano. (arma suggests war) (I.1)

onomatopoeia: use of words that sound like their meaning
click, clack.
magno cum murmure montis (I.55)

personification: attribution of human characteristics to something not human
Mother nature cares for us all.
Fāma...ingrediturque solo et caput inter nubila condit (4.173-94)

pleonasm: the use of superfluous words to enrich the thought
I saw the UFO with my own eyes. (as opposed to someone else's eyes?)
Āmēns animī "mindless in his mind" (4.203)

polysyndeton: use of more conjunctions (Gr. *syndeton*) than are needed
He ran and laughed and jumped for joy.
Eurusque Notusque ruunt creberque procellis Africus (I.85-6)

simile: explicit comparison using words "like" or "as" (sicut, similis, velut, quālis, quam)
Just as the sands in the hourglass, so are the days of our lives.
Quālis apēs...exercet labor... "just as work busies the bees" (I.430-6)

synecdoche: the use of the part to express the whole, a type of metonomy
I drove a new set of wheels off the lot today. (wheels = car)
summersāsque obrue puppēs "rush over the sunken ships" (decks suggest ships, I.69)

synchesis (interlocking word order): ABAB order often used with pairs of nouns and adjectives
saevae memorem ***Iunonis*** *ob* *iram* *(Adj.1 – Adj.2 – Noun1 –Noun2)* (I.4)

tmesis: the separation of a compound word into two parts
I didn't want that comic book any-old-how.
Bis collo squamea circum terga dati. (=circumdati) (2.218-19)

transferred epithet (enallage): the transfer of an adjective from its proper object to a related object
*saevae memorem Iunonis ob iram (Juno, not the anger, is mindful) (*1.4)

Alphabetized Core Vocabulary (5 or more times)

The alphabetized list includes all 275 words in the Vergil selections that occur five or more times. The number at the end of each entry indicates how many times the word occurs in the commentary. These same dictionary entries are found in an running core list in the introduction.

ā, ab, abs: (away) from, by, 25
accipiō, -ere, -cēpī, -ceptus: receive, take, 7
ad: to, toward, at, near (acc.) 29
adversus, -a, -um: facing, opposite, straight on, 5
Aenēās, -ae, acc. -ān m.: Aeneas, 23
Aeolus, -ī m.: Aeolus (king of the winds), 5
aequor, -oris n: sea, the level (sea), 11
agmen, -inis n.: column, formation (of troops), 5
agō, -ere, ēgī, āctus: drive, lead, do, 9
aiō, ais, ait; aiunt: say, speak; assert, 7
alius, -a, -ud : other, another, else, 9
altus, -a, -um: high; deep; **altum, ī n.**: (deep) sea, 28
amor, -ōris m.: love, 9
Anchīsēs, -ae, acc. -ēn m.: Anchises 8
anima, -ae f.: breath, life; soul, spirit, 5
animus, -ī m: mind; spirit; courage; anger, 19
annus, -ī m: year, 5
ante: before, in front of (acc.); before, previously, 10
antrum, -ī n.: cave, 5
aperiō, -īre, -uī, apertus: open; reveal, 5
āra, -ae f.: altar, 8
ardeō, -ēre, arsī, arsus: burn, be eager to (inf.), 8
arma, -ōrum n: arms; weapons and armor, 18
arx, arcis f: citadel, (fortifed) hilltop, 12
aspiciō, -ere, spexī, spectus: to look at, see, 9
at, ast: but, yet, however, at least, 10
āter, ātra, ātrum: dark, black, 7
atque, ac: and; as, 38
aura, -ae f.: breeze, air, 6
aut: or; **aut...aut**: either...or, 31
bellum, -ī n: war, 11
caelum, -ī n.: sky, 13
capiō, -ere, -cēpī, captus: take, seize, catch, 5
caput, -itis n.: head; life, 10
causa, -ae f: reason, cause; for the sake of (gen), 7
celer, -eris, -ere: swift, quick, 6
circum: around (acc.), 12
clāmor, -ōris m.: shout, noise, 5
classis, -is f: fleet, 8
comes, -itis m./f.: companion; comrade, 5
coniūnx, -iugis m/f: spouse, husband, wife, 6
cor, cordis n.: heart, 5
corpus, -oris n.: body, 11
corripiō, -ere, -uī, -reptus: snatch (up), 6
crēdō, -ere, -didī: believe, trust, 5
crūdēlis, -e: cruel, bloody, 6
cum: with; when, since, although, 23
cūnctus, -a, -um: all, whole, entire, 5
cūra, -ae f.: care, concern; worry, anxiety, 7
cursus, -ūs m.: course, running; haste, 6
Danaus, -a, -um: Danaan (Greek), 7
dē: (down) from; about, concerning, 10
dea, -ae f: goddess, 7
dēmittō, -ere, -mīsī, -missum: drop, sink, 5
dēsero, -ere, -ruī: desert, forsake, abandon, 6
deus, -ī m: god, 19
dexter, -tra, -trum: right (hand), favorable, 9
dīcō, -ere, dīxī, dictus: say, speak, tell, 18
Dīdō, -ōnis f.: Dido, 11
dīvus, -a, -um: divine; *noun*, god, goddess, 12
dō, dare, dedī, datum: give; grant, allow, 27
dolor, -ōris m: pain, grief, 6
domus, -ūs f.: home, house(hold); 8
dōnum, -ī n.: gift, offering, prize, 6
dūcō, -ere, dūxī, ductus: lead, draw; consider, 9
dulcis, -e: sweet, pleasant, fresh, 7
dum: while, as long as, until; provided that, 6
ē, ex: out of, from (abl.), 8
ego, meī (pl **nōs, nostrum**): I (pl. we) , 43
eō, īre, iī, itus: go, 10
errō (1): wander, 10
et: and; also, even, too, 173
etiam: also, even, 7
extrēmus, -a, -um: farthest, outermost, 5
faciō, -ere, fēcī, factum: do, make, 7
fāma, -ae f.: fame, rumor, reputation, 9
fātum, -ī n: fate, 18
ferō, ferre, tulī, lātus: bear, endure, carry, report, 25
ferrum, -ī n.: iron; sword, weapon, tool, 7
fīnis, -is m./f.: end, border; territory 5
flamma, -ae f: flame, 8
flūctus, -ūs m: wave, 11
for, fārī, fātus sum: speak, say, tell, 7
fortis, -e: strong, brave, 5
fuga, -ae f.: flight; haste, 5
fugiō, -ere, fūgī: flee, escape; avoid, 5

furō, -ere, -uī: rage, rave, seethe, 7
gemitus, -ūs m.: groan, lament, sob, 5
gēns, gentis f: race, people, clan, 11
genus, -eris n: birth, lineage, family, race; kind, 7
gerō, -ere, gessī, gestus: carry (on), wage, 5
gravis, -e: heavy, serious, severe 5
harēna, -ae f.: sand, 6
heu: hail! hey! (to grab attention); alas! ah! 7
hic, haec, hoc: this, these, 73
hīc: here, 13
hinc: from here, hence, from this place, 7
hūc: to this place, hither, 5
iactō (1): to throw (back and forth), toss, 7
iam: now, already, 19
īdem, eadem, idem: same, the same, 6
ignis, -is m: fire; lightning, 15
ille, illa, illud: that, those, 41
immānis, -e: immense, huge, 6
imperium, -ī n.: power, command; empire, 6
imponō, -ere, -posuī, -positus: impose, place on, 5
īmus, -a, -um: bottom of, lowest (part) of, 5
in: in, on, among (abl.); into, against (acc.), 55
incipiō, -ere, incēpī, inceptum: begin, undertake, 6
ingēns, -entis: huge, immense, 13
inter: between, among, during (acc.), 8
intereā: meanwhile, in the meantime, 5
invideō, -ēre: hate, envy, 6
ipse, -a, -um: himself, herself, myself, -self; very, 22
īra, -ae f: anger, rage; passion, 11
is, ea, id: he, she, it, they; this, that, these, those; 5
Ītalia, -ae f: Italy, 11
iubeō, -ēre, iussī, iussus: order, command, 9
Iūnō, Iūnōnis f: Juno, 9
Iuppiter, Iovis, Iovī, Iovem Iove m: Jupiter, 9
labor, -ōris m.: labor, hardship, task, 8
lacrima, -ae f.: tear, 5
laetus, -a, -um: happy; fertile, 5
lateō, -ēre, -uī: lie hidden, hide; escape notice of, 5
lātus, -a, -um: wide, 6
latus, -eris n.: side, 5
Libya, -ae f: Libya, 5
līmen, -inis n.: threshold, doorway, 5
lītus, -oris n: shore, coast, beach, 15
locus, -ī m. (pl. locī, loca): place, 8
longus, -a, -um: long; *adv* far, 10
lūmen, -inis n.: light, lamp; eye; life, 5
lux, lūcis f.: light, daylight; life, 5
magnus, -a, -um: great, large, 19
manus, -ūs f.: hand, 9
mare, -is n: sea, 5
medius, -a, -um: middle (part) of, middle, 12
metus, -ūs f.: dread, fear, 5
meus, -a, -um: my, mine, 10
mīror, -ārī, -ātus sum: wonder, be amazed at, 5
misceō, -ēre, -uī, mīxtum: mix (up), 7
miser, -era, -rum: miserable, wretched, 6
moenia, -ium n: walls; defense, city-walls; 7
mōlēs, -is f: mass, structure; burden, 5
mōns, montis m.: mountain, 5
morior, morī, mortuus sum: die, 5
moveō, -ere, mōvī, mōtus: move, upset, 7
multus, -a, -um: much, many, 9
mūrus, ī m.: wall, 8
nam, namque: for; indeed, truly, 6
nātus, -ī m.: son (male having been born) 8
nāvis, -is f.: ship, 11
nē: lest, that not, so that not; no, not, 5
-ne: *indicates a yes/no question*; whether, or, 9
nec: nor, and not; **nec…nec**: neither…nor, 30
nōmen, -inis n.: name, fame, renown 5
nōn: not, 22
noster, -ra, -rum: our, ours, 10
nox, noctis, f.: night, 7
nūbēs, -is f: cloud, 6
nūllus, -a, -um: not any, no(one, thing), 6
nūmen, -inis n: divine power, approval, 7
nunc: now, 15
Ō: O! oh!, 14
oculus, -ī m.: eye, 12
omnis, -e: all, every, whole, entire, 27
ōra, -ae f.: shore, coast, border, 5
ōrō (1): plead, beg; pray for, entreat, 8
ōs, ōris n.: mouth, face, 10
parēns, -entis m./f.: parent, 6
pars, -tis f.: part, side, direction; some…others, 5
pater, -tris m: father; ancestor, 13
patria, -ae f.: fatherland, country, 8
pectus, -oris n: chest, breast; heart, 12
per: through, over, by, 45
pēs, pedis m.: foot, 5
petō, -ere, -īvi: seek, head for; ask, 14
pietās, -tātis f: piety, devotion, 6
poena, -ae f.: punishment, penalty, 5
pōnō, -ere, posuī, positum: put, place (aside), 5
pontus, -ī m: sea, 9
populus, -ī m: people, 6
porta, -ae f.: gate, 6
possum, posse, potuī: be able, can, 5

post: after, behind (acc.), later, 5
premō, -ere, pressī, pressum: (sup)press, control, 5
prīmus, -a, -um: first; leading, 23
prior, prius: earlier, before, 6
puer, -ī m.: boy, child, 6
pulcher, -chra, -chrum: beautiful, pretty; noble, 5
puppis, -is f.: deck, ship, 5
quaerō, -ere, quaesīvī, -sītus: search for, ask, 5
quālis, -e: which/what sort; such as, just as, like, 7
que: and, 273
quī, quae, quod (quis? quid?): who, which, what, that; *after sī*: any, some, 136
rapiō, -ere, rapuī, raptum: snatch, seize; kidnap, 7
referō, -ferre, -tulī, -lātus: carry back; report, say, 5
rēgīna, -ae f: queen, 10
rēgnum, -ī n: kingdom, kingship, rule, 14
regō, -ere, rēxī, rectus: rule, lead, direct, 13
rēs, reī, f.: thing, matter, affair; circumstance, 11
rīpa, -ae f.: bank, 8
Rōmānus, -a, -um: Roman, 5
ruō, ruere, -ī: rush (over), fall; plow, 8
sacer, -cra, -crum: sacred, holy; rite, ritual, 5
saevus, -a, -um: savage, fierce, 7
sanguis, -inis m: blood, 6
saxum, -ī n.: rock, 11
scopulus, -ī m.: rock, cliff, crag, 6
sē: him-, her-, it-, themselves, 20
sed: but, 15
sēdēs, -is f.: seat; home, dwelling, foundation, 7
servō (1): save, perserve, keep, 6
sī: if, whether, 26
sīc: thus, so, in this way, 17
sīdus, -eris n.: star, constellation, 7
simul: at the same time, together, 7
socius, -ī m.: comrade, ally, 6
sōlus, -a, -um: alone, only, sole, 5
somnus, -ī m.: sleep; dream 5
soror, sorōris f.: sister, 5
sors, sortis f.: lot, lottery; luck, 5
spēs, -eī f.: hope, expectation, 6
stō, -āre, stetī, status: stand, stop, 6
sub: under, beneath; near, 13
subeō, -īre, -iī, itus: go up to, approach, 6
sum, esse, fuī, futūrus: be, 55
summus, -a, -um: top of, highest, 9
surgō, -ere, -rēxī, -rēctus: raise, rise up, surge, 5
tacitus, -a, -um: silent, speechless, still, 5
tālis, -e: such, 15
tandem: finally; at length, pray, 5
tantus, -a, -um: so great, so much, so many, 18
tectum, -ī n.: roof; shelter, house, building, 6
tellūs, -ūris f.: land, earth, 6
tēlum, -ī n.: spear, arrow, projectile, 6
templum, -ī n.: temple, 5
tendō, -ere, -dī, tentus: stretch; strive, hasten, 8
teneō, -ēre, -uī, -tus: hold; grab, 11
tergum, -ī n.: back (part of the body), rear, 5
terra, -ae f: land, ground, earth, 20
Teucrus, a, um: Teucrian, Trojan, 10
tollō, -ere, sustulī, sublātus: raise, lift up; destroy, 5
torqueō, -ēre, torsī, tortum: twist, turn, 5
tot: so many, 8
tōtus, -a, -um: total, entire, whole, 8
Troia, ae f: Troy, 13
Trōs, Trōis: Trojan, 5
tū, tuī (*pl.* vōs, vestrum) : you, 44
tum, tunc: then, at that time; 18
tuus, -a, -um: your, yours, 11
Tyrius, -a, -um: Tyrian, of Tyre; Carthaginian, 8
ubi: where; when, 10
ūllus, -a, -um: any(one, thing), 5
umbra, -ae f.: shade, shadow, ghost, 12
unda, -ae f.: wave, 14
ūnus, -a, -um: one, alone; **ūnā**, together, 10
urbs, urbis f: city, 27
ut: so that, that; as, when; how, 11
varius, -a, -um: various, 5
vastus, -a, -um: vast, enormous, 7
ve, vel: or (either or both options hold true), 8
veniō, -īre, vēnī, ventus: come, go, 14
ventus, -ī m.: wind, 11
vertex, -icis m.: peak; whirlpool, 5
vester, -ra, -rum: your, yours, 5
videō, -ēre, vīdī, vīsus: see; *videor*, seem, 24
vincō, -ere, vīcī, victus: conquer, 5
vir, -ī m: man, husband, 22
vīs, vīs f : force, power; *pl.* **vīrēs**, strength, 7
vocō (1): call, name; summon, 8
vōx, vocis f.: voice, utterance; word, 8
vulnus, -eris n.: wound, injury, 7
vultus, -ūs m.: expression, face, 6